Advisory Board

Glencoe/McGraw-Hill's advisory board of marketing educators provides up-to-date research to address the needs of today's workplace. The board has provided its expertise and experience to establish the foundation for this innovative, real-world, marketing education program. Glencoe/McGraw-Hill would like to acknowledge the following individuals for their support of this project:

D1404022

Exploring Sports and Entertainment Marketing

As part of the Glencoe Marketing Series, this first edition of *Sports and Entertainment Marketing* focuses on the real-world business perspective by using examples from the marketing world to illustrate features, concepts, and activities. Information on featured companies, organizations, their products, and services is included for educational purposes only, and does not represent or imply endorsement of the Glencoe marketing program. The following are some of the companies represented in the feature *Hot Property* and throughout the text:

 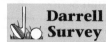

Table of Contents

Table of Contents

Table of Contents

Table of Contents

Welcome to *Sports and Entertainment Marketing*

Welcome to *Sports and Entertainment Marketing*—part of the Glencoe Marketing Series. Get ready to learn about one of the most exciting—and competitive—businesses in the world. Sports and Entertainment Marketing is a subject that you can relate to and make your own. After all, it is all around us—not just at ballparks and theaters, but at schools, on television and radio, in stores, and on the Internet.

Understanding the Unit

The units introduce you to the sports and entertainment industries, types of products, marketing strategies, and careers in these popular fields. Each unit opens with a preview and concludes with application activities featuring a reading activity from *BusinessWeek* magazine, as well as a marketing simulation. The 16 chapters in *Sports and Entertainment Marketing* are divided into five units:

UNIT 1: Marketing and Sports & Entertainment

UNIT 2: Sports Marketing

UNIT 3: Sports Marketing Mix

UNIT 4: Entertainment Marketing

UNIT 5: Entertainment Marketing Mix

Previewing the Unit

Each unit opener spread focuses on the content of the upcoming unit.

Unit Opener Photo

The unit opener photo illustrates a concept relevant to the upcoming unit. Ask yourself, "How does the photo relate to the content of the unit?"

Unit Overview

The *Unit Overview* provides a brief road map of the unit chapters.

In This Unit...

The titles of the unit chapters are listed on the left-hand side of the unit opener spread. Think about what you can learn in each chapter. A quotation helps you focus on what is to come.

Unit Lab Preview

The *Unit Lab Preview* prepares you for *Dream Machine, Inc.*, the unit's culminating real-world simulation and hands-on activity.

The Marketing Wheel

This visual representation of the National Marketing Education Standards highlights the two main parts of marketing—the foundations and the functions. The functions of marketing relate to how marketing is applied in the retail business world: Distribution, Financing, Marketing-Information Management, Pricing, Product/Service Management, Promotion, and Selling. The functions or foundations addressed in each unit are listed on this page.

Closing the Unit

UNIT 1 ACTIVITIES

BusinessWeek News

NINTENDO BEEFS UP ITS ARSENAL

With the video-game business in the midst of a bruising fight, Nintendo Company is beefing up its arsenal. Its latest weapon is *Metal Gear Solid: The Twin Snakes,* an action thriller featuring sword-wielding ninjas and antiterrorist commandos. That's quite a departure for a company known for characters such as the mild-mannered plumber Mario and Pokémon's lovable "pocket monsters." But [otherwise], Nintendo risks being picked off by archrivals Sony and Microsoft.

The once-undisputed King of Gameland remains the world's largest game-software publisher, and it dominates the handheld game market with its hugely successful Game Boy Advance. But Nintendo has sold only 9.6 million GameCube video-game consoles since September, 2001, far short of its 13.8 million target. Nintendo President Satoru Iwata concedes that the year has been a challenge. "But then, that's what I enjoy," says Iwata, a former game developer. "We need to feel a sense of crisis to bring out the best in us."

That sense of crisis has led Iwata to rethink Nintendo's business plan. He has moved to sharpen Nintendo's lineup of titles. The new version of *Metal Gear Solid,* developed exclusively for Nintendo, is a first step. To maintain the momentum, Iwata has lined up a *Star Wars* epic from Lucas Arts Entertainment Company, and a futuristic *F-Zero* car-racing game from Sega

Corporation, and other sports and action titles to push Nintendo's software lineup from 180 titles to 320.

Yet, if Nintendo hopes to attract more of the boys and young men who are flocking to PS2 and Xbox, Iwata needs to come up with a thrilling lineup of sports and adventure games.

Another concern is that Nintendo continues to stay clear of online gaming, while Sony and Microsoft are taking the plunge. "Consumers aren't ready to pay for such services, so how do you make money?" asks Iwata. Microsoft thinks it can make plenty of money with Internet games, and so far, it has attracted 500,000 subscribers who pay $50 a year for its Xbox Live.

Iwata firmly believes Nintendo has a future in digital entertainment. Nintendo's creators are hard at work on next-generation stars to replace the company's aging lineup of Mario and Pokémon. Iwata may have the skills to do that, but he'll have to pack plenty of firepower to climb to the top of the video-game business.

By Irene M. Kunii with Jay Greene

■ CREATIVE JOURNAL

In your journal, write your responses:

CRITICAL THINKING
1. What is the target market for action video games?

APPLICATION
2. If you were developing a new video game to appeal to the target market for Nintendo games, what sports or related films would you use as inspiration to create the game? Why? Describe your game.

Go to businessweek.com for current *BusinessWeek On...*

BusinessWeek NEWS

A reading and writing exercise entitled *BusinessWeek News* concludes each unit. A relevant excerpt from a real *BusinessWeek* article caps the unit content.

■ UNIT LAB

UNIT 1 ACTIVITIES

Dream Machine, Inc.

You've just entered the real world of sports and entertainment marketing. Dream Machine, Inc., is a sports and entertainment marketing company that serves college and professional sports teams, professional athletes, sporting events, sports arenas, and major sports product corporations, as well as performing arts companies, television networks, and movie studios. As an entry-level employee, you will have the opportunity to work on a variety of clients' projects.

Turn On the Electric Channel—Create a Web Site

SITUATION Last year during summer break, you worked for a concession stand at a local minor league ballpark. With interest in minor league baseball growing, along with the winning stats of the team, attendance at the ballpark increased. The stand sold more T-shirts, pennants, and caps than ever before. This year, your former manager has her hands full. She remembers that you were knowledgeable about the Internet and wants you and Dream Machine to develop a Web site for selling team merchandise, especially because the home team may win the championship.

ASSIGNMENT Complete these tasks:
- Plan your basic e-tail store with one or two unique features to attract your customers.
- Estimate your start-up costs including design, shipping, maintenance, and storage.
- Create a final report.

TOOLS AND RESOURCES To complete the assignment, you will need to:
- Conduct research at the library, on the Internet, or by phone.
- Ask other sporting-goods stores about experiences with Web sites.
- Have word-processing, spreadsheet, and presentation software.

RESEARCH Do your research:
- Find out the most important characteristics of a sporting-goods Web site.
- Go to other similar Web sites and identify and assess their features.
- Get cost estimates for designing and implementing basic Web sites with purchasing features.

REPORT Prepare a written report using the following tools, if available:
- *Word-processing program:* Prepare a written report with a site map outline and list of features, as well as a market overview and customer analysis.
- *Spreadsheet program:* Prepare a chart comparing other competitor Web sites with yours. Prepare a budget chart with your estimates.
- *Presentation program:* Prepare a ten-slide visual presentation with key points, some visuals, and little text.

PRESENTATION AND EVALUATION
You will present your report to your silent partner and the bank that may finance your plan. You will be evaluated on the basis of:
- Knowledge of the e-tail Web-site business
- Continuity of presentation
- Voice quality
- Eye contact

■ PORTFOLIO
Add this report to your career portfolio.

■ UNIT LAB

Dream Machine, Inc.

At the end of each unit, the unit lab simulation *Dream Machine, Inc.* will take you on an exciting journey through the world of sports and entertainment marketing.

Understanding the Chapter

E ach unit of *Sports and Entertainment Marketing* includes two to five chapters. Each chapter focuses on one specific area, such as branding, licensing, sponsorships, or promotion and advertising.

Previewing the Chapter

The chapter opener resources are designed to capture your interest and set a purpose for reading.

The chapter opener photo focuses on the chapter topic. You might ask yourself, "How does this photo relate to the chapter title?"

Chapter Objectives

The objectives help you identify exactly what you are expected to know upon completion of the chapter.

Using the Sections

Each chapter of *Sports and Entertainment Marketing* is divided into two or three sections. By using the activities and resources in each section, you can maximize learning.

AS YOU READ ...

You Will Learn lists the knowledge you can expect to learn.

Why It's Important explains how the chapter concepts relate to your world.

Key Terms list major terms presented in each section.

Case Study

Each chapter opens with the *Case Study*, Part 1, that presents a real-world marketing situation. Critical-thinking questions help focus content. Part 2 continues within the chapter.

Photographs and Figures

Photographs, illustrations, charts, and graphs reinforce content. Captions with questions guide you.

Quick Check

The section-ending *Quick Check* helps you to review and respond to what you have read.

Understanding the Features

Special features in each chapter are designed to interest and promote your understanding of chapter content. Features incorporate activities, such as critical-thinking questions, to help you integrate what you have learned.

World Market

World Market presents interesting stories of sports and entertainment practices as well as profiles of businesses and venues around the world.

Hot Property

Hot Property profiles successful or creative sports and entertainment marketing businesses, both large and small. Two critical-thinking questions focus on chapter topics.

Profiles in Marketing

Profiles in Marketing provides insight through personal interviews of successful or noteworthy individuals working in the real world of sports and entertainment marketing. A chapter-related, critical-thinking question follows the feature. The "Career Data" column gives the education, skills, outlook, and career-path information for this career.

THE Electronic CHANNEL

The Electronic Channel links chapter content to the expanding world of e-marketing, e-commerce, e-promotion, and e-tailing.

Game Point

Game Point presents brief, memorable facts to illustrate sports and entertainment issues, trends, and history.

ETHICAL PRACTICES

Ethical Practices links chapter content to current ethical issues in marketing, as well as legal, community-service, and character-education issues and practices.

Math Check

Math Check provides a math problem related to chapter discussions.

TECH NOTES

Technology is today's number-one marketing trend. *Tech Notes* highlights the wide range of technological applications enhancing sports and entertainment marketing today. An exercise directs you to the book's Web site at **marketingseries.glencoe.com**.

Worksheets and Portfolio Works

At the end of each chapter's text, before the review section, special write-on worksheet pages provide review and skill-building activities related to chapter content.

Chapter Worksheets

Two one-page worksheets give you the opportunity to complete an activity or exercise and apply the chapter content in a variety of interesting formats.

Portfolio Works

The *Portfolio Works* worksheet at the end of each chapter guides you through the development of an employability portfolio. The portfolio is developed throughout the course. You can assess, reflect, and plan for your career. Record what you have learned and how you would demonstrate those necessary values, skills, personal qualities, and knowledge. These activities provide the foundation for a career development portfolio. Save these pages for a prospective employer to demonstrate your combination of marketing knowledge and workplace skills needed to succeed in a sports and entertainment marketing career.

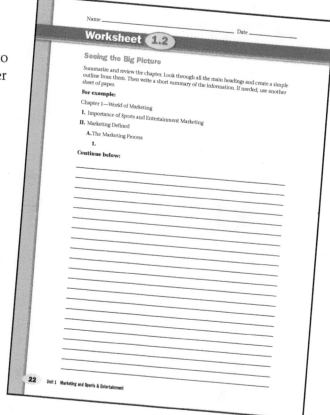

You can also include in your portfolio: documents that demonstrate your marketing competencies, employability skills, career goals, service and leadership activities, as well as employment letters, a résumé, and a job application form.

Building an employability portfolio helps you relate what you learn in school to the skills you will need to succeed on the job. When you have completed the project, you will have a visual résumé to use in your job search.

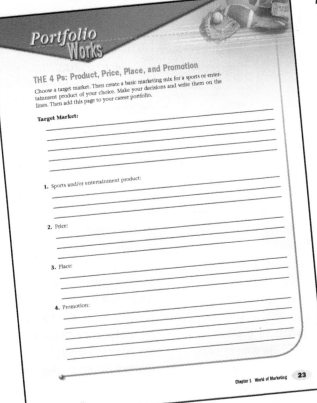

Understanding Assessments

At the end of each chapter, *Chapter Review and Activities* presents a chapter summary with key terms, recall and critical-thinking questions, and a variety of activities targeting academic and workplace skills.

Chapter Summary

The *Chapter Summary* is a bulleted list of the main points developed within each section, related to the chapter objectives. The key terms are listed with page references alongside the summary points.

Cross-Curriculum Skills

These skill-building exercises are divided into two categories: work-based learning and school-based learning. *Work-Based Learning* activities are hands-on projects that help you develop identified Foundation Skills and Workplace Competencies. *School-Based Learning* activities ask you to apply academic skills, such as math, science, and literacy skills, to real-life scenarios.

Chapter 1 — Review and Activities

CHAPTER SUMMARY

Section 1.1 What Is Marketing?

marketing (p. 6)
marketing concept (p. 7)
market (p. 7)
needs (p. 8)
wants (p. 8)
target market (p. 8)
demographics (p. 10)
marketing mix (p. 10)
channel of distribution (p. 11)

- Marketing involves the process of developing, promoting, and distributing products, or goods and services, to satisfy customers' needs and wants.
- Successful businesses understand the marketing concept as the need to satisfy their customers, while also trying to reach their organization's goals.
- Businesses use demographic information, such as age, income, occupation, gender, ethnic background, and educational level, to develop their marketing plans.
- The marketing mix is a combination of product, price, place, and promotion decisions that are focused on the target market.

Section 1.2 Economics of Marketing

economics (p. 12)
GDP (p. 12)
profit (p. 12)
competition (p. 13)
copyright (p. 14)

- Economics is the study of the choices and decisions that affect making, distributing, and using goods and services. In the free enterprise system, profit is a business's motivation. But risk is also a factor. Competition helps to encourage quality products at competitive prices.
- Intellectual property rights are intangible and protect a creator's property or products by patents, copyrights, and trademarks.
- Some types of business ownership include sole proprietorship, partnerships, corporations, and Subchapter S corporations.
- Sports and entertainment have an economic impact on countries, cities, and communities because events and products can generate revenue.

CHECKING CONCEPTS

1. Define and give an example of the term marketing.
2. Explain the marketing concept.
3. Describe the concept of demographics.
4. Explain the marketing mix.
5. Explain the concept of economics.
6. Name four types of business ownership.
7. Define intellectual property rights.

Critical Thinking

8. Describe how sports and entertainment affect national and local economies.

24   Unit 1 Marketing and Sports & Entertainment

CROSS-CURRICULUM SKILLS

Work-Based Learning

Thinking Skills—Seeing Things in the Mind's Eye
9. Think of a movie or television show that may have no promotional products. What character from the movie or TV show would make a good promotional toy? Describe the toy.

Interpersonal Skills—Serving Customers
10. You work in an athletic shoe store. Teenagers come into the store but do not buy. You believe the store needs to display more products that teens prefer. What brands of shoes would you choose to display? Why?

School-Based Learning

History
11. Use the Internet and/or the library to find information on advertisements for the first talking movie, released in 1927. Write a short report about how the movie was advertised.

Art
12. Create a collage from magazine or newspaper ads of sports products with appealing packaging. Explain to the class why the designs are effective.

DECA CONNECTION

Role Play: Tournament Director

SITUATION You are to assume the role of director for an amateur tennis tournament. Because of the tournament's size, two different tennis clubs and several hotels within the same proposed town must be used. The town mayor (judge) is unsure about presenting this project to the town council.

ACTIVITY Convince the town mayor (judge) to support hosting your event.

EVALUATION You will be evaluated on how well you meet the following performance indicators:
- Explain the economic impact of sports and entertainment events on a community/area.
- Describe factors that influence the demand for services.
- Explain the concept of competition.
- Explain the concept of economic resources.
- Describe trends in sports and entertainment marketing.

INTERNET ACTIVITY

Use the Internet to access MGM's Web site and answer these questions.
- Name five operating units of this company.
- List three consumer products marketed by MGM.
- Identify this company's type of ownership and explain what that is.

➡ For a link to the MGM Web site to do this activity, go to marketingseries.glencoe.com.

marketingseries.glencoe.com

Chapter 1 World of Marketing   25

Checking Concepts

Seven review questions help you check your understanding of the text by defining terms, describing processes, and explaining concepts. The last exercise asks you to use your critical-thinking skills.

DECA Connection

In every chapter review section, the *DECA Connection* offers specially created, DECA-approved role-play activities. These activities provide opportunities to practice for DECA's participating events that relate to sports and entertainment marketing, and are based on a real DECA role-play situation.

Internet Activity

In every chapter-review section, the *Internet Activity* provides a Web-based research activity. Resources for each exercise can be found through the book's Web site **marketingseries.glencoe.com**.

The DECA Connection

DECA is an association of marketing students that sponsors skill-building events. It is a co-curricular club with chapters in more than 6,000 high schools. The membership includes representation from all 50 states, four U.S. territories, the District of Columbia, and two Canadian provinces. All DECA activities further student development in one or more of the following areas: leadership development, social intelligence, vocational understanding, and civic consciousness. Through individual and group DECA activities with the marketing education instructional program, students develop skills to become future leaders in the areas of marketing and management.

DECA Builds Leadership Skills

The structure of a DECA chapter encourages leadership development for student members. Each chapter elects officers who, with the membership, choose an annual program of work. Committee chairpersons may organize and execute the activities in the program. Local activities encourage every member to act responsibly as a leader or member of a group. Chapter activities focus on the advantages of participating in a free enterprise system, marketing research, and an individual's civic responsibility.

National DECA provides opportunities for local chapter officers and members to receive additional training. Annual Regional Conferences are held in the fall each year. In the spring, students may attend the Leadership Development Academy at the Career Development Conference (CDC). During the summer, students can attend a State Officer Leadership Institute. The skills and leadership qualities gained are shared with all members of the chapter. The recognition received by individuals and teams within a DECA chapter serve as a showcase of the marketing program to your local school and community.

The following is a listing of events.
Individual Series Events:
- Apparel and Accessories Marketing Series
- Business Services Marketing Series
- Food Marketing Series
- Full Service Restaurant Management Series
- Marketing Management Series
- Quick Service Restaurant Management Series

- Retail Merchandising Series
- Vehicles and Petroleum Marketing Series

In addition, there are Management Team Decision Making Events, one of which is:
- Sports and Entertainment Marketing Management Team Decision Making Event

The *Sports and Entertainment Marketing* Web Site

The *Sports and Entertainment Marketing* Web site draws on the vast resources of the Internet to expand your exploration of career topics.

The student site includes the following:
- Chapter Objectives
- Interactive Practice Tests for each chapter with automatic scoring
- Math exercises and help with solving *Math Check* exercises
- E-flashcard games
- Web links for doing feature exercises from *Tech Notes, The Electronic Channel,* and *Internet Activities*
- DECA Competitive Events practice
- National Skills Standards
- Disability Support Links

At the *Career Clusters* Web site, you can explore career options with print and .pdf resources as well as links to job-search tips, external career planning sites, and educational resources.

Reading Strategies

How can you get the most from your reading? Effective readers are active readers. Become actively involved with the text. Think of your textbook as a tool to help you learn more about the world around you. It is a form of nonfiction writing—it describes real-life ideas, people, events, and places. Use the reading strategies in the *Power Read* box at the beginning of each chapter along with strategies in the margins to help you read actively.

 PREDICT Make educated guesses about what the section is about by combining clues in the text with what you already know. Predicting helps you anticipate questions and stay alert to new information.

Ask yourself:
- What does this section heading mean?
- What is this section about?
- How does this section tie in with what I have read so far?
- Why is this information important in understanding the subject?

 CONNECT Draw parallels between what you are reading and the events and circumstances in your own life.

Ask yourself:
- What do I know about the topic?
- How do my experiences compare to the information in the text?
- How could I apply this information in my own life?
- Why is this information important in understanding the subject?

 QUESTION Ask yourself questions to help you clarify meaning as you read.

Ask yourself:
- Do I understand what I've read so far?
- What is this section about?
- What does this mean?
- Why is this information important in understanding the subject?

RESPOND React to what you are reading. Form opinions and make judgments about the section while you are reading—not just after you've finished.

Ask yourself:
- Does this information make sense?
- What can I learn from this section?
- How can I use this information to start planning for my future?
- Why is this information important in understanding the subject?

More Reading Strategies

Use this menu for more reading strategies to get the most from your reading.

BEFORE YOU READ . . .

SET A PURPOSE
- Why are you reading the textbook?
- How does the subject relate to your life?
- How might you be able to use what you learn in your own life?

PREVIEW
- Read the chapter title to preview the topic.
- Read the subtitles to see what you will learn about the topic.
- Skim the photos, charts, graphs, or maps. How do they support the topic?
- Look for key terms that are boldfaced. How are they defined?

DRAW FROM YOUR BACKGROUND
- What have you read or heard concerning new information on the topic?
- How is the new information different from what you already know?
- How will the information that you already know help you understand the new information?

AS YOU READ . . .

PREDICT
- Predict events or outcomes by using clues and information that you already know.
- Change your predictions as you read and gather new information.

CONNECT
- Think about people, places, and events in your own life. Are there any similarities with those in your textbook?
- Can you relate the textbook information to other areas of your life?

QUESTION
- What is the main idea?
- How do the photos, charts, graphs, and maps support the main idea?

VISUALIZE
- Pay careful attention to details and descriptions.
- Create graphic organizers to show relationships that you find in the information.

NOTICE COMPARE AND CONTRAST SENTENCES
- Look for clue words and phrases that signal comparison, such as *similarly, just as, both, in common, also,* and *too.*
- Look for clue words and phrases that signal contrast, such as *on the other hand, in contrast to, however, different, instead of, rather than, but,* and *unlike.*

NOTICE CAUSE-AND-EFFECT SENTENCES
- Look for clue words and phrases, such as *because, as a result, therefore, that is why, since, so, for this reason,* and *consequently.*

NOTICE CHRONOLOGICAL SENTENCES
- Look for clue words and phrases, such as *after, before, first, next, last, during, finally, earlier, later, since,* and *then.*

AFTER YOU READ . . .

SUMMARIZE
- Describe the main idea and how the details support it.
- Use your own words to explain what you have read.

ASSESS
- What was the main idea?
- Did the text clearly support the main idea?

- Did you learn anything new from the material?
- Can you use this new information in other school subjects or at home?
- What other sources could you use to find more information about the topic?

UNIT 1

MARKETING AND SPORTS & ENTERTAINMENT

"To succeed, you need to find something to hold on to, something to motivate you, something to inspire you. **"**

—Tony Dorsett
Athlete

UNIT OVERVIEW

The sports and entertainment industries are two of the most profitable industries in the United States. Marketing sports and entertainment products is also a global business. Chapter 1 examines and reviews the basic principles of marketing and economics, including demographics and the marketing mix, with special emphasis on sports and entertainment marketing. Chapter 2 examines the history and background of sports and entertainment marketing and the legal issues and business risks. Focusing on the similarities between marketing sports products and entertainment products, Chapter 2 also discusses the differences that can help marketers successfully target the consumer.

■ UNIT LAB

Preview

Consider all the e-tail Web sites. eBay sells sports memorabilia, and teams offer sports products. Is the Internet a good place to sell team merchandise?

These functions are highlighted in this unit.
- Promotion
- Product/Service Management
- Distribution
- Selling
- Pricing
- Marketing-Information Management

Chapter 1

World of Marketing

Chapter Objectives

- Define marketing.
- Explain the marketing concept.
- Define demographics.
- Explain the marketing mix.
- Explain economics and free enterprise.
- Identify intellectual property rights.
- Explain the different types of business ownership.
- Explain the economic impact of sports and entertainment.

OLYMPIC BENEFITS?

Cities hosting the Olympic Games face huge costs for improvements for infrastructure, such as streets and highways, arenas, transportation and medical services, security, cultural events, and many other necessities for handling so many people and events. However, the Olympics has a huge impact on the economy of a community. In 1996, Atlanta, Georgia, hosted the Centennial Olympic Games. That year there were 111 local sponsors and 125 licensees within the United States, generating $725 million. The Olympic Organizing Committee took advantage of the market and the large number of companies that wanted to be associated with the Games. It was one of the few Games that actually didn't lose money. Some people criticized the Games, though, saying the great number of businesses over-commercialized the Olympics. The International Olympic Committee (IOC) stresses to all organizing committees that sport should be the priority of the Olympic Games. However, the IOC realizes that if cities don't reap benefits, they won't apply to host the Olympics.

ANALYZE AND WRITE

1. List the potential profits for a city that hosts the Games.
2. What might be some disadvantages for a city hosting the Olympic Games?

Case Study Part 2 on page 17

POWER READ

Be an active reader and use these reading strategies:

PREDICT what the section will be about.

CONNECT what you read with your life.

QUESTION as you read to make sure you understand the content.

RESPOND to what you've read.

What Is Marketing?

AS YOU READ ...

YOU WILL LEARN

- To define marketing.
- To explain the marketing concept.
- To define demographics.
- To explain the marketing mix.

WHY IT'S IMPORTANT

Marketing terms and concepts provide the foundation for further study of sports and entertainment marketing.

KEY TERMS

- marketing
- marketing concept
- market
- needs
- wants
- target market
- demographics
- marketing mix
- channel of distribution

marketing the process of developing, promoting, and distributing products, or goods and services, to satisfy customers' needs and wants

PREDICT

Choose one of the key terms and define it in your own words.

The Importance of Sports and Entertainment Marketing

Today, more than at any time in history, the sports and entertainment industries have become two of the most profitable industries in the United States. Fans spend billions of dollars each year on recreation and related products and services. Sports and entertainment also reach around the globe because entertainment is a main export of the United States. Because these are booming industries, sports and entertainment vendors, or salespeople, compete for a share of the customer's dollar. With so many businesses competing for attention, an organized marketing plan with strategies that target specific consumers is essential. This is the foundation of sports and entertainment marketing.

Marketing Defined

Marketing is defined as the process of developing, promoting, and distributing products, or goods and services, to satisfy customers' needs and wants. *Goods* are tangible products, such as sports equipment, while *services* are intangible products, such as theater tickets. For example, the theater ticket provides entrance to the play, which is a service.

The Marketing Process

Developing products involves studying consumers to determine what they want, and then designing the products that will satisfy their needs and wants. If you were asked to fill out a questionnaire or take part in a survey, you were part of a marketing research study. Your input may have helped to develop a new product or design a new advertising campaign.

Promotional activities help to educate consumers, create interest and desire, make a sale, and create an image for a company and its products. Do you recognize the following slogans: "Just Do It" and "The Breakfast of Champions"? Can you fill in this blank: "Take the _____ Challenge"? Can you name the company with the golden arches? If you know Nike, Wheaties, Pepsi, and McDonald's, respectively, you have been exposed to marketing. All the newspaper, magazine, radio, television, direct mail, and Internet advertising you see and hear are part of promotion.

Where do you buy a pair of athletic shoes or a theater ticket? Do you buy these products over the Internet, or do you go to a retail store or a theater? *Distribution* is the means of getting the product into the hands of the customer. Buying and selling are also involved in distribution. Some companies sell their products directly to the customer through direct-marketing efforts, such as direct mail, telephone solicitation, or the Internet. Others use intermediaries, such as wholesalers and retailers, to distribute their products. But how do companies address their need to satisfy the customers' needs and wants?

The Marketing Concept

Successful organizations recognize the importance of their customers and follow a marketing concept. The **marketing concept** is the idea that organizations need to satisfy their customers while also trying to reach their organizations' goals. Therefore, to be profitable, businesses must focus their efforts on customers' needs and wants.

The Market

The first step in creating a marketing concept involves identifying customers. Potential customers are referred to as a market if they meet certain criteria. A **market** consists of potential customers with shared needs who have the desire and ability to buy a product. Identifying the

CONNECT

Have you ever participated in a survey? What was the topic?

marketing concept idea that organizations need to satisfy their customers while also trying to reach their organizations' goals

market potential customers with shared needs who have the desire and ability to buy a product

Hot Property

Got to Be the Shoes

He rises into the air with his legs flared and a basketball held high. It's hard to forget the slam-dunk image of Michael Jordan—especially when it's associated with millions of athletic shoes. Nike, the company behind the shoes, first took flight by importing Japanese athletic shoes in 1962. Since then the company, founded by college track coach Bill Bowerman and his track student Phil Knight, has become its own instantly recognizable brand. Nike's effort to expand its appeal across different sports and different cultures has pushed its revenue past the $10 billion mark.

THE SPORTS LIFESTYLE

From the beginning Nike focused on creating innovative, high-tech products that would appeal to rising stars and sports enthusiasts. In 1985, Nike signed talented rookie Michael Jordan to an endorsement deal. Jordan was a marketing force that could carry Nike beyond the inner circle of athletics. Michael Jordan demonstrated an exciting

new style that inspired athletes, nonathletes, and fans. When people bought Air Jordan Court Shoes for under $200, they bought a connection to a champion's winning image and spirit. Sales surged.

Nike has worked to repeat this connection and the financial pay-off worldwide by carefully assembling a variety of diverse stars to represent their products. In 2000, Nike watched golf sales soar after Tiger Woods endorsed the Nike Tour Accuracy Golf Ball. In countries where soccer reigns supreme, Nike sought endorsements from high-profile clubs like Manchester United and the Korean World Cup team. In 2003, the company's efforts to diversify its appeal paid off, with international sales exceeding U.S. sales for the first time.

1. Why does Nike seek athletes to help market the company's products?
2. What do you think attracts buyers most about Air Jordans—the performance of the shoe or the image of Michael Jordan?

market, or potential customers, is important because businesses need to know whom they need to satisfy. For example, you might be included in the market for sneakers if you have the desire and money to purchase them. Perhaps you feel the need and have a desire to buy an automobile, but you do not have the money. In that case, you would not be included in the automobile market.

NEEDS AND WANTS Organizations spend lots of money to learn about their customers' needs and wants. **Needs** occur when people experience a lack of basic necessities such as food, clothing, or shelter. **Wants** are things that people desire based on personality, experiences, or information about a product. For example, you may get thirsty (a need), and from your past experience, you desire Gatorade (a want). For our purposes, we will use both terms, needs and wants, interchangeably.

TARGET MARKET Satisfying customer needs is not an easy task. For example, each member of your family may have the need for a pair of athletic shoes. Would everyone want exactly the same shoe? Probably not. Companies such as Nike and Reebok recognize the differences in customer needs and create shoes for tennis, golf, running, walking, basketball, and so on. Each type of shoe is designed for a smaller group of people within the larger market for athletic shoes. This smaller, homogeneous—or similar—group is called a target market. A **target market** is a specific group of consumers that an organization selects as the focus of its marketing plan. Having a clear picture about the target market makes developing a marketing plan easier to accomplish.

needs a lack of basic necessities such as food, clothing, or shelter

wants things that people desire based on personality, experiences, or information about a product

target market a specific group of consumers that an organization selects as the focus of its marketing plan

Figure 1.1

Demographics

CUSTOMER PROFILING Do businesses know who might buy their products? They conduct market research to find out and customize their marketing and advertising efforts. Demographic research was used to create these four sample profiles developed by Cohorts, a marketing tool offered by the firm Looking Glass. *Create your own profile by describing the characteristics of your demographic group.*

Cohort Segment Name	Description	Median Age	Median Income
Eric & Rachel	**Young, Married Starters** Young, childless renters whose lifestyle patterns include outdoor activities like camping, fishing, and running, as well as automotive work and video games.	28	$20,000
Jason	**Male Students and Grads** Physically active, technologically inclined young men finishing school or embarking on their first job.	26	$17,000
Megan	**Fit and Stylish Students** Young, fashion-conscious, career-minded female students who enjoy music, aerobic sports, and the latest in high tech.	26	$17,000
Danny & Vickie	**Teen-Dominated Families** Middle-aged, middle-income families whose teen-dominated households keep busy with outdoor activities, computers, and video games.	42	$57,000

Profiles in Marketing

ATHLETIC NETWORKING

Andrea Bonner
Director of Client Services
The Active Network

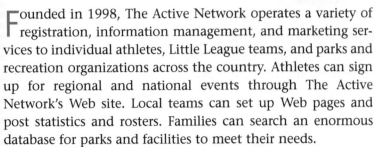

Founded in 1998, The Active Network operates a variety of registration, information management, and marketing services to individual athletes, Little League teams, and parks and recreation organizations across the country. Athletes can sign up for regional and national events through The Active Network's Web site. Local teams can set up Web pages and post statistics and rosters. Families can search an enormous database for parks and facilities to meet their needs.

At The Active Network, Andrea Bonner has a diverse job, handling a number of different tasks: "I wear a hundred hats," she says. "It's up to me to manage and organize the business development department, which includes developing processes and procedures to help our efforts flow smoothly, providing training and leadership to the team, and ensuring that our clients are getting the absolute best service as we partner with them on promotional programs."

Andrea has a bachelor's degree in marketing from the University of Texas. She originally planned to go into banking or consulting but found marketing to be her most interesting subject. She interned at an advertising firm when she was 20. She spent the next 18 years in the advertising business before shifting into her current career.

According to Andrea, leadership skills are important, as is "extreme organization. The drive to keep hammering at even the most elusive problems is important, along with the ability to laugh often."

Why do you think organizational skills would be important in a marketing career?

Career Data: Director of Marketing Services

Education and Training Degrees in communications, public relations, and general business

Skills and Abilities Writing skills, multitasking skills, and leadership skills

Career Outlook Faster than average growth through 2010

Career Path A college degree can lead to an entry-level marketing position. Even if the degree doesn't exactly match the company's field, the skills learned are always useful.

Mass Marketing vs. Market Identification

Businesses have not always identified their target markets to promote products. Back in the 1950s, mass marketing was more common. Mass marketing involves promoting products with one key message that is directed to everyone. Today marketing efforts are much more sophisticated due to availability of information and computer technology. Market-research companies provide clients with data to determine consumers' lifestyle characteristics (see **Figure 1.1**). There are many such market-research firms doing business today.

demographics statistics that describe a population in terms of personal characteristics

marketing mix a combination of four basic marketing strategies, known as the 4 Ps—product, price, place, and promotion

ⓥ **DESIGN IN THE MIX**
Marketing decisions include finding the right products and promoting them. Product image and packaging promote sales. *Do you think a sports drink would sell if the label had an old-fashioned design? Why?*

The U.S. census provides information about the demographics of our nation. **Demographics** are statistics that describe a population in terms of personal characteristics. There are many characteristics, but some of the most common demographic categories include age, income, occupation, gender, ethnic background, and educational levels. The United States compiles demographic information every ten years. Businesses use that information to develop their marketing plans.

The Marketing Mix

Marketers use a tool to develop marketing strategies called the marketing mix. The **marketing mix** is a combination of four basic marketing strategies, known as the 4 Ps—product, price, place, and promotion. To be effective, all 4 Ps in a marketing plan must focus on the target market.

Product Decisions

Product decisions involve the goods, services, or ideas used to satisfy consumer needs. Designing, naming, and packaging a product are major considerations. To design a product, marketers determine what the consumer needs. For example, filmmakers create movies for specific audiences, taking into consideration what sells best. Also, makers of protein bars produce their energy bars for athletes to address their energy needs. Advant Edge brand has 26 grams of protein, while the Power Bar brand has 9 grams, and Zone Perfect brand has 16 grams. Notice the names of each protein bar. A good name is another product decision.

Package designs are also part of the product decision. The materials used for the package must take into account how the product will be sold. Protein bars need to be packaged in material that prevents spoilage. Since protein bars are displayed on shelves in self-service food stores, the colors and design of the package are very important. Package design often influences customers' buying decisions.

Price Decisions

Price also influences customers' buying decisions. Price decisions involve the exchange process between the customer and the seller. Businesses must ask how much should be charged for the good or service. The cost of making or buying a product for resale is one factor in determining the price to charge customers. Other factors include the expenses related to marketing the product, competition, and of course, what the consumer is willing to pay. For example, to reach different target markets with different needs and income levels, Nike prices its running shoes from $70 to well over $100. Businesses that sell protein bars price individual bars from $1.29 to $2.69.

Place Decisions

Place decisions involve making the product available to the customer. Thus, marketers must determine how and where their target market shops. If customers normally shop in retail stores, then the product needs to be sold to retailers for resale to customers. Infomercials and the Internet offer the option of selling a product directly to the customer.

There are other options and considerations when determining a **channel of distribution,** or the path a product takes from the producer to the consumer. Some businesses use a combination of channels. For example, Nike has a Web site where you can purchase products directly or locate a retail store that carries Nike products. Nike sells its products to retailers, such as Foot Locker, Champs, and Sports Authority. Nike also has its own retail stores and factory-outlet stores. Protein bars can be purchased in supermarkets, convenience stores, health stores, and gyms, and through Internet Web sites hosted by the manufacturers, as well as Internet retailers. For entertainment customers, theater tickets can be sold directly from the theater or through a broker, such as Ticketmaster or Telecharge, by telephone or Internet.

Promotion Decisions

Promotion decisions involve how the goods or services are communicated to the consumer. Promotions may use any combination of advertising, sales promotion, publicity, and personal selling.

Besides many other forms of promotion, Nike uses print and broadcast media to promote its products. You will see Nike ads and articles in magazines geared to sports enthusiasts. Its television commercials run during sporting events, such as major golf tournaments and the Super Bowl. Its Web site is a source of communication with its customers around the world. Its familiar slogan, "Just Do It," became a household phrase. Endorsements from athletes, such as Tiger Woods, also help to promote its image as a top brand in the industry. Nike's sponsorship of athletic events helps to generate positive publicity.

Thus, the marketer makes promotion decisions involving selection of media, as well as the message to be delivered that will contribute to the entire marketing plan. The plan should help to develop, promote, and distribute products—goods and services—to satisfy customers' needs and wants.

THE Electronic CHANNEL

Buzz Power

"Word-of-mouth ramped up to warp speed" is one definition of Internet buzz, says *BusinessWeek*. It's the marketing by-product of e-mail, instant messaging, bulletin boards, and chat rooms. The influence of buzz is so powerful that researchers monitor consumer opinions online. Positive buzz can increase profits for products, books, films, TV, music, and fashion, and determine popularity of athletes and celebrities. With public resistance to banner ads and pop-ups, a little buzz "zooms" a long way.

➡Read an article about buzz and list examples of it through **marketingseries.glencoe.com.**

channel of distribution path a product takes from the producer to the consumer

Quick Check

RESPOND to what you've read by answering these questions:

1. Define marketing and the marketing concept. _____

_____

2. Explain the concept of a market. _____

_____

3. What is the marketing mix and what is its relationship to a target market? _____

_____

Economics of Marketing

YOU WILL LEARN

- To explain economics and free enterprise.
- To identify intellectual property rights.
- To explain the different types of business ownership.
- To explain the economic impact of sports and entertainment.

WHY IT'S IMPORTANT

Knowing the relationship between marketing and economics is important for businesses that operate in free enterprise systems.

KEY TERMS

- economics
- GDP
- profit
- competition
- copyright

economics the study of the choices and decisions that affect making, distributing, and using goods and services

GDP (gross domestic product) the value of all goods and services produced within a country

profit the money left after all costs and expenses of a business are paid

Economic Basics

The marketing decisions and plans made by sports and entertainment businesses help determine profits from their products, or goods and services. Those decisions and plans also economically affect the countries, cities, and communities that use the products. The economics of marketing sports and entertainment have a great impact globally as well as locally.

Economics is the study of the choices and decisions that affect making, distributing, and using goods and services. These choices and decisions are made due to limited resources. People and countries have unlimited needs and wants but only limited resources. Thus, they must choose between options available to them. For instance, you may want to buy tickets for a sporting event and a concert, but you don't have enough money to do both. What do you do? You must decide between the two options.

Gross Domestic Product

Countries must consider the unlimited needs of its people and businesses when making economic decisions. With limited resources from taxpayers, those decisions are often difficult. To make those decisions, governments study several economic indicators. One measure of economic growth is the gross domestic product (GDP). The United States' **GDP** is the value of all goods and services produced within the country. The sector of agriculture accounts for about 2 percent of the GDP; the industry sector is 18 percent; and the services sector is 80 percent of the U.S. GDP. An increase in the GDP is a positive indicator, or sign, of economic growth. Spending by consumers, businesses, and the government helps to increase economic growth and the GDP. Every time you purchase movie tickets or buy sports equipment, you are actually helping the economy and the GDP.

In the United States, businesses make economic decisions all the time. They decide what will be produced and how it will be produced, based on what consumers buy. They are able to make those decisions because of our free enterprise system. In a *free enterprise system,* profit is a business's motivation. There are no guarantees, because risk is also part of a free enterprise system. Competition helps to encourage quality products at competitive prices. Let's take a closer look at the characteristics of free enterprise.

Profit

Profit is the money left after all costs and expenses of a business are paid. Profit allows companies to stay in business. Of course, the goal of most sports and entertainment events is to make a profit. Profitable businesses help the free enterprise system and economy by providing employment and paying taxes on their profits. When the economy slows down, people lose jobs. High unemployment is bad for the economy because fewer people have money to spend, and consumer confidence is lost. Because consumers are not buying, fewer products need to be produced, which negatively affects the GDP.

Risk

Not all businesses are profitable. As with most businesses, there is a financial risk, or possible loss, involved with sports and entertainment events. Each week entertainment news programs announce the ticket sales, or box office, for popular movies. However, they usually do not report how much it costs to produce the movies. A movie that does not attract audiences may fail to make a profit. The same is true for a sporting event.

There are other risks that must be handled by businesses, such as unforeseen happenings. Poor weather conditions might prevent events from occurring. Just think of how much money might be lost if a singer cancels a concert for health reasons. Also, lawsuits from spectators who fall while in the theater or on arena property or athletes who are injured by spectators are examples of more risks that must be considered and handled. Companies handle risks in several ways, one of which is through insurance. Proper employee training and event planning that take safety into consideration may also help reduce or manage risks.

Competition

Another characteristic of free enterprise is **competition**, which is the struggle among companies for customers. This dynamic is the basis of the free enterprise system, founded on the theory that only the strongest will survive. That is, only those organizations that provide the best products at the best relative prices will stay in business.

PRICE COMPETITION Competition that is based on price follows the concept of *demand elasticity and available substitutes*. In other words, when there are many substitutes for a product, demand for the product is elastic. That means that a change in price affects demand for the product. The theory is that when you lower your price, demand will increase; when you raise your price, demand will decrease. Companies that use price as a competitive tool recognize this concept of demand elasticity and offer lower prices than those of their competitors.

Supply and demand relate to pricing decisions. *Supply* is all the products available for sale. *Demand* is the customers' desire to buy products. In supply-and-demand theory, when there is a limited supply and high demand for products, businesses can charge higher prices. For example, when there are only a certain number of seats in a theater or sports arena, and a very popular band or game is scheduled, prices may be high. When a great number of products are available with low demand for them, prices need to be lower to encourage people to buy the products. As price goes up, demand will go down, because fewer people will be able to afford the product. Businesses that

competition as a characteristic of free enterprise, the struggle among companies for customers

PREDICT

Has a major sporting event affected your community? In what way?

want to increase demand will lower their prices. For example, when a theatrical play is no longer drawing large audiences, its ticket prices may be lowered.

NON-PRICE COMPETITION Not all organizations use price to compete. Non-price competition involves factors other than price, such as quality, service, or image. Companies try to create loyal customers by focusing on product quality, personalized service, and/or ongoing relationships with customers. In those instances, the supply-and-demand principles may not apply. A very popular recording artist, play, sporting event, or product (good or service) can charge a high price and still generate strong demand. For example, a round of golf that would normally cost $100 might cost you three or four times more if you want to play on a prestigious golf course such as the Pebble Beach Golf Course in Pebble Beach, California.

Property Ownership and Intellectual Property Rights

Inherent in the free enterprise system is the right to own property and to start a business. Property may be tangible items, such as buildings, theaters, stadiums, and equipment, or it may be intangible items, such as services. For example, sports and entertainment events are considered to be services. The money invested in these businesses does not usually come from the government; it comes from personal investors in a free enterprise system. Intellectual property rights are also intangible and are protected by patents, copyrights, and trademarks, but they also protect profits earned from selling products as well. For example, an idea or script made into a film is intellectual property. It is intangible. However, a toy modeled after a character in the film is a product, also protected by copyright law.

Copyrights

Copyright is the legal protection of a creator's intellectual property or products. Books, films, video games, and music are copyrighted, or registered in the Library of Congress for the life of the author plus 70 years. For example, if you wanted to use a clip from a copyrighted film for a television commercial, you would have to get permission. You also would pay for that in the form of a payment, or *royalty*. Every time a talk show airs a movie clip, the TV station pays the filmmakers a royalty.

With computer technology, it has become relatively easy to illegally copy music, movies, and other copyrighted material. The Internet has allowed this practice to be more widespread, which causes businesses to lose revenue.

Patents

Patents are granted for 20 years to protect owners of patented products. The patented product cannot be used without the inventor's or owner's permission. Patented inventions are protected from others making, using, importing, selling, or offering them for sale. For

copyright the legal protection of a creator's intellectual property or products

example, according to the U.S. Patent and Trademark Office (USPTO), thousands of patents are granted on golf-related equipment and gadgets. The Nike driver (patent no. 6,280,348), used by Tiger Woods, is one of 1,400 patents associated with golf clubs. Another 1,000 patents are associated with golf balls. Titleist, a major manufacturer of golf balls, has more than 100 of its own golf-related patents.

Trademarks

Trademarks on words, names, symbols, sounds, or colors that distinguish goods and services are also registered with the USPTO. Trademarks can be renewed over and over again. The MGM lion is trademarked, as are the names Coke, Reebok, and Disney. Visit **www.uspto.gov** for more information on U.S. patents and trademarks. Trademarks are important to businesses because consumers come to expect certain quality and service from trademarked products. For example, individuals or companies that make "knock-off," or fake, Reebok shoes do not use the same quality materials or craftsmanship to produce the shoes. Thus, a company's image, reputation, and profits are linked to its trademark. That is why a trademark must be protected.

Types of Business Ownership

In the free enterprise system, entrepreneurship is business ownership. Entrepreneurs take financial risks in hopes of getting a return on their investment. There are several forms of business ownership used by sports and entertainment enterprises.

Sole Proprietorship

Sole proprietorship of a business involves only one owner. For example, some sports memorabilia or local sporting-goods shops may be owned by one person or a family. The benefits of being a sole proprietor include ease in starting and ending a business, as well as complete control over the business. All decisions are made by the one owner, and all profits belong to that owner. The disadvantages include lack of finances to expand, unlimited liability, and the time an owner must devote to running the business. Unlimited liability means that creditors may take an owner's personal property to satisfy a debt.

Partnership

When there are two or more owners, the business is a *partnership*. The advantages of a partnership include shared financial investment, shared responsibilities, and shared expertise, as well as the ability to expand. Disadvantages include unlimited liability and difficulty in withdrawing. Also, the death of a partner dissolves the partnership. There is the possibility of disagreements among partners, and they must share profits. It is a good idea to prepare a partnership agreement (contract) before starting a business. The contract should cover the percentage of investment for each partner, share in profit and losses, partners' responsibilities, as well as how the partnership will handle the death of a partner.

X-TREME HISTORY
The first skateboard contest was held at a school in Hermosa Beach, California, in 1963. In 1964, surfing legend Hobie Alter teamed with sponsor and partner Vita-Pakt juice to form the company Hobie Skateboards.

A partnership may have a "silent partner," making the business a *limited partnership*. In a limited partnership, there must be at least one general partner who assumes unlimited liability. For example, George Steinbrenner is the general partner of the New York Yankees baseball team. In 1973, Mr. Steinbrenner put together a group of investors (silent partners) to buy the New York Yankees from CBS. All the limited partners enjoy limited liability. Limited liability means that only an individual's investment in the business is lost when there is financial failure.

Corporation

A *corporation* is a business entity that has the ability to conduct business and enter into contracts apart from its owner or owners. A corporation must be chartered, which requires providing information to the state in which the business plans to operate. A corporate charter is a license to do business. The information needed for a business to be incorporated might include:

- Name

- Number of shareholders

- Type of business

- Products

- Selling location

- Members of the board of directors

The owners of a corporation are called stockholders or shareholders. The corporation can generate a great deal of money, or capital, for operating expenses by selling shares of stock. You can be a

MAIN STREET ON WALL STREET **The Walt Disney Company is a large corporation with many business units, including amusement parks and movie studios— all owned by stockholders.** *Do you think a corporation is the best type of ownership for this company? Why?*

 marketingseries.glencoe.com

stockholder by buying stock in a company. Stockholders elect a board of directors. The board of directors hires people to run the company. For example, Big 5 sporting goods is a corporation owned by stockholders. Its stock symbol is DKS. In the entertainment world, Metro-Goldwyn-Mayer (MGM) is a corporation that provides entertainment products around the world. Its stock is listed on the New York Stock Exchange with the symbol MGM.

Advantages of a corporation include the ability to generate capital investment, limited liability for its owners, ability to hire experts to run the company, ability to expand, and ease with which owners can join and leave the corporation. Its disadvantages include its complex structure; higher tax rate; double taxation (taxes on company and shareholders); and increased government regulation.

Subchapter S Corporation

Another form of business ownership is a *Subchapter S corporation*. This type of corporation must follow all the same government regulations as a corporation, but it is taxed like a partnership. There are several restrictions to qualify as a Subchapter S corporation. For example, there can be no more than 35 shareholders, and no more than 80 percent of its revenue can come from foreign sources.

Economic Impact

Broadway in New York City, Walt Disney World® in Orlando, Florida, and the 2004 Olympics in Athens, Greece, all have something in common. The host locations all benefit economically from sports and/or entertainment events and marketing. For example, plays on and off Broadway attract theatergoers to New York City. Theatergoers who travel by automobile must pay bridge or tunnel tolls and parking fees. They may also have lunch or dinner, which supports the local restaurants. Disney World in Orlando attracts tourists who support local hotels, restaurants, and car-rental services, as well as airlines. The economic impact of sports and entertainment marketing on Athens, Greece, is even more dramatic, because its positive effects continue long after the Olympic Games are over with improvements in roads, new hotels, restaurants, and profits that are reinvested in the local economy.

Case Study PART 2

OLYMPIC BENEFITS?
Continued from Part 1 on page 5

In 2002, Salt Lake City, Utah, hosted one of the most successful Olympic Winter Games. Over $2,071 million was generated in marketing revenue, including the broadcast of the games as well as the sponsorship and partnership, ticketing, licensing, and coin programs. Between 1996 and 2003, direct spending related to the Olympics was $2.1 billion. In total, the 2002 Games generated $4.5 billion, including $1.5 billion in income to Utah workers and business owners, as well as $450 million in taxes for governments. This activity included income from construction, souvenirs, travel, hotel, food, and other extensions of the Games.

In comparison to Atlanta in 1996, Salt Lake City had 53 local sponsors and 69 licensees, a big drop in partnerships. However, this smaller number of sponsors and licensees actually generated $840 million—a $116 million increase! This success by the Organizing Committee is impressive, given that Atlanta hosted the larger-scale Summer Games versus the smaller Winter Games. A survey of European, Asian, and Latin-American markets noted one long-term benefit for the Winter Games: 80 percent of respondents indicated that they now recognize the state of Utah, describing it as the "American West."

ANALYZE AND WRITE

1. Identify the products and the related products produced by the Olympic Games.
2. Refer to your list of benefits from Case Study, Part 1. What are the long-term benefits for a host city that may occur five to ten years after the Games are over?

World Market

Marketing a Mountain

On May 29, 1953, Sir Edmund Hillary and his Sherpa guide, Tenzing Norgay, were the first to climb to the summit of Mt. Everest. The pair could never have known that their story would "market" the mountain and cause many people to follow in their footsteps.

As part of the mountain range forming Nepal's northern border, Mt. Everest is the highest point on Earth. Over five miles tall, it has become the ultimate quest for mountaineers seeking recreation. It's also a marketer's paradise. At $70,000 per expedition, teams from all over the world wait for their chance to participate in this historic sport of mountain climbing. To date, about 10,000 adventurers have attempted the climb, and only 2,000 have made it to the top. Nearly 200 have died reaching for its heights. Although the tourist dollar (over $50 million annually) is a boost to the Nepalese economy, there is a down side. For example, trash—aluminum ladders, climbing rope, camp refuse—litters the mountain.

Describe how this particular "sporting event" affects the economy of Nepal.

NEPAL

Local Events

On the local level, sporting events and entertainment venues and events economically affect areas in which they operate because they draw audiences. With more people who attend an event, there are more workers needed for crowd control, ticket collection, concession sales, and security. In many cases, these same customers generate business for local merchants, who in turn hire local people to work for them. Spectators support sporting events by buying tickets and merchandise from stadium concessions, as do movie- and theatergoers. Events and theaters need employees. All the workers at a concert, movie, or baseball game have jobs, which help improve the local economy. Add to that all the income and employment from parking, hotels, taxi services, and restaurants, and you can see a huge economic impact on the community as shown in **Figure 1.2.**

For example, the Sports and Events Committee of Chattanooga, Tennessee, estimated the economic impact to be $20 million for all the sporting events hosted there. The Sports Council of Atlanta, Georgia, is proud of the many sporting events it has attracted and the resulting economic impact on the community. The council estimated the impact of the 2003 National Basketball Association (NBA) All-Star Game to be $34.27 million. That might be why Los Angeles got involved in hosting the 2004 NBA All-Star Game with weekend events planned around the game to further boost the economy of the area.

High School Events

Many competitive sports careers begin in high school through events. High school sports draw enthusiastic crowds and aspiring athletes alike. In some states such as Florida and Texas, high school football games can draw more fans than local college games, especially if rival teams are playing. For example, in Odessa, Texas, the average attendance can number 20,000 spectators. High school basketball games in Indiana can draw more than 40,000 fans to Hoosier Dome.

There are many opportunities for marketing efforts on this level that can also have economic impact. You have probably attended football and basketball games in support of your high school teams and witnessed all types of promotional efforts, from halftime contests to local radio ads to being entertained by team mascots. Besides building school spirit and encouraging your athletes, high school sporting events and projects can generate money for athletic programs. Some high schools have fund-raising drives to support their teams. Also, profits from concession stands and program sales provide income. Motivated students can also solicit sponsors among local businesses, such as fast-food restaurants, local radio stations, and other businesses. Even large corporations have sponsorship programs for high school athletics. Participating in marketing efforts for high school sports is a good way to learn about sports marketing and earn needed money for school programs, equipment, and facilities. Even on this level, sports marketing has an economic impact on the community.

Figure 1.2

Event Impact

ECONOMIC EFFECTS Ticket sales to major events like the Olympics and world fairs are only one source of revenue. Everyone involved in these events can profit before, during, and after the event. *Name three businesses that might benefit from the Super Bowl taking place in their community.*

The Olympics

Hosting the Olympic Games creates a huge economic impact on a region before, during, and after the event. Before, Olympic Committee members must visit the site several times to check on the preparations for the Olympics. Representatives from various countries and their athletes also visit to see what it would be like to compete in the environment. Add employees of the media, sponsors, and other interested organizations to that number of visitors, and you can get an idea about the economic impact on an area before the Games even begin.

During the Games, spectators arrive, along with all the people associated with the Games, such as athletes and their families, dignitaries, sponsors, and media personnel. Most of the Olympic sites expect the economic impact to continue well after the Games are over because of publicity during the Games. In addition, all these people who visit before, during, and after the Games need transportation and places to sleep and eat. That means new jobs for residents of the area—as well as an increase in the country's gross domestic product.

Think of the media exposure that Athens, Greece, will have as a tourist destination for years to come. The increase in tourism contributes to Greece's GDP and employment. The economic impact of marketing this sports entertainment event has been felt in all host countries, cities, and communities around the world. It is one reason that the sports and entertainment industries have become such profitable industries.

Quick Check ✓

RESPOND to what you've read by answering these questions.

1. Explain the concept of economics. _____
   _____
   _____
   _____

2. What are three characteristics of a free enterprise system? _____
   _____
   _____
   _____

3. What is the economic impact of sports and entertainment events on a community? _____
   _____
   _____
   _____

Worksheet 1.1

Word Mapping

Word maps can help you remember new words and make connections as you learn. Choose one of the key terms from this chapter. Fill in the word map chart below. You can use this form for any word or concept you learn in any subject at school.

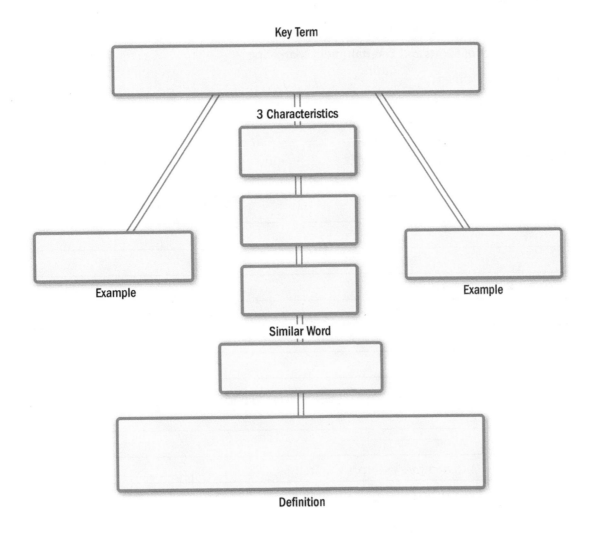

Key Term

3 Characteristics

Example

Example

Similar Word

Definition

Worksheet 1.2

Seeing the Big Picture

Summarize and review the chapter. Look through all the main headings and create a simple outline from them. Then write a short summary of the information. If needed, use another sheet of paper.

For example:

Chapter 1—World of Marketing

  I. Importance of Sports and Entertainment Marketing

 II. Marketing Defined

    A. The Marketing Process

        1.

Continue below:

_____
_____
_____
_____
_____
_____
_____
_____
_____
_____
_____
_____
_____
_____
_____
_____
_____
_____
_____
_____
_____
_____
_____

THE 4 Ps: Product, Price, Place, and Promotion

Choose a target market. Then create a basic marketing mix for a sports or entertainment product of your choice. Make your decisions and write them on the lines. Then add this page to your career portfolio.

Target Market:

_____

_____

_____

_____

_____

1. Sports and/or entertainment product:

_____

_____

_____

2. Price:

_____

_____

_____

3. Place:

_____

_____

_____

4. Promotion:

_____

_____

_____

_____

_____

CHAPTER SUMMARY

Section 1.1 What Is Marketing?

marketing (p. 6)
marketing concept (p. 7)
market (p. 7)
needs (p. 8)
wants (p. 8)
target market (p. 8)
demographics (p. 10)
marketing mix (p. 10)
channel of distribution
    (p. 11)

- Marketing involves the process of developing, promoting, and distributing products, or goods and services, to satisfy customers' needs and wants.

- Successful businesses understand the marketing concept as the need to satisfy their customers, while also trying to reach their organization's goals.

- Businesses use demographic information, such as age, income, occupation, gender, ethnic background, and educational level, to develop their marketing plans.

- The marketing mix is a combination of product, price, place, and promotion decisions that are focused on the target market.

Section 1.2 Economics of Marketing

economics (p. 12)
GDP (p. 12)
profit (p. 12)
competition (p. 13)
copyright (p. 14)

- Economics is the study of the choices and decisions that affect making, distributing, and using goods and services. In the free enterprise system, profit is a business's motivation. But risk is also a factor. Competition helps to encourage quality products at competitive prices.

- Intellectual property rights are intangible and protect a creator's property or products by patents, copyrights, and trademarks.

- Some types of business ownership include sole proprietorship, partnerships, corporations, and Subchapter S corporations.

- Sports and entertainment have an economic impact on countries, cities, and communities because events and products can generate revenue.

CHECKING CONCEPTS

1. **Define** and give an example of the term marketing.
2. **Explain** the marketing concept.
3. **Describe** the concept of demographics.
4. **Explain** the marketing mix.
5. **Explain** the concept of economics.
6. **Name** four types of business ownership.
7. **Define** intellectual property rights.

Critical Thinking

8. **Describe** how sports and entertainment affect national and local economies.

CROSS-CURRICULUM SKILLS

Work-Based Learning

Thinking Skills—Seeing Things in the Mind's Eye

9. Think of a movie or television show that may have no promotional products. What character from the movie or TV show would make a good promotional toy? Describe the toy.

Interpersonal Skills—Serving Customers

10. You work in an athletic shoe store. Teenagers come into the store but do not buy. You believe the store needs to display more products that teens prefer. What brands of shoes would you choose to display? Why?

School-Based Learning

History

11. Use the Internet and/or the library to find information on advertisements for the first talking movie, released in 1927. Write a short report about how the movie was advertised.

Art

12. Create a collage from magazine or newspaper ads of sports products with appealing packaging. Explain to the class why the designs are effective.

 **CONNECTION**

Role Play: Tournament Director

SITUATION You are to assume the role of director for an amateur tennis tournament. Because of the tournament's size, two different tennis clubs and several hotels within the same proposed town must be used. The town mayor (judge) is unsure about presenting this project to the town council.

ACTIVITY Convince the town mayor (judge) to support hosting your event.

EVALUATION You will be evaluated on how well you meet the following performance indicators:

- Explain the economic impact of sports and entertainment events on a community/area.
- Describe factors that influence the demand for services.
- Explain the concept of competition.
- Explain the concept of economic resources.
- Describe trends in sports and entertainment marketing.

 **INTERNET ACTIVITY**

Use the Internet to access MGM's Web site and answer these questions.

- Name five operating units of this company.
- List three consumer products marketed by MGM.
- Identify this company's type of ownership and explain what that is.

For a link to the MGM Web site to do this activity, go to **marketingseries.glencoe.com**.

Chapter 2

Sports and Entertainment: Connections and Contrasts

Chapter Objectives

- Discuss the history of sports and entertainment.
- Discuss the impact of sports and entertainment history on today's markets.
- Explain how sports and entertainment marketers use tools to sell their products.
- Explain risks and risk management of sports and entertainment events.
- Identify differences between marketing sports and entertainment products.

NEW KIND OF KICK

When most skateboard-related companies were maintaining an uncivilized street edge, Ken Block and Damon Way took their skate-shoe company in the other direction. The two friends started the DC Shoe Company in a San Diego, California, apartment in 1994, aiming to use nothing less than the highest-tech materials and unique fashion-forward designs. They styled their advertising with slick concepts, challenging the "street" style that dominated skateboard magazine ads at the time. A serious approach to shoemaking combined with a team of highly respected skaters—including Way's brother Danny, who endorsed the product. The company quickly expanded its shoe line, started making clothing, and began branching out to other sports. Ken and Damon even considered distributing products outside the skate-shop world. Historically, this kind of expansion has been bad luck for a skateboard company. So how could DC find ways to market its shoes, grow as a company, and keep its street credibility?

ANALYZE AND WRITE

1. Do you think that champion skateboarder Danny Way helped sell DC Shoes? Why?

2. If you were going to tie DC products to an entertainment market, what strategies might you use?

Case Study Part 2 on page 35

POWER READ

Be an active reader and use these reading strategies:

PREDICT what the section will be about.

CONNECT what you read with your life.

QUESTION as you read to make sure you understand the content.

RESPOND to what you've read.

History of Sports and Entertainment

AS YOU READ ...

YOU WILL LEARN

- To discuss the history of sports and entertainment.
- To discuss the impact of sports and entertainment history on today's markets.

WHY IT'S IMPORTANT

When you know the history and development of a career field, you are better able to make an informed decision about pursuing that career area.

KEY TERMS

- consumers
- discretionary income
- kinetoscope
- vendors
- product

PREDICT

Name an athlete and an entertainer from the early 20th century.

consumers people who use products

discretionary income money left to spend after necessary expenses are paid

kinetoscope a device used to view a sequence of moving pictures

Sports and Entertainment Connections

What are the connections between sports and entertainment? What do you do when you go to a baseball game or to a movie? Eat buttered popcorn? Walk down the aisle in a stadium or theater? Find your seat and then check out the view? Wait for your favorite star to give a great performance? Do you feel excitement when the screen lights up—or when the players run onto the field as the umpire announces, "Play ball!" What do sports and entertainment events have in common? They have thrilled and entertained people for centuries—since the ancient Olympic Games and Greek plays.

A Brief History of Leisure

Sports and entertainment are leisure activities for the purpose of enjoyment. Sports and entertainment marketers have always sold *participation* in sports or entertainment events to consumers. **Consumers** are people who use products. The growth of the sports and entertainment industries has relied on consumers with free time; **discretionary income,** or money left to spend after necessary expenses are paid; and a desire for recreation.

In America organized sports and entertainment used to be pastimes just for wealthy consumers. In the mid- to late 1800s, only the wealthy had the time and the discretionary income needed to go to the theater, the ballet, horse races, and tennis matches. The working classes had little time away from daily labor. Workers also earned lower wages, which made it difficult for them to spend money on sports or entertainment.

However, labor unions fought for and won higher wages, better working conditions, and reasonable working hours for their members. Workers then had a few extra pennies to spend and more time to attend organized sports and entertainment events. The development of technology and some new inventions also made entertainment more available to the working classes.

Entertainment for Everyone

The creation of public transportation meant that a working-class family without a costly horse and buggy could ride the trolley or bus across town to see an opera or watch a baseball game. Thanks to public transportation, by the 1890s, both wealthy and working-class families were seeking out similar forms of entertainment.

In the late 1890s, Thomas Edison invented the **kinetoscope,** a device for viewing a new phenomenon—moving pictures. Soon both factory workers and owners would stop along the same boardwalk, look into a kinetoscope, and be amazed at the sight of speeding trains and racing horses. The invention of the kinetoscope, also called the Vitascope, signaled the birth of the film industry. Other inventors, such as the Lumière brothers and George Eastman, also contributed to motion picture technology. Further inventions such as the nick-elodeon helped the entertainment industry grow from the era of silent movies to full-sound films in 1927 when *The Jazz Singer* premiered as the first talking movie.

By the end of World War I in 1918, Canadian-born actress Mary Pickford was the world's first international movie star. In sports, Babe Ruth set records in baseball that would stand for decades. Sports and entertainment became staples in everyday life in America through the 1920s. Both forms of entertainment were a welcome distraction from the hardships of the Great Depression in the 1930s. During the 1940s, they became a relief from the trauma of World War II.

Further advances in technology in the 1950s and beyond meant that people grew up with television, local movie theaters, sports franchises, Disneyland, and more time and money to spend on recreation.

Development of Sports and Entertainment Marketing

William "Bill" Veeck was a key figure in the development of sports marketing. In the 1940s, he owned baseball teams such as the Cleveland Indians and the Chicago White Sox. While owner of the White Sox, he drafted the first African-American player to the American League, Larry Doby. However, Veeck is best known for his sports marketing innovations. He believed that consumers wanted to be involved in more than just the final score. So, he conceived of marketing activities and events that surrounded baseball games. Veeck introduced grandstand-style entertainment to the fans. Fireworks, dazzling scoreboards, special-event nights, and the Grandstand Managers' Day, in which fans determined the St. Louis Browns' play for a day, were just some of the activities that Veeck marketed to the fans. By taking a game and turning it into a concept that appealed to both fans and the media, he made sporting events more profitable. Fans enjoyed the new experiences and came to more games because Veeck presented a more interesting "show," or product, and sold more advertising.

Adolph Zukor, founder of Paramount Pictures and pioneer in creating the Hollywood studio system, also knew how to sell to a crowd. In the 1900s, a movie was a ten-minute series

SPORTS AND ENTERTAINMENT The show *I Love Lucy* starring Lucille Ball and Desi Arnaz was one of the most popular sitcoms of the 1950s. Sports and entertainment often overlap. *Do entertainers integrate sports into their acts today?*

AHEAD OF THE PACK

Charles Howard
Sports Marketer/Horse Owner
Seabiscuit

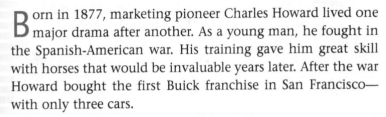

Born in 1877, marketing pioneer Charles Howard lived one major drama after another. As a young man, he fought in the Spanish-American war. His training gave him great skill with horses that would be invaluable years later. After the war Howard bought the first Buick franchise in San Francisco—with only three cars.

The Right Bet In 1936, Howard returned to his love for horses, spending $8,000 to buy a horse named *Seabiscuit,* an underdog by anyone's standards. His first trainer said the horse was "dead lazy." He was small, clumsy, and awkward. However, in 1938, Howard took Seabiscuit on a tour of race-tracks across the country. He won nearly every race he ran. On November 1, 1938, Seabiscuit faced the only horse that was expected to beat him, the Triple-Crown-winning *War Admiral*. Again, Seabiscuit triumphed—and continued to win, despite injuries, until retirement in 1940.

The horse was an enormous hit with the public who identified with the little horse that beat the odds. "Seabiscuit Limited" trains would transport fans to racetracks. Everything from fashionable hats and wallets to toys and wastebaskets were tagged with Seabiscuit's name. The horse's image promoted products and businesses alike.

A born salesman, Charles Howard placed his "athlete" in front of the public, catering to the press with the latest news—and champagne. Some say he invented sports marketing because he understood that he needed more than a great horse.

List some examples of promotions tied to Seabiscuit.

Career Data:
Sports Marketer

Education and Training Bachelor's or master's degrees in business, marketing, or general education

Skills and Abilities Excellent communication skills, strong organizational skills, and creativity

Career Outlook Faster than average growth through 2010

Career Path Entry-level positions provide experience. Real-world skills are crucial for advancement in sports marketing.

CONNECT

Have you ever attended a special-event night at a baseball game? If so, what was the event?

of moving pictures produced by Edison to sell projection machines. However, Zukor had show business in mind. He was one of the first film producers to draw big box-office crowds and own a chain of theaters, making Paramount the leading studio of the teens and 1920s. He marketed early movies such as *The Prisoner of Zenda* as "Famous Players in Famous Plays." As an entertainment marketer, he capitalized on the appeal of dramatic stories and popular stars of the day.

Marketing Today

Today sports and entertainment marketing professionals cannot simply rely on the entertainment value of their products. Just as athletes compete for points to win and TV programs compete for ratings, sports and entertainment **vendors,** or sellers of products, compete for a share of the money people spend on recreation. With many new media vying for consumer attention, an organized strategy that targets specific consumers to specific products is essential. This is the foundation of sports and entertainment marketing.

Sports and entertainment marketing directs consumers toward sports and entertainment products. A **product** is a good or service that any for-profit industry sells to its customers. It is not enough to sell tickets to a single ball game or a concert. Marketers want to sell season tickets, have patrons return for the sequel, and purchase goods related to that team or entertainer.

Similarities and Differences in Marketing

Sports and entertainment are closely related. But are they the same thing? Watch a Lakers or Knicks game on television, and you see celebrities, such as Spike Lee, Jack Nicholson, or Salma Hayek, sitting courtside watching star athletes such as Shaquille O'Neal or Keith Van Horn. Flip though a *People* magazine, and you find stories about famous sports or entertainment stars. The status and exposure of sports stars on television, in magazines, and in advertising are equal to, if not greater than, those of Hollywood celebrities. Their images are used to sell clothes, perfume, athletic shoes, cars, and even barbeque grills. This overlap makes defining the differences between sports and entertainment a difficult task.

Sports has spawned a huge entertainment-based industry beyond the competition between organized teams. Sports has produced TV channels, movies, books, video games, theme restaurants, fashion trends, and magazines—all of which blur the line between the sports and entertainment industries. In the sections that follow, we will look at the similarities and differences between the two industries and the marketing considerations for each one.

MARKETING SERIES *Online*

Remember to check out this book's Web site for sports and entertainment marketing information and more great resources at marketingseries.glencoe.com.

vendors sellers of products

product a good or service that any for-profit industry sells to its customers

QUESTION

Besides tickets, what do sports and entertainment marketers want to sell?

Quick Check

RESPOND to what you've read by answering these questions.

1. Name two inventions that helped to enable more equal access to entertainment for the wealthy and the working classes by the 1890s. _____

   _____

2. Who was a key figure in the development of sports marketing? _____

   _____

3. How did Adolph Zukor help the entertainment market grow? _____

   _____

Similarities in Marketing

AS YOU READ . . .

YOU WILL LEARN

- To explain how sports and entertainment marketers use tools to sell their products.
- To explain risks and risk management of sports and entertainment events.

WHY IT'S IMPORTANT

Knowledge of the basic tools, copyright law, and risks regarding sports and entertainment marketing helps marketers achieve success.

KEY TERMS

- promotion
- endorsement
- core product
- ancillary product
- revenue
- piracy
- royalty
- product tie-in
- cross-promotion
- convergence
- synergy
- risks
- risk management

PREDICT

Choose one key word and explain what you think it means.

Changes in Marketing

As discussed in Chapter 1, the marketing mix, or Four Ps—product, place, price, and promotion—has been the basis for marketing many products and services over the last few decades. Some marketers consider *people* as a fifth P in the marketing mix. **Promotion** is any form of communication used to persuade people to buy products through advertising, publicity, personal selling, or sales.

Thirty years ago marketers did not have today's marketing tools, such as the Internet, e-commerce, Direct TV, TiVo, video, CDs, CD burners, DVDs, MP3s, PCs, PDAs, interactive gaming, and virtual advertising. New technologies have broadened the scope and reach of marketing messages, and they can be entertainment products themselves. What happens when the products for sale are also the marketing tools? It changes the way products are marketed.

Marketing Similarities

Marketing professionals are split over whether sports and entertainment products belong in the same category. After all, a sports event is a form of entertainment, just as a film or concert is a form of entertainment. However, professionals do agree that both sports and entertainment products are similar in that they are marketed differently than traditional consumer products. The marketing of sports and entertainment products differs from marketing traditional products in four areas: product, place, price, and promotion. **Figure 2.1** on page 34 illustrates these differences.

Product

Sports and entertainment *products* are different from traditional consumer products. By nature, sports and entertainment products are often not physical goods that can be stacked on a store shelf. Entertainment presentations and athletic competitions are both dynamic and can be used to promote unrelated products. For example, ESPN-themed restaurants do not sell tickets to a game. They sell burgers and drinks by using the appeal of sports. Also, golf celebrities, such as Tiger Woods, sell everything from cars to watches to clothing. Woods uses his appeal as a sportsman to promote these non-sports-related products.

ENDORSEMENT **Endorsement** is approval or support of a product or idea, usually by a celebrity lending his or her image or name to

Worldwide Buzzing

They frequently stake out their subjects while lurking around a corner, hunkering down in a car, or perching in a tree. They're not the police—they're freelance photographers called paparazzi. Often traveling in groups, they track celebrities for candid snapshots and quick cash. The word *paparazzi*—Italian for "buzzing insects"—comes from the 1959 film *La Dolce Vita* ("The Good Life"). An annoying photographer in the movie was named *Signor Paparazzo*. You don't have to be Italian to be a paparazzo, but you do have to be quick, aggressive, and patient. Some paparazzi make a career out of

following a single celebrity. These avid photographers often bother entertainers and sports figures, whose pictures are sold to the highest bidder. Privacy laws do little good. The tabloid market is big, and consumers are eager to have the latest unauthorized photos of Madonna, Shaq, or De Niro.

Do you think celebrities have a right to privacy or are paparazzi just doing a job?

a product. Celebrity endorsement is not used only in sports marketing. It is an important tool in entertainment marketing as well. A music, fashion, TV, or film celebrity endorsement is a powerful marketing tool. All celebrities have a *public persona,* or a personality perceived by the public. This may be based on their skills and behavior in public. Fans identify with and admire many celebrities. This identification makes the fans feel connected to celebrities. If a high-profile athlete says that a particular sports energy drink works for her, her fans may trust her endorsement and buy the product to get the same results.

However, marketers must match their products with the correct celebrities. To create an effective endorsement, the celebrity who endorses a product should be popular with people who would buy the product. Can you imagine former heavyweight boxing champion George Foreman endorsing CoverGirl Cosmetics? Despite his celebrity status, George Foreman would be unlikely to get an endorsement contract with CoverGirl Cosmetics. Instead, CoverGirl uses singer Faith Hill, who appeals more to the people who are the primary consumers of cosmetic products.

promotion any form of communication used to persuade people to buy products

endorsement approval or support of a product or idea, usually by a celebrity

CORE AND ANCILLARY PRODUCTS In sports and entertainment marketing, examples of a **core product,** or main product, include the sports event, movie, stage show, or book. The **ancillary product** is a product related to or created from the core product. For example, an ancillary product could be an amusement-park ride based on a movie, or core product. A DVD recording can be the ancillary product of a stage show, which is the core product. A movie studio can release an animated movie in theaters and then later release it on DVD as an ancillary product. Fans can view a boxing match at an arena and later see it as an ancillary product on network or pay-per-view TV.

core product the main product, such as sports event, movie, stage show, or book

ancillary product a product related to or created from the core product

Figure 2.1

Comparing the Four Ps

FINDING THE RIGHT MIX Sports products and entertainment products are each unique, but both benefit from a good marketing mix. *In what ways are traditional consumer products marketed differently than sports and entertainment products?*

Marketing-Mix Component	Traditional Consumer Product	Entertainment Product	Sports Entertainment Product
	Light Bulb	**Movie**	**Baseball Game**
Product Who is my customer?	Someone in the dark who needs a light bulb	Someone who wants to be entertained by a plot/character	Someone who wants to be entertained by sports
Place Where will I sell the product?	In a local hardware store, grocery store, or online	In local theaters, stores, online, through pay-per-view TV, or cable/satellite TV	At local stadiums, in sports bars, online, through pay-per-view TV, or cable/satellite TV
Price How do I compete for customers?	Price better for quality than the competition and increasing sales	Consumer choice to buy a movie ticket is not based on price. Price is largely set and based on what theaters can charge and what people will pay.	Consumer choice to buy a baseball ticket is not based on price. Price is set and based on what sports teams can charge and on what people will pay.
Promotion How do I inform customers?	Advertising in print and on TV, and having in-store promotions	Great Web site; in-theater and TV previews; stars on late-night TV/talk shows, in magazines and books, and on lunch boxes and billboards; action figures and collectibles	Games on TV; selling jerseys; giving away prizes at games; family days at the stadium; talk radio; ads; sports shows; high-profile players on TV, in magazines, and on billboards; bobblehead dolls; trading cards

revenue gross income

Companies can market sports and entertainment products as core and ancillary products. Companies can earn additional **revenue**, or gross income, by using those core and ancillary products as promotional tools to promote and market even more unrelated products. For example, the characters in a movie, the core product, can be sold later as toys, lunchboxes, T-shirts, sheets, and pajamas, which are ancillary products. A hockey team, as a core product, can generate jerseys, caps, posters, bumper stickers, and even miniature Stanley Cups, which are ancillary products.

CONNECT

How much do you spend for tickets and concessions when you go to the movies?

Place

The changing nature of the *place* component in the marketing mix has affected traditional marketing more than sports and entertainment marketing. E-commerce has changed where most people shop for traditional consumer products. Business people once thought that the mall would signal the end of local merchants and their stores on Main Street, U.S.A. This has occurred in some areas, but now the mall is competing with customers shopping at home on the Internet.

Successful sports and entertainment marketing strategies have always appealed to the desire to go out to a special event. Fans will still go to see a movie in a theater or will drive to a ballpark to see a game. The *occasion* appeal of the event contributes to the entertainment value of the process. When fans get home, they can also go online and purchase a soundtrack and book version of a film. They can download player statistics from a sports Web site, or they can catch the highlights of the game on television.

Price

Pricing sports and entertainment products is radically different from pricing traditional consumer products. Movie theaters rarely lower their ticket prices to compete with other first-run theater chains. Even when theaters offer reduced matinée prices, other theaters do the same thing. In fact, prices for movies and sports tickets have risen steadily over the last ten years.

Price is set and adhered to uniformly, based on what theaters and sports teams can charge—and what people will pay. However, customers may believe that they are getting more for their money. "More" might include stadium seating in googolplex cinemas, nachos in addition to popcorn, and stadiums with sushi bars and hotdog stands. This kind of perception separates sports and entertainment marketing from the marketing of other consumer products.

Case Study **PART 2**

NEW KIND OF KICK

Continued from Part 1 on page 27

While DC Shoes has grown quickly, Block and Way have ensured that it has stayed true to its skateboarding roots. They've limited their expansion to sports such as snowboarding, BMX, and surfing—activities that skateboarders respect and often do. DC has also involved musicians and artists in its marketing mix by making limited-edition shoe designs influenced by punk bands, drum-and-bass collectives, graffiti artists, and designers.

DC-sponsored skaters play a role in keeping the brand current as well. When Danny Way strapped on a skateboard and jumped out of a helicopter onto a ramp to perform the world's largest "air," every skateboard magazine covered the story. Likewise, DC Shoes has not abandoned independent skate shops for mall chains. DC reserves certain models for skate shops only. As a result of its loyal and savvy marketing practices, DC Shoes now has a staff of 150 employees and makes more than $100 million annually.

ANALYZE AND WRITE

1. How has DC used cross-promotion to market its skateboards?
2. If you were to market DC Shoes, where would you advertise? Why?

PRICE PROBLEMS Price becomes an issue when highly paid players and celebrities go on strike for salary increases. Fan loyalty can be damaged. Many fans cannot understand the justification for athletes or celebrities striking to get even richer.

Other pricing issues include ticket scalping and piracy. *Ticket scalpers* are unauthorized ticket sellers who stand outside a game or concert and offer tickets at a higher price, especially if tickets are difficult to obtain. They keep any profit they make. **Piracy** is the unauthorized use of an owner's or creator's music, movies, or other copyrighted material. Any intellectual property can be copyrighted. *Intellectual property* is an idea, concept, or written or created work that is protected by copyright. Piracy can occur online when consumers use file-sharing software to download copyrighted material without permission. Street vendors also sell copies

piracy the unauthorized use of an owner's or creator's music, movies, or other copyrighted material

of copyrighted goods that are pirated or *bootlegged,* which means produced and distributed without authorization.

When people purchase entertainment in a store, or use it in another form for profit, a portion of the profit called a royalty usually goes to the artist or owner. A **royalty** is a payment for material that has been copyrighted, or legally declared as belonging to the creator. When consumers copy and distribute illegal copies of entertainment material, they cut the property owner out of the profits.

royalty a payment for material that has been copyrighted, or legally declared as belonging to the creator

Promotion

Sports and entertainment marketing uses two tools to *promote* goods: product tie-ins and cross-promotion. **Product tie-in** is the use of ancillary products such as merchandise as promotional tools. For example, if you buy a Happy Meal® at McDonald's®, the free toy included with the meal might be a character from the newest Disney film or a popular sports figure modeled as a bobblehead doll.

product tie-in use of ancillary products such as merchandise as promotional tools

cross-promotion any form of communication through which one industry relies on another industry to promote its product

Cross-promotion is any form of communication through which one industry relies on another industry to promote its product. In film promotion, celebrities use their personal appeal to persuade viewers to buy tickets to their movies. The star of a new movie will do TV promotions by appearing on late-night and daytime talk shows. The same celebrity will also give exclusive interviews to magazines and newspapers.

Web sites are another important cross-promotional tool. Web sites provide information and highlights of a product, while hosting links to other products. Web sites also market by *word-of-mouth.* Chat rooms, user ratings, and online voting surveys use consumers to spread news about a product. This word-of-mouth talk, or *buzz,* about a film or a team can translate into increased ticket sales.

Convergence—Part of the Marketing Mix

convergence the overlapping of product promotion

Convergence is the overlapping of product promotion. For example, a studio may use TV advertising to promote a movie that may one day be sold to television. Web sites are used both as promotional tools and as sources of revenue, hosting links and online shopping for merchandise. This convergence, or overlap, expands the potential for profit in sports marketing and entertainment marketing. Marketers must consider all the elements , obstacles, and opportunities involved in marketing sports and entertainment. They must develop marketing strategies that understand this convergence, or overlap.

SYNERGY One of the biggest similarities between sports and entertainment marketing is the potential for convergence and cross-promotion. Convergence and cross-promotion help to develop product synergy. **Synergy** is a combined action that occurs when products owned by one source promote the growth of related products.

Oprah Winfrey represents a good example of how synergy works. Oprah created an image as a "lifestyle guru." She has a TV show as her core product and uses that visibility and viewership to promote ancillary businesses, such as her magazine, her production company, and the products she endorses. Synergy occurs again when the magazine steers readers back to viewing the show.

synergy a combined action that occurs when products owned by one source promote the growth of related products

QUESTION

What is an example of convergence?

Figure 2.2

Risk Insurance Coverage

TAKING NO CHANCES Companies can buy insurance to protect against four different risks listed in this chart. *If you were planning a rock concert, what would you insure?*

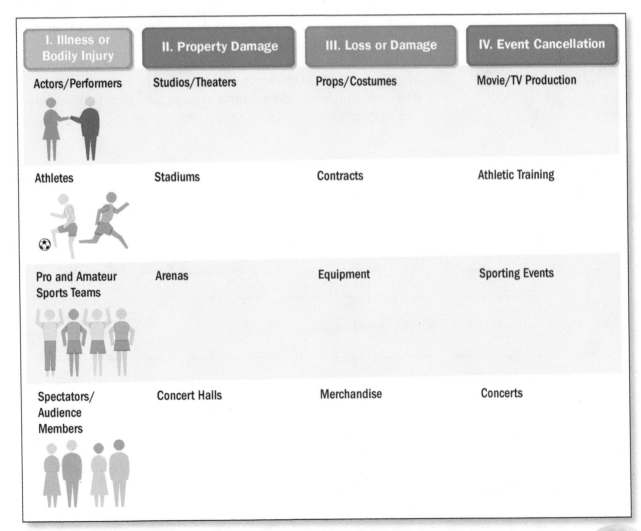

I. Illness or Bodily Injury	II. Property Damage	III. Loss or Damage	IV. Event Cancellation
Actors/Performers	Studios/Theaters	Props/Costumes	Movie/TV Production
Athletes	Stadiums	Contracts	Athletic Training
Pro and Amateur Sports Teams	Arenas	Equipment	Sporting Events
Spectators/ Audience Members	Concert Halls	Merchandise	Concerts

Long before wrestling entertainer Hulk Hogan and Hulkmania, there was Ed "Strangler" Lewis in the 1920s, whose career and fortune were knocked down by The Great Depression in the early 1930s.

risks unforeseen events and obstacles that can negatively affect business

risk management a strategy to offset business risks

Risks and Risk Management

Creating synergy is a goal of sports and entertainment marketing. However, synergy is not easy to achieve. In any industry, there are **risks**, or unforeseen events and obstacles that can negatively affect business. The business of sports and entertainment is especially risky because of the unpredictable nature of the products.

For example, highly paid athletes and entertainers are subject to injury and illness. They may also be suspended if caught using any type of illegal substance. This can mean a losing season for a ball club or expensive production delays for a movie studio. Concert promoters can plan events at major arenas for thousands of people, but a singer with a sore throat can cancel the whole show.

Successful sports and entertainment marketers realize there are many risks in their businesses. So they develop **risk management**, which is a strategy to offset business risks. Sports and entertainment risk-management firms are hired to identify potential risks. They help write contracts and purchase insurance policies to protect their clients from industry-related risks. **Figure 2.2** on page 37 illustrates some of the items covered by a risk insurance policy.

Some insurance policies will reimburse business owners for both direct and indirect losses. For example, when a stadium fire causes the cancellation of an event, insurance will pay for the loss of profit to the business as well as the cost to repair and reopen the stadium. Similarly, if a fan is injured while at a football game, insurance will pay for the fan's claim related to bodily injury.

Both sports products and entertainment products share risks that highlight the similarities that exist between the two types of products. However, differences do exist that require marketers to adjust marketing strategies for each specific industry.

Quick Check

RESPOND to what you've read by answering these questions.

1. What is celebrity endorsement? _____

_____

_____

2. What is the difference between a core and an ancillary product?_____

_____

_____

_____

3. Give an example of synergy. _____

_____

_____

Differences in Marketing

Different Players, Different Games

From a marketing point of view, sports products and entertainment products are dynamic goods and services. However, each type of product has distinctions. For example, entertainment is based on creative ideas that can be fashioned to fit the tastes of a target audience, but sport is based on athletic ability and competition.

Because the two areas are based on different things, consumers are attracted to sports or entertainment for different reasons. For instance, you probably would not go see a terrible movie twice, but you might keep going to a sports game, even if your team was experiencing a losing streak.

The differences between sports and entertainment can be found in three areas:

- Consumer loyalty

- Product

- Revenue stream

Differences in Consumer Loyalty

Sports fans enjoy the drama of real competition and the unpredictability of each game. A team can win at the last second in overtime. If sports fans feel their team is trying to win, the team can retain its consumer loyalty. **Consumer loyalty** occurs when consumers are happy with a company's product and become repeat customers. For example, consumer loyalty may mean always watching one team play on television because you like that team the best.

Fans usually support one or two teams. Sports marketers target a core group of fans and work on maintaining their team loyalty, or consumer loyalty. While sports marketers are always looking for ways to attract more fans to games, most sports franchises spend more effort marketing a winning season to their target markets than trying to appeal to new and different consumer groups.

In contrast, the entertainment consumer is not motivated by brand or team loyalty, but by a desire for satisfying entertainment. Furthermore, the entertainment industry is subject to trends that dictate "what's hot and what's not." If a company's movie, book, sitcom, amusement ride, video game, magazine, CD, DVD, or video does not deliver the expected level of entertainment, the consumer will quickly turn to the competition.

Entertainment marketers target each product to a well-defined consumer group. An individual artist might successfully maintain a

AS YOU READ ...

YOU WILL LEARN

- To identify differences between marketing sports and entertainment products.

WHY IT'S IMPORTANT

There are few differences between marketing sports products and entertainment products, but knowledge of the differences helps marketers target the correct consumer.

KEY TERMS

- consumer loyalty
- sponsorship

consumer loyalty consumers' attitude that occurs when they are happy with a company and become repeat customers

PREDICT

Before reading the section, think of one difference between watching a sports game and watching a movie.

loyal fan base, but entertainment production companies have difficulty creating that same kind of consumer loyalty. Production companies offer a variety of products targeting a variety of consumers. Therefore, unlike fans who follow only one sports team, film and music fans will usually see films made by more than one production company, or will buy CDs produced by many different record labels.

Because of this difference in consumer loyalty, marketers must identify the different marketing goals for sports consumers and for entertainment consumers:

- **Job of the Entertainment Marketer:** Find a Winning Formula. Try to KNOW what consumers want. CREATE that product.

- **Job of the Sports Marketer:** Find a Winning Team. KNOW what consumers want. Try to DELIVER that product.

Differences in Product

Another big difference between sports product and entertainment product is the consistency, or stability, of the sports product and the variability, or changeability, of the entertainment product. In marketing a traditional product, marketers have plenty of time to conduct research, run tests, and plan launches and promotions.

To some extent, sports as a product has that same luxury because its core product remains the same—a sports team, event, or facility. For entertainment products, however, marketers have to predict a trend or fad, and then change the product to satisfy audience demand. For example, a movie release may be postponed or cancelled because the movie's subject matter is too sensitive due to current events. In the case of the 2003 movie *Phone Booth,* the plot revolved around a man pinned in a phone booth by a gunman. Its premiere coincided with real-life shootings in the Washington, D.C., metro area. Therefore, the studio 20th Century Fox postponed the movie's release. Sports events are usually not subject to the same variables.

Differences in Revenue Stream

Both sports and entertainment have their own streams of revenue. Entertainment products can be developed into merchandise, used for promotion, and create profit through sales of ancillary products, licensing, and royalties. Because there are so many different types of entertainment products, the streams of revenue created by marketing products are very diverse. A single film can generate many ancillary products. The film can be sold to cable TV and pay-per-view TV, and also rented as videos and DVDs. The film can also be the basis for a game, TV series, book, or clothing line. The products that make use of the original creative idea or characters make a profit for the owner through sales, royalties, and licensing fees.

However, with the exception of a championship game, one sporting event does not usually produce the same amount of revenue from merchandising and royalties as might an entertainment event. For example, a single, regular-season National Football League (NFL) game probably does not have more economic impact than a Rolling Stones concert. However, sporting events do have their own streams of revenue from tickets sales, media advertising, video games, and so on.

Sponsorship Differences

Sponsorship is the promotion of a company in association with a property. For example, a company sponsors, or gives money to, another person or company to fund a project or production in exchange for something, such as advertising. Watch a NASCAR (National Association for Stock Car Auto Racing) race, and you will see sports sponsorship. Different companies sponsor each car and driver. In return, the company logo is displayed on the car and on the driver's suit and helmet. The company benefits from the increased advertisement. The driver benefits from additional income.

Sponsorship is different from endorsement. The sponsoring company is not lending a name or image to a sports product, which is endorsing.

Another example of sponsorship is corporate boxes in stadiums. Sponsorship money buys advertising and privileges at sporting events, such as the use of company boxes. Corporations use them as a marketing tool to entertain and network with their own clients.

Math Check

REAPING REVENUE
A charity baseball game earned $6,010 in ticket sales, $837 in T-shirt sales, $1,500 in advertising, and $375 in parking. What was the total revenue?

➡ For tips on finding the solution, go to marketingseries.glencoe.com.

sponsorship the promotion of a company in association with a property

Hot Property

Beyond the Gridiron

Once upon a time, the Super Bowl was a sports contest, pitting the newly formed National Football League and American Football League against each other. That was in 1967. Since then the Super Bowl has become much more than a football championship.

MILLIONS AT STAKE

Today the Super Bowl is a media event that makes millions of dollars for stadiums, advertisers, television networks, and record companies. Even entertainment trade magazines such as *Daily Variety* analyze ratings and marketing strategies, as well as game plays, to track profit potential.

Beginning in 1982, the Super Bowl has consistently pulled television audiences of over 70 million viewers—and sometimes over 90 million. The network that broadcasts the game profits by charging high rates for advertisers to reach those viewers. In 2004, companies paid CBS an average of $2.25 million for 30 seconds of commercial time. The high cost of purchasing time raises the stakes for producing commercials. Some sponsors debut new commercials at the Super Bowl.

In addition to innovative ads and corporate sponsorships, the Super Bowl features performers from the recording industry in pre-game, halftime, and post-game shows. Stars such as U2, Sting, Aerosmith, and Shania Twain are included to attract a broader audience than the football game could draw by itself. That means higher ratings for the network and higher profits for advertising sponsors.

1. Why is the Super Bowl important to networks and advertisers?
2. What do you think viewers remember most after watching the Super Bowl—the game, the commercials, or the halftime show?

QUESTION

 Where do advertisers place their names at sports games?

Another source of sponsorship revenue comes from selling stadium-naming rights. Bank One Ballpark in Arizona, Citizens Bank Park in Philadelphia, and Minute Maid Park in Houston each bears the name of a corporate sponsor. The sponsors pay for the privilege of having stadiums named after their businesses.

Advertising and Broadcast Rights

Virtual advertising is a new phenomenon that has also created revenue for sports teams and venues. Besides buying advertising banners on scoreboards and seats, companies can now pay to have their logos digitally overlaid onto a billboard during a televised game. Fans at the game do not see the digital sign, but viewers at home can watch a new brand logo pop up on the screen every few minutes.

Sports franchises also earn revenue by landing local broadcast deals with television companies. TV networks make million-dollar deals with sports leagues for exclusive rights to broadcast games. Notre Dame's football team is the only team to make an exclusive national broadcast deal with a network—NBC. This is an example of companies recognizing the marketability of sports and using it to attract viewers to their stations. As a result, the networks sell more advertising.

Summary

As technology advances, the overlap between entertainment media and products will cause the lines to blur between sports and entertainment. However, sports and entertainment products remain separate. This separation, or difference, is enough to require different approaches for marketing products. Sports and entertainment are separated by differences in consumer loyalty, product, and revenue streams.

The desire for entertainment is as old as civilization, whether it is sport, dance, art, or song. If modern consumers continue to have time and discretionary income available, they will continue to spend them on recreation. Marketers are in a good position to harness that desire to market sports entertainment and products.

Quick Check ✓

RESPOND to what you've read by answering these questions.

1. List two differences in consumer loyalty between sports and entertainment. _____

   _____

   _____

2. What are differences between marketing sports products and entertainment products? _____

   _____

3. Describe one way in which the stream of revenue in sports differs from the stream of revenue in

   entertainment. _____

Worksheet 2.1

Expanding Products

Name three favorite movies as core products and list some ancillary products for each film. Think of some new ancillary products that would help market each film and create more revenue.

Core product:

Film Title	Film Title	Film Title
1. _____	2. _____	3. _____
_____	_____	_____
_____	_____	_____

Ancillary products:

New ancillary products:

Worksheet 2.2

The Wide World of Marketing

Give examples of the differences between marketing sports and marketing entertainment.

Marketing Sports

Consumer loyalty

_____

_____

_____

Product

_____

_____

_____

Revenue stream

_____

_____

_____

Marketing Entertainment

Consumer loyalty

_____

_____

_____

Product

_____

_____

_____

Revenue stream

_____

_____

_____

Portfolio Works

EXPLORING MARKETING CAREERS

Go to the library or the Internet and find five careers in sports and entertainment marketing that interest you or may be unfamiliar to you. Do the following exercises. Then add this page to your career portfolio.

1. List five careers.

_____

_____

_____

2. Use the Internet to explore at least one career. Describe that career.

_____

_____

_____

3. List your skills and interests. Then list the jobs that match these skills and interests. Create names for the jobs if they are applicable.

Skills/Interests	Possible Jobs
_____	_____
_____	_____
_____	_____

4. Review your list of skills and interests. What stands out? Think of as many jobs as you can that relate to your skills and interests.

_____

_____

_____

_____

_____

5. Describe an ideal job that involves these skills. Include the location of the ideal job and the kinds of coworkers, customers, and employees you would meet.

_____

_____

_____

CHAPTER SUMMARY

Section 2.1 History of Sports and Entertainment

consumers (p. 28)
discretionary income (p. 28)
kinetoscope (p. 28)
vendors (p. 31)
product (p. 31)

- Sports and entertainment marketing during the early 20th century helped create the foundation of sports and entertainment marketing.

- The history of sports and entertainment reveals how strategies and technological advances such as special events at sports events, the kinetoscope, sound technology, television, and the Internet all influence marketing today.

Section 2.2 Similarities in Marketing

promotion (p. 33)
endorsement (p. 33)
core product (p. 33)
ancillary product (p. 33)
revenue (p. 34)
piracy (p. 35)
royalty (p. 36)
product tie-in (p. 36)
cross-promotion (p. 36)
convergence (p. 36)
synergy (p. 37)
risks (p. 38)
risk management (p. 38)

- Sports and entertainment marketers use the same tools, such as the marketing mix, including product, place, price, and promotion strategies to sell their products.

- To offset risks or unforeseen events and obstacles in sports and entertainment events and businesses, risk management is used to identify risks and obtain insurance.

Section 2.3 Differences in Marketing

consumer loyalty (p. 39)
sponsorship (p. 41)

- Differences between marketing sports and entertainment products are based on consumer loyalty, product, and revenue streams.

CHECKING CONCEPTS

1. **Identify** three people in sports and entertainment history.
2. **Discuss** one way that sports and entertainment history has affected marketing today.
3. **Name** three different marketing tools.
4. **Define** royalty.
5. **Give an example** of a royalty.
6. **Give an example** of cross-promotion for a film.
7. **Describe** one risk involved in a sports event.

Critical Thinking

8. **Explain** one method of risk management for one risk.

CROSS-CURRICULUM SKILLS

Work-Based Learning

Basic Skills—Writing

9. Imagine you work at a sports marketing agency. You must write a banner ad for a new sports drink. Write the ad and read it in class.

Interpersonal Skills—Teaching Others

10. Create a chart or graphic organizer that explains cross-promotion. Display it and discuss it in class.

School-Based Learning

History

11. Using the Internet and library, research and write a one-page report about two athletes and two film stars of 1930.

Language Arts

12. Write a radio script to advertise a local business that is sponsoring a charity bicycle race. Read it to your class.

 **CONNECTION**

Role Play: Marketing Director

SITUATION You are to assume the role of marketing director for a semi-pro wrestling tournament. Community groups select the wrestlers they wish to see compete in a match and use the event as a fundraiser. The director (judge) wants to increase the number of events on the schedule, but he or she is unsure about how to identify the event—as a sporting event or an entertainment event.

ACTIVITY Present a product/service management plan for this event to the director (judge).

EVALUATION You will be evaluated on how well you meet the following performance indicators:

- Develop strategies to position product/business.
- Describe factors used by marketers to position products/business.
- Describe the role of customer expectations in services marketing.
- Explain the concept of product mix.
- Explain the role of customer service in positioning/image.

 **INTERNET ACTIVITY**

The Clio is the award for advertising achievement. The Clio is awarded to those judged best in the fields of television, print media, radio, integrated media, innovative media, design, Internet, and student work.

- Access the Web site for the Clio Awards.
- Read three press releases.
- Choose one press release, write a summary, and read it to your class.

For a link to the Clio Awards to begin this exercise, go to **marketingseries.glencoe.com**.

BusinessWeek News

NINTENDO BEEFS UP ITS ARSENAL

With the video-game business in the midst of a bruising fight, Nintendo Company is beefing up its arsenal. Its latest weapon is *Metal Gear Solid: The Twin Snakes,* an action thriller featuring sword-wielding ninjas and antiterrorist commandos. That's quite a departure for a company known for characters such as the mild-mannered plumber Mario and Pokémon's lovable "pocket monsters." But [otherwise], Nintendo risks being picked off by archrivals Sony and Microsoft.

The once-undisputed King of Gameland remains the world's largest game-software publisher, and it dominates the handheld game market with its hugely successful Game Boy Advance. But Nintendo has sold only 9.6 million GameCube video-game consoles since September, 2001, far short of its 13.8 million target. Nintendo President Satoru Iwata concedes that the year has been a challenge. "But then, that's what I enjoy," says Iwata, a former game developer. "We need to feel a sense of crisis to bring out the best in us."

That sense of crisis has led Iwata to rethink Nintendo's business plan. He has moved to sharpen Nintendo's lineup of titles. The new version of *Metal Gear Solid,* developed exclusively for Nintendo, is a first step. To maintain the momentum, Iwata has lined up a *Star Wars* epic from Lucas Arts Entertainment Company, that is a futuristic *F-Zero* car-racing game from Sega

Corporation, and other sports and action titles to push Nintendo's software lineup from 180 titles to 320.

Yet, if Nintendo hopes to attract more of the boys and young men who are flocking to PS2 and Xbox, Iwata needs to come up with a thrilling lineup of sports and adventure games.

Another concern is that Nintendo continues to stay clear of online gaming, while Sony and Microsoft are taking the plunge. "Consumers aren't ready to pay for such services, so how do you make money?" asks Iwata. Microsoft thinks it can make plenty of money with Internet games, and so far, it has attracted

500,000 subscribers who pay $50 a year for its Xbox Live.

Iwata firmly believes Nintendo has a future in digital entertainment. Nintendo's creators are hard at work on next-generation stars to replace the company's aging lineup of Mario and Pokémon. Iwata may have the skills to do that, but he'll have to pack plenty of firepower to climb to the top of the video-game business.

By Irene M. Kunii with Jay Greene

CREATIVE JOURNAL

In your journal, write your responses:

CRITICAL THINKING

1. What is the target market for action video games?

APPLICATION

2. If you were developing a new video game to appeal to the target market for Nintendo games, what sports or recent films would you use as inspiration to create the game? Why? Describe your game.

 Go to businessweek.com for current *BusinessWeek* Online articles.

UNIT LAB

Dream Machine, Inc.

You've just entered the real world of sports and entertainment marketing. Dream Machine, Inc., is a sports and entertainment marketing company that serves college and professional sports teams, professional athletes, sporting events, sports arenas, and major sports product corporations, as well as performing arts companies, television networks, and movie studios. As an entry-level employee, you will have the opportunity to work on a variety of clients' projects.

Turn On the Electric Channel—Create a Web Site

SITUATION Last year during summer break, you worked for a concession stand at a local minor league ballpark. With interest in minor league baseball growing, along with the winning stats of the team, attendance at the ballpark increased. The stand sold more T-shirts, pennants, and caps than ever before. This year, your former manager has her hands full. She remembers that you were knowledgeable about the Internet and wants you and Dream Machine to develop a Web site for selling team merchandise, especially because the home team may win the championship.

ASSIGNMENT Complete these tasks:
- Plan your basic e-tail store with one or two unique features to attract your customers.
- Estimate your start-up costs including design, shipping, maintenance, and storage.
- Create a final report.

TOOLS AND RESOURCES To complete the assignment, you will need to:
- Conduct research at the library, on the Internet, or by phone.
- Ask other sporting-goods stores about experiences with Web sites.
- Have word-processing, spreadsheet, and presentation software.

RESEARCH Do your research:
- Find out the most important characteristics of a sporting-goods Web site.

- Go to other similar Web sites and identify and assess their features.
- Get cost estimates for designing and implementing basic Web sites with purchasing features.

REPORT Prepare a written report using the following tools, if available:
- *Word-processing program:* Prepare a written report with a site map outline and list of features, as well as a market overview and customer analysis.
- *Spreadsheet program:* Prepare a chart comparing other competitor Web sites with yours. Prepare a budget chart with your estimates.
- *Presentation program:* Prepare a ten-slide visual presentation with key points, some visuals, and little text.

PRESENTATION AND EVALUATION
You will present your report to your silent partner and the bank that may finance your plan. You will be evaluated on the basis of:
- Knowledge of the e-tail Web-site business
- Continuity of presentation
- Voice quality
- Eye contact

PORTFOLIO
Add this report to your career portfolio.

UNIT 2
SPORTS MARKETING

" The crowd makes the game. "
—Ty Cobb

The sports market is vast and growing due to the "wide world of sports" that are played and viewed by the public today. From Olympic swimming championships to Super Bowl games, the sports industry is big business that requires effective marketing strategies. Chapter 3 introduces sports marketing with a history of the business, which continues to expand into the 21st century, as well as an overview of the many categories of sports. Chapter 4 answers the question, "Who is the sports consumer?" Finally, the variety of sports that generate sports goods and services is examined with a discussion on how marketing sports products impacts the economy.

■ UNIT LAB

Preview ⌐

⌐ Consider the different types of sports products on the market today. Sports apparel is a huge segment of the sports industry. Is producing sportswear a good strategy for a clothing company? Why?

These functions are highlighted in this unit:

- Promotion
- Selling
- Distribution
- Product/Service Management
- Pricing
- Financing

Chapter 3

The Sports Market

Chapter Objectives

- Define sports marketing.
- Identify the different categories of sports.
- Differentiate between amateur sports and professional sports.
- Discuss the significance of international sports.
- Explain the significance of women's sports.

CARDBOARD COLLECTIBLES

Once upon a time, sports trading cards were made with simple designs on cheap cardboard and packaged with a stick of chewing gum. The target market for these cards was children. In 1988, Upper Deck changed the look of trading cards when it introduced its first set of baseball cards. Superior photography, high-end graphics, acid-free paper, and a higher price tag were aimed specifically at the collector's market. The Upper Deck brand was an immediate success. Basketball, football, hockey, auto racing, and other sports cards were added in subsequent years. Upper Deck also introduced new ideas, including randomly distributed hologram cards, special sets honoring all-star legends and prospects, and second releases of cards for every sports season to include rookies and traded players. However, other brands of trading cards followed Upper Deck's formula, offering their own special sets, autographed cards, and other premiums. How would Upper Deck keep the upper hand in the industry?

ANALYZE AND WRITE

1. Why was Upper Deck able to charge twice as much as previous card companies for its product?
2. Can you think of other examples of products that were originally intended for children, and then were repackaged for an adult market?

Case Study Part 2 on page 63

POWER READ

Be an active reader and use these reading strategies:

PREDICT what the section will be about.

CONNECT what you read with your life.

QUESTION as you read to make sure you understand the content.

RESPOND to what you've read.

Sports Marketing Profile

AS YOU READ ...

YOU WILL LEARN

- To define sports marketing.

WHY IT'S IMPORTANT

The sports industry is growing and ranks as one of the top industries in the United States, which presents new marketing and career opportunities.

KEY TERMS

- sports marketing

sports marketing all the marketing activities designed to satisfy the needs and wants of sports consumers

PREDICT

Why do you think sports marketing is a growing business?

Sports Appeal and Marketing

"Touchdown!" "Score!" "Goal!" "Grand slam!" "Slam dunk!" Where were you the last time you heard these words? Chances are you were watching television, listening to the radio, or sitting in the stands watching a game. People spend time and money on sports because they are entertained by the competition and spectacle of sports. Sports marketers sell sports, games, goods, and services to these fans.

What Is Sports Marketing?

Marketing and sports marketing are two terms that apply to different characteristics of marketing. *Marketing* is defined as the process of developing, promoting, and distributing products, or goods and services, to satisfy customers' needs and wants. With that understanding, **sports marketing** can be defined as all the marketing activities designed to satisfy the needs and wants of sports consumers. Chapters 3 through 9 of this book focus on sports marketing and all the activities of the sports consumer. Sports marketing might focus on the sport of football, baseball, or hockey, as well as all the other activities that revolve around a sporting event, such as event planning, promotion, financing, and sponsorship.

Sports marketing has two major components—the marketing of sports and marketing through sports. For example, the promotion of the Super Bowl, the Indianapolis 500, and the Olympics through television or radio advertisements is considered the *marketing of sports*. On the other hand, when Nike, Gatorade, and Goodyear promote their products by using a connection to sports, such as a sports personality as a spokesperson, those companies are *marketing through sports*.

A Brief History

The beginnings of sports marketing can be traced through several events and people. Many sports marketing firsts took place in the 20th century, such as the longest running endorsement deal in sports history. In 1923, Wilson Sporting Goods signed professional golfer Gene Sarazen to a deal that lasted until Sarazen died in 1999.

As discussed in Chapter 2, one of the most influential people in sports marketing was William "Bill" Veeck. During the mid-1900s, Bill Veeck realized that consumers were missing something very important when they attended baseball games. Veeck knew that the key to making sporting events profitable was to get people interested in watching the game as well as in the activities and events that surround the game. He believed that if he made the spectators' time fun and memorable, they would return to more games. Veeck was able to take an ordinary baseball game and turn it into something appealing for both the fans and the media. He introduced the concepts of player names on jerseys, ballpark giveaways, exploding scoreboards, and Wrigley Field's ivy-covered walls.

One of Veeck's most famous promotions took place in August 1951 on the 50th anniversary of the American League. He hired stage performer Eddie Gaedel. Gaedel was about three and a half feet tall and weighed 65 pounds. Wearing a St. Louis Browns uniform with the number "1/8," Gaedel jumped out of a cardboard birthday cake and then stepped up to home plate to bat. The crowd enjoyed it, and Veeck planned to use Gaedel again, but the American League president was outraged by the performance and banned little people from Major League Baseball. Veeck had a knack for taking sporting events to a different level of entertainment through many other promotions. Because of his innovations, he was inducted into the Baseball Hall of Fame.

In the 1960s, linking athletes to corporations was the brainchild of agent Mark McCormack, founder of the International Management Group (IMG). McCormack's client and friend, golfing legend Arnold Palmer, was one of the first professional athletes to associate with corporations in a promotional role. The concept and industry of sports marketing developed and expanded during the 20th century.

THE Electronic CHANNEL

From X-Games to E-Tainment

The cyber-revolution has positioned the Internet as a major channel for sports marketing. Case in point: ESPN Internet Ventures. From its humble beginnings in 1979 as a small cable TV station in Bristol, Connecticut, the Entertainment and Sports Programming Network evolved into ESPN, Inc. Then ESPN.com became the hub of ESPN on the Internet, covering sports, X-sports, sports business news, and offering video games, e-tail stores, ESPN magazine, and more.

➡ Find and list types of sports covered on a sports Web site through **marketingseries.glencoe.com.**

Figure 3.1

Ranking Sports

Rank	Industry	Size in billions of dollars
1	Real estate	850.0
2	Retail trade	639.9
4	Health service	443.4
5	Construction	277.6
8	Utilities	205.3
★11	Sports	152.0
15	Insurance carriers	115.4
18	Legal services	100.5
25	Auto repair, services, parking	60.5

SOURCE: *Sport Marketing Quarterly*, 6, 4

BIG BUSINESS The sports industry competes well against other industries in the Top 25 rankings. *Do you think the sports industry is still growing?*

MARKETING THE TEAM

Curt Gruber
Vice President of Marketing
Chicago Rush Arena Football

Football might be a seasonal activity, but the behind-the-scenes work of running a team never takes a holiday.

"Whether it is during the off-season or playing season, marketing a professional sports franchise is a full-time job," says Curt Gruber, whose football franchise is still very young. "This is especially true when the team is new to the market, like the Chicago Rush."

Gruber says his daily duties include media planning, advertisement development, designing ticket-sales promotions, and working with corporate sponsors to bring the Rush brand to retail and service outlets. "Organization is the most important skill in this position," he says. "When daily tasks jump between advertising/media planning one day to designing a game-day program the next, you have to stay focused.

"You must also be a student of your business—and ask: What are other teams doing? What are other entertainment venues doing? Do you know everything possible about your consumers—and about your competitor's consumers?"

Education Gruber has a bachelor's degree in philosophy and Spanish, and an MBA in international management. However, he doesn't necessarily recommend a specific study path for students wanting to get into sports marketing. Rather, he says it is the level of effort a student puts into his or her education that is important, whatever path the student chooses.

"Professional athletes achieve success through hard work and dedication," he says. "Similarly, I think most students will succeed in school, and later in their careers, based on the amount of effort they put forth into their studies."

In what ways does a good sports marketer have to be a "student" of the business?

Career Data: Team Marketing Executive

Education and Training
Bachelor's or master's degree in business, marketing, or general education

Skills and Abilities
Communication skills, organizational skills, creativity

Career Outlook As fast as average growth through 2010

Career Path Entry-level positions provide experience with a sports franchise. Real-world skills are crucial for advancement.

CONNECT
What might be one marketing-related job at a sporting-goods company?

Studying Sports Marketing

Sports marketing is more than promoting sports events and finding a sponsor for your next game. It is more than the film character Jerry Maguire shouting, "Show me the money!" Sports marketing takes a simple game and turns it into an interesting and exciting event. Television shows such as *Monday Night Football* got started by applying the principles of sports marketing. Because it is a multibillion-dollar industry (see **Figure 3.1**) with an appeal to many people, sports marketing, like general marketing, is studied in high school and college to prepare students for professional careers.

Careers in Sports Marketing

With the growth of the sports industry, new sports, and more than 20 new leagues in the last decade, employment possibilities for marketers are expanding. Sports journalists have opportunities to work on new publications and books about sports. Sporting goods are a big growth industry as well, and related companies provide a variety of job opportunities.

You can see that the sports industry is substantial. Many people make it possible. The sports agent's job is only one of the many careers in sports marketing. In fact, sports marketing careers include a variety of jobs. Examples of a few jobs include:

- Scriptwriter

- Producer

- Ticket agent

- Luxury-box sales representative

- Food and merchandise sales representatives

- Group-ticket salesperson

These are just a few of the careers in sports marketing. Because sports marketing is a growing industry that involves action, creativity, and dedication, there are many opportunities for motivated students.

Game Point !

→ **MAJOR LEAGUE INDUSTRY**
    With $213 billion in revenue, the sports business industry is one of the largest and fastest growing industries.

QUESTION
Is it true that only a few jobs are available in sports marketing?

Quick Check ✓

RESPOND to what you've read by answering these questions.

1. Define sports marketing. _____

_____

_____

2. Name a pioneer of sports marketing and identify his or her contribution. _____

_____

_____

3. Name three jobs in sports marketing. _____

_____

_____

Categories of Sports

AS YOU READ ...

YOU WILL LEARN

- To identify the different categories of sports.
- To differentiate between amateur sports and professional sports.
- To discuss the significance of international sports.
- To explain the significance of women's sports.

WHY IT'S IMPORTANT

Understanding the categories of sports and knowing how each applies to sports marketing helps a marketer develop good marketing strategies.

KEY TERMS

- amateur athlete
- NCAA
- professional athlete
- Title IX
- extreme sports

amateur athlete a person who does not get paid to play a sport

PREDICT

Choose one key term and define it in your own words.

Variety of Sports

Sports and sporting events can be classified into several categories, including amateur, high school, college, and professional. This section will explain the categories of sports and how each one varies and applies to sports marketing. These categories will give you an understanding of how a sports marketer can make the most of the different and specific characteristics.

Amateur and Professional Sports

A sports consumer may enjoy watching certain forms of amateur, high school, or college sports more than he or she enjoys professional sports. People enjoy sports for different reasons. For example, consider how your family and friends react when they watch you and your peers play in a high school game. The excitement they display while watching soccer or baseball might surprise you. Their enthusiasm is based on their interest in you and your school. Similarly, many sports consumers who enjoy watching basketball might get more excited during the NCAA "March Madness" in college basketball finals because they find this classification of basketball more competitive than professional basketball. Sports consumers are attracted to professional sporting events, but they also find interest in the sport and the classification or level of the sport.

Amateur Sports

An **amateur athlete** is a person who does not get paid to play a sport. Therefore, a high school, college, or any other type of athlete, including a recreational player, is considered an amateur athlete because he or she is not paid to play. Other than pay, there are no limitations regarding being an amateur athlete. To be an amateur, an athlete needs to have only the desire and drive to play a sport.

Amateur sporting events attract a large number of fans, attention, and money. Many communities have youth leagues, senior leagues, and a variety of other athletic organizations that attract people who have a strong interest in participating or watching a particular athletic event. Because so many people are interested in playing the sport, it has become common to see these amateur sporting events attracting a number of interested spectators and sponsors.

Young Amateur Sports

Youth-league basketball tournaments in major cities attract many people. Interest may come from the players' families and friends to potential sponsors, such as soft-drink and health-care product manufacturers or local businesses. In addition, there are booths from sponsors and banners hanging around the court aiming to attract a target market to their products. Colleges and universities may be represented at these types of tournaments because they know that amateur events attract teenagers who might be interested in attending their schools.

Recreational Sports

Many people get involved in recreational sporting events. For some, involvement may start when they are five or six years old, playing in a peewee league. As interest in a particular sport continues, a boy or girl has the opportunity to join a variety of recreational youth leagues, including the Boys and Girls Clubs of America, the YMCA and YWCA, and a whole range of other youth organizations. One of the biggest and oldest amateur sporting organizations, the Amateur Athletic Union (AAU), was established in 1888 as a nonprofit organization to encourage children and adolescents to explore sports that they may not otherwise have an opportunity to play. Many of these youth organizations cannot function without the help of community funds and donations. As a result, many local businesses, such as pizza shops and automobile dealers, will sponsor youth teams.

As adults, people can continue to participate in recreational sporting events. Adult leagues present a full range of sporting events including softball, soccer, and basketball, as well as downhill skiing, rowing, and rugby. These team sports also attract much-needed financial support from the community and various businesses.

Recreational sports also include a variety of nontraditional events that, though noncompetitive, are classified as sports. A few popular examples are scuba diving, rollerblading, skydiving, and rock climbing. These recreational events inspire people to improve their skills and exercise their physical abilities while enjoying recreational time.

High School Sports

If you have ever gone to a pep rally at your school, chances are you have seen the impact that high school sports have on school spirit. If your school wins a big game, and the news is printed in the local newspaper, the entire community is proud of its team. As a result, community morale is high. Many high schools and communities put much effort and enthusiasm into their sporting events.

Some people debate the issues involved with educational institutions spending money and energy in support of sporting events. Because of these controversies, high school organizations such as the National Federation of State High School Associations (NFHS) set guidelines and make sure that students benefit from a balanced educational and athletic experience.

TECH NOTES

Pay-Per-View Webcasts

A growing number of sports fans are choosing to pay for the opportunity to watch live broadcasts of baseball games, NASCAR races, and other sporting events on the Internet. Many viewers are introduced to these Webcasts by free trial subscriptions and discounted season passes. Fans can customize a viewing experience by selecting video clips of their favorite players and creating their own personal highlight reel.

➥Write a paragraph that compares Webcasts to pay-per-view television after reading information through **marketingseries.glencoe.com**.

A Coach Who Cares

Critics believe that high-paying salaries have shadowed the love of the game for many athletes and coaches. At Fresno State University, that isn't so. The men's track and field teams were about to be dropped to save money. Coach Bob Fraley's solution was to work for no pay. He gave up $95,000 a year to save the dreams of future athletes and an athletic program with a "proud history." In fact, Fraley says he is thankful: "This university has done more for me than I could ever pay back. I can do this, and I want to."

In many communities, high school sports are part of a tradition. This tradition encourages people in the community to rally around the games. Disney's *Remember the Titans* is one motion picture that examines and details the power that high school sports has on a community as well as the power that a community has on high school sports.

Location Considerations

Regional influences affect the popularity of sports in the United States. In many southern states, high school football games take on the importance of college or professional football. In the central states and in New England, the sport of ice hockey interests many communities. People from Vermont, for example, may also be skilled at and interested in skiing. People growing up on the coast of California may develop skills and an interest in surfing. The natural resources of a specific climate and geographical location encourage the popularity and development of specific sports.

College and University Sports

Sporting events at the college level are very popular and extremely competitive in all regions. In fact, many people consider collegiate sports to be more competitive than professional sports. To appeal to the wide range of student interests, colleges offer a variety of sports events. At large universities the types and number of sports offered are greater because the student population is larger. For example, at large universities, sporting events such as rowing, water polo, and fencing become highly competitive. In most cases, these schools also have large budgets. Ohio State University's athletic budget is one of the highest in the NCAA each year. The budget provides the university with the best possible facilities and support staff to encourage winning teams.

NCAA Sports

NCAA (National Collegiate Athletic Association) a national organization that governs college athletics and oversees important decisions pertaining to athletics

The National Collegiate Athletic Association, or **NCAA**, is a national organization that governs college athletics and oversees important decisions pertaining to athletics (similar to the NFHS for high school sports). The guidelines and rules of the NCAA are posted on its Web site at www.ncaa.org. As an example of an NCAA rule, players are not allowed to accept any form of payment from a school or from companies. This kind of rule encourages legitimate, amateur competition without unfair influence from businesses or individuals. The NCAA regulates all collegiate athletics, including the marketing of sporting events. If rules and regulations are broken, the NCAA has the power to eliminate teams from playing for an entire season and can terminate an athlete's college scholarship.

To keep schools on a competitive level, the NCAA created divisions determined by the characteristics of a school and the level of competitiveness of the athletes. For example, schools are ranked as Division I, Division II, or Division III—based on student population, financial stability, and player ability. The NCAA ranking has an important economic impact on schools and communities, because the ranking of sports draws larger crowds to games. Higher divisions draw more spectators. As more people are attracted to a particular sporting event, there is more opportunity for the university to benefit from name recognition.

Perhaps the most heavily marketed collegiate sporting event is the NCAA Division I Men's Basketball Championship tournament, known as March Madness, where one loss by a team means elimination from the tournament. During this event, marketing efforts by competing schools are intense. Each school uses this time to get its name known and to attract potential markets. Potential markets can be the athletic fans wanting to buy school-brand apparel, or they can be prospective students interested in attending the school.

CONNECT

Do you think college athletes should earn money for playing sports?

Professional Sports

A professional athlete is an athlete who has the will and ability to earn an income from a particular sport. A professional athlete's income is paid by his or her employer, who is the team or organization. However, the professional athlete's employer may depend on major corporations to pay the athlete's salary, as in the case of professional race car drivers.

professional athlete an athlete who has the will and ability to earn an income from a particular sport

Hot Property

Sports Television

The first words spoken on the Entertainment and Sports Programming Network, ESPN, said it all: "If you're a fan, what you'll see in the next minutes, hours, and days may convince you you've gone to sports heaven." ESPN has been delivering its own brand of "sports heaven" for over 20 years.

Hockey PR man Bill Rasmussen founded the cable network on September 7, 1979, promising round-the-clock sports coverage. However, the early days at the station were uncertain. ESPN did not have deals in place with the major professional and college sports leagues and was forced to fill the time with lesser events. ESPN's distinctive anchor personalities and thorough coverage of these events would have to keep viewers' attention. The tactic succeeded. A few sports leagues signed on for partial coverage—and then more. Before too long ESPN had the coverage it needed to make it an important destination for fans. Now owned by Disney and co-branded with ABC Sports, ESPN dominates the sports-television industry that it helped create with additional channels such as ESPNEWS, ESPN2, ESPN Classic, and others.

DIVERSIFICATION

ESPN is widely received throughout the United States by nearly 87 million homes. It covers over 65 sports and has diversified properties to include radio, Internet, print magazines, and even restaurants. The ESPN Enterprises division is dedicated to finding and developing products that meet and create demand from the public. In marketing themselves to advertisers, ESPN emphasizes the draw of sports for men, especially those with higher-than-average incomes. Advertisers hoping to reach that market find the perfect partner in ESPN's array of properties.

1. What programming niche does ESPN fill?
2. Why do you think ESPN added more channels?

In addition to the salary a player receives from the team, extremely talented athletes have opportunities to earn other income from major corporations seeking endorsement services from the athlete. On rare occasions, the additional income from major corporations can be higher than the athlete's actual team salary. For example, at the age of 18, basketball player LeBron James signed a three-year, $12.96 million deal with a one-year option at $5.8 million with the Cleveland Cavaliers. That amount was minor compared to his seven-year endorsement deal with Nike, worth over $90 million, added to $10 million for other endorsement deals.

Teams as Businesses
Professional sports are perhaps the most costly and heavily marketed of all sports categories. Teams are considered fully functional businesses whose main purpose is to get the best players in order to win events that will attract fans who have a desire to purchase tickets and merchandise.

Professional Sports Entertainment
In professional sports both entertainment and athletic characteristics of marketing are involved. Gene Upshaw, the former Oakland Raider and Hall of Famer, once stated, "I don't see the NFL as athletes versus the owners, but instead it's professional football versus all the other entertainment choices out there—the movies, music, and theater." In fact, marketing methods can be similar for these overlapping forms of entertainment because they have overlapping target markets. This is why professional sporting organizations hire the best marketing personnel to attract the right target market. This is also why major corporations are welcomed sponsors—they help attract audiences to various products as well as to the sport itself.

New England Patriots owner Robert Kraft owns Gillette Stadium, which cost $345 million to build. Aside from having a field that is dedicated to football, the stadium features two large clubhouses that are sponsored by Fidelity Investments. Both clubhouses have working fireplaces, chef stations, and several appealing amenities for high-paying corporate ticket holders. In addition to the luxury clubhouse, there is a McDonald's fast-food restaurant above each end zone. By the way, the stadium has a capacity of 68,000 seats, with 6,000 club seats in midfield that go for as much as $6,000 each over ten years. To show the success of this undertaking, more than 50,000 fans have put down a deposit to be on a waiting list for season tickets to see the Patriots in action.

Other Categories of Sports
Besides the main categories of sports and sporting events, the world of sports has a category for the Olympic Games. Sports and sports marketing have also broadened in the last few decades to encompass an even wider world of sports, including athletes with disabilities, international sports, women's sports, and extreme sports.

SLAM DUNK Professional basketball is ranked as one of the top three favorite spectator sports in the United States, a close second to football and baseball. *Do you think fans watch more professional basketball games than college basketball games? Why?*

Olympic Sports

Have you ever wondered how the Olympics began? According to legend, the ancient Olympic Games were founded by Heracles (the Roman Hercules), a son of the Greek god Zeus. The first recorded evidence of the Olympic Games shows that the first Olympic competition was held in 776 B.C. in Olympia, Greece. In 776 B.C., the only event at the Olympics was a run of approximately 192 meters (210 yards). Several years later other events such as discus, javelin, jumping, and wrestling were added. The ancient Olympic Games grew and continued to be played every four years for nearly 1,200 years. In 393 A.D., Roman emperor Theodosius I abolished the Games because of their pagan influences.

Olympic Revival

More than 2,500 years later in 1890, a young Frenchman named Pierre de Coubertin began the revival of the Olympic Games. Coubertin organized a meeting with 79 delegates, who represented nine countries, and advocated the revival of the Olympic Games to them. The delegates voted unanimously to reinstate the Olympic Games. The delegates also decided to have Coubertin organize an international committee to plan the games and oversee issues and decisions. This committee became the International Olympic Committee (IOC).

In April 1896, Athens was chosen for the revival of the Olympic Games. Since it was not well publicized internationally, contestants were not chosen by nation. Instead, athletes traveled to Athens at their own expense. Events included pole vaulting, sprints, shot put, weight lifting, swimming, cycling, target shooting, tennis, marathon, and gymnastics. Approximately 300 athletes from 13 countries participated.

Present-Day Olympics

The Olympic goal is: "To contribute to building a peaceful and better world by educating youth through sports practiced without discrimination of any kind and in the Olympic spirit, which requires mutual understanding with a spirit of friendship, solidarity and fair play." Each time the Olympics are held every four years, the IOC increases its global membership. By 2002, the Salt Lake City, Utah, Winter Games included 77 member nations with 2,399 athletes who competed in the 78 winter events.

However, the Olympics have experienced problems along the way, such as terrorist attacks, illegal drug use, and boycotts. The

Case Study | PART 2

CARDBOARD COLLECTIBLES
Continued from Part 1 on page 53

To maintain its leadership in the industry as other card companies were making premium collectibles, Upper Deck brought card collecting into the 21st century by offering exclusive access to sports-related Web sites. Upper Deck has used its clout to enter the autographed memorabilia market, selling authenticated photographs, footballs, basketballs, hockey pucks, jerseys, and other objects. The company has also expanded into international sports, licensing and creating products for Swedish hockey, Manchester United soccer, and basketball in the Philippines. In the United States, Upper Deck has added products related to the entertainment industry, including the *Space Jam* movie, the *Survivor* reality television show, and the CardCaptors franchise. All of these product innovations have kept Upper Deck on top.

ANALYZE AND WRITE

1. What steps did Upper Deck take to ensure its leadership position in the industry?
2. Why might a collector be more likely to buy authenticated sports memorabilia from Upper Deck than from an independent seller?

QUESTION

In what year were the Olympic Games revived?

Ancient Entertainment

In the summer of 776 B.C., a cook named Coroebus in Olympia, Greece, ran toward the altar of Greek god Zeus and crossed the finish line to take first place in history's first Olympics. The event, a 210-foot race called the *stadion*, was the only contest. There was no second place, and there were no women competitors. By law, the only spectators were men.

More than 2,500 years later, the world's most prestigious games will have come full circle. In 2004, the Olympics were held in the capital city of Athens. Over 10,500 young women and men from 200 countries signed to compete for the gold, silver, and bronze medals in 35 individual and team sports, from aquatics to weightlifting.

Today women participate in all events except baseball and boxing, while men compete in everything except softball. Unlike ancient times, millions cheer for the athletes, and Greece was given the opportunity to promote its unique attractions to the world on a grand scale.

What is most different about today's Olympic Games compared to those of the past?

IOC had to determine methods to keep the Olympics in business. As a result, during the 1984 Olympic Games in Los Angeles, California, the IOC allowed 43 corporate sponsors to sell "official" licensed Olympic products. With new corporate sponsors, the 1984 Olympic Games became the first Games since 1932 to make a profit ($225 million).

The Amateur Rule

The amateur rule has prohibited professionals from competing in Olympic events and plagued athletes and officials since the beginning of the Olympic Games. Eventually, individual sporting groups began to determine whether professionals should be allowed to compete in the Olympics. The amateur rule was finally overturned in 1986. As a result of this ruling, the 1990s saw professional athletes competing in the Olympics, and television viewership increased.

Perhaps most memorable was the formation of the U.S. men's basketball team in 1992, known as the "Dream Team," that included professional athletes such as Michael Jordan, Erwin "Magic" Johnson, and Larry Bird. The IOC believed that if Olympic athletes played with the best players in the world, everyone would benefit. Every team that played the Dream Team considered it an honor to be on the court with them. From a sports marketing perspective, the Dream Team was responsible for the enormous boost in popularity of basketball on an international basis.

The Wide World of Paralympics

In 1948, Sir Ludwig Guttman organized a sports competition involving World War II veterans with spinal cord related injuries in England. Four years later competitors from Holland joined the competition, and the international movement now known as the *Paralympics* began. Olympic-style games for athletes with disabilities were organized for the first time in Rome in 1960. In Toronto in 1976, other groups with disabilities were added, and the idea of merging different groups for international sports competitions was born. The Paralympic Games continue to be held in the same year as the Olympic Games.

Special Olympics

In 1968, Eunice Kennedy Shriver organized the First International Special Olympics games at Soldier Field in Chicago, Illinois. The concept began in the early 1960s when Shriver started a day camp for people with developmental disabilities. She saw that these individuals were far more capable in sports and physical activities than many experts had thought. The Special Olympics offer year-round training and competition in 26 Olympic-type summer and winter sports. Since 1968, millions of children and adults have participated in the Special Olympics. Special Olympics currently serve one million people in more than 200 programs in more than 150 countries.

International Sporting Events

In the early days of ABC Sports on the ABC television network, producer Roone Arledge realized that American television viewers might be interested in watching sports from around the world. He visualized traveling the world with cameras, filming people in various countries playing sports native to their countries. He created *The Wide World of Sports*, a weekly television show that brought unusual

Math Check

WINNING WAYS
If the number of athletes participating in the Special Olympics is about 1 million, and that number is expected to increase by one-third for the next Olympics, how many athletes may participate?

➡ For tips on finding the solution, go to **marketingseries.glencoe.com.**

◀ **PERSONAL BEST These Special Olympics athletes train as rigorously as athletes who compete in the centuries-old Olympic Games.** *Do you think companies can benefit from sponsoring events such as the Special Olympics? Why?*

 marketingseries.glencoe.com

sporting events into homes, exposing everyone to sports such as world wrist-wrestling from Petaluma, California, cliff diving from Mexico, and world figure skating from Prague in the Czech Republic. *The Wide World of Sports* introduced the public to sports icons such as basketball entertainers the Harlem Globetrotters, boxing legend Muhammad Ali, daredevil Evel Knievel, and sportscaster Howard Cosell. Advances in media technology and the globalization of television brought sports to all corners of the globe.

Soccer (known as *football* outside the United States) is one of the world's most popular sports. With devotion to World Cup soccer, international fans show extreme passion for their favorite soccer teams. Other well-known international sporting events such as the Tour de France bicycle race have slowly gained American interest, as athletes spend a rigorous 28 days racing their bikes over 2,200 miles. American Lance Armstrong has won the race at least five times, capturing an audience in the United States. Other popular international sports include cricket, rugby, and jai alai—each providing new entertainment to the sports consumer and new challenges to sports marketers.

Title IX a law that bans gender discrimination in schools that receive federal funds

Women's Sports

The status of women in sports has advanced in the 20th century and especially in the last 20 years, opening up new markets for sports, with more progress ahead (see **Figure 3.2**). As early as 1932, Olympic gold medalist Mildred "Babe" Didrikson Zaharias not only excelled at most sports, including track, golf, basketball, softball, boxing, and others, she was also an impressive sports promoter. She had a signature line of golf clubs, wrote books, and made personal appearances. Playing at the amateur and professional levels, Zaharias's all-around skills inspired women and men, as well as sports marketers, at a time when few women received public recognition for their athletic abilities.

Title IX to the Present

On June 23, 1972, the enactment of Title IX (nine), the Education Amendment, advanced girls' participation in sports. **Title IX** is a law that bans gender discrimination in schools that receive federal funds. As a result, over a 20-year period, the number of girls participating in high school sports programs has increased nearly tenfold. In 1970–71, only 294,000 high school girls competed in interscholastic sports in the United States. By 1998–99, more than 2,652,000 girls were participating. Prior to Title IX, few colleges offered sports scholarships for women. By 1995–96, female athletes received more than $212 million in scholarships.

A key player in the advancement of women's sports was tennis star Billie Jean King. She dominated women's tennis for nearly two decades, winning her first Wimbledon title in 1962, and went on to win 20 Wimbledon titles. In 1972, *Sports Illustrated* named Billie Jean King "Sportswoman of the Year," the first time the annual sports award was given to a woman. In 1973, she challenged male tennis professional

Bobby Riggs, who had publicly proclaimed that no woman could beat him. The event was dubbed "The Battle of the Sexes." King defeated Riggs, and remained a significant figure in women's sports history.

Since then other successful women in modern-day professional sports have emerged, including golf pro Annika Sorenstam, tennis stars Martina Navratilova, Chris Evert, Venus and Serena Williams, soccer star Mia Hamm, and racecar driver Sarah Fisher. Professional sports organizations have also experienced breakthroughs. For example, in 1991, the Washington Wizards named Susan O'Malley as the first female president of an NBA franchise.

Figure 3.2

Women and the Olympics

1900	Women are included on the Olympic program, competing in golf and tennis.
	Tennis player Charlotte Cooper of Great Britain becomes the first female Olympic champion.
1966	Gender verification tests for women are adopted in international sport.
1968	In Mexico City, Enriqueta Basilio becomes the first woman to light the Olympic flame.
1976	Rowing and basketball become Olympic events for women.
1984	The first women's Olympic marathon is won by Joan Benoit of the United States.
	Women's cycling, synchronized swimming, and rhythmic gymnastics are added to the Olympic program.
1996	3,626 women compete at the Olympic Games in Atlanta—32 percent more than in Barcelona, with inclusion of women's soccer, softball, and triple-jump events.
	The IOC holds its first World Conference on Women and Sport.
1998	The IOC (International Olympic Committee) includes women's ice hockey in the Winter Olympic program in Nagano, Japan.
2000	New women's events for the Sydney, Australia, Olympics include the triathalon, the trampoline, water polo, weight lifting, and tae kwon do.

SOURCE: www.olympic.org

MOVING AHEAD New practices by the Olympic Games represent some advances made in women's sports in the 20th century. *Do you think women's professional sports will grow? Why?*

Women's amateur and professional sports organizations have also taken substantial steps to involve women in sports. For example, on April 24, 1996, the NBA Board of Governors approved the formation of the Women's National Basketball Association (WNBA). WNBA teams began to play in June 1997. Since then, the WNBA has grown and produced a variety of new basketball superstars such as Lisa Leslie and Sheryl Swoopes.

Extreme Sports

extreme sports sports that involve nontraditional, daring methods of athletic competition

Extreme sports are sports that involve nontraditional, daring methods of athletic competition. Though extreme sports have been around for several generations, officially, they are relatively new to sports-marketing efforts. In the 1980s, the skateboarders, rollerbladers, stunt bikers, and snowboarders of Generation X helped launch this new style of sport. With the interest in these sports catching the attention of the public, several television stations and magazines directed their efforts toward extreme sports. Along with these efforts, corporations began to market products toward a new target market by promoting extreme sport drinks, clothing, and other merchandise.

The efforts of skateboarding legend Tony Hawk, skiing and snowboard legend Warren Miller, and surfing legend Kelly Slater have promoted the marketing movement of extreme sports. In addition, efforts by ESPN and the X Games have added to the success of extreme sports. Extreme sports have also caught the attention of major corporations selling products from sport drinks to clothing to video games.

Extreme sports is one of the many categories of sports whose characteristics help identify target markets. Sports marketers use these categories and characteristics to sell games, teams, and products.

Quick Check

RESPOND to what you've read by answering these questions.

1. What are the four main categories of sports?_____
_____
_____

2. Which category is the most costly and marketed of all categories?_____
_____
_____

3. List three other categories, besides professional and amateur sports, that reflect the "wider" world of sports. _____
_____

Worksheet 3.1

The Many Faces of Sports Marketing

1. Choose a famous athlete such as Michael Jordan or another prominent athlete. Write the athlete's name and sport on the lines.

_____

_____

2. Learn more about the person and his or her product endorsements and other activities through Internet research, sports magazines, or newspapers. Write a few significant facts on the lines.

_____

_____

_____

_____

_____

_____

3. In the space below, create a diagram or graphic organizer. Write the name of the person in a center circle and draw boxes around the center circle. Give each box a title that represents the person's activities, such as clothing and footwear endorsements, television commercials, or book deals. Write information in each box. Draw a line from each box to the center circle.

Worksheet 3.2

Sporting News

1. Search the Internet, newspapers, and magazines for sports-marketing related stories.
2. Summarize two of the stories you find and identify their categories.

Summary 1:

_____

_____

_____

_____

_____

_____

_____

_____

_____

_____

_____

Summary 2:

_____

_____

_____

_____

_____

_____

_____

_____

_____

_____

_____

3. Exchange papers with another student and edit each other's summaries.
4. Make a bulletin board of the summaries in your classroom.

Portfolio Works

EXPLORING SPORTS MARKETING CAREERS

Go to the library or the Internet and find five careers in sports marketing that interest you or may be unfamiliar to you. Do the following exercises. Then add this page to your career portfolio.

1. List the five careers.

_____

_____

_____

2. Use the Internet to explore at least one career. Describe it.

_____

_____

_____

3. List your skills and interests. Then list the jobs that match these skills and interests. Create names for the jobs if applicable.

Skills/interests	Possible jobs
_____	_____
_____	_____
_____	_____
_____	_____

4. Review your list of skills and interests. What stands out? Think of as many sports marketing jobs as you can that relate to your skills and interests.

_____

_____

_____

5. Describe an ideal job that involves these skills. Include the location of the ideal job and the kinds of coworkers, customers, and employees you would meet.

_____

_____

_____

_____

CHAPTER SUMMARY

Section **3.1** **Sports Marketing Profile**

sports marketing (p. 54)

- Sports marketing includes all activities designed to meet the needs and wants of the sports consumer through exchange processes. Sponsorships are focused on the actual event or game, but marketing through sports occurs when sponsors promote their products to the consumer by using a connection to sport.

Section **3.2** **Categories of Sports**

amateur athlete (p. 58)
NCAA (p. 60)
professional athlete
   (p. 61)
Title IX (p. 66)
extreme sports (p. 68)

- Sports and sporting events can be classified into categories such as amateur, high school, college, and professional sports.

- An amateur athlete has the desire to play but does not get paid, while a professional athlete has the will and ability to earn a living playing sports. Many fans enjoy both professional and amateur sports, but some may find amateur sports more exciting and competitive.

- Media exposure of sports has opened up the world to new possibilities and new sports to be marketed.

- Athletes such as Babe Zaharias, Billie Jean King, and others have helped women's professional and amateur sports advance in the 20th century. The enactment of Title IX in 1973 enabled more girls to participate in school sports. More diverse sports markets are one result.

CHECKING CONCEPTS

1. **Define** sports marketing.
2. **Explain** the difference between the marketing of sports and the marketing through sports.
3. **Identify** the different categories of sports.
4. **Explain** why the sports consumer is not just attracted to professional sports.
5. **Name** one difference between an amateur athlete and a professional athlete.
6. **Name** five or more international sports.
7. **Identify** one significant female athlete in sports history.

Critical Thinking

8. **Discuss** some factors that contribute to the popularity of extreme sports.

CROSS-CURRICULUM SKILLS

Work-Based Learning

Basic Skills—Writing

9. Write a letter to your favorite sports franchise and explain why it is your favorite team. Also request a media guide or other team information.

Interpersonal Skills—Teaching Others

10. Using key terms from this chapter, create your own crossword puzzle. Trade puzzles with another student and help solve it.

School-Based Learning

Math

11. Brad and Nigel each bought a ticket to a baseball game for $10. Brad also paid $8 for a hot pretzel and soft drink and $5 for a program. Nigel paid $3.50 for a soft drink. They had $40. Brad wanted to buy a T-shirt at $10. Was there enough money?

Social Studies

12. Choose an American team from any sport and identify players from at least three countries. Then find the countries on a world map.

 CONNECTION

Role Play: Marketing Director

SITUATION You are to assume the role of marketing director for an athletic shoe manufacturer. Your company will produce three new shoe designs for the fall season. Sales are forecasted to be high. A buyer (judge) from a retail chain isn't convinced that the demand will change for this season.

(ACTIVITY) Advise the buyer (judge) for the retail chain on how to prepare for the fall season.

EVALUATION You will be evaluated on how well you meet the following performance indicators:

- Explain the principles of supply and demand.
- Describe factors that influence the demand for services.
- Explain the nature and scope of purchasing.
- Explain the concept of competition.
- Describe the nature of current economic conditions.

 **INTERNET ACTIVITY**

The NCAA regulates college teams and athletes. View its Web site to do the following exercises:

- Write down three rules for college athletes.
- Find out when the NCAA began and why.
- What is the NCAA Clearinghouse?

➡ For a link to the NCAA to do this exercise, go to **marketingseries.glencoe.com**.

Chapter 4

Sports Products

Section 4.1

The Consumer and Sports Products

Section 4.2

Economic Impact of Sports Marketing

Chapter Objectives

- Define the sports consumer.
- Explain market segmentation.
- Identify sports products.
- Explain the differences between sports goods and services.
- Differentiate between the product line and product mix.
- Explain the economic impact of sports marketing.

MICHAEL
JORDAN

ARENA PRODUCT ADVANTAGE

Sports products can be many different goods and services, from basketballs and shoes to tennis lessons and a great game at the ballpark.

On April 6, 1992, Oriole Park at Camden Yards opened as the first retro-style park designed for baseball. The park is located in downtown Baltimore, Maryland, near the famed Inner Harbor.

Camden Yards met with rave reviews because of the natural grass turf, an asymmetrical playing field, seats angled to the action, and a turn-of-the-century atmosphere. Fans responded by buying tickets. In 1992, season attendance reached 3,567,819. From 1995 to 1998, Camden Yards led the American League in fan attendance. These numbers were boosted when Cal Ripken, Jr., broke Lou Gehrig's record in 1995, and the Orioles won their division in 1997.

Since that time, however, there has been a decline in attendance, along with a stream of losses. By 2003, the Orioles ranked 11th in league attendance and finished in fourth place in the American League Eastern Division.

ANALYZE AND WRITE

1. What businesses rely on fan attendance?
2. Identify reasons for decreased attendance.

Case Study Part 2 on page 87

POWER READ

Be an active reader and use these reading strategies:

PREDICT what the section will be about.
CONNECT what you read with your life.
QUESTION as you read to make sure you understand the content.
RESPOND to what you've read.

The Consumer and Sports Products

AS YOU READ...

YOU WILL LEARN

- To define the sports consumer.
- To explain market segmentation.
- To identify sports products.
- To explain the differences between sports goods and services.
- To differentiate between the product line and product mix.

WHY IT'S IMPORTANT

Understanding the sports consumer, who uses sports products offered by sports businesses and organizations, helps marketers to create effective marketing plans.

KEY TERMS

- sports consumer
- market segmentation
- sports products
- tangible products
- intangible product
- product line
- product mix

sports consumer a person who may play, officiate, watch, or listen to sports, or read, use, purchase, and/or collect items related to sports

PREDICT

Review the headings in this section and define *sports products* in your words.

The Sports Consumer

The consumer is the target of sports marketing because the consumer, as a customer, makes purchases and helps sports organizations to make a profit. A consumer is a person who uses an actual product. A **sports consumer** is a person who may play, officiate, watch, or listen to sports, or read, use, purchase, and/or collect items related to sports. Hundreds of thousands of people are sports consumers. A purchase by the sports consumer, as a customer, is like a vote because the purchase equals a decision of approval. If a fan buys a ticket to a professional wrestling event, he or she is supporting the event and encouraging it to grow.

There are many reasons a consumer, as a customer, chooses to purchase or not purchase a ticket. Perhaps the consumer dislikes the sport, the event will take place at an inconvenient time, or the consumer believes the price of the ticket is too expensive. The goal of planning marketing strategies is to encourage the consumer to act as a customer and purchase tickets or merchandise—and this is the job of sports marketing personnel.

Consumer Decisions

Many factors affect the sports consumer's decision to spend money on or participate in sports. These factors can be classified in two categories: the consumer's environmental factors and the consumer's individual factors.

Environmental factors that influence a consumer's involvement in sports can include family and friends; society's attitudes and values; cultural differences related to class, race, and gender; climate and region; and of course, marketing influences, such as commercials.

One *individual factor* might include self-concept or self-image. For example, if a teenager views herself as an athletic individual, she may be more inclined to play volleyball, tennis, softball, or other sports. Another individual factor relates to self-development or stage of life. For example, National Football League (NFL) researchers have found that 60 percent of fans of any sport say they became fans by the age of 11. Other individual factors that affect money spent on and participation in sports are physical characteristics related to the ability to play a sport, learned characteristics regarding the ability to learn athletic skills, and motivation and attitude.

With all these factors that influence the sports consumer, sports marketers must consider a combination of these factors to make effective decisions about marketing plans.

Sports Consumers and Market Segmentation

U nderstanding market segmentation of the sports consumer market is important in order to sell products and services. **Market segmentation** is a way of analyzing a market by specific characteristics to create a target market. These characteristics include geographics, demographics, psychographics, and product benefits. Geographics are a consideration of where the consumer lives. Demographics are statistics that describe a population in terms of personal characteristics such as gender, race, religion, and earnings. Psychographics include characteristics that are easier to change, such as attitudes or opinions the consumer has toward recreational activities. Marketers also study consumers' behaviors, needs, and wants regarding specific product benefits to consumers.

Market Segmentation Shifts

The market segmentation of the sports consumer market can change. Sports marketing professionals must constantly check current consumer approval ratings. Consider the sports-consumer market for golf. Several years ago this market included mostly men, ages 30–60, with incomes of $50,000–$175,000 per year. Because of the tremendous success and the marketing of young golfer Tiger Woods, a new consumer market of teenagers developed for golf. Thus, the marketing segment shifted for golf, and the Professional Golfers Association (PGA) gained new sponsors who sell to this market. Take a look at the list of sponsors that back Tiger Woods:

- Nike

- Wheaties (General Mills)

- Upper Deck

- Coca-Cola

Veteran PGA sponsors also noticed Tiger Woods' influence. Companies such as Gatorade, Quaker Oats, Adidas, Pepsi-Cola, and Chapstick sponsored PGA tournaments before Tiger Woods, but now their advertisements also focus on teenagers.

The purchases made by a sports consumer show support for sports teams, athletes, and sponsors. Therefore, it is crucial that the sports marketer carefully plans a program that targets the right sports consumer to maximize sales.

market segmentation a way of analyzing a market by specific characteristics to create a target market

SHIFTING MARKETS **Since Tiger Woods began to dominate the golfing world, new worlds opened up for sports marketing professionals.** *Which new top athlete would you choose to appeal to teenagers or young-adult consumers? Why?*

Sports Products

sports products the goods, services, ideas, or a combination of those things related to sports that provide satisfaction to a consumer

Sports products are goods, services, ideas, or a combination of those things related to sports that provide satisfaction to the consumer. The product of sports can also provide the consumer with basic needs, such as entertainment, sociability, or even achievement. For example, the product of a monster-truck race can include music and celebrity appearances to entertain spectators. Besides sports products in the form of goods and services, sports products can also be athletes. The athlete who demonstrates more than one skill is considered a valuable "product" by the team that contracts the athlete.

Many people share in the process of marketing sports products—owners, sponsors, communication firms, city governments, taxpayers, and consumers. For example, the marketing process occurs when the members of the National Association for Stock Car Auto Racing (NASCAR) work with a variety of companies to get sponsors for automobiles or events. Television and radio networks also sell airtime to these sponsors so that consumers can be targeted with a variety of products and services. The racecar owners must appeal to city governments for permits, as well as to taxpayers to convince

---

Hot Property

More Than Home Runs

Louisville Slugger®

Legend has it that the Louisville Slugger brand of baseball bats was created around 1884. As the story goes, young John A. "Bud" Hillerich offered slumping big-leaguer Pete Browning a custom-made bat from his father's wood shop. The story may or may not be true, but no one argues that Hillerich created a memorable brand.

BASEBALL HISTORY

Instead of blasting the airwaves with commercials, Louisville Slugger uses tradition to sell its products. The company has its very own museum dedicated to baseball history and to the company's place in that history. The museum shows how baseball greats such as Babe Ruth, Joe DiMaggio, and Hank Aaron swung customized Louisville Slugger ash-wood bats into the record books. There you can see the signatures of these legends and thousands more branded into the side of Louisville Slugger bats. While baseball stars have bats made just for them, fans can feel like stars by buying a bat signed by a big leaguer or one with their own signature. Nonprofessionals buy 1 million signature bats each year.

The company pioneered the use of celebrity endorsements when it signed baseball player Honus "The Flying Dutchman" Wagner in 1905. Now the bat maker boasts stars such as Alex Rodriguez and Jason Giambi. However, big-name players have not kept challengers from going after Louisville Slugger's business. So far, the company still claims a 60-percent share of the Major League market. Only time will tell if it can continue to maintain its lead. No matter what happens, Louisville Slugger has bragging rights as the official bat of Major League Baseball. It's a tradition.

1. How does Louisville Slugger market its product?
2. Do you think stars like Alex Rodriguez can inspire fans to buy more Louisville Slugger bats?

them that racing events will help the local economy. The city government, communication firms, sponsors, and owners all work together so the consumer will have a memorable experience and will return to other events.

Types of Sports Products

Products can be goods or services. Unlike typical consumer products, sports products include a broader range of products. Unique to sports are these products that can be classified as goods or services, or both:

- **Sporting events**—These events are the core product of sports—games, events, and competitions on all levels. They include athletes and the arenas where the events take place.

- **Sports information**—This sports product involves news, statistics, schedules, and stories. Television, radio, online, and print media provide sports information.

- **Sports training**—This product is usually a service such as instruction that is provided through fitness centers, sport camps, and lessons.

- **Sporting goods**—These products usually include a wide range of goods, such as equipment, licensed merchandise, collectibles, and memorabilia, as well as apparel and accessories.

There is a difference between goods and services regarding planning and implementing the sports marketing process. Because services, such as providing a game to be watched, are produced by the players and consumed by the spectators simultaneously, there is no formal channel of distribution. However, when you purchase a tangible good, such as a baseball bat or a skateboard, it must be produced by a manufacturer and sent to a retailer (such as Sports Chalet) to sell to the customer. This kind of channel of distribution requires careful planning and managing.

Sports Goods

Items such as skateboards, balls, exercise equipment, and bats are **tangible products,** or physical goods that offer benefits to the consumer. Customers buy tangible products at stores or other retailing outlets. You can easily identify tangible products such as athletic shoes, baseball cards, and so on. However, there are other sports products that can also include services. When you buy a hot dog or soda and a game souvenir, such as a Rally Monkey, at a baseball game, you have purchased goods, but customer service is also involved in the exchange at the baseball stadium. Thus, many sports products can fall between the categories of goods and services.

ETHICAL PRACTICES

Protecting Young Athletes

Being approached by a sports agent is not always a dream come true. Unethical agents who are motivated by greed might do anything to lure promising athletes into professional sports by offering gifts and lies. If an athlete forfeits his or her eligibility to play college sports, a chance at a scholarship and education could be lost forever. To protect young athletes from being exploited, Nebraska Congressman Tom Osborne introduced the Sports Agent Responsibility and Trust Act—or SPARTA. This act protects athletes and punishes unethical agents with severe civil fines.

CONNECT

What is the most important quality that you look for when buying athletic shoes?

tangible products physical goods that offer benefits to the consumer

QUALITY OF GOODS There are two basic questions to ask about characteristics, or quality dimensions of goods, when judging the quality of manufactured products:

- Does the product conform to design specifications in the manufacturing process?

- How well does the product perform its function in the opinion of the consumers, or end users, of the goods?

The consumer's opinion or perception about the quality of the products is most important to marketing professionals (see **Figure 4.1.**). Many sports organizations attempt to increase the quality of their products, but they risk losing customers if they raise prices as a result. For example, if a sports franchise increases the price of tickets, it may lose the loyalty of the average fan. However, the franchise might find another target market that is willing to spend more money for higher-quality goods, such as luxury suites at the ballpark or special athletic shoes.

Figure 4.1

Characteristics of Quality Goods

JUDGING GOOD QUALITY
A company might use these standards to raise the quality level of its product, but consumers' perception of quality is what matters most. *Can you think of another characteristic, or "quality dimension," to use for measuring quality in a product?*

Quality Dimension of Goods	Consumers' Questions
Performance	How well does the product perform its core function? (Does the athletic running shoe increase your performance?)
Features	Does the product offer additional benefits? (Are the golf-club heads made with titanium?)
Conformity to specifications	Are there many reports of defects? (Does the baseball have the correct number of stitches?)
Reliability	Does the product perform with consistency? (Does the weight machine keep the proper level of weight when being used?)
Serviceability	Is the service system efficient, competent, and convenient? (If you have a problem with the strings on a tennis racket, will the manufacturer quickly address your problem?)
Aesthetic design	Does the product's design look and feel like a high-quality product? (Does the golf club look good and feel good when striking the ball?)

SOURCE: Adapted from D.A. Garvin, "Competing on the Eight Dimensions of Quality." *Harvard Business Review* (November–December 1987) © 1987 by the President and Fellows of Harvard College; all rights reserved. Reprinted by permission of Harvard Business School Press.

Profiles in Marketing

VIRTUAL GAMES

Brian Movalson
Global Brand Manager
EA SPORTS™

Career Data:
Brand Manager

Education and Training
Bachelor's or master's
degrees in communications
or general business; classes
in languages and public
speaking

Skills and Abilities Excellent
communication, writing,
interpersonal, and
organizational skills

Career Outlook As fast as
average growth through
2010

Career Path Employees starting in entry-level marketing
positions can work their way
up. Business degrees are
helpful.

Brian Movalson started his career in the *real* sports world. After earning a bachelor's degree in communications from the University of Michigan, he went to ABC-TV to work on *Monday Night Football*. Seven years later, his experience led him to EA SPORTS, a key brand of Electronic Arts, one of the world's leading electronic-game companies. EA SPORTS has created cool action-game franchises such as *NBA Live, NBA Street, NASCAR Thunder*™, *Knockout Kings*™ for boxing, and *SSX* for snowboarding.

"I realized that the video-game console was becoming like the microwave—everybody is going to have one," he says. "So I focused on how I might work for a great company in that business."

On the Job As global brand manager, Brian is responsible for the EA SPORTS identity as it appears in thousands of products, events, and endorsements worldwide. This includes every-thing from video games to invitational basketball tourna-ments to Web sites to product licensing.

Brian supervises a staff of three employees, and together they work with a larger marketing group of about 40 people. He says that the bulk of his time is spent communicating with partners on various projects. "I have a lot of phone calls, hun-dreds of e-mails, and meetings throughout the day. At any one time, I probably have 50 different projects going."

He says that communication skills, both written and oral, are absolutely essential in his position. "My job really comes down to a lot of communication—that's what marketing is, communicating a message.

"Working with sports, you have to have a passion for sports and a great interest," he adds. "You can't fake that enthusiasm."

How can communication skills help in developing new sports video-game products?

EA SPORTS, the EA SPORTS logo, and Knockout Kings are trademarks or reg-istered trademarks of Electronic Arts, Inc., in the U.S. and/or other countries. NBA, NASCAR, and NASCAR Thunder are trademarks of their respective owners.

intangible product a non-physical service such as tennis lessons, personal training, and sports camps

QUESTION

What are some examples of intangible sports products?

Got Game—and More

The Women's National Basketball Association (WNBA) has come a long way in a few years since April 1996 when it was first formed. By 2001, WNBA games had been seen by 60 million fans in 167 countries. Fostering this global audience, the WNBA.com Web site provides many services for its followers: draft notices, player information, news, statistics, standings, game schedules, highlights, a virtual box office, fantasy games, and even an e-tail store.

➡ Visit the e-tail store and list some of the products available at WNBA.com through marketingseries.glencoe.com.

product line a group of closely related products manufactured and/or sold by a company

Sports Services

In contrast with a sports product, a sports service is an **intangible product**, or nonphysical service such as tennis lessons, personal training, and sports camps. Sports camps, or sports fantasy camps, appeal to many older amateur athletes. The Los Angeles Dodgers Adult Baseball Camp in Vero Beach, Florida, sells its top-rated service of playing with celebrities and getting professional advice for about $4,200 per session. Besides meals and lodging, the price includes tangible goods, such as a uniform, cap, autographed baseball, baseball cards, photo, certificate, and commemorative pin.

Other intangible products, or services, may include the experience of attending a sporting event. However, stadiums advertise and sell their *tangible* appeal in the form of good seats, well-designed interiors, or good parking facilities.

QUALITY OF SERVICE Sports organizations and businesses try to identify characteristics of service quality to help market their services to sports consumers. In the 1980s, researchers Parasuraman, Zeithaml, and Berry identified some key characteristics for good service to all types of consumers. Their ten dimensions of service quality are called SERVQUAL and include these areas to judge: tangibles (appearance of facilities), reliability, responsiveness, competence, courtesy, credibility, security, access, communication, and understanding the customer.

Later, researchers McDonald, Sutton, and Milne used those service-quality dimensions to create a new guide just for sports called TEAMQUAL. They used these dimensions, or characteristics, to evaluate sports spectators' opinions of a National Basketball Association (NBA) team:

- **Reliability**—ability to perform promised services dependably and accurately

- **Assurance**—knowledge and courtesy of employees and their ability to convey trust and confidence

- **Empathy**—the caring, individualized attention provided by the professional sports franchise for its customers

- **Responsiveness**—willingness to help customers and provide prompt service

- **Tangibles**—appearance of equipment, personnel materials, and venue

Sports Product Classifications

You know that products can be classified as goods as well as services. Sports businesses or organizations that offer a variety of products classify their products by product line and product mix. A **product line** is a group of closely related products manufactured and/or sold by a company. These products satisfy a class of needs and may be used together, sold to the same customer group, sold through the same type of outlets, or have the same price range. For example, a sporting goods company such as Spalding® sells several product lines. The Infusion basketball product lines include Infusion Professional and Infusion All Surface products. The common characteristic in these product lines is that the basketballs are equipped with the Infusion Dual-Action Micro Pump that is designed to release air at anytime.

A **product mix** is the total assortment of products that a company makes and/or sells. For example, Wilson® Sporting Goods makes a variety of different product lines that are closely related, but its product mix is extensive with equipment in several sports categories, such as tennis, baseball, basketball, football, hockey, and softball. For example, the product mix under the baseball product line includes bats, bags, baseballs, gloves, mitts, protective equipment, uniforms, and accessories. Many companies will specialize in a limited product mix. However, a company such as Adidas has a broad product mix with everything from shoes and clothing to deodorant and watches. Nike also has an extensive product mix; nevertheless, it continues to expand by adding golfing to its product line.

Math Check

SPARE CHANGE
Tasha makes $40,000 per year. Her discretionary income is 8 percent of that. Does she have enough money for tennis lessons that cost $75 per month?

➡️For tips on finding the solution, go to **marketingseries.glencoe.com**.

Figure 4.2

Sports Product and Extensions

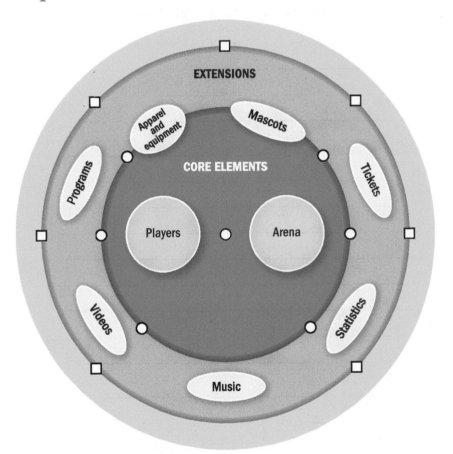

The Sporting Event

RIPPLE EFFECTS The main sporting event is just one type of sports product that generates more sports products, or product extensions. *Identify the product extensions in this diagram.*

product mix the total assortment of products that a company makes and/or sells

Sports Products and Product Extensions

Sports businesses and organizations, like any consumer-driven business, want to offer whatever products will sell. However, sports products differ from typical consumer products because sports products have the ability to generate a greater variety of related products, or product extensions (see **Figure 4.2** on page 83). For example, a Super Bowl football game is a core, or main, sports product. From that one event, product extensions develop, and sports consumers purchase them. Super Bowl programs, tickets that can be saved as collectibles, videos, statistics in the news, related television programs, and T-shirts are all product extensions of the core product, which is the sporting event.

Sports products, or goods and services, have the potential to generate income and affect the economy with one or more related products—all of which become the focus of marketing activities for businesses, organizations, and consumers.

Quick Check ✓

RESPOND to what you've read by answering these questions.

1. What are four characteristics needed to analyze the market segmentation of sports consumers?

_____

_____

_____

_____

2. How is a purchase by the sports consumer similar to a vote? _____

_____

_____

_____

_____

_____

_____

_____

3. Define product mix. _____

_____

_____

_____

_____

Economic Impact of Sports Marketing

Economic Effects

What are the economic effects of purchasing a sports product? When you decide to go to a professional game or event, you might use the telephone or the Internet to purchase tickets. Maybe you make arrangements to drive to the arena or ballpark. If you cannot arrange for your own transportation, you might arrange for public transportation. When you arrive, you may be hungry, or you may wish to purchase a souvenir. If you enjoyed your experience at the sporting event, you might return and pay for more events.

Consider all the aspects of the economy that are affected by a sporting event. Each part of the consumer's experience has an economic impact. From the moment the consumer inquires about a ticket, there is impact on the economy. The consumer's decisions activate a system that is run by people who are trained to know the needs and expectations of the consumer. If the system is successful in getting the consumer to spend money, and the consumer has had an enjoyable experience, then profits result. Money spent at sporting events is divided among all of the groups involved in the sporting event. As a result, the local economy also improves.

A Day at the Ballpark

Each decision you make keeps people involved in the event employed in jobs at the ballpark or arena, such as a ticket agent, parking garage attendant, food and merchandise vendor, sanitation attendant, and others. Tax dollars are spent for roads, arena construction, public transportation, and police.

Each decision the consumer makes involves an **opportunity cost**, which is the loss of the opportunity that is passed up in order to receive something in exchange. Opportunity-cost decisions affect sports marketing because the consumer decides to spend his or her discretionary income to have an enjoyable experience.

A satisfied customer will tell others about a pleasurable experience at the event. Other people will be interested and will attend later events. This chain reaction continues to have a positive effect on the local economy. As the economy grows, then more infrastructure is needed to support the athletic event. **Infrastructure** is the physical development of an area, including the major public systems, services, and facilities of a country or region needed to make a location function. Six of these functions include: power and water supplies, public transportation, telecommunications, roads, and schools—all of which support residents and tourists alike. This entire process, from beginning to end, contributes to the economy.

AS YOU READ ...

YOU WILL LEARN

- To explain the economic impact of sports marketing.

WHY IT'S IMPORTANT

Profits from sports products and sporting events impact local and regional economies.

KEY TERMS

- opportunity cost
- infrastructure
- sports franchise
- grassroots marketing

PREDICT

Pick one key term and define it in your own words.

opportunity cost the loss of the opportunity that is passed up in order to receive something in exchange

infrastructure the physical development of an area, including the major public systems, services, and facilities of a country or region needed to make a location function

A European Sports Market

It is no wonder that Germany is a world power in athletics. School children take classes on the history and culture of the Olympics. Two of the country's universities teach only sports and physical education. The German Sports Federation has signed up more than two million volunteer coaches and officials. Plus, one out of every three Germans is a member of one of 62,000 sports clubs in the country. Germany also boasts Olympic training facilities, one of Europe's largest indoor ski slopes, and 34 national parks. Having so many sports outlets, Germans spend billions of Euros (Europe's currency) on sporting goods, making Germany the largest sports market in Europe.

In addition, each year German workers have three to six weeks off—more vacation time than for any Western country. Leisure has become a major pursuit and sports a major industry. As a result, American manufacturers are prospering in that market because German consumers frequently ask for sports equipment made in the United States.

Explain why Germans purchase a large amount of sports products.

CONNECT

How much money would you pay for a season ticket to see your favorite sports team?

"The Sunshine State"

Did you know that the state of Florida, known as "The Sunshine State," is the number one tourist destination in the world? It welcomes over 30 million tourists every year. Along its beaches and coasts, business establishments seek profits. Motels, hotels, resorts, restaurants, plazas, and malls fill this state that used to be covered with wetlands, marshes, and orange groves.

With the establishment of Walt Disney World in 1971, Orlando, Florida, became known worldwide as "theme-park central." The city of Orlando has also established itself as the high-technology hub of Florida. Throughout the state, Florida shows signs of economic growth. Because of the growth, professional sports have also become a part of Florida's economy—and Walt Disney World added its Wide World of Sports complex as a result.

Case Study: Sports Economy in Orlando

The Orlando Magic joined the National Basketball Association (NBA) for the 1989–90 season. But nearly four years before the team sank its first basketball, local developer and banker Jim Hewitt began promoting the idea of Orlando as the hometown of an NBA sports organization—also known as a franchise. A **sports franchise** in sports is an agreement or contract for a sports organization to sell a parent company's (i.e., a national sports league) good or service within a given area. By selling Orlando Magic T-shirts, caps, and other

sports franchise an agreement or contract for a sports organization to sell a parent company's (i.e., a national sports league) good or service within a given area

items, the investors were able to convince the residents of Orlando to make $100 deposits on season-ticket reservations. All of this was done to impress the NBA with a show of support from central Florida fans. The Orlando Magic franchise had only a short period of time in which to establish itself as a competitor. By drafting star center Shaquille O'Neal in 1992, the Magic became competitive instantly—and became one of the league's most popular teams. In addition, the Orlando Magic became another attraction for Orlando residents and tourists. The team continues to bring in millions of dollars each year to the city's economy.

Economic and Marketing Challenges

A profitable business is one that makes money. Sports marketing helps businesses make money as consumers have fun, but marketers often face challenges, obstacles, and limitations while pursuing success. Consider the marketing challenges faced by the New York Yankees or the Los Angeles Dodgers compared to the challenges faced by lesser-known teams such as the Columbus Clippers or the Las Vegas 51s. Many professional teams deal with similar as well as different challenges faced by semi-professional or minor league teams. They must use different methods for marketing.

For example, the Los Angeles Sparks, which are supported by the NBA, have won the Women's National Basketball Association national championship two seasons in a row. However, on ESPN, their championship win was announced immediately after the results of a fishing tournament. The WNBA has become an organization drawing millions of viewers and spectators around the world. The players are very talented, playing a game that is as competitive as the men's game. However, the media gave the WNBA national championship announcement lower-profile exposure. Improving media exposure is the challenge for the team's marketers.

The efforts of the Los Angeles Lakers' marketing team compared to the efforts of the Los Angeles Sparks' marketing team are very different. They are both professional basketball teams, and both play in the same arena, but the target market for each team is significantly different. Therefore, the marketing activities and sponsors for these two events are different.

Case Study — PART 2

ARENA PRODUCT ADVANTAGE
Continued from Part 1 on page 75

With a decline in game attendance and a low ranking in the 2003 season, the Baltimore Orioles considered new marketing strategies. They offered almost 40 games with promotions and giveaways. Six nights were Esskay Dollar Dog Nights sponsored by the Esskay Company located in Baltimore, Maryland. Esskay is the official hot dog for the Baltimore Orioles, as well as for the Baltimore Ravens, the Washington Wizards, and the Washington Redskins. Fans could purchase a maximum of four hot dogs for $1 each on Dollar Dog Night. Eighteen more home games were designated as Bargain Nights. Fans could purchase an Upper Reserve seat for $8 and a super hot dog and soda at a combo price.

The Baltimore Orioles are working on improving the team and improving the fan experience at the game.

ANALYZE AND WRITE
1. Looking at both parts of this case study, identify the sports products and the products that use sports to sell the product.
2. Identify the reasons Esskay would want to remain the official hot dog of the Baltimore Orioles.

QUESTION
If the target market for two teams is different, what two other factors differ?

> **LOCAL SUPPORT All professional-league sports teams make an effort to give back to their communities. Charity fund-raising games and personal appearances not only benefit a team's image but also provide assistance to people in need.** *Find out what community or charitable activities your favorite team sponsors.*

grassroots marketing marketing activity on a local community level

Grassroots Marketing Efforts

To gain support, a team such as the Sparks is heavily involved in grassroots marketing. The term **grassroots marketing** refers to marketing activity on a local community level. For example, helping and assisting the community with charity and fund-raising events is a grassroots activity. To get to essential community support, many sports teams have to appeal to local residents. The grassroots marketing concept helps build a relationship between the community and the team. A positive relationship between the community and the team can help the economy of an area or neighborhood improve.

In fact, a community's economic health can depend on local sporting events. A successful team attracts spectators who buy sports products such as tickets, food, and souvenirs. A ticket purchase is more than just a pass to a game—it also affects several aspects of the community. In turn, the trust and the support of the local community for sporting events positively affect many local businesses. Economic success promoted by sports marketing for events and products on a local level can extend to regional and national levels, affecting the global community.

Quick Check

RESPOND to what you've read by answering these questions.

1. What is opportunity cost? Give an example. _____

_____

_____

2. List six functions of an infrastructure of a community. _____

_____

_____

3. Why is grassroots marketing an important part of sports marketing?_____

_____

_____

Worksheet 4.1

Sports News

Choose one of your favorite sports events. Identify the event as an amateur or professional event. Find out what products are sold in connection with the event. Include a sketch, diagram, or photo of the products. Write an article about the event and its product extensions.

Event: _____

Product	Product

Article: _____

_____

_____

_____

_____

_____

_____

_____

_____

_____

_____

_____

_____

_____

_____

_____

_____

Worksheet 4.2

Sports Economy

1. Choose a favorite professional sports team from the Minor or Major League. Contact the chamber of commerce in the team's city. Ask about the economic impact the home team has on that city's economy. Record your findings below.

Sports Team	Home City	Economic Impact in Dollars
_____	_____	_____
_____	_____	_____

2. List types of products and services sold as a direct and indirect result of the sports team.

_____

_____

_____

_____

_____

_____

_____

_____

_____

_____

_____

_____

_____

_____

_____

_____

_____

_____

Portfolio Works

TYPES OF SPORTS PRODUCTS

1. Over the next two weeks, chart the types of sports products you use or a friend uses. List at least five products. Classify them as goods or services or both.

Name of Product	Goods	Service	Overlap
1)			
2)			
3)			
4)			
5)			
6)			
7)			
8)			
9)			
10)			

2. For each product, name one thing you would change about the product and explain why. Also, if you think the product does not need changing, explain why.

Name of Product	Product Change
1)	
2)	
3)	
4)	
5)	
6)	
7)	
8)	
9)	
10)	

Add this page to your career portfolio.

CHAPTER SUMMARY

Section 4.1
The Consumer and Sports Products

sports consumer (p. 76)
market segmentation
(p. 77)
sports products (p. 78)
tangible products (p. 79)
intangible product
(p. 82)
product line (p. 82)
product mix (p. 83)

- A sports consumer is a person who may play, officiate, watch, or listen to sports, or read, use, purchase, and/or collect items related to sports.

- Market segmentation is a way of analyzing a market by specific characteristics to create a target market. It considers consumer characteristics, such as geographics, demographics, psychographics, and product benefits.

- Sports products are goods, services, ideas, or a combination of those things related to sports that provide satisfaction to the consumer.

- Goods are tangible products, whereas services are intangible. There is a difference between goods and services regarding planning and implementing the marketing process.

- A product line is a group of closely related products manufactured and/or sold by a company, but a product mix includes the total assortment of products made and/or sold by a sports company.

Section 4.2
Economic Impact of Sport Marketing

opportunity cost (p. 85)
infrastructure (p. 85)
sports franchise (p. 86)
grassroots marketing
(p. 88)

- A sporting event has a wide-reaching impact on a local economy, providing jobs and revenue for teams, cities, as well as vendors. Grassroots marketing involves helping and assisting the local community with various fundraising events.

CHECKING CONCEPTS

1. **Describe** how a marketer views a sports consumer.
2. **Name** the four characteristics that need to be considered when analyzing the market segment of sports consumers.
3. **Describe** what happens when the correct sports consumer is targeted by a sports-marketing plan.
4. **Identify** the sports product.
5. **Explain** how sports goods and sports services differ.
6. **Compare** a product line and product mix.
7. **Define** grassroots marketing.

Critical Thinking

8. **Explain** five dimensions of service quality and how they apply to a sports team.

CROSS-CURRICULUM SKILLS

Work-Based Learning

Basic Skills—Speaking

9. Research one company that makes sports-related products. Include history, athlete endorsements, and marketing information. Give a five-minute speech in class about that company.

Basic Skills—Writing

10. Use the Internet or library to research team mascots. Write a summary of your findings and present it to the class.

School-Based Learning

Social Studies

11. Use the Internet or library to research sports products that are most popular in another country. Write two paragraphs about your findings.

Writing

12. Use the Internet or library to research your favorite athlete. Write a report about the athlete that includes a history of the person's life and products tied to the athlete.

 CONNECTION

Role Play: Marketing Director

SITUATION You are to assume the role of marketing director for an event-planning company that is heavily involved in the revitalization of the downtown area of your city. You are on the committee to study whether the town should build a new venue for the baseball and football teams, or if a separate venue should be built for both.

(ACTIVITY) Determine the needs of a town for a venue site and present it to the committee chair (judge).

EVALUATION You will be evaluated on how well you meet the following performance indicators:

- Describe factors used by marketers to position products.
- Explain the concept of product in sports and entertainment marketing.
- Determine services to provide customers.
- Describe the role of customer expectations in services marketing.
- Describe current issues and trends in sports and entertainment marketing.

INTERNET ACTIVITY

Use the Internet to access information about the Olympics.

- · Click on Sports News.
- Choose one of the top sports stories.
- Share what you learned with another classmate.

➡ For a link to the official Olympic site to begin this exercise, go to marketingseries.glencoe.com.

WHEN TO RUN WITH NIKE?

Perhaps no company has cashed in more successfully on America's fascination with sports than Nike. In the 40 years since its co-founding by CEO Phil Knight and the late University of Oregon track coach, Bill Bowerman, Nike has grown from a maker of shoes for track-and-field athletes into the world's leading purveyor of sportswear and sneakers—for everyone from major leaguers to wannabes.

Nike's pace slowed in the late 1990s. But the company has come to grips with challenges such as price resistance to $200 basketball shoes and changing tastes on the part of consumers who once treated sneakers as high fashion.

Among the variety of factors that have revived the company, perhaps the most crucial is growth overseas, where it gathered 53 percent of revenues in 2002, a figure that's expected to rise to 55 percent, thanks to major gains in the soccer market.

Customizing for Customers

That's partly because the Nike-endorsed Brazilian team won the World Cup in 2002. But it's also because Nike has begun customizing its shoe designs for overseas markets. In Latin America, its customers often play soccer on beaches or rocky roads instead of grass fields. So Nike has made its shoes for that market more durable.

At the same time, Nike is continuing to reinvigorate sales by playing up its shoes' durability and comfort over the high-fashion look—and by lowering prices. Customer resistance led to an 8 percent reduction, to $58, in Nike's average sneaker price.

Nike's sudden focus on affordability dovetailed with its decision to go retro in an effort to appeal to baby boomers, its second-largest customer group after young men. Its Nylon Cortez iD sneaker, priced at $70, is a hit with boomers who still remember the original model from 1968. Retro models have even caught on with younger consumers.

More important, consumers aren't willing to pay as much for sportswear, now that "high-end [athletic shoes] are no longer also high fashion," says Cohen [NPD market analyst]. Many young males now go for Timberland boots, instead, he says. All those factors account for about a two-point decline in Nike's share of the market over the past year. Still, Nike's financial results and stock price continue to improve—perhaps a sign that it's yet a force to be reckoned with.

By Olga Kharif

CREATIVE JOURNAL

In your journal, write your responses:

CRITICAL THINKING

1. What strategies have helped Nike improve sales?

APPLICATION

2. Imagine you are planning for and promoting a new sports show or item of clothing. Name and describe the product and its target market. Explain why this product would be successful. Then write a slogan for advertising the product. Share your ideas with the class.

 Go to businessweek.com for current *BusinessWeek* Online articles.

UNIT LAB

You've just entered the real world of sports and entertainment marketing. Dream Machine, Inc., is a sports and entertainment marketing company that serves college and professional sports teams, professional athletes, sporting events, sports arenas, and major sports product corporations, as well as performing arts companies, television networks, and movie studios. As an entry-level employee, you will have the opportunity to work on a variety of clients' projects.

Get Creative—Design a New Product

TOOLS AND RESOURCES To complete the assignment, you will need to:
- Conduct research at the library, on the Internet, or by talking to retailers.
- Ask sports-minded individuals what new features would better meet their needs.
- Have word-processing, spreadsheet, and presentation software.

SITUATION You are employed by a clothing manufacturer that wants to enter the sports-apparel market. Your company's sales have been flat in the last few years. Management wants to invest in new ideas to boost sales. As product manager, you will have the opportunity to design and market a new sports-apparel line for your company. You believe that product innovation and aggressive marketing are needed to increase sales. The vice president of marketing wants to hear your ideas, based on research you conduct.

ASSIGNMENT Complete these tasks:
- Research sports-apparel manufacturers to determine their market share.
- Research various sports to find out what new apparel line might be profitable.
- Research trends and opportunities.
- Based on your research, make recommendations for a new sports-apparel line.
- Make a report to your vice president of marketing.

RESEARCH Do your research:
- Research target markets for sports apparel.
- Research total sales for the sports apparel industry in the past three years.
- Research new product innovation.
- Determine trends and opportunities.

REPORT Prepare a written report using the following tools, if available:
- *Word-processing program:* Prepare a report of trends and opportunities in the sports-apparel industry, your product design, and characteristics of the target market.
- *Spreadsheet program:* Prepare a chart comparing competitors of your product. Prepare a chart to list sports-apparel industry sales for the past three years.
- *Presentation program:* Prepare a ten-slide visual presentation with key points, sketch of your product, market-share chart, and illustration of the target market.

PRESENTATION AND EVALUATION
You will present your report to the V.P. of marketing. You will be evaluated on the basis of:
- Your knowledge of the sports-apparel industry and competitors
- Rationale for your new product idea
- Continuity of presentation
- Voice quality
- Eye contact

PORTFOLIO
Add this report to your career portfolio.

UNIT 3

SPORTS MARKETING MIX

" You give 100 percent in the first half of the game, and if that isn't enough, in the second half you give what's left. "

—Yogi Berra
Baseball player and manager

UNIT OVERVIEW

A ll types of sports, sports products, and athletes can benefit from effective marketing strategies. Developing a marketing mix is a strategy used to market the goods and services offered by the sports industry. Unit 3 focuses on all the components of the marketing mix. In Chapter 5, you will learn how pricing considerations are applied to sports products. Chapter 6 examines place decisions and the role of market research. The promotional strategies and methods found in Chapters 7 and 8 include different types of branding and licensing, as well as promotional methods and media marketing. Chapter 9 explains the elements of good marketing plans. You will also learn about careers in sports marketing.

■ UNIT LAB

Preview

In-line skating is growing among recreational and fitness skaters. Your company is looking for innovative products to take advantage of this trend.

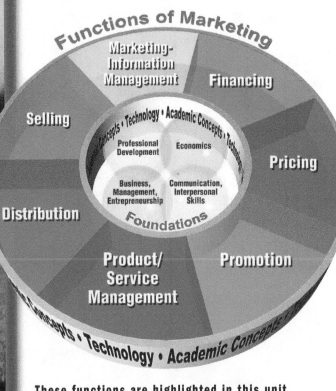

Functions of Marketing

- Marketing-Information Management
- Financing
- Selling
- Pricing
- Distribution
- Promotion
- Product/Service Management

Foundations
- Professional Development
- Economics
- Business, Management, Entrepreneurship
- Communication, Interpersonal Skills

Concepts • Technology • Academic Concepts • Technology • Academic Concepts • Technology • Academic Concepts

These functions are highlighted in this unit.

- Promotion
- Product/Service Management
- Selling
- Pricing
- Marketing-Information Management

Chapter 5

Product and Price Decisions: Sports

Section 5.1

Product Design

Section 5.2

Pricing and Strategies

Chapter Objectives

- Differentiate between a product item and product line.
- Classify products as consumer goods or business goods.
- Explain the seven steps in developing a new product.
- Identify the stages in a product's life cycle.
- Define price and the role it plays in determining profit.
- Describe the factors that affect pricing decisions.
- Identify pricing strategies.

FROM OLD TO GOLD

Sports products can include goods, services, or ideas. A state-of-the-art arena, such as Staples Center in Los Angeles, is a product that provides sports services and also sells goods such as memorabilia and souvenir T-shirts. Popular throwback jerseys made by Mitchell & Ness are also sports products.

Since 1904, Mitchell & Ness has had a long history as a sporting-goods company in Philadelphia, Pennsylvania. Then in 1985, the company started making throwback baseball jerseys using original materials. The retro uniform tops were made of heavy Pendleton wool flannel, authentic in their look, feel, and design. Sales for the shirts, originally made for older fans, exploded in 1998 when hip-hop artists began wearing shirts such as Nolan Ryan's rainbow Astros jersey from the 1970s. The company began offering vintage NBA, NFL, MLB and NHL jerseys.

Demand for vintage jerseys has grown—and so has the competition. Nike and Reebok now offer vintage uniforms at lower prices because of their volume sales. How has Mitchell & Ness maintained its success?

ANALYZE AND WRITE

1. Give examples of other businesses that have profited by reviving old products.
2. Will throwback jerseys continue to sell and have a long life cycle? Why?

Case Study Part 2 on page 109

POWER READ

Be an active reader and use these reading strategies:

PREDICT what the section will be about.

CONNECT what you read with your life.

QUESTION as you read to make sure you understand the content.

RESPOND to what you've read.

Product Design

YOU WILL LEARN

- To differentiate between a product item and product line.
- To classify products as consumer goods or business goods.
- To explain the seven steps in developing a new product.
- To identify the stages in a product's life cycle.

WHY IT'S IMPORTANT

Product development is one of the Four Ps of the marketing mix. Making decisions about a product's design is important to its success with the target market.

KEY TERMS

- product item
- consumer goods
- business goods
- point of difference
- focus group
- commercialization
- repositioning

PREDICT

Why do you think pricing is an important factor in marketing sports products?

product item specific model or size of a product

consumer goods goods purchased and used by the ultimate consumer for personal use

Product Defined

The world of sports generates many products. As you learned in Chapter 4, a sports product is a good, service, or idea that satisfies consumers' needs. Products are one of the essential components in the marketing mix. A product can be tangible, such as a baseball bat (good), or intangible, such as watching a professional baseball game (service). Demonstrating good sportsmanship and supporting the Special Olympics are ideas that can be marketed as well.

Product Item and Line

A **product item** is a specific model or size of a product. Nike's Air Flight Lite basketball shoe is a product item. The entire group of Nike athletic shoes would be called a product line. As discussed in Chapter 4, a product line is a group of closely related products that are sold by a company. Nike has three product lines: athletic clothing, athletic footwear, and sports equipment, which make up its product mix, or combination of product lines sold by the same company.

Product Classifications

Products can also be classified as consumer goods or business goods. **Consumer goods** are purchased and used by the ultimate consumer for personal use. **Business goods** are purchased by organizations for use in their operation. Thus, depending on the intended use of the product, the same product could be both a consumer good and a business good. For example, if you purchased a pair of Nike athletic shoes in a retail store, the shoes would be considered a consumer good. When Nike athletic shoes are purchased by retailers for resale purposes, they become business goods. With this understanding, marketers recognize that two different marketing approaches are necessary to reach the two different types of customers. Promoting Nike products might involve television advertising on sporting events. Promoting Nike products to retail chain stores, such as Foot Locker or Sports Authority, might involve discounts for volume purchases.

Point of Difference

Organizations design their products to make them stand out in the marketplace. Therefore, products need to have a point of difference. A **point of difference** is a unique product characteristic or benefit that sets the product apart from a competitor's product. A baseball team that wins the World Series has a big point of difference when compared to competing teams. Companies, such as Nike, with certain product brands work hard to communicate their products' unique features and benefits to establish a point of difference in the marketplace. For example, Nike is constantly introducing and patenting new shoe designs that improve the product's durability and performance. One of the reasons for new product failures is the lack of a point of difference. Thus, product planning is crucial to the success of a product.

Steps in New Product Development

There are usually seven steps in developing a new product. Not all steps are followed each time. Let's look at how a typical new product is developed.

Step 1—SWOT Analysis

The first step involves analysis of the company's strengths (S) and weaknesses (W), as well as external opportunities (O) and threats (T) in the marketplace (SWOT). This SWOT analysis helps to develop a product that matches the company's objectives; it also provides focus for the other steps in the process.

Step 2—Idea Generation

Step 2 involves generating new product ideas. New ideas can come from many sources, such as consumers, employees, research and development departments, and even competitors. By analyzing customer complaints and/or merchandise returns, an organization can get ideas for new product designs. Employees can provide ideas in special work sessions. The sales staff can also get feedback from channel members or from consumers, depending on the type of product. Research and development departments have responsibility for coming up with new ideas for products.

Studying the competition can help generate new product ideas as well. For example, Nike might decide to create a new golf shoe after learning that New Balance (a competitor) has just created a specially

Game Point

> **X-TREME GROWTH SPURT**
> Extreme growth with extreme risk describes the X-treme sports niche for the last five years. For example, a sport such as snowboarding has jumped 113 percent with a target market of close to 5.5 million "risk-takers" buying products, according to American Sports Data, Inc.

◄ **CREATIVE THINKING**
Sports marketing professionals need new ideas to create products that can be marketed to old and new customers. *What would be the point of difference for a child's golf shoe?*

Handheld Stats

The use of handheld computers continues to grow. Special computer software made for handheld computers now allows coaches to keep track of statistics and scouting information. After collecting information at a game, users can calculate team and individual statistics, download the stats to a desktop computer, then print out detailed reports. The reports can be faxed or e-mailed to local media outlets or used by coaches to adjust game strategy.

➡Discuss the use of handheld computers as a coaching tool after reading information through **marketingseries.glencoe.com**.

focus group a panel of six to ten consumers who discuss opinions about a topic under the guidance of a moderator

CONNECT

Have you ever bought a new product when it was first introduced?

commercialization process that involves producing and marketing a new product

designed shoe for child golfers. At this point the company should write a protocol. A *protocol* is a statement that identifies a target market, specifies customers' needs and wants, and explains the new product and what makes it unique (point of difference). The target market for Nike would be children who need a reasonably priced, quality golf shoe. Nike's points of difference could be bright colors in its shoe design—and Tiger Woods' endorsement of the new golf shoe.

Step 3—Screening and Evaluation

Step 3 involves screening and evaluating the new product idea. The product idea is evaluated to see if the company has the technology needed to make the product and to see if it meets the company's objectives. The researchers can also evaluate the product idea with consumers. Focus group sessions provide feedback on the proposed product design. A **focus group** is a panel of six to ten consumers who discuss their opinions about a topic under the guidance of a moderator. The moderator asks specific questions to get the panel members to talk about their ideas and opinions. The group's feedback is invaluable for a company to determine possible customer acceptance of the unproven product.

Step 4—Business Analysis

Step 4 involves the business analysis. In this step, financial aspects of making and marketing the product are reviewed. The company must determine what is needed to take this product idea to market. Product researchers analyze legal factors to see if the product can be patented or copyrighted for protection against competitors.

Step 5—Development

Step 5 involves development of the actual product. If a product idea passes the business analysis, then the company can develop a prototype for the product. A *prototype* is the first model of the product. In this stage, the company tests its production capabilities to see if the product can be produced at a reasonable cost. Complex technical problems, as well as standards for quality and safety, are addressed in this stage of development.

Step 6—Test Marketing

In Step 6, the product is tested in the marketplace. Test marketing involves offering the product for sale in a small geographic area. Marketers test all aspects of the marketing mix (product, place, price, and promotion) during this step. The results of test marketing can help in projecting sales and market share for the new product. Not all new products go through this step because of the costs and the influence of competitors. Competitors can actually ruin a test market by flooding the geographical area with special promotions or by reducing its prices during this phase.

Step 7—Commercialization

Commercialization is a process that involves producing and marketing a new product. In Step 7, the company offers the product in the

 marketingseries.glencoe.com

Snow Business

There's no business like snow business—but in sunny Spain? Spain has always had great outdoor skiing. However, a new sports arena that recently opened in Madrid makes swooshing down the slopes a year-round sport. Named *Parque de Nieve* (Spanish for "Snow Park"), its 17th century building is advertised as Europe's largest indoor ski facility.

A single slope that measures 820 feet long and 65 feet wide has a respectable incline of about 20 percent—and there's nothing like giving Mother Nature a little help. Two giant compressors generate frozen mist from 17 cannon-like devices installed in the ceiling. Freezing temperatures ranging from 28 to 32 degrees Fahrenheit add icy realism to the virtual environment. Although there are a number of snow domes across Europe, the park's communication director points out that this new ski arena also has a mountain theme.

Maintaining a wintry playground is expensive; it costs $57,000 per month for electricity. However, business has been brisk: "As a way of satisfying the craving to ski, it's pretty good," said one stoked customer.

What kind of test marketing could a sports company do to project the success of a sports arena such as a ski park in the United States?

marketplace for sale to the final consumer. There is full-scale production during the launch of this new product. Some companies use regional rollouts, which involve launching the new product in certain geographic areas over a set time period. This process allows production to build up gradually and also allows the company to evaluate its marketing activities. This is just the beginning of a product's life cycle.

Product Life Cycle

The product life cycle represents the stages that a product goes through during its life in the marketplace. There are four stages in the product life cycle—introduction, growth, maturity, and decline. (See **Figure 5.1** on page 104.)

Introduction

The introduction stage occurs when a product is first introduced into the marketplace. Marketers focus on promoting consumer awareness and getting customers to try the new product. To accomplish those objectives, companies spend millions of dollars to educate the consumer through advertising and promotion. For example, think about the sports drink Gatorade. When it was first introduced, consumers did not know what this product could do for them. The company had to educate consumers about Gatorade's capability of restoring an athlete's energy lost during active play in hot weather. Gatorade was competing with bottled water in the marketplace when it was originally introduced. At that time, its only flavor was lemon-lime.

Figure 5.1

A Product's Life Cycle

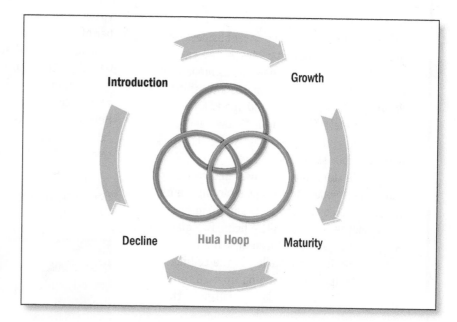

Product pricing can be high to cover research and development costs. This type of pricing is called *skimming pricing.* However, companies may use *penetration pricing* instead. They will price a new product low in comparison to a competitor's product in order to quickly generate demand for the product.

A major task during the introduction stage involves distribution of the new product in the marketplace. Convincing retailers to carry the new product can be challenging, depending on the type of product and available shelf space. Getting Gatorade on supermarket shelves required marketers to convince store owners that this product would be popular with consumers.

QUESTION

What is one major task during the introduction stage of the product life cycle?

Growth

In the growth stage, more competitors enter the marketplace if they see that a new product is successful. For example, Powerade and Sportsade joined the race for the sports-drink market as Gatorade became popular. To be competitive at this stage, the product may be improved by adding new features or new products in that line. For example, in the growth stage, Gatorade added new flavors (orange and fruit punch), package sizes, and types of containers to remain the market leader.

At this stage adding distribution outlets is important too. Gatorade increased its distribution from convenience stores and supermarkets to include vending machines, fountain service, and snack bars to take advantage of its growth stage.

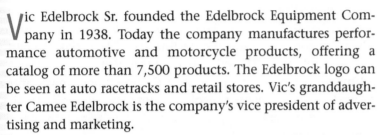

Profiles in Marketing

THE RACER'S EDGE

Camee Edelbrock
Vice President of Advertising
and Marketing
Edelbrock Corporation

Vic Edelbrock Sr. founded the Edelbrock Equipment Company in 1938. Today the company manufactures performance automotive and motorcycle products, offering a catalog of more than 7,500 products. The Edelbrock logo can be seen at auto racetracks and retail stores. Vic's granddaughter Camee Edelbrock is the company's vice president of advertising and marketing.

Camee holds a degree in communications arts and sciences from the University of Southern California. She started working for the family business in 1982, became director of advertising in 1987, and moved up to vice president in 1993. She is credited with bringing the company into the computer age—she updated the firm's advertising department and introduced desktop publishing, which expanded the company's catalog business.

"I wear many hats," she says. "Copywriting, art directing, design, production, public relations, and project management." She says her workload is consistently heavy and that there is always a new project to work on: "My mind works 24/7."

Communication According to Camee, the most important skills in her job are not necessarily the nuts-and-bolts technical details but rather being able to communicate with fellow employees. She emphasizes that listening is just as important as speaking.

She also stresses the importance of having dedication and focus. A company that produces thousands of products also produces thousands of marketing opportunities. It is important to choose carefully and creatively, seeing every project through to completion through all the stages of a product's life cycle.

How would communication skills help in determining the life-cycle stage for a particular product?

Maturity

The third stage of a product's life cycle is maturity, when sales begin to slow down for the product category or just the product. Repeat customers may stop buying the product, and new buyers may be difficult to attract in this stage. To keep the product alive, a company may make changes to the product to distinguish it from competitors' products. Marketers may also focus on identifying new buyers for the product in the maturity stage.

Decline

When sales and profits begin to drop, a product or product category goes into the decline stage. Technological advances can cause entire product categories to enter the decline stage. Just look at eight-track tapes, cassettes, and CDs. What will be the next stage for these products? Individual products move into decline when newer and more improved models replace the older ones. For example, in the golf industry, new drivers, irons, putters, and woods are introduced each year by golf club manufacturers.

You may wonder what happens to products when they reach the decline stage. A company may drop many of them from its product line. Products in decline that are kept in the product line get little or no marketing support. The main reason a company may keep a product is to satisfy requests from loyal customers who still use that particular product.

Product Life-Cycle Considerations

Not all products fit the life-cycle pattern. For example, since Pepsi purchased Quaker Oats (owner of the Gatorade brand) in 2001, Gatorade sales have continued to increase from $85 million in 1983 to over $2 billion in 2003. In fact, the sports-drink market appears to still be growing. Thus, Gatorade may still be in the growth stage. Consumer demand in the sports-drink market and its own product sales will determine how long Gatorade can stay in the growth stage.

On the other hand, fads have a very short life cycle. *Fads* are products that become popular quickly and lose popularity just as quickly. In the 1980s, Koosh balls and boom boxes were very popular, but consumers soon lost interest. A product that requires a lot of information to educate the consumer will stay in the introduction stage for a long period of time. A new sports drink, however, would probably not stay in the introduction stage very long because consumers already know the benefits that sports drinks have to offer.

Management of the Product Life Cycle

Product managers need to manage a product through its life cycle. Managers can accomplish that task in three ways:

- Modify the product.

- Market the product.

- Reposition the product.

Product Modification

Modifying the product requires changing a product's characteristics. Changes can be made to the product's features, appearance, package design, or quality. A company markets this new and improved product with its new look in hopes of increasing sales. For example, in addition to the original Gatorade Thirst Quencher, you can purchase Gatorade Fierce, Gatorade Frost, Gatorade Ice, and Gatorade Xtremo—all product modifications of the original lemon-lime Gatorade.

Market Modification

Modifying the market is a strategy to find new customers or to encourage current customers to use more of the product. For example, Gatorade introduced a new version of its product (Gatorade Frost) to target a new market: anyone in a hot environment who gets thirsty. The target market is different for Gatorade Frost than for the other types of Gatorade, which all target athletes specifically.

Repositioning

Repositioning a product involves changing a product's image in relation to its competitor's image. A change in any of the four Ps of the marketing mix can be enough to reposition a product. For example, New Balance decided to redesign its athletic shoes for older people who have wider feet and often have foot problems. By repositioning its athletic shoes for this niche market, New Balance no longer had to compete directly with companies such as Nike and Reebok. Part of New Balance's repositioning included promoting its products to podiatrists so they would recommend New Balance shoes to their patients.

repositioning changing a product's image in relation to a competitor's image

MARKETING SERIES *Online*

Remember to check out this book's Web site for pricing information and more great resources at marketingseries.glencoe.com.

Quick Check

RESPOND to what you've read by answering these questions.

1. Explain the seven steps involved in developing a new product._____

_____

_____

_____

2. Name the four stages in the product life cycle._____

_____

_____

_____

3. What three things can be done to manage a product through its life cycle?_____

_____

_____

Pricing and Strategies

AS YOU READ ...

YOU WILL LEARN

- To define price and the role it plays in determining profit.
- To describe the factors that affect pricing decisions.
- To identify pricing strategies.

WHY IT'S IMPORTANT

Pricing is one of the Four Ps of the marketing mix—product, price, place, and promotion. It plays a significant role in determining a product's success.

KEY TERMS

- price
- prestige pricing
- odd-even pricing
- target pricing
- markup
- cost-plus pricing
- non-price competition
- market share
- price lining
- bundle pricing
- loss-leader pricing
- yield-management pricing
- price fixing

price the value placed on goods or services being exchanged

PREDICT

Choose one key term in this section and write your own definition of it.

Pricing

How much would you pay for season tickets to see your favorite football team? Businesses struggle with a similar question: "How much will someone pay for _____?" All types of businesses use price in the exchange process. However, the concept of price goes by many names. For example, you pay tuition for college and interest on a loan. Professionals such as doctors and lawyers charge you a fee. To use some bridges and roads, you must pay a toll. When you take a bus or train, you pay a fare. You pay rent for your apartment. You could even barter a signed baseball bat for a special baseball card. Bartering means trading goods or services for someone else's goods or services. So, **price** is defined as the value placed on the goods or services being exchanged.

Pricing and Profit

Price is important in a business because it helps determine a company's profit or loss. Each item that is sold in a business carries a price. When you multiply the number of items sold by its sales price, you arrive at the sales revenue a company generates from its operation. To determine if a firm earned a profit or suffered a loss, subtract the cost of goods sold and the company's expenses from the money it generated in sales revenue. Here is a simple example: A company sells 1,000 baseball bats at $175 each to generate revenue of $175,000. Let's assume the company purchased those baseball bats for $90 each. The cost of goods (baseball bats) sold would be $90,000. Let's say the expenses of running the business totaled $60,000. In this case, the business would earn a profit of $25,000 ($175,000 minus $150,000 equals $25,000).

Pricing and the Marketing Mix

Price plays a significant role in the marketing mix. As you recall from Chapter 1, all four Ps of the marketing mix (product, price, place, and promotion) must be directed to the target market. What a person in the target market is willing to pay becomes a major question to be answered. Marketing efforts must price the product correctly to fit the target market's pocketbook. For example, the Rollerblade in-line skating company carries a wide range of in-line skates. The lower-priced skates are sold in Wal-Mart and Target stores for value-oriented customers. The higher-priced, more advanced skates are sold in specialty shops that cater to serious in-line skaters.

Pricing Considerations and Strategies

Consumer perception, demand, cost, product life-cycle stage, and competition affect price decisions. Each of these factors may influence businesses and the pricing strategies they use.

Consumer Perception

What is the relationship of price and quality in a consumer's mind? Many consumers believe that the higher the price, the better the quality of an item. Marketers will price goods and services high to attract customers who have that perception. Thus, the image of a product is closely related to its price. A very good quality product at a low price may not sell as well as it would at a higher price. **Prestige pricing** is pricing based on consumer perception. Very expensive sports watches, sports equipment, and apparel will be priced well above the average market price to attract consumers who may judge a product's quality by its price.

Another strategy related to consumer perceptions is odd-even pricing. **Odd-even pricing** is pricing goods with either an odd number or an even number to match a product's image. Odd-priced items, such as $25.99, suggest a bargain. Even-priced items reflect a quality item. Thus, more expensive goods are often priced with even numbers such as $100.

Target pricing is pricing goods according to what the customer is willing to pay. Manufacturers estimate the target price and then work backwards to determine how much to charge wholesalers and retailers for that item. They know that the wholesalers and retailers need to make a profit too. So, they figure the markup each will add onto the product to set a price. In some cases, product modifications are required to ensure the target price is achieved.

Demand

Demand is related to price in many ways. If a product is in high demand, and there is a limited supply, its price will be high. Popular sporting events (high demand) with a limited number of seats (supply) may be able to charge a high price for tickets to that event. Companies may even create this situation by producing a limited edition of an item so it can be priced high. For example, a limited edition of baseball cards for a popular player or special occasion may be priced higher than one that is produced in very large quantities.

Whenever there is a large supply of an item and demand is not great, dealers may lower prices to increase demand for that item.

Case Study — PART 2

FROM OLD TO GOLD

Continued from Part 1 on page 99

Big companies such as Nike and Reebok can manufacture large runs of vintage clothing at a lower cost than the smaller sporting goods company Mitchell & Ness. However, they cannot match the same attention to detail or use the old-fashioned methods of construction to recreate old uniforms accurately. In fact, the size of large manufacturers can work against them. Part of the appeal of a retro uniform is that it is unique. Consumers who wear vintage uniforms do so to recall favorite players. Also, retro styles are unique and make a statement about being individual. In 2002 and 2003, sales of vintage NBA uniforms have tripled, and with 47 NFL players, 30 MLB players, and 15 NHL players under contract for vintage uniforms, Mitchell & Ness's roster looks good for the future.

ANALYZE AND WRITE

1. How is Mitchell & Ness's small company size beneficial to business? Explain.
2. What might be some ways for Mitchell & Ness to expand its offerings?

prestige pricing pricing based on consumer perception

odd-even pricing pricing goods with either an odd number or even number to match a product's image

target pricing pricing goods according to what the customer is willing to pay

Math Check

COVERING EXPENSES
What is the dollar markup and markup percentage for a pair of baseball cleats that cost the business $24? The retail price of the cleats is $60.

➡ For tips on finding the solution, go to marketingseries.glencoe.com.

markup difference between the retail or wholesale price and the cost of an item

cost-plus pricing pricing products by calculating all costs and expenses and adding desired profit

Retailers may do this near the end of a season when there is still a supply of merchandise that has not sold at the regular price.

As a general rule, demand will be lower for a higher-priced item, such as an expensive racing bicycle or set of golf clubs, because fewer people can afford to buy it. If that same product were priced lower, more people would be able to purchase it and demand for it might increase. Supply-and-demand theory is based on *elastic demand,* which means that a change in price will affect demand.

However, there are four situations when the price will have no effect on demand. In those situations, demand is *inelastic.* Inelastic demand occurs when a product is a necessity; there are no substitutes; the price increase is not significant relative to the customer's income; or there are time restraints. For example, let's say you are at a sporting event, and you need to buy orange juice immediately due to a health condition such as diabetes. You would pay any price for that orange juice because it is an immediate necessity.

Many Nike sports products are high priced, but demand remains high for them. Why? One reason is because consumers believe that there is no substitute for that Nike product. These brand-loyal customers will pay the higher price.

Cost

Since a business needs to make a profit, the price of an item must be higher than the cost a business paid for it. Two pricing strategies related to cost are markup and cost-plus pricing. Markup pricing is used by wholesalers and retailers who buy goods for resale. **Markup** is the difference between the retail or wholesale price and the cost of an item. The markup must be high enough to cover expenses and ensure a profit.

Let's say a sports retailer purchases a pair of athletic shoes for $25 (cost). To cover expenses and ensure a profit, the retailer sells those shoes for $49.99 per pair. In this case, the dollar markup is $24.99 ($49.99 retail price – $25 cost = $24.99 markup). Markup may also be reported as a percentage. The markup percentage may be based on the retail price. Using the above example, the markup on retail would be 50 percent ($24.99 markup divided by $49.99 retail price). Markup can also be calculated based on the cost of the item. In that case, the markup based on cost would be 100 percent ($24.99 markup divided by $25 cost).

Retailers will often use a product-line pricing strategy when marking up the entire line of products. *Product-line pricing* involves setting different markup percentages for each product so that the average markup is achieved for the entire line of goods. In this case, the markup on one model of in-line skates may only be 20 percent, but for another model it may be 75 percent. When you average all the markups for all models, the total may be 50 percent.

Manufacturers and service providers generally use **cost-plus pricing**, which is pricing products by calculating all costs and expenses and adding desired profit. In this case, the cost of making the item or providing the service is determined first. Then the amount of money to ensure a profit is tacked onto that amount to arrive at a price

MUST-HAVES Sportswear items such as tennis shoes and sweatshirts were once relatively low-priced and affordable—that is, until sports fashions became cool designer merchandise. *Do you think high-priced sportswear will continue to be popular? Why?*

charged to customers. For example, food-service providers at sporting events determine the salaries of their employees, the cost of food supplies, and rent. Then they add their intended profit to set the prices to charge for food service.

Newness of the Product

As previously discussed, when introducing a new product, marketers may decide to price the item very high to recover the costs of development—or they may price it low to create immediate demand for the product. As previously mentioned, pricing a new item high is called skimming pricing. Pricing below the competition is called penetration pricing.

Competition

Businesses find out what their competitors are charging for the same items they are selling. If they want to compete on price, they lower their prices to draw customers away from their competitors. If they do not want to compete on price, they use **non-price competition**, which is competition between businesses based on quality, service, and relationships. If a product is better quality than the competition's product, a business can charge a higher price. If a business offers special services, it can charge a higher price. If a business has developed a relationship with its customers, it may be able to price items higher because of customer loyalty.

non-price competition competition between businesses based on quality, service, and relationships

Pricing Objectives and Strategies

Pricing objectives are the goals that a company wants to achieve through pricing. In addition to the considerations and factors already discussed, businesses often have additional goals that may change the pricing of its goods. Two common pricing objectives involve increasing profit and improving market share.

Profit Objective

A company may have an objective to earn a higher profit. Sometimes costs and expenses increase, but the company knows that it cannot

Aquatic Therapy

Have you ever heard of aquatic sports therapy? While recovering from a foot injury, Lynda Huey learned quite a bit about it. She discovered that training in water helps build up strength and flexibility in the injured area without causing strain. She took this knowledge, combined it with her experience as an athlete and a coach, and started a business helping elite athletes recover from injuries. Her clients have included track stars Jackie Joyner-Kersee, Inger Miller, and Carl Lewis.

CREATING HER OWN NICHE

After working with world-class athletes, Lynda Huey found that nonathletes could also benefit from her therapeutic techniques. She teamed with Tanya Moran, M.S., P.T., to develop physical-therapy plans that could work for anyone. She then applied her experience and knowledge and wrote a book called *The Complete Waterpower Workout Book* and started a company called Complete PT. There,

physical therapists guide patients through a recovery regimen that includes both aquatic and land-based physical therapy.

Huey then built her business even further. Services now include training actors for underwater stunts, consulting on therapy-pool designs, and selling water-workout equipment. Her Web site features articles that she's written, while also advertising her books and workout videos. Currently she's promoting her books, co-written with Robert Klapper, M.D.: *Heal Your Hips: How to Prevent Hip Surgery—And What to Do If You Need It* and *Heal Your Knees*. Through these books, Huey has expanded her business beyond a handful of athletes to address more global health concerns. As Huey finds new ways to market aquatic therapy, she also finds new audiences who can benefit as clients.

1. How has Lynda Huey capitalized on her knowledge of aquatic therapy?
2. What kind of business that sells goods and services could you build around what you know?

CONNECT
Have you ever bought a new product at a high price and later saw it priced much lower?

market share the percentage of the total sales of all companies that sell the same type of product

price lining selling all goods in a product line at specific price points

charge more for its product. In that case, a business may add a surcharge. For example, a football team may keep its set prices but add a user fee to the ticket price. A business may reduce some of the unneeded features or size of a product to keep the price in line with the competition's price.

Market Share Objective

A company may have another objective to gain a higher market share. **Market share** is the percentage of the total sales of all companies that sell the same type of product. A product such as Gatorade may have an 80 percent market share, which means that its sales represent 80 percent of all sports drinks sold by all sports-drink companies. The other sports drinks represent the remaining 20 percent of the sports-drink market. If a company wants to increase its market share, it may lower the price of its product to do so.

Special Pricing Strategies

A few special pricing strategies include price lining, bundle pricing, loss-leader pricing, and yield-management pricing. (See **Figure 5.2**.)

Price lining is selling all goods in a product line at specific price points. For example, a business may decide to sell its warm-up suits at

Figure 5.2

Pricing Strategies

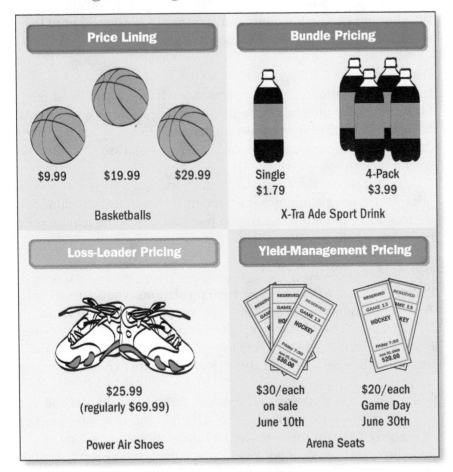

Price Lining

$9.99 $19.99 $29.99

Basketballs

Bundle Pricing

Single
$1.79

4-Pack
$3.99

X-Tra Ade Sport Drink

Loss-Leader Pricing

$25.99
(regularly $69.99)

Power Air Shoes

Yield-Management Pricing

$30/each
on sale
June 10th

$20/each
Game Day
June 30th

Arena Seats

THE PRICE IS RIGHT
Businesses know that consumers will pay different prices for items in different circumstances. *Why does bundle pricing make sense?*

three price points: $39.99, $59.99, and $79.99. This type of pricing strategy makes it easier for customers to make purchasing decisions. Businesses also benefit because it is easier to take later markdowns. Inventory control is simplified as well.

Bundle pricing is selling several items as a package for a set price. In this case, the products purchased individually would cost more than the package price. Customers benefit because of the lower price. Businesses benefit because sales are generally higher and more product is sold.

Loss-leader pricing is pricing an item at cost or below cost to draw customers into the store. Then they will buy other products while at the store. Their total purchases for the shopping visit will more than cover the money lost on the loss leader.

Yield-management pricing is pricing items at different prices to maximize revenue when limited capacity is involved. For example, seats in a sports arena or stadium are limited by seating capacity. A business may price its seats differently to maximize revenue. Some seats are priced higher than others due to their location or the time they are purchased. Some teams, such as the New York Mets, use *tiered pricing,* charging more for tickets to home games against more competitive opponents that might draw more attendance.

bundle pricing selling several items as a package for a set price

loss-leader pricing pricing an item at cost or below cost to draw customers into the store

yield-management pricing pricing items at different prices to maximize revenue when limited capacity is involved

QUESTION

What are some items sold by yield-management pricing?

price fixing an illegal practice whereby competitors conspire to set the same prices

Price Adjustments and Regulations

To maintain the integrity of a published price, marketers will often make price adjustments by offering discounts or allowances. When offering these discounts and allowances, businesses need to be sure they are not breaking any pricing regulations.

Discounts and Allowances

Discounts and allowances may be used to change a published price. Manufacturers will offer discounts for buying in large quantities or buying prior to the buying season. They also offer functional or trade discounts to wholesalers and retailers, as well as cash discounts for paying their invoices early.

Like discounts, allowances are reductions taken from the quoted price. One type of allowance is a trade-in. If a business will allow you to trade in an old model when you purchase a new model, the price reduction would be called a trade-in allowance.

Regulatory Factors

Pricing is subject to some government regulations. The Sherman Anti-Trust Act prohibits price fixing and predatory pricing. **Price fixing** is an illegal practice whereby competitors conspire to set the same prices. *Predatory pricing* is setting a very low price in order to drive competitors out of business. Both of these practices restrict competition and are illegal.

Price discrimination was originally prohibited by the Clayton Act and later by the Robinson-Patman Act. *Price discrimination* is the practice of charging different prices to similar buyers. However, as long as the price discrimination does not lessen competition, it is generally considered legal. If products are priced right, and the other Ps of the marketing mix are effective, marketing efforts will be successful.

Quick Check ✓

RESPOND to what you've read by answering these questions.

1. How is pricing related to profit and the marketing mix? _____
   _____
   _____

2. List five factors that affect price decisions. _____
   _____
   _____

3. What are two common pricing objectives and special pricing strategies? _____
   _____
   _____

Worksheet 5.1

Steps in New Product Development

Usually there are seven steps in developing a new product. Although not all steps are followed each time, you need to be familiar with each of the steps. Match the name of each step to its description. Write the correct letter on the line beside the information terms.

STEPS:

A. screening and evaluation

B. commercialization

C. business analysis

D. SWOT analysis

E. test marketing

F. development

G. idea generation

_____ **1.** producing and marketing

_____ **2.** focus group sessions

_____ **3.** looking at a company's strengths, weaknesses, and external threats and opportunities

_____ **4.** making the product

_____ **5.** financial and legal factors reviewed

_____ **6.** protocol written

_____ **7.** trying the product in the marketplace

Name _____ Date _____

Worksheet 5.2

Comparing Prices

Visit two sporting-goods stores or discount stores with sporting-goods departments. Record the brand name and the price of the sports equipment listed below for each store.

Item	Brand	Store #1 Price	Store #2 Price
1. basketball			
2. baseball glove			
3. tennis racket			
4. tennis balls			
5. football			
6. soccer ball			
7. ice skates			
8. rollerblades			
9. volleyball			
10. hockey stick			
11. swimming goggles			
12. baseball bat			
13. exercise mat			
14. fishing rod			
15. golf balls			

What pricing strategies do you think each store is using?

_____

_____

_____

_____

_____

Portfolio Works

EXPLORING SPORTS PRODUCTS

Consider all of the sports products you use (remember that a product can be a good, service, or idea). Do the following exercises and write them down on the lines provided below. Then add this page to your career portfolio.

1. Brainstorm a list of your favorite sports products and write them down on the lines provided below.

_____

_____

_____

_____

_____

2. Choose three products from your list to research on the Internet. Write the product name and the Web-site address you used for your research.

_____

_____

_____

_____

_____

3. What did you learn about each product?

_____

_____

_____

_____

_____

4. Would you like a career associated with any of the products you researched? Why?

_____

_____

_____

_____

_____

CHAPTER SUMMARY

Section 5.1 Product Design

product item (p. 100)
consumer goods (p. 100)
business goods (p. 101)
point of difference
    (p. 101)
focus group (p. 102)
commercialization
    (p. 102)
repositioning (p. 107)

- Product items are specific models or sizes of a product, whereas product lines are groups of closely related products sold by a company.

- Products can be classified as both goods or services and as consumer goods or business goods, depending on their use.

- The seven steps of new product development are SWOT analysis, idea generation, screening and evaluation, business analysis, development, test marketing, and commercialization.

- A product goes through four stages in its life cycle: introduction, growth, maturity, and decline.

Section 5.2 Pricing and Strategies

price (p. 108)
prestige pricing (p. 109)
odd-even pricing (p. 109)
target pricing (p. 109)
markup (p. 110)
cost-plus pricing (p. 110)
non-price competition
    (p. 111)
market share (p. 112)
price lining (p. 112)
bundle pricing (p. 113)
loss-leader pricing (p. 113)
yield-management
    pricing (p. 113)
price fixing (p. 114)

- Price is the value placed on the goods or services being exchanged. Price helps determine a company's profit or loss, and it is part of the marketing mix.

- Consumer perception, demand, cost, product life-cycle stage, and competition affect pricing decisions.

- To reach pricing objectives to make a profit and improve market share, retailers use various pricing strategies: price lining, bundle pricing, loss-leader pricing, and yield-management pricing.

CHECKING CONCEPTS

1. **Explain** the difference between product item and product line.
2. **Name** the ways products can be defined and classified.
3. **Explain** the seven steps used in developing a new product.
4. **Identify** the four stages in a product's life cycle.
5. **Define** price.
6. **Explain** how price determines a company's profit.
7. **Identify** the factors that may influence pricing strategies.

Critical Thinking
8. **Define and compare** markup and cost-plus pricing.

CROSS-CURRICULUM SKILLS

Work-Based Learning

Basic Skills—Math

9. Calculate the quarterly profit if 10,000 soccer balls sold for $9 each. The balls cost the store $5 each. The expense of running the store was $25,000 during the quarter.

Thinking Skills—Reasoning

10. Your line of "Cool Wear" athletic T-shirts has reached the maturity stage. List three ways you can avoid the decline stage.

School-Based Learning

Language Arts

11. Read newspaper ads for two businesses that sell sporting goods. Write down the prices of products they sell that are similar.

Science

12. Research and list three areas of science that a sporting goods manufacturer might use to develop better sports equipment.

 CONNECTION

 INTERNET ACTIVITY

Role Play: Marketing Consultant

SITUATION You are to assume the role of a marketing consultant hired by the Athletic Booster Club of Main Valley High, a brand-new high school. The president (judge) wants you to create a pricing plan for its line of Spiritwear to be sold at events. All shirts come in a variety of colors and are sized S, M, L, and XL in adult and youth sizes. Short-sleeved T-shirts cost the club $5; long-sleeved T-shirts cost $10; and sweatshirts cost $15.

ACTIVITY Design a price plan for the line and present it to the president (judge).

EVALUATION You will be evaluated on how well you meet the following performance indicators:

- Explain factors affecting pricing decisions.
- Identify strategies for pricing new products (for imitative new products and for innovative new products).
- Select approach for setting a base price.
- Set prices.
- Adjust prices to maximize profitability.

Use the Internet to access the Gatorade Sports Science Institute (GSSI) and answer the following questions:
- For what sports team is Gatorade named?
- When did scientists begin testing Gatorade and why?

➡ For a link to the GSSI to answer these questions, go to **marketingseries.glencoe.com.**

Sports Market Research and Outlets

Chapter Objectives

- Define market research.
- Explain how businesses use market research.
- Identify the steps used in the research process.
- Explain how businesses make the place decision as part of the marketing mix.
- Discuss direct and indirect channels of distribution.

A PLACE FOR ATHLETES

After sports marketers research their customers, they make decisions about where to distribute or place their products. A football, baseball, or basketball player is considered a sports product, and agents such as Bill Duffy help athletes find their place in sports.

It's not surprising that Bill Duffy is involved in the National Basketball Association (NBA). In college, he shared a room with former Boston Celtic great Kevin McHale, and he was drafted by the Denver Nuggets in 1982. However, his ultimate calling was not to play on the court, but to be a sports agent. His agency, Bill Duffy and Associates Sports Management (BDA), helps young players get drafted higher and earn top dollar.

As the NBA has grown, so have BDA's duties. Teams now draft players after one, two, or no years of college. Such young players often need guidance off the court as well as on the court. Also, more players are coming from around the world. How can a sports agent adjust to these changes?

ANALYZE AND WRITE

1. How might an agent "distribute" an athlete's image?
2. How would an agency's duties change as the NBA changes?

Case Study Part 2 on page 133

POWER READ

Be an active reader and use these reading strategies:

PREDICT what the section will be about.

CONNECT what you read with your life.

QUESTION as you read to make sure you understand the content.

RESPOND to what you've read.

The Research Process

AS YOU READ ...

YOU WILL LEARN

- To define market research.
- To explain how businesses use market research.
- To identify the steps used in the research process.

WHY IT'S IMPORTANT

Market research provides data so that good decisions can be made for both businesses and consumers.

KEY TERMS

- market research
- secondary research
- primary research
- observation method
- census
- sample

market research the process of systematically collecting, recording, analyzing, and presenting data related to marketing goods and services

PREDICT

Why would population information be useful to sports marketers?

Research and the Marketing Concept

For a business to be successful, it must know its customers. The goal of the marketing concept, as explained in Chapter 1, is to satisfy customers' needs and wants. How do you know what your customers need and want? You do research.

Small, medium-sized, and large companies all do research. Small-business owners who have direct access to their customers get to know their likes and dislikes by reviewing sales data and by talking to their customers. For example, a sporting-goods store owner may approach you after a purchase to ask you how you like something you recently bought at the store. That is research. **Market research** is the process of systematically collecting, recording, analyzing, and presenting data related to marketing goods and services. Product development, pricing, promotional activities, distribution, and customer satisfaction are areas where information generated by market research can be beneficial.

Business owners may not be able to personally ask each and every customer about their level of satisfaction. Larger companies that try to monitor the degree of customer satisfaction with products or services may do so through more formal measures, such as surveys and focus groups. Marketers may conduct surveys to ensure customer satisfaction. They may conduct focus groups to see how consumers feel about a product or advertising campaign. For example, a minor league baseball team might distribute questionnaires to determine what it needs to do to maintain fan loyalty. Fans can be questioned about their likes and dislikes. The results of such a survey would allow the minor league baseball team to decide how to spend its limited yearly budget.

Steps in the Research Process

There are five steps that market researchers take to conduct formal market research studies:

1. Identify the problem.

2. Conduct secondary research.

3. Select and design primary research.

4. Collect data.

5. Report and analyze data.

World Market

Global Relaxation

In a world that is increasingly tense, many people seek relaxation by taking classes in the Asian art of Tai Chi. One of the largest schools for this ancient art is The Academy of Tai Chi in Australia. The academy explains that *Chi* is the energy that brings the universe to life. It comes from food, water, and air. The flow of Chi (or life energy) through the body is necessary for good physical and mental health, and can be generated through practicing Tai Chi.

Sometimes called "meditation in motion," it is exercise without the jumping, aerobics, running, or weights. In Tai Chi, the feet are always grounded to the Earth, while the body makes graceful, deliberate movements in sequence. Popular in Australia since the 1970s, Tai Chi is practiced all over the world—in community centers, beaches, city parks, or any place that offers good lighting and flat ground. Deceptively easy-looking, Tai Chi can take some people a lifetime to master.

Demographic research tells us that more women than men practice the art of Tai Chi. What might be the reason(s) for this difference?

AUSTRALIA

Identify the Problem

The first step is to identify the problem. Identifying the problem requires asking a question that research can help answer. For example, imagine a golf ball manufacturer. One question the manufacturer might ask would be: "What can we do to improve the image of our golf ball to stand out from all the rest on the market?" The objectives might be to determine how golfers select their golf balls, or to find out the current image of that particular brand among that product's target market.

Conduct Secondary Research

Secondary research is published data that have been collected for some other purpose. *Data* are recorded facts and figures that are organized and analyzed in some way. Secondary research can include internal data from a company, such as sales reports and reports on merchandise returns and complaints. Secondary data may also come from external sources, such as books, magazine articles, the Internet, or from companies that specialize in market research.

Some research companies sell research reports by product category. For example, American Sports Data, Inc., sells sports-related research data to interested companies. A.C. Nielsen provides research on television viewing habits throughout the nation. Networks monitor these reports when they broadcast different kinds of sports events. Entertainment and media companies use the data from the Nielsen ratings to determine what kinds of programs people are watching and what kinds of rates they can charge for advertisements during these programs.

secondary research published data that have been collected for some other purpose

Game Point !

> DRIVING RANGE
In 1999, golfer Tiger Woods participated in his first automobile endorsement. In hopes of gaining a new market of Tiger's youthful peers, while keeping its older customer base, Buick signed Tiger to a five-year deal.

ETHICAL PRACTICES

Beyond Nations and Races

True sportsmanship sees beyond color and race. During the 1936 Olympics in Berlin, Germany, Jesse Owens (an African-American athlete) was competing in the long jump against Germany's Luz Long. During his qualifying jumps, Owens faulted. One more fault, and he would have been disqualified. Wanting to compete against the best, Luz Long gave Owens some pointers. His advice helped Jesse Owens win the gold medal. After the competition, Long took winner Owens by the arm, and together, they paraded around the stadium before Hitler and thousands of stunned spectators.

primary research original research conducted for a specific marketing situation

CONNECT

If you wrote a school report on the history of golf balls, would you use more secondary or primary research?

The United States government conducts many different kinds of research. The best known research is the U.S. Census, which is a survey of the entire population that takes place every ten years. Its findings help businesses address the ever-changing demographic environment. The U.S. Census provides information about the population in terms of age, race, income, household, educational attainment, residence, and other demographic factors. You can access this public information free by visiting the U.S. Census Web site at **www.census.gov**.

SECONDARY BEFORE PRIMARY Secondary research is conducted before primary research because secondary data may actually answer all or part of a research problem or question. The United States Golf Association may issue a press release regarding its policy on golf ball design, which may include information about which types of balls are legal and which ones are not. Such a report would be helpful secondary research as background information for the study. In addition, a golf magazine may have conducted research about golf balls and published that report in its magazine. That article would be considered secondary data. However, the article may not include everything to know regarding the objectives of a study. It may provide background information about the different types and brands of golf balls—but not about how golf balls are selected or the image of any particular brand. For that information, you need to conduct primary research.

Select and Design Primary Research

Primary research is original research conducted for a specific marketing situation. In the case of the golf ball manufacturer, primary research is needed because the secondary research is not sufficient to answer the research question.

The type of research for primary research depends on the objectives and subjects of the study. The subjects are those members of the population who are being studied. In the case of the golf ball manufacturer, only golfers would be part of the study's population. The types of golfers could be further separated into private country club golfers and public golf course golfers. Other subgroups might be men, women, and children golfers. The more specific the characteristics of the population, the easier it is to select the primary research method.

There are three types of research methods:

- Experiment
- Observation
- Survey

EXPERIMENT An experimental design for research has two parts, or *variables*. You need to have an independent variable and a dependent variable. The independent variable is the variable that is being manipulated, or changed. The dependent variable is the one that is affected by the change made by the independent variable. For example, changing the ticket price to a minor league baseball game (independent variable) to see if ticket sales increase (dependent variable) would be an example of an experimental design. Having a machine hit different brands or types of golf balls (independent variable) to see how far each one flies (dependent variable) is also an experiment. Experiments let you draw conclusions from the interaction of the variables.

OBSERVATION The **observation method** is a research technique that involves watching actual behavior and recording it. Some methods of recording, or taking down information about, behavior include text or writing, audio, and video.

observation method research technique that involves watching actual behavior and recording it

The observation method allows freedom for interpretation. For example, if you want to learn which types of sports video games appeal to younger children, you might use the observation method. In this case, you might bring children to a facility with a two-way mirror and provide them with several choices of video games. You would then watch them to see which games they selected, which ones they played the longest, and which ones they seemed to enjoy the best. You might also take down their comments and note their body language.

For research for the golf ball manufacturer, an observer may watch customers in a specialty golf store to see what they do when they purchase golf balls. The observer could mark down answers to the following questions: How long do they take when deciding on their golf ball purchase? Are golf balls purchased along with other purchases, or are the golf balls a customer's only purchase? Do customers study any displayed literature on golf balls? The answers to these questions are provided by observing. Because the information is recorded, researchers can reexamine the observations later to help answer the research question.

QUESTION
Why is observation a good form of research?

SURVEY The survey method involves asking questions of participants in a study. The survey could be basic or it could be specific to a particular product or service. The questions could be for a focus group or panel or part of a written or verbal questionnaire.

Focus Groups A focus group or panel involves six to ten participants who are brought together to discuss their feelings, reactions, and attitudes regarding a product, promotion, or some other topic. A moderator asks questions and seeks responses from the participants. The interaction among focus group participants is often videotaped for later analysis by the research specialists. Focus groups are considered to be qualitative research: The data collected are subjective, so no statistical analysis can be made. However, important information can be discovered as the researcher interprets the data based on the responses gathered from the participants.

In the golf ball manufacturer example, focus groups could be used to discover how golfers feel about the golf balls they use. Are they important? If so, what features make them important? How do the customers feel about particular brands? What images do those brands hold in their minds? Are customers looking at price or at the newest technology as their main purchase criteria? Some of the information gathered in focus group sessions becomes the basis for a questionnaire that will be given to larger numbers of people at a later time.

MARKETING SERIES *Online*

Remember to check out this book's Web site for market-research information and more great resources at **marketingseries.glencoe.com**.

Hot Property

Keeping It Real

Darrell Survey

If you paid a top golfer hundreds of dollars every time she used your golf club, you'd want to be sure she was really using it. Right? That's where the Darrell Survey Company comes in. During the opening rounds of professional tour events, including each stop on the PGA and LPGA circuits, employees from the Darrell Survey check golfers' bags and identify and record what equipment they are using.

The Darrell Survey Company began in 1932 when Eddie and Virginia Darrell started the business of "spying" on golfers' equipment. Back then some players would switch gear, such as balls and clubs, on the sly. Eddie Darrell made this scam much more difficult. By checking each player's gear, he ensured that golf pros stayed honest and did not use another company's equipment. The service also enabled companies to track the popularity of its products.

THE GOLF AUTHORITY

Today Susan Naylor and her brother John Minkley carry on Darrell's legacy. Naylor bought the company from Darrell's widow in 1980 and runs the business in much the same way that Darrell did years ago. Company employees still travel to tour stops and personally check each golfer's equipment. They carefully record the information, and then they release the results to manufacturers who pay for the inside story. In addition, the Darrell Survey publishes an annual almanac, which summarizes its findings for the year.

Manufacturers use these data to advertise their products and to track trends. Players use the information as a guide. With research from the Darrell Survey, companies can make claims such as, "Ours is the most popular golf ball on the PGA Tour." These claims make a powerful impact on sales, as golfers at all levels try to find the winning equipment to be champions.

1. How does the Darrell Survey Company help golf-equipment manufacturers?
2. Why does a Darrell Survey verification make advertisements more trustworthy?

Questionnaires Questionnaires, such as the sample in **Figure 6.1**, are written surveys that can be administered in person, by telephone, fax, mail, or online. Since questionnaires are written documents, these data can be easily quantified, or measured, counted, sorted, and put into different categories. Quantitative research allows for statistical analysis, which includes things such as correlations—or connections or similarities between different kinds of data—and numerical percentages of responses to the total number of people responding. In the golf ball example, a telephone survey could be used to ask specific questions based on golf ball purchases (e.g., price, brands, location of retailer, and type). Other questions can relate to demographic information about the person who is responding: age, gender, golfing ability, and golf club affiliation, if any. Market researchers can correlate, or interrelate, the information about purchases with the demographic information when reporting and analyzing the data.

Collect Data

The method of collecting data depends on the survey tool and the characteristics and needs of the population being surveyed. For example, if you were doing research for a minor league baseball team, you might ask every tenth person who entered the stadium to

Figure 6.1

TV Sports Survey Questionnaire

1. Why do you watch television (TV) sports?
- ☐ to relax
- ☐ for entertainment
- ☐ I do not watch TV sports
- ☐ other (explain) _____

2. Approximately how many hours do you spend watching TV sports during the week?
- ☐ 1 or less
- ☐ 2–4 hrs
- ☐ 5 or more hours

3. Approximately how many hours do you spend watching TV sports on the weekend?
- ☐ 1 or less
- ☐ 2–4 hrs
- ☐ 5 or more hours

4. How many television sets do you have in your household?
- ☐ 0
- ☐ 1–2
- ☐ 3 or more

5. Approximately how many live sports events do you attend during the week?
- ☐ 0–1
- ☐ 2–3
- ☐ 4 or more

6. Approximately how many live sports events to you attend during the weekend?
- ☐ 0–1
- ☐ 2–3
- ☐ 4 or more

7. Which of these television sports do you watch? Check all that apply.
- ☐ basketball
- ☐ football
- ☐ hockey
- ☐ tennis
- ☐ curling
- ☐ swimming
- ☐ other _____

8. Would you be interested in a cable channel that showed classic sports events?
- ☐ yes
- ☐ no
- ☐ maybe

GET TO KNOW YOUR MARKET
Questionnaires can determine the habits of consumers in a specific market. *What might be a common characteristic of the group of people to whom this survey is given?*

ON-SITE DATA COLLECTION
Mall intercepts and in-store surveys take advantage of avid shoppers who have the time to browse and shop.
What might be some disadvantages of the data obtained from a mall intercept for an advertising campaign?

Math Check

MEASURING TEAM SPIRIT
Nicolas is doing a survey on how often his classmates attend school sporting events. Sixteen people attend two per month; 12 people attend one per month; and two people attend three per month. What is the average number of events attended by his classmates per month?

➡For tips on finding the solution, go to marketingseries.glencoe.com.

census a study that counts everyone in the research population

sample a number of people who are representative of a study's population

complete a customer satisfaction survey. If you wanted everyday and immediate responses to a new product or new advertising campaign, you might conduct a mall intercept. In a mall intercept, researchers approach shoppers in a mall and ask if they would like to participate in a research study. Those who agree are shown the products or ads and are asked questions about their opinions.

Many participants in various surveys do not expect to go out of their way to complete the surveys. Telephone surveys are more successful if they are brief. Mail and fax surveys require a cover letter and a way of returning the questionnaires, such as a prepaid envelope. Many survey participants are compensated, or given a gift, coupon, or something of value for their participation in the study.

Advantages and Disadvantages Each of the research methods has advantages and disadvantages related to time, cost, and accuracy of data collected. Mail and fax questionnaires have the added problem of return rate. Not everyone returns questionnaires on time or at all. Online surveys are also conducted by companies on their own Web sites or, at other times, by online research companies. Care must be taken with online surveys to avoid duplication of responses by one participant. If one participant completes the same survey 20 times, the results of the survey will be inaccurate.

CENSUS The population or subjects of a study have to be determined early in research planning. If that population that is being surveyed is a small group, then a census can be taken. A **census** is a study that counts everyone in the research population. For example, a small pro shop that is affiliated with a private golf club might conduct a census among all 50 active women golfers to determine which tournaments they would like scheduled in the coming season. However, the golf ball manufacturer does not have the same ability to access all golfers who buy golf balls. Therefore, a census is not possible in the case of the manufacturer.

SAMPLE In those instances when a census is not possible, a sample is used to collect data. A **sample** is a number of people who are representative of a study's population. In the case of the golf ball manufacturer, data from the focus group sessions might indicate that private club golfers and public golfers differ in their attitudes about the game and the golf balls they use. In that case, the sample would have to reflect both types of golfers. To contact a select group, the golf ball manufacturer may have to purchase names and telephone numbers from a research company that sells such specialized lists. The size of the sample would need to be large enough to represent the population under study.

In addition to determining sample size, you must decide how to locate and select those people who are part of your study's population. If you have a complete list of all members of the population, you can randomly select their names from a pool, or use a computer program. If you use a random-selection process, the results represent the entire population. If a complete list of members of the population is unavailable, you must use a non-random sample, such as the mall intercept group. You can make sure they are qualified for the study by asking specific questions. Some qualifying questions for the golf survey might be:

1. Do you golf?

2. If yes, how often do you golf during the golf season?

3. Do you belong to a private golf course?

4. Are you between the ages of 21 to 59?

By asking qualifying questions, you can help to ensure that the sample is actually representative of the population you hope to study.

DATA MINING Data mining is a process of collecting data from one or more existing databases and looking for relationships among the data. Computers and people use special data-mining software to analyze, find, and predict patterns and connections that might remain hidden from traditional statistical analysis. Data mining is used to find out and predict information such as:

- Market segmentation

- Customer or client profiling

- Fraud detection

- Success or failure of promotions

- Credit risk or acceptability

For example, a sporting-goods catalog company might learn from data mining that younger men buy more clothing at the beginning of the season at full price, but older men wait for specials or competing sales. This information might come from recorded transactions combined with survey information. A catalog company could design specialized catalogs with different product codes for each age group and send them out at different times of the year. These codes from the catalog are recorded electronically and used in data mining.

Report and Analyze Data

You have learned about different ways that data can be recorded and collected. For this data to be useful, it needs to be reported and analyzed. It is important to be very specific and clear in report language.

Virtual Focus Groups

Traditionally, a focus group is a face-to-face discussion session led by a moderator. Information collected during the discussion is used by market researchers to better understand a problem. Now market researchers are also conducting these discussions in Internet chat rooms. Members of these virtual focus groups never meet in person, and they can be recruited through other online venues, such as bulletin boards and e-mail surveys.

➡ Learn about and discuss the effect one virtual focus group had on a sports drink by reading the article through **marketingseries.glencoe.com**.

REPORTING QUALITATIVE-RESEARCH DATA Qualitative, or subjective, research data are reported in paragraph format. No conclusions can be drawn from qualitative data, only inferences—that is, an interpretation drawn from the facts. That is not to say that qualitative data are not useful to marketers. This data provides insight into a problem, which researchers must be able to detect if they hope to find answers to the research question.

REPORTING QUANTITATIVE-RESEARCH DATA Quantitative, or objective, data can be reported in graphs and charts, with analysis, or interpretation, written in accompanying paragraphs of text. It is a good idea to link the report information to the objectives of the study when writing the formal report. For example, a company wants to know how many people buy golf balls in the winter to determine if production of golf balls should continue in December. It is easy to make correlations with quantitative data. However, you cannot conclude anything because surveys involve the subjective reactions of people.

Unlike numbers, people are not consistent from day to day. Thus, you can suggest or infer something, but you cannot conclude anything about any given data. For example, let's say the survey indicated that most private-club golfers purchased their golf balls at their pro shops. Using this information, you could not conclude that all private golf club members only buy their golf balls at their pro shops. Why? Because the golf club manufacturer did not survey all golfers in all private golf clubs. Your interpretation might be: "It appears that most private golf club members buy their golf balls at their respective golf clubs."

Research and Interpretation
Both market research and the interpretation that follows can reveal expected and unexpected results. All the data, observations, and analyses that are recorded and reported can be used to help make decisions about how to satisfy the needs and wants of customers.

Quick Check

RESPOND to what you've read by answering these questions.

1. Name the five steps in the research process. _____

_____

_____

2. What is the difference between secondary and primary research? _____

_____

_____

3. What are the three types of primary research methods? _____

_____

_____

Outlets—the Place Decision

Place Decision

One of the Four Ps of the marketing mix is place, as discussed in Chapter 1. Place decisions involve how you get your product into the hands of your customer. As you recall, all four marketing-mix decisions must focus on the target market. So the first consideration regarding a decision about a product's distribution is to determine the type of customer you have.

There are two basic types of customers depending on the intended use of the product. There are business customers and ultimate consumers. Business customers or organizational buyers purchase products for use in the operation of a business. Ultimate consumers, or customers, buy products for their own personal use. The same product, such as a treadmill, may be sold to gyms or to hotels for use in gyms and sold to ultimate consumers for home use. Reaching each type of customer requires a different channel of distribution because their needs and shopping habits are completely different. Thus, how and where customers shop are important factors in deciding on a channel of distribution.

Channels of Distribution

A channel of distribution is the path a product takes from the producer or manufacturer to the consumer. The channel of distribution may be direct or indirect, as illustrated in **Figure 6.2** on page 132. Let's look at examples and reasons why companies use direct, indirect, as well as multiple channels of distribution.

Direct Channels

A **direct channel** of distribution is the path a product takes without the help of any intermediaries between the producer and consumer. Certain products require direct contact with customers for a sale to take place. For example, business products that have a high unit value are marketed directly from the producer to the business user. The company SRI Sports sells its Astroturf brand synthetic turf directly to colleges and professional sports teams for their playing fields. Reebok has its own Web site where customers can buy its products directly from the factory.

DISTRIBUTING SERVICES Services are distributed directly to customers. An independent personal trainer works directly with his or her clients. One popular service offered to Web surfers is fantasy sports leagues. Personal services such as fantasy sports games require direct

AS YOU READ . . .

YOU WILL LEARN

- To explain how businesses make the place decision as part of the marketing mix.
- To discuss direct and indirect channels of distribution.

WHY IT'S IMPORTANT

The right decisions need to be made about the distribution of a company's products to customers. If customers do not have access to products, they cannot buy them.

KEY TERMS

- direct channel
- direct marketing
- indirect channel

direct channel the path a product takes without the help of any intermediaries between the producer and consumer

PREDICT

Why are services considered an example of direct marketing?

How do you usually purchase tickets to sports events?

contact with the customer and a direct channel of distribution. Players may log onto sports sites at ESPN.com, CBS SportsLine, and Yahoo! Sports to pick players and coaches from existing teams to play fantasy football and other sports.

All sporting events are considered to be services. Tickets can be sold directly to patrons through a team's box office. The means to achieve direct distribution are varied. Companies may use their own sales force or partner with independent Web sites. For example, fans can go to the Yankee Stadium box office to buy tickets to an upcoming New York Yankees game.

direct marketing marketing activities to sell products directly to customers through the use of a customer database

DIRECT MARKETING Direct marketing involves marketing activities to sell products directly to customers through the use of a customer database. A company can use its existing customer database, or a list of current and potential customers, to solicit business over the telephone, by fax, by mail, or by e-mail.

Telephone Sales Telephone sales are selling activities in which a live person or a recording calls a number in the database to inform the potential customer about a product or service. Many companies and businesses use telemarketing efforts to get the word out about new product offerings. Telemarketing can produce immediate sales. However, there are restrictions regarding the times of day when telemarketers can call. In addition, there is legislation to curtail telemarketing efforts called the "National Do Not Call Registry." Anyone who

Figure 6.2

Distribution Channels

THE RIGHT PATH Adding distribution channels may cost a business more money. *Why would a business give up or add a distribution channel?*

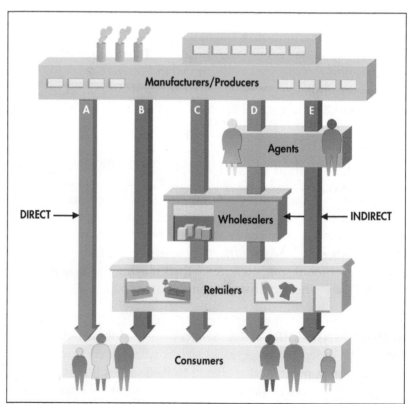

does not want to receive telemarketing calls may register his or her phone number with the government for free.

Print Using print media is a popular and time-honored way to apply direct-marketing techniques. Print media can also be combined with other media for more marketing exposure. Catalog companies are becoming so sophisticated that they can publish specialized versions of their catalogs based on customers' buying habits. Advertising in magazines and on television can generate direct sales through the use of an 800 number.

Television Television can also be used to make a marketing impact. Fitness-equipment companies in particular have made use of television infomercials to sell weight or exercise machines directly to the public. Infomercials are 30-minute television advertisements of an educational nature. The Home Shopping Network (HSN) is another tool for direct marketing by product manufacturers. It is a TV channel that shows products and services available for purchase—24 hours a day. Customers can order the products seen on the Home Shopping Network by calling and ordering.

E-mail and the Internet Direct-mail marketing can also be done using e-mail. The Internet allows us to obtain information without leaving our homes. It also enables us to purchase merchandise from any location in the world with access to a computer.

Photos and descriptions of services and products can be placed in an e-mail, or potential customers can click on a link included in the e-mail to go to a Web site that gives them more information. However, customers are more likely to respond to this method of distribution if they have requested the e-mail information themselves. Unsolicited electronic mail, or *spam*, is one of the biggest concerns Web users have today.

Indirect Channels

An **indirect channel** of distribution is the path a product takes using intermediaries, or people or services in the middle of a transaction, between the producer and consumer. For example, a manufacturer of sporting goods might sell its products to retailers, who in turn sell those products to customers. Agents, wholesalers, and retailers are all intermediaries.

AGENTS Agents do not take ownership of the goods they sell. They simply bring buyers and sellers together for a fee. They often exist in

Case Study   PART 2

A PLACE FOR ATHLETES
Continued from Part 1 on page 121

Bill Duffy and Associates Sports Management helps young players by providing more than just contractual advice. With connections in entertainment, health, and tax fields, BDA Sports opens doors for clients in movies and video production, gives health analysis and nutritional advice, and provides tax experts. BDA players have also been regularly featured on video game boxes.

Bill Duffy also works with international players. After seeing Yao Ming play in 1998, he spent four years working to get the 7'4" center out of China and into the NBA. Yao was picked first in the 2002 draft, and Duffy represented two of the other first four picks as well. Such dedication and accomplishments inspired *Sports Illustrated* to rank Duffy as number 20 on its 2003 list of 101 Most Influential Minorities in Sports.

ANALYZE AND WRITE
1. Describe some of the extra services that BDA offers its clients. Why would these appeal to a player who hasn't graduated college or is from another country?
2. What are some challenges that may come with the globalization of the NBA?

QUESTION
What makes e-mail a good method for marketing directly to consumers?

indirect channel the path a product takes using intermediaries between the producer and consumer

Weaving a Ticketweb

Venues both large and small offer electronic ticketing, or use services such as Ticketmaster or Ticketweb to offer tickets. When you order online, you pay a convenience fee—but you never have to wait *in* line. You can choose to have paper tickets shipped to you for a price. But more often than not, people decide to use the "Will Call" option that allows people to pick up tickets at the time of the event.

→Learn how to purchase a ticket online by going to a link to an intermediary Web site through **marketingseries.glencoe.com**.

multiple locations and manage ticket sales electronically. Agents can be brick-and-mortar stores, online, or telephone services. Ticketmaster is an example of an agent intermediary. You might go to a Ticketmaster outlet in a local retail store or contact Ticketmaster by phone or online to buy a ticket. This is more convenient for the buyer and the seller than waiting in line at a box office. In addition, in this way, it is easy for tickets to be sold before the date of an event.

WHOLESALERS A manufacturer of sporting goods may sell its products to wholesalers. Wholesalers are resellers who buy goods, store them, and sell them in smaller quantities to retailers or sports organizations. The wholesaler's function helps reduce the number of sales contacts that a manufacturer has to make in order to sell products.

RETAILERS Retailers are resellers too, but they sell their goods directly to the customer. A sporting-goods retailer such as Sports Authority sells products to customers for their personal use. Sports Authority and other sporting-goods businesses can purchase their products from both wholesalers and manufacturers, depending on the product as well as the needs of their businesses.

Multiple Channels

The use of multiple channels involves more than one type of distribution channel to reach customers. For example, Nike is an athletic-shoe and apparel company that uses multiple channels to sell its products to customers. Nike has its own Web site and its own retail stores to promote and sell its own products. It also sells its products to retailers such as Foot Locker, who in turn sells those products to their customers.

→ **INFOMERCIAL SUCCESS**
Infomercials often sell home or personal improvement items such as exercise equipment. Infomercials usually air late at night or early in the morning when fewer people are watching television. *What are some advantages of airing infomercials or commercials at this time?*

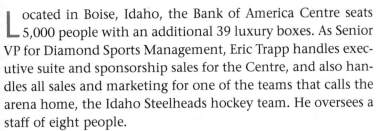

Profiles in Marketing

MANAGING THE VENUE

Eric Trapp
Senior Vice President
Diamond Sports Management

Located in Boise, Idaho, the Bank of America Centre seats 5,000 people with an additional 39 luxury boxes. As Senior VP for Diamond Sports Management, Eric Trapp handles executive suite and sponsorship sales for the Centre, and also handles all sales and marketing for one of the teams that calls the arena home, the Idaho Steelheads hockey team. He oversees a staff of eight people.

"My workload will vary from season to season," Eric says. "During the actual hockey season most of our time is spent implementing what we have sold and entertaining our clients. During the off-season most of our time is spent selling, budgeting, and planning our strategies for the upcoming season."

Eric has bachelor's degrees in both advertising and telecommunications, with a minor in marketing. He has 12 years of marketing experience, working with a variety of baseball, hockey, and tennis teams. He says sales experience is very helpful, as are desktop publishing skills.

Entertainment Product While many consumers might not think of entertainment as a product, savvy marketers do—entertainment fights for consumer dollars alongside countless other ways to spend money. Eric says it's important to keep this in mind.

"Each customer will have different needs and objectives, and it is our job as an organization to show them how our entertainment product will fulfill their personal or organizational needs," he says. "We also strive to think out of the box and provide a new and unique experience each and every game."

Why might desktop publishing skills be valuable to a marketing professional?

Career Data: Arena Manager

Education and Training Bachelor's or master's degrees in advertising, marketing, sales, or general business; real-world job experience

Skills and Abilities Writing skills, networking skills, strong interpersonal skills, and people skills

Career Outlook Faster than average growth through 2010

Career Path Many sports marketers begin working with small, regional teams and work their way up to the big leagues.

Russell Athletic, a sports-apparel company, outfits many Major League Baseball teams. Direct distribution is the best way to reach professional sports franchises. Some Russell Athletic clothing is also sold through the MLB Web site, and the rest of its athletic clothing line is sold to sporting-goods retailers for resale to customers.

Not all products involve physical goods. Sporting leagues and organizations, such as Major League Baseball, also sell the right to broadcast their games to television and radio networks. Many sporting events sell their rights to Internet companies for broadcast. For example, MLB has also sold rights to broadcast its games online through Real.com and MLB.com (a subsidiary of MLB). Turner Sports Interactive has the rights to show NASCAR and PGA Tour events on the Web. The use of multiple channels not only increases product and service exposure, it also provides an opportunity to reach different parts of the consumer market.

Trying It Out

Every business needs to sell its products in order to survive. Many businesses will start with one distribution channel and experiment with others until they find the mix that lets their business grow. It's up to each individual business or organization to carefully research and identify what to produce, for whom, and what method of delivery will get the product out into the marketplace to be sold.

Quick Check ✓

RESPOND to what you've read by answering these questions.

1. What does the place decision involve? _____

_____

_____

_____

_____

_____

2. List several direct distribution methods. _____

_____

_____

_____

_____

_____

3. What are three basic types of intermediaries in an indirect channel of distribution? _____

_____

_____

_____

_____

_____

Worksheet 6.1

Market Research: Making Observations

Attend four sporting events at your school or in your community. Notice the products that are marketed at each event, including clothes with the school logo worn by students. Record your observations below.

Sporting Event #1

_____

_____

_____

Sporting Event #2

_____

_____

_____

Sporting Event #3

_____

_____

_____

Sporting Event #4

_____

_____

_____

Evaluating Information

1. What marketing tools did you notice at each of the events?

_____

_____

2. How effective is each of these tools?

_____

_____

Worksheet 6.2

Analyze Direct-Marketing Distribution

Collect catalogs and other direct-mail materials about sports equipment, games, and sports clothing and gear. Choose one category (equipment, games, clothing, or gear) and answer the following questions.

1. Why do you think this type of distribution was chosen for the merchandise?

_____

_____

_____

_____

_____

2. Do you agree or disagree that this is an effective means of distribution for the merchandise? Explain.

_____

_____

_____

_____

_____

3. What advantages and disadvantages does direct marketing provide for this type of merchandise?

_____

_____

_____

_____

_____

4. What other means of distribution would you choose for this merchandise?

_____

_____

_____

_____

_____

Portfolio Works

CHOOSING A CHANNEL OF DISTRIBUTION

You are the owner of a shop that specializes in making clothing with sports logos.
You have the license to make clothing for the local university's sports teams.

1. On a separate sheet of paper, design a chart or graphic organizer that lists all the channels of distribution. Also list the advantages and disadvantages of each channel for your clothing.

2. Write a short report describing which channels of distribution you chose. Explain why you chose these channels.

_____

_____

_____

_____

_____

_____

_____

_____

_____

_____

_____

_____

_____

_____

_____

_____

_____

_____

_____

_____

_____

_____

Add this page to your career portfolio.

CHAPTER SUMMARY

Section 6.1 The Research Process

market research
(p. 122)
secondary research
(p. 123)
primary research (p. 124)
observation method
(p. 125)
census (p. 128)
sample (p. 128)

- Market research is the process of systematically collecting, recording, analyzing, and presenting data related to marketing goods and services. It provides data so that intelligent business decisions can be made regarding marketing products.

- Market research is used for product development, pricing, promotional activities, distribution, and customer satisfaction.

- The five steps to conducting formal market research are identify the problem, do secondary research, select and design primary research, collect data, and report and analyze data.

Section 6.2 Outlets—the Place Decision

direct channel (p. 131)
direct marketing (p. 132)
indirect channel (p. 133)

- Businesses use market research to determine their business customers and their ultimate consumers who are their target markets. Knowing the type of customer a retailer has is the first consideration regarding the place decision, or product distribution decision.

- A direct channel is the path a product takes without help between the producer and the customer. An indirect channel uses intermediaries to get a product from the producer and to the customer.

CHECKING CONCEPTS

1. **Define** market research.
2. **Explain** how businesses use market research.
3. **List** the steps used in the market-research process.
4. **Explain** the three primary research methods and when each should be used.
5. **Describe** how primary research data are collected, reported, and analyzed.
6. **Identify** how businesses make the place decision as part of the marketing mix.
7. **Explain** the appropriate channels of distribution for a product.

Critical Thinking

8. **Explain** why a city government would conduct market research before bringing in a minor league baseball team.

CROSS-CURRICULUM SKILLS

Work-Based Learning

Basic Skills—Listening Skills and Writing

9. Write or call the marketing manager of a Minor League sports team. Ask the manager about the marketing research methods the team uses and the effectiveness of each method. Write a summary of your findings and share it with the class.

Interpersonal Skills—Participating as a Team Member

10. Form a focus group of eight students. The group will discuss and compare different brands of soccer balls. Write a report based on the focus group's reactions.

School-Based Learning

Computer Technology

11. Use the Internet to research a sports team and its marketing in a foreign country. Give an oral report to the class.

Arts

12. Work with four students to prepare and present a multimedia presentation of a major sports team. Contact the team's marketing department for materials.

Role Play: Marketing Researcher

SITUATION You are to assume the role of market researcher for a national chain of sporting-goods stores. The company is planning to open its first location in a large city. There are two possibilities: an indoor mall location in the suburbs or a stand-alone location in a downtown area.

ACTIVITY Determine the market research needed to make the location decision and present it to your manager (judge).

EVALUATION You will be evaluated on how well you meet the following performance indicators:

- Assess marketing-information needs.
- Identify information for marketing decision making.
- Describe sources of secondary data.
- Explain factors to consider when selecting a store site.
- Describe techniques for processing marketing information.

INTERNET ACTIVITY

Use the Internet to access American Sports Data, Inc.

- Click on one of the market research studies on the left side of the screen.
- Write a fact sheet about the research.
- Post the fact sheet in the classroom for your class-mates to read.

➡ For a link to American Sports Data, Inc., to begin this exercise, go to **marketingseries.glencoe.com**.

Chapter 7

Branding and Licensing

Chapter Objectives

- Explain the concepts of branding and brand equity.
- Discuss the types of brands.
- Describe how to develop an effective brand name.
- Discuss product licensing and how licensed goods are merchandised.
- Explain the importance of sports sponsorships and endorsements.
- Discuss how companies choose sports endorsers for their products.

RACE FOR THE PRIZE

To fund their races, the National Association for Stock Car Auto Racing (NASCAR) receives race fees from track owners, annual fees from driving teams, a percentage of television revenue and licensed merchandise, and other sponsorship money. NASCAR's 75 million fans each support a favorite driver by buying the products of that driver's sponsor. They demonstrate a 72 percent loyalty to sponsor brands, double that of any other sport.

When restrictions on the advertising of tobacco products began in the 1970s, R.J. Reynolds Tobacco Company shifted its promotion money to the sponsorship of NASCAR. The Winston Cup, NASCAR's premier racing series, was established, and both sides benefited for over 30 years. By 2000, NASCAR was the number one spectator sport in the United States and the number two rated sport on television. However, R.J. Reynolds could not continue its sponsorship, due to increased costs from tobacco lawsuits, taxes, and declining market share. NASCAR needed to find a new title sponsorship.

ANALYZE AND WRITE

1. Why are NASCAR fans considered loyal to sponsor brands?
2. Why did NASCAR need to find a new title sponsorship?

Case Study Part 2 on page 153

POWER READ

Be an active reader and use these reading strategies:

PREDICT what the section will be about.

CONNECT what you read with your life.

QUESTION as you read to make sure you understand the content.

RESPOND to what you've read.

Branding

AS YOU READ ...

YOU WILL LEARN

- To explain the concepts of branding and brand equity.
- To discuss the types of brands.
- To describe how to develop an effective brand name.

WHY IT'S IMPORTANT

Branding develops an image and customer loyalty for a product and company. Recognizable brands differentiate products and companies from competitors.

KEY TERMS

- brand
- brand name
- trademark
- brand equity
- manufacturer brand
- co-branding
- intermediary brand
- generic brand

brand a name, word or words, symbol, or design that identifies an organization and its products

brand name a word or words, letters, or numbers representing a brand that can be spoken

trademark a device that legally identifies ownership of a registered brand or trade name

PREDICT

Give an example of a brand.

The Importance of Branding

The appeal and influence of sports can be seen on television, in apparel, and in advertising. With such exposure, sports organizations and companies strive to develop strong identities, or brands, to differentiate themselves from one another. A **brand** is a name, word or words, symbol, or design that identifies an organization and its products. Nike's logo, the "swoosh," is an example of a branding strategy.

What's in a Name?

A **brand name** is a word or words, letters, or numbers representing a brand that can be spoken, such as "Gatorade" or "Los Angeles Lakers." A *trade name* is the legal name of a company, such as Reebok. Companies that want to have exclusive rights to a brand name or a trade name will register those names with the U.S. Patent and Trademark Office in Arlington, Virginia. When a brand name or trade name is registered, it also becomes a trademark. A **trademark** is a device that legally identifies ownership of a registered brand or trade name.

Branding is important for building customer loyalty. Customers come to expect the same quality from the brands they buy or the teams that they watch. Once satisfied, they become repeat customers. Branding helps a company to introduce new products in a line of products. Customers familiar with the original brand are more likely to trust a new product with the same brand. Branding also creates an image for the product.

Brand Personality

The Yankee baseball team has been recognized as an outstanding franchise. Its ads point out that during a 100-year span, the franchise has won 26 world championships. This accomplishment makes the Yankees the most successful, or winning, franchise in professional sports history. Thus, the Yankees have a brand personality as a winning team. Its pinstripe uniform and logo are well known by fans and competitors.

A brand personality involves attaching human traits to a brand name. For example, Nike and other sports footwear companies often have professional athletes endorse their products to create a "winning" brand personality. Similarly, Skechers brand sport footwear tries to develop a cool, hip brand personality through its ads.

Brand Equity

Brand equity is the value a brand has beyond its actual functional benefits. When a brand becomes very popular, its value becomes a competitive advantage because most consumers equate the brand with quality. Thus, customers are generally willing to pay a higher price for products with brand equity.

Brand equity is developed over years of promoting a brand-name product to consumers. Establishing that brand name in the minds of consumers requires three basic steps:

1. **Develop** the brand in the customer's mind as part of a class of products. Example: Gatorade is a sports drink.

2. **Link** the product's brand name to its function and make some type of emotional connection with the product. Example: Gatorade helps athletes to perform better in athletic events.

3. **Help** consumers think and feel the way you want them to regarding your product. Example: Gatorade is the best product of choice for successful athletes.

Sports teams try to accomplish the same goals. For example:

1. **Develop** the brand in the consumer's mind as part of a class of products. Example: The Yankees are a professional baseball team.

2. **Link** the product's brand name to its function and make some type of emotional connection with the product. Example: The Yankees fans think positively about the club and players.

3. **Help** consumers think and feel the way you want them to regarding your product. Example: Yankees fans stick with their team through good and bad seasons because of the bond they have with the team.

Brand equity also has financial value through licensing. Allowing another company to use a brand name, patent, or any other item for a fee or royalty is called *licensing*. For example, the National Football

brand equity the value a brand has beyond its actual functional benefits

CONNECT

Do you or your family purchase brand-name products? Why or why not?

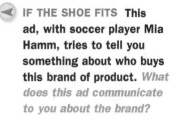

◄ **IF THE SHOE FITS** This ad, with soccer player Mia Hamm, tries to tell you something about who buys this brand of product. *What does this ad communicate to you about the brand?*

manufacturer brand a brand owned by the producer of the product

co-branding a branding strategy that combines one or more brands to increase customer loyalty and sales for each product

League (NFL) may allow a clothing manufacturer to use its name or logo to produce and sell hooded sweatshirts. Logos, or distinctive symbols, immediately identify a company or organization. Licensing will be discussed in more detail in Section 7.2.

Types of Brands and Strategies

There are three types of brands and several branding strategies. The three basic types of brands are:

- Manufacturer brands

- Intermediary brands

- Generic brands

Manufacturer Brands

A **manufacturer brand** is owned by the producer of the product. Manufacturers may use multi-product branding, multi-branding, and co-branding.

MULTI-PRODUCT BRANDING This is used when the manufacturer uses one name for all its products. The major advantage of multi-product branding is that a strong promotional campaign can be developed to create an image for all products. For example, Nike basketball, running, soccer, golf, hockey, and skateboard lines use multi-product branding. Nike is capitalizing on its name and image to sell all the product lines it manufactures. Another strategy is brand extension. For example, within the Nike golf line, clubs, balls, footwear, and apparel all bear the Nike name. A brand-extension strategy uses an existing brand name for an improved or new product in the product line. There are several different Nike Forged Titanium drivers. If a new driver is introduced, the Nike name will be part of the brand name.

MULTI-BRANDING Manufacturers sometimes practice multi-branding, which means that each product in a product line has a distinctive name. This strategy is used for products that target different consumers. For example, Procter & Gamble's deodorant product line includes three antiperspirants/deodorants: Secret for women, Old Spice for men, and Sure for men or women.

One of the advantages of multi-branding is that each product has its own distinct image. If a new product fails, its failure will not affect the other products produced by the manufacturer. One of the major disadvantages of multi-branding is cost. The cost of creating separate promotional plans for each product can be very expensive.

CO-BRANDING The branding strategy called **co-branding** combines one or more brands to increase customer loyalty and sales for each product. Two different manufacturers may partner to produce one product. Co-branding works well when the products complement each other. Credit card companies, such as MasterCard and Visa, have been co-branded with airlines, automobile manufacturers, and sports organizations. For example, General Motors and the Professional

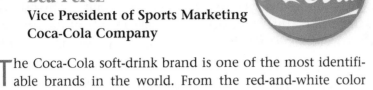

Profiles in Marketing

MARKETING THE REAL BRAND

Bea Perez
Vice President of Sports Marketing
Coca-Cola Company

The Coca-Cola soft-drink brand is one of the most identifiable brands in the world. From the red-and-white color scheme to the distinctive lettering, Coca-Cola products are easy to recognize.

As vice president of sports marketing for Coca-Cola, Bea Perez works with how that brand is used in the world of sports. She oversees the marketing department for all sports activities in North America—including NCAA sports, NASCAR racing, NHL hockey, and PGA Tours. She is responsible for all league and athlete relationships that Coke has throughout the country.

On a typical day, she might be negotiating a contract with a league or an athlete. She works with her marketing department to make sure everything is running smoothly, finding new opportunities while patching up any problems that arise.

Perez says that being able to collaborate on large projects with others, both inside and outside the company, is crucial. "Also, persuasive selling—internal or external—and negotiation are part of the job." She adds, "Strategic thinking is important—looking at the bigger picture and the long-term picture."

Perez has been with Coca-Cola for ten years. She started at the company working on Hispanic marketing, then gradually moved into sports.

"I love the people I work with," Perez says. "It's an incredible brand with incredible people."

Why are negotiation skills in sports marketing important?

Career Data:
Vice President of Sports Marketing

Education and Training
Bachelor's or master's degree in advertising, marketing, or public relations

Skills and Abilities
Interpersonal skills, time-management skills, organizational skills, multitasking skills, patience, and resourcefulness

Career Outlook Faster than average growth through 2010

Career Path Marketing degrees are an excellent starting point, as are degrees in sales and public relations.

Golfers' Association (PGA) have a co-sponsored MasterCard. Co-branding can also be seen on Web sites. For example, on the NFL Web site, you might see the notation, "powered by Sportsline.com." On the Sportsline.com Web site, you will see a link to the NFL Web site. This co-branding reinforces both of the products in the eyes of consumers.

Intermediary Brands

An **intermediary brand** carries a name developed by the wholesaler, retailer, or catalog house. Intermediaries contract with manufacturers to make products that are sold under their own private labels. Sporting-goods catalog houses such as Gander Mountain and Cabela's use their names as private labels.

intermediary brand a brand that carries a name developed by the wholesaler, retailer, or catalog house

Generic Brands

A **generic brand** represents a general product category and does not carry a company or brand name. For example, you would find a can with the generic label "peas" in a supermarket. However, it is unlikely that you would find many generic brands of apparel or equipment in the sports industry. One of the only exceptions might be in fishing-supplies stores where you would buy bait or handmade fly-fishing lures. In those cases, the words describing the contents of the package, that is, the word *worms,* would be all that you would see on the container.

Developing Brand Names

Choosing and developing a good brand name requires thought and planning. There are a few guidelines to follow. (See **Figure 7.1** for examples of successful brand names.) The brand name should:

- Offer a benefit.
- Be simple.
- Be different and positive.
- Reflect an image.
- Be previously unregistered.

Offer a Benefit

A good brand name will offer the customer value. The sports drink Gatorade was given that name because it helped the University of Florida football team, the Gators, play better when it was hot. The team actually became known as the "second-half" team because of the team's stamina in the second half of the game. The sports *drink* ("ade") served to *help* (sounds like "aid") the Gators, and so the name "Gatorade" became a well-known brand name.

generic brand a brand that represents a general product category and does not carry a company or brand name

---

Figure 7.1

Branding Success

PUT YOUR BEST FOOT FORWARD Good branding gives a consumer a strong emotional association with the brand and/or product. *Do you recognize any of these brands? What do you associate with them?*

Top 5 Athletic Shoe Brands		
Rank	**Brand**	**Retail Dollar Share**
1	Nike	34%
2	Reebok	13%
3	Adidas	6%
4	New Balance	5%
5	Easy Spirit	2%

 marketingseries.glencoe.com

Hot Property

Good Hydration

Question: How do you beat water as the must-have drink for thirsty athletes?

Answer: Develop a product scientifically formulated to hydrate them better.

In 1965, doctors at the University of Florida developed a new kind of beverage called Gatorade to prevent their football team from becoming dehydrated. Due to playing in heat and humidity, the University of Florida Gators tended to run out of energy because they lost fluids through sweating. Gatorade replaces fluids and electrolytes the players lose and provides them with extra carbohydrates to power them through the second half of a game.

SPREADING THE WORD

As the Gator football team started winning in the 1960s, other college and professional football teams took notice of the drink. After the Gators won the Orange Bowl championship in 1967, Gatorade signed to supply the beverage to the entire NFL. Since then, Gatorade has built its brand through sponsorship deals with the top pro leagues of nearly every sport. Now Gatorade is the official sports drink of the NFL, MLB, the NBA, U.S. Soccer, and other organizations.

Gatorade hasn't limited itself to ball sports: It has also made inroads into professional car racing. For example, Gatorade made a deal with the International Speedway Corporation to create Gatorade-branded victory lanes and refueling stations for thirsty crews. Through these deals and the endorsements of top athletes, such as Michael Jordan, Gatorade has created a memorable brand image in the minds of consumers. According to the New York-based Beverage Marketing Corporation, Gatorade boasted an 84 percent share of the sports-drink category in 2002.

1. How has Gatorade created consumer awareness of its brand?
2. Why do you think consumers want to drink Gatorade?

Be Simple

A simple name is more memorable. Nike is a simple name. Other simple brand names in the sports-footwear industry include Reebok, Adidas, Puma, Gravis, and Fila.

Be Different and Positive

The Puma brand has a positive association as it projects an image of a fast animal in the cat family, such as a cougar or mountain lion. In addition, team names are usually simple and distinctive: Yankees, Red Sox, White Sox, Giants, Orioles, and Angels.

Reflect an Image

Branding should say something about the product. For example, since the 1930s, Wheaties cereal has used athletes on its packaging and is known as The Breakfast of Champions. Images of successful athletes from track and field, baseball, golf, football, hockey, swimming, figure skating, boxing, gymnastics, tennis, soccer, and numerous other sports have been featured on Wheaties boxes. This positive association with the sports industry helps to create a distinctive image of Wheaties as the Breakfast of Champions.

Be Previously Unregistered

A brand name cannot be previously registered with the U.S. Patent and Trademark Office. You can go to the government Web site (**www.uspto.gov**) and conduct a search to see if a name already exists. For example, Country Club Industries, a small California company, wanted to register "Sport Powerace" as a new brand of drinking water. The Coca-Cola Company opposed that registration because it was too similar to its registered brand-name sports drink, Powerade. Government agencies may also restrict the use of certain words that may be misleading to consumers. For example, using the word *heart* in connection with food products might mislead a consumer into thinking a given product is good for one's heart.

Make It Last

Choosing a name, symbol, device, or slogan for a business or organization is a critical process. It communicates the type of business and products to customers. A good brand name and symbol will last over time. For example, the Nike "swoosh" was created in 1971 for $35 by a student of founder Phil Knight. The design was based on the "wing" of the goddess Nike, and it has represented that company for over 30 years. Effective branding comes from understanding the product and the organization—and from understanding how to get the message across to consumers.

Quick Check

RESPOND to what you've read by answering these questions.

1. What are the three steps involved in developing brand equity? _____

_____

_____

_____

_____

2. Name the three types of brands. _____

_____

_____

_____

3. What rules should be followed when developing a good brand name? _____

_____

_____

_____

_____

Licensing

Licensing and Merchandising

Licensing is an agreement that gives a company the right to use another's brand name, patent, or other intellectual property for a royalty or fee. The *licensor* is the company or individual granting the license for a fee in this legally binding contract. The *licensee* is the company or individual paying for the rights to use the licensor's name or property. Licensed merchandise can bear the name, logo, or other characteristics of the licensor.

Licensed Products

In sports marketing, a company may pay a fee to use a league's, team's, or individual's name, image, or logo on a product or on the product's packaging. Any time you see a sports figure featured on a box of cereal, or a sport team's logo on a T-shirt, you know that company is paying a fee to that sports figure or team (licensor). For example, the National Football League (NFL) grants product licenses to companies that want to use the NFL logo or any NFL team's logos on the goods they make and sell. You may see Reebok (licensee) selling its jerseys and hats with the NFL logo. A visit to the NFL Web site will give you an idea of the manufacturers that have licensing agreements with the NFL. College sports teams also have licensing agreements with product manufacturers. Individual sports figures grant licensing agreements as well. For example, Tiger Woods has a licensing agreement with Nike. There are advantages for sports organizations and companies, as shown in **Figure 7.2** on page 152.

THE PRODUCTS Licensing agreements can apply to just about any product imaginable. Apparel, key chains, toys, sports equipment, food products, credit cards, video games, and household items are just a few items that can make use of licensing agreements. Souvenirs at sporting events, such as baseball caps and pins, are also licensed products.

The licensor must be careful to select products that reflect the image its brand name has in the public eye. If the licensing agreement is with a company that produces poor-quality merchandise, the licensor's image may be damaged. Licensees also need to select the right events, leagues, teams, and/or individuals for their products. For example, the Olympic Games have a prestigious and high-profile image around the world. Licensed products carrying the Olympic logo are viewed positively. Winning teams and players help sell licensed merchandise. A team that makes it to the World Series in baseball will

AS YOU READ ...

YOU WILL LEARN
- To discuss product licensing and how licensed goods are merchandised.
- To explain the importance of sports sponsorships and endorsements.
- To discuss how companies choose sports endorsers for their products.

WHY IT'S IMPORTANT
Licensing, sponsorships, and endorsements generate income for sports organizations and events. The activities also offer companies access to their target markets.

KEY TERM
- licensing

licensing an agreement that gives a company the right to use another's brand name, patent, or other intellectual property for a royalty or fee

PREDICT
List some advantages and disadvantages of using a sports organization to promote the image of a product.

JUST BUY IT Sports-affiliated merchandise should reinforce the positive image of the particular sport or athlete. *What kind of an image does this merchandise project?*

create excitement and will generate sales of licensed products. Teams or players that are in a slump will not receive the same enthusiasm from fans, who are potential customers.

Merchandising Licensed Goods

In the past most licensed merchandise could be purchased only at the event venue. Today licensed merchandise is made available through many channels of distribution. You can purchase licensed goods in department stores, chain stores, league-sponsored retail outlets, and through the Internet. Most sports organizations have their own Web sites where people can buy licensed products. Some have their own retail stores, such as stores owned by the United States Golf Association (USGA) or the Washington Redskins.

Retail stores that carry licensed goods use that fact to promote those products. As you will see in the next section on sponsorships,

---

Figure 7.2

Benefits of Licensing

TEAMWORK Sports organizations and companies or manufacturers can benefit from licensing agreements. *Is the relationship between sports organizations and companies equal? Why?*

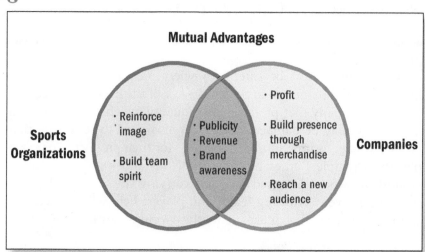

Mutual Advantages

Sports Organizations
- Reinforce image
- Build team spirit

- Publicity
- Revenue
- Brand awareness

- Profit
- Build presence through merchandise
- Reach a new audience

Companies

special promotional deals create partnerships between the licensor and the licensee to help boost store traffic and subsequent retail sales of licensed products. Sweepstakes and contests are run by a sponsor, with the prize being tickets to the sporting event. These promotions are advertised in print, broadcast, and online media. However, you must visit the retail stores that carry the licensed products to enter; or you must purchase the product and mail proof of purchase to the sponsor. At the retail locations, posters and signs promote the sweepstake or contest. Thus, the sponsor provides promotional support and activities that help to increase product sales.

Some licensed products are used as promotional incentives for customers to buy a product. For example, if you subscribe to the magazine *Sports Illustrated,* you may receive a free video of that year's most celebrated athlete. The video of the athlete would be the licensed product.

Sponsorships and Endorsements

Two forms of licensing are *sponsorships* and *endorsements.* One of the most recognizable sports logos in the world is the five- ringed logo of the Olympic Games. Companies pay top dollar for the right to be identified as one of the sponsors of the Olympic Games. NASCAR is another brand that takes advantage of licensing. If you have ever attended a NASCAR event, you would have seen company logos on all the racing cars and on the uniforms of the racers. At golfing events, you may see a golfer wear a shirt or a hat with a company logo on it. In the supermarket, you may see a cereal box with a sports figure on it. These examples involve agreements called sponsorships or endorsements.

Sponsorships

Sports events generate income from broadcast rights, ticket sales, merchandising, and sponsorships. Sponsorships are the promotional vehicles that financially support sports events. All of the major sports organizations, including the Olympics, NASCAR, PGA, NFL, NHL, MLB, NBA, WNBA, and NCAA, use sponsorships to help finance their operations. Promotional packages for sponsors may include licensing rights, stadium promotions, product sampling, signage, product sales, billboards, hospitality opportunities, receptions with the athletes, free tickets, and on-site merchandising opportunities. Additional benefits may include exposure of a sponsor's products through use by the athletes or the organization.

Case Study   PART 2

RACE FOR THE PRIZE
Continued from Part 1 on page 143.

With sponsorship money from R.J. Reynolds Tobacco about to be withdrawn, NASCAR needed a new title sponsor. So, as of 2004, the Winston Cup became known as the Nextel Cup when NASCAR selected Nextel to be its new title sponsor. With Nextel as sponsor, NASCAR has no government restrictions for developing the family market, including young people who may have potential NASCAR loyalty.

NASCAR is taking advantage of Nextel's image by incorporating technology into the races, which may attract a new audience. Kiosks that demonstrate new phones are replacing tents where packs of cigarettes had been given away. Wireless phones are used to receive messages about specific races and drivers. Nextel is able to promote all aspects of NASCAR—tracks, races, teams, and drivers—on television, on the Internet, through wireless communication, and other media.

ANALYZE AND WRITE
1. What market are NASCAR and Nextel hoping to reach? Why is this market important?
2. In what ways might Nextel use technology in this sponsor partnership?

CONNECT
Name a product or service that you associate with a sports figure.

QUESTION

How might buying unlicensed counterfeit team merchandise affect the team itself?

IMPORTANCE OF SPONSORSHIPS Operating sports events and sports leagues requires a significant amount of money. Sports organizations need the money generated from corporate sponsors to help pay their costs and expenses. Professional players' salaries in major league sports and prize-money events, such as the Super Bowl or other tournaments, cost more money each year. Multinational sporting events such as the Olympics could not exist without the support of sponsors.

What do sponsors get out of the deal? Sponsors get exposure of their products through their promotional efforts and free publicity. With the Olympics, for example, the exposure is international due to media coverage around the world. Sponsoring companies can use sports events to target their consumers and promote their products. The objectives may be to enhance their image by associating with the event and to increase their sales revenue. Sponsors must weigh the costs of sponsorship against their objectives.

Sponsorships can be seen in promotional activities. For example, an official Olympics sponsor may use the five-ringed Olympic Games logo on product packages. If a company such as Kodak buys the rights to sponsorship, its film and camera products would be sold exclusively at the Olympics. Kodak would also be included in the official Olympics program. Association with the Olympics helps to build a positive image for the company and its products. To capitalize on that positive image and to increase sales, Kodak might provide stores with display signs promoting Kodak's sponsorship of the Olympics and may run a contest or sweepstakes. These coordinated promotional efforts help generate store traffic and sales of its products. The publicity surrounding the Olympics will also add value to the promotional efforts of its sponsors.

TYPES OF SPONSORSHIPS Sponsorships can be flexible. A company can sponsor a team for a length of time or just sponsor an event. A company may agree to sponsor portions of a sporting event. For example, a company can sponsor the half-time portion of a football game or the first quarter of a basketball game. This is especially common during sports events that are broadcast. You might see that XYZ company has sponsored an "XYZ Star of the Game" or an "XYZ Halftime Report." These strategies integrate the company name into the game itself, providing a form of direct advertising.

- **Signage** Sponsors can also buy signage at a stadium. During a game that is seen in person or on television, sponsors' names may appear on the scoreboard, floorboards, rafters, or even rotating electronic screens. This is signage. If the event is broadcast on television, the company receives direct advertising without buying airtime.

NASCAR is an organization that offers a variety of sponsorship opportunities. A company can purchase the right to place its message or logo on various parts of a race car. A company can promote its product on the dashboard, side door, rear panel, top, hood, or wheel area. Along with the race track, different parts of the drivers' and pit crews' uniforms are also available for logos and names.

The Branded Tour

In France bicycling is serious business—at least for three weeks each July. Established in 1903, the Tour de France is the world's most prestigious and difficult bicycle race. Covering more than 2,200 miles over the countryside, the best cyclists from many nations race at top speeds. They travel across flatlands, up and down steep mountain slopes, around breakneck curves, and through wind, rain, and heat. Crowds cheer the cyclists on—and none do so more loudly than the race's sponsors.

Sponsorship From large corporations to small businesses, sponsors provide cash, top equipment, and training in return for advertising exposure. Company logos are placed on team jerseys, vehicles, signs, and media advertisement. At the race's end, the world watches the winner pedal down the broadest avenue of Paris, the Champs-Elysées, and then cross the finish line.

The U.S. Postal Service sponsors American Lance Armstrong and his team. Some feel this sponsorship wastes federal dollars. What do you think?

PREMIUM SPONSORS A company must pay more to be the official or title sponsor, but it receives more options and opportunities. Two examples of premium sponsorships are *entitlements* and *product exclusivity*.

- **Entitlements** Entitlement occurs when there is one major sponsor for an event. For example, NASCAR signed a 10-year contract with Nextel, a cell-phone service provider, to be its title sponsor. Nextel gains much exposure through its title sponsorship because NASCAR is popular with an estimated 75 million fans in over 100 countries.

The PGA grants entitlement sponsorships for almost all of its tour events. A visit to the PGA Web site and a look at its schedule of events will show you how many of its events are sponsored exclusively by one company. Some of the scheduled events include the Buick Invitational, Mercedes Championship, NEC Invitational, Sony Open, AT&T National Pro-Am, Nissan Open, Chrysler Classic, Ford Championship, Honda Classic, Bell South Classic, Shell Houston Open, Wachovia Championship, American Express Championship, John Deere Classic, Franklin Templeton Shootout, and ConAgra Foods Skins Game.

- **Facility Entitlements** There are also facility entitlements through which a company purchases the promotional rights to an entire stadium. Several large companies have done this and renamed stadiums and arenas to publicize their sponsorships. Heinz Field in Pittsburgh, Pennsylvania, and FedExField near Washington, D.C., are just two examples. This type of entitlement gives the company exposure in all the events that are held at the stadium during the season and off-season.

■ **Product Exclusivity** Product exclusivity is another premium sponsorship whereby only one product in a product category is granted sponsorship. This exclusivity agreement prevents competitors from selling or promoting their products during the sponsored events. On-site products and on-site merchandising are available with this premium sponsorship. For example, if Coca-Cola is an official sponsor of the Olympic Games, only Coca-Cola soft drinks can be sold at the Games. The concession stands will contain only Coca-Cola products. This kind of on-site merchandising that excludes the competition results in increased profits, as well as exposure of sponsored products.

There are many kinds of companies that can affiliate with a sporting event. For example, if you visit NASCAR's Web site and select sponsors from the menu, you will see all the official sponsors, many of which are local companies. In addition, some of them include sponsors such as Coca-Cola (official soft drink), Dasani (official water), Domino's Pizza (official pizza), Kellogg's (official cereal), and Visa (official card). The Olympics also offer product exclusivity to its official sponsors. The Olympics Web site includes a list of sponsors and their product exclusivity for the upcoming Olympic Games. In each product category, there is only one sponsor.

Endorsements

As you learned in Chapter 2, an endorsement is a statement of approval of a product, service, or idea made by an individual or organization speaking on behalf of the advertiser. Endorsements involve using a celebrity or public figure to represent and promote a company and that company's products. Companies pay sports figures so they can use their images in print and broadcast media, as well as on product packaging, billboards, and collectibles. The company may also require a set number of public appearances by the sports figure at various events sponsored by the company. The sports figure lends familiarity and credibility to the product. The public may think, "If the sports figure likes the product, then it must be good."

ASSOCIATION Endorsements may simply involve an association with the product. Some companies that make products unrelated to sports want their products associated with an athlete. Though there is no direct relationship between the product and the athlete, the company believes that association will help sell the product. Of course, all companies want to use successful athletes—ones who will project a positive image for their products.

For example, Annika Sorenstam, a professional golfer, sells Kentucky Fried Chicken on broadcast ads. For years, basketball legend Michael Jordan endorsed Hanes wear. In each example, the product had no relation to the sport with which the athlete was affiliated. Nonetheless, the companies believe these spokespersons help to sell their products.

DEMOGRAPHIC MATCH A company may choose a sports figure who matches the demographic profile of its customer base. To reach a target market of African Americans, a company may choose a successful African-American athlete who has peer recognition. For example, General Mills has a licensing agreement with NASCAR. Bill Lester, an African-American NASCAR driver, is featured on a package of Honey Nut Cheerios. To reach the customer base with an interest in female athletes, Multi-Grain Cheerios packages have featured five top Women's National Basketball Association (WNBA) players: Sheryl Swoopes of the Houston Comets, Lisa Leslie of the Los Angeles Sparks, Sue Bird of the Seattle Storm, Tamika Catchings of the Indiana Fever, and Chamique Holdsclaw of the Washington Mystics.

SUCCESSFUL CAREERS Top sport endorsers come from all sports, but they have one thing in common—they all have successful careers. Golfer Tiger Woods is a number one sports endorser because of his winning record and winning attitude. Some of the products that Tiger Woods endorses are Nike golf equipment and apparel, as well as Buick automobiles. Two other top product endorsers are soccer player Mia Hamm and professional tennis player Anna Kournikova.

In addition, players who look promising attract endorsement deals. One such player is LeBron James, a former high school basketball star from Akron, Ohio. Before he graduated from high school to set foot on a professional basketball court for the NBA's Cleveland Cavaliers in 2003, he was being asked to endorse products. James negotiated endorsement deals with Nike for $90 million, with Upper Deck trading cards for $6 million, and with Coca-Cola to endorse Sprite and Powerade. However, some athletes do not get compensated with millions of dollars but are given services or goods, such as cell phones.

Some sports celebrities are so outstanding that companies create product lines using a celebrity's name, such as Michael Jordan. Nike has a complete line of Air Jordan basketball shoes. In this case, Jordan's earnings from endorsements surpassed his earnings from playing basketball. Another top sports celebrity is Lance Armstrong, a professional cyclist who won the Tour de France multiple times. The Oakley sunglasses company designed the Lance Armstrong Signature Series. In both of these cases, the match between the products and successful athletes makes the endorsement deals effective.

IMAGE Endorsements sell products when the endorser has a positive image and is popular. In fact, image is a major factor when companies decide to renew contracts with their endorsers. Sports celebrities who endorse products of major companies must be role models in the public eye. For better or for worse, their personal lives are part of the image that they project for all the products they endorse. Most endorsement contracts have clauses, or statements, in them that will release the company from the contract if that celebrity's image is tainted due to problems with the law or his or her athletic performance. Even if a contract cannot be cancelled, it may not be renewed. A company will no longer use the celebrity because it does

Math Check

THE WEARING OF THE GREEN

Green Cleaners sponsors the local softball team. They purchase team uniforms and provide free environmentally safe uniform cleaning. In addition, any customer who brings in the most recent game program will receive $5 off any order of at least $50. What is the percentage of the promotional discount?

➡ For tips on finding the solution, go to marketingseries.glencoe.com.

ETHICAL PRACTICES

Team Spirit

Athletes can sometimes make a bigger impact off the field or court. While the players of the Women's National Basketball Association (WNBA) have been making their mark on basketball courts all over the country, they've especially affected their communities. The WNBA has raised money to educate women and raise awareness of breast cancer. It is also involved in Read to Achieve, a program that encourages families to read to their young children. The program collects over 200,000 books annually. Reading and Learning centers are open nationwide.

not want its products associated with a person who is not seen as a positive role model.

Sports figures must be very careful to monitor their public image. Bad publicity can mean the end of these profitable endorsement deals. It has happened to athletes with high-paying endorsements. Sports figures such as Mike Tyson, the boxer, and Ben Johnson, the former Olympic Gold medalist, lost present and future endorsement deals. Companies that contracted with them to endorse their products did not want to be associated with damaged public images. An athlete's image and private life are key factors when companies choose spokespersons for their products.

Sports Appeal

Sports and sporting events appeal to many different demographic groups. Companies associate their products with well-known sports organizations to reach new customers and strengthen their relationships with their existing customers. Through licensing, sponsorships, and endorsements, companies can generate positive publicity and achieve their marketing goals of increasing brand awareness and sales.

Quick Check ✓

RESPOND to what you've read by answering these questions.

1. Name two forms of licensing. _____

_____

_____

2. How do sponsorships benefit the sports organization and the sponsor? _____

_____

_____

_____

3. What do companies consider when selecting a sports celebrity for endorsement of a product?

_____

_____

_____

Worksheet 7.1

Differentiating Three Types of Brands

Visit a sporting-goods retail store or the sporting-goods section of a large store. Choose 15 products. Notice whether the products are manufacturer brands, intermediary brands, or generic brands. List each product under one of the categories—manufacturer brands, intermediary brands, or generic brands.

Manufacturer Brands	Intermediary Brands	Generic Brands
_____	_____	_____
_____	_____	_____
_____	_____	_____
_____	_____	_____
_____	_____	_____
_____	_____	_____
_____	_____	_____
_____	_____	_____
_____	_____	_____
_____	_____	_____
_____	_____	_____
_____	_____	_____

1. Which category of brand has the most products?

   _____

2. Why do you think this category of brand has the most products?

   _____

   _____

   _____

   _____

   _____

Worksheet 7.2

Corporate Sponsorships

Attend three different professional sports games or watch three sports games on television. Then answer these questions for each game:

- What types of sponsorships are present?
- Is a company sponsoring the entire game or only a portion of it, such as halftime events?
- Is a company buying signage at the stadium?
- Is a company's logo being used on equipment?

Record your observations, and then compare them with those of other students.

Game #1 _____

_____

_____

_____

_____

_____

_____

Game #2 _____

_____

_____

_____

_____

_____

_____

Game #3 _____

_____

_____

_____

_____

_____

_____

Portfolio Works

DEVELOPING BRAND EQUITY

You are the marketing director of a major soft-drink company. The company is about to launch a new sports drink. Explain the three steps involved in developing brand equity and how you will apply these steps to the new product.

Step 1:

_____

_____

_____

_____

_____

_____

_____

Step 2:

_____

_____

_____

_____

_____

_____

_____

Step 3:

_____

_____

_____

_____

_____

_____

_____

Add this page to your career portfolio.

CHAPTER SUMMARY

- Branding is important in developing an image and consumer loyalty for a product and/or a company. Recognizable brands help to differentiate products and companies from those of their competitors. Brand equity is the value a brand has beyond its functional benefits.

- There are three types of brands that help build customer loyalty—manufacturer, intermediary, and generic. Each uses different strategies to identify products.

- Developing an effective brand name helps create an image for a product. Development guidelines include: Offer a benefit; be simple; be different and positive; reflect an image; and be previously unregistered.

- Licensing generates income for sports organizations and events through licensed products, sponsorships, and endorsements.

- Sponsorships and endorsements offer companies access to their target markets through positive image-building relationships and promotions. They also generate needed income for operating expenses.

- Companies select sports celebrities for product endorsements by using criteria such as an athlete's demographic target market, success, and image.

CHECKING CONCEPTS

1. **Define** brand and brand name.
2. **Explain** the concept of branding and its components.
3. **Explain** how brand equity is developed.
4. **Differentiate** between the three basic types of brands.
5. **Define** co-branding.
6. **Explain** product licensing.
7. **Explain** why sponsorships and endorsements are important to sports organizations and sponsors.

Critical Thinking

8. **Discuss** the importance of an athlete's image to a company that is choosing an endorser.

CROSS-CURRICULUM SKILLS

Work-Based Learning

Basic Skills—Writing

9. Access the Web site for the Brand Names Education Foundation to learn about protection of brand names. Choose one sports-related topic and write a short report about your research.

Thinking Skills—Creative Thinking and
Basic Skills—Writing

10. Imagine you are the agent for a major sports figure. Your job is to arrange an endorsement that will benefit your client's professional goals. Write a letter to a potential sponsor.

School-Based Learning

Language Arts

11. Write a statement in an endorsement contract that explains the image your company expects from the endorser.

Arts

12. Use a computer or art supplies to create a name and logo for a sports product of your choice. Post your flyer in class.

 CONNECTION

Role Play: Marketing Director

SITUATION You are to assume the role of assistant marketing director for a beverage company. Your company created a new beverage targeted to young athletes—a noncarbonated fruit sports drink that is vitamin and calcium fortified. The company has used sporting events for promoting its other products and is seeking similar opportunities for the new product.

ACTIVITY Present to your boss, the marketing director (judge), a rollout plan for marketing the new beverage.

EVALUATION You will be evaluated on how well you meet the following performance indicators:

- Explain the use of branding in sports marketing.
- Explain the nature of a promotional plan.
- Explain the types of promotion.
- Develop promotional plan for a business.
- Determine sponsorship opportunities.

 INTERNET ACTIVITY

As a class, make a list of professional or college sports franchises, such as the NFL or the NCAA. Choose an organization and use the Internet to access its Web site and find its merchandising section.

- Make a list of all the products and brand names that are part of the company.
- Next to each product or brand, write a short description of the product.
- Post your research in class.

➡ For a link to these companies to begin this exercise, go to **marketingseries.glencoe.com**.

Chapter 8

Sports Promotion

Chapter Objectives

- Define event marketing.
- Explain promotion and the promotional mix in sports marketing.
- Identify the roles of advertising and sales promotion in sports marketing.
- Describe the use of technology in promotion.
- Identify the roles of public relations and personal selling in sports marketing.
- Explain the types and steps of selling.

CALLING ONLINE ATHLETES

Many professional athletes, from world-class soccer players to big-league baseball players, begin their careers playing in local games and contests. The services provided by Active.com can help both pro and amateur athletes compete.

In 1998, Active.com was launched to help runners, cyclists, swimmers, and other athletes find and enter races advertised across the United States. Before Active.com existed, participants would find out about events through flyers, local publications, and word of mouth. Enrollment in events involved sending a check in the mail or going to a community center weeks in advance. Many athletes would arrive at dawn to register for a race, only to find out it was filled to capacity. However, for a small surcharge, Active.com allowed computer users to sign up online for events. The company also provided a calendar of events and training tips. Active.com was an instant hit in the sports community, becoming the industry's number one online registrar for participatory sports. Then in 2000, many dot-com businesses began to fail. How did Active.com survive?

ANALYZE AND WRITE

1. Why would athletes pay to register online?
2. Why would athletes be a good market for an online service?

Case Study Part 2 on page 173

POWER READ

Be an active reader and use these reading strategies:

PREDICT what the section will be about.

CONNECT what you read with your life.

QUESTION as you read to make sure you understand the content.

RESPOND to what you've read.

Planning the Promotion

AS YOU READ ...

YOU WILL LEARN

- To define event marketing.
- To explain promotion and the promotional mix in sports marketing.

WHY IT'S IMPORTANT

Developing an effective promotional mix and corresponding budget requires an understanding of event marketing and types of promotions.

KEY TERMS

- event marketing
- promotional mix

event marketing all activities associated with the sale, distribution, and promotion of a sports event

PREDICT

What do you think event marketing means?

Event Marketing

Events can be associated with a sanctioned sports league or a one-time promotional event. When the Yankees play the Red Sox at Yankee Stadium, the event is part of a sanctioned league, the National League. The Skins Golf Game is a one-time promotion, generally presented during the off-season in golf. The Olympics and Special Olympics are one-time promotions, as is the Super Bowl. **Event marketing** is all activities associated with the sale, distribution, and promotion of a sports event.

Managing Organizations

Sanctioned league events are presented by sports franchises. These franchises have administrative support and marketing departments that promote the sports events. Revenue is generated through broadcast-media contracts, ticket and stadium sales, licensing agreements, and sponsorships. The particular league determines the rules and schedules for the competitions. Usually, a commissioner heads a league and is the person who makes the final decisions regarding disputes and rulings. Licensing, sponsorships, and special promotions are governed by league policies.

Internationally, various organizations govern worldwide sports competitions. For example, FIFA is the Fédération Internationale de Football Association. The FIFA Congress is the legislative branch of that organization and provides guidelines for soccer, or "football," which is the name of the sport in many countries. Its six confederations and national associations have similar structures so competitions are consistent at the local level. Each governing body at the global, national, and local levels runs competitions to comply with FIFA statutes.

One-time promotions are usually organized by a committee that is responsible for the sporting event. For example, the Olympic Committee is responsible for planning the winter and summer Olympic Games. Several years in advance of the event, the committee selects a site and begins site planning. Planning includes getting the selected city ready for the actual competitive events, as well as for the hospitality, or hotel, needs of the athletes and patrons. The committee also sells sponsorships to financially support the event.

Promotion in Sports Marketing

Promotion for sports is like promotion for any product. Its functions are to generate sales, attract a targeted audience, and help create a positive image. All sports events are business ventures and, therefore, must produce revenue to cover expenses. Promotion of the event by the league or event committee helps to create interest and ticket sales, as well as draw an audience of radio listeners and television viewers. When more people come to the games and listen and watch the games, more revenue can be generated by the league or event. Advertising rates and sponsorships for these venues are based on the size of the audience. Thus, winning teams and popular events that attract a large number of people can charge more for sponsorships and licensing agreements. For example, the Super Bowl charges approximately $2.25 million for a 30-second television spot. Why? Because the number of viewers is extraordinary.

Each sporting event targets fans of the sport and potential customers of the products being promoted by the sponsors. Fans should be viewed as a company's clientele. All marketing efforts need to attract those fans to the stadium or their television sets. Loyal fans, like loyal customers, are needed for repeat ticket sales and regular viewing.

The images that sports events, organizations, leagues, teams, and players project are a direct result of marketing efforts. Sponsors rely on positive images to promote their products. Association with these positive images helps to build the company's name and product brands in the minds of fans and the general public. For example, Wheaties brand cereal and the American College of Sports Medicine became partners in order to promote health and physical fitness. Fitness information is printed on Wheaties boxes and featured on the Wheaties Web site. This marketing partnership helps the Wheaties brand promote its image as the "The Breakfast of Champions."

Promotional Mix

Companies involved in sports marketing of products must decide what types of promotion will best suit their needs. The different forms of promotion can be combined into a company's promotional mix. The **promotional mix** is any combination of advertising, sales promotion, publicity, and personal selling.

For example, Russell Athletic ran a promotion with the theme, "Are you Russell Athletic material?" To reach their 12- to 25-year-old target market, Russell Athletic decided to use print, broadcast, stadium signage, online advertising, and sales promotions. Russell ran print ads in *Sports Illustrated* and *Men's Fitness,* and ran television commercials on ABC, ESPN, and ESPN2 television networks. One television commercial used a football player, and another one used a baseball player, both of whom were working out in Russell apparel in the commercials. To connect with college basketball, Russell purchased signage in post-season games held at the National Invitational Tournament (NIT) sites. Online ads were also purchased on espn.com, Yahoo! Sports, and si.com (*Sports Illustrated*).

Each company must decide on its own promotional mix. It must decide which combination of media will provide the best return for the money spent on promotion for the particular product.

THE Electronic CHANNEL

Turn on the Web

Where can you watch live baseball, highlights, and replays at any time? On TV? On video? It's available online through MLB.TV—that's *dot-TV,* not dot-com. Viewer fees make this sports outlet a profitable business. In fact, Web business contributes to a growing portion of sports revenue—an estimated 15 percent in 2004. The Internet has been friendly to sports, as cyber giants such as Yahoo! and AOL offer sports online. Auto racing and golf are also using the medium. However, football dealmakers are reluctant to embrace Webcasts if television revenue is lost in the deal.

➡️ Find out and list monthly rates for MLB.TV through **marketingseries.glencoe.com.**

promotional mix any combination of advertising, sales promotion, publicity, direct marketing, and personal selling

CONNECT

When you see a favorite athlete on a product label, do you remember the brand?

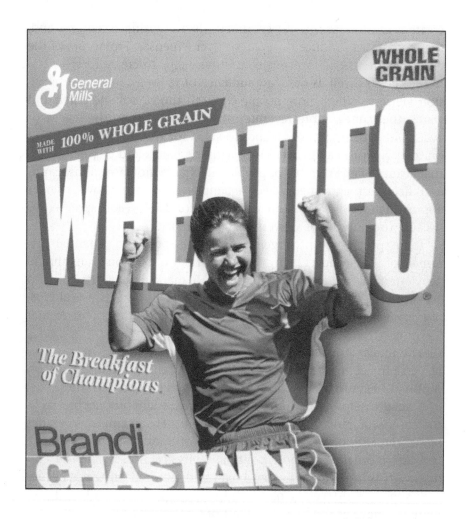

Game Point

AD BUDGETS

A 2004 Super Bowl ad cost $2.25 million for a 30-second spot on a show that airs once. But weekly *Monday Night Football* ads run $272,900 each for 30 seconds.

QUESTION

What is the disadvantage of using the percentage-of-sales method to create a promotion budget?

Promotional Budget

The promotional budget can be a determining factor in deciding the promotional mix. There are three ways to determine a promotional budget:

- Percentage of sales

- Competitive parity

- Objective-and-task method

Percentage of Sales

Sports organizations may use a set percentage, or portion, of last year's sales or the coming year's sales to decide on the funds for the promotional budget. The problem with the *percentage-of-sales method* to form a budget is its direct connection with sales. If sales were low the previous year, then the new promotional budget may not be enough to do all the promotions a company may need to do to stay competitive in the coming year. The total funds still need to be calculated for the other elements of the company's promotional mix. The benefit of this method is that it is easy to calculate.

Competitive Parity

When using *competitive parity,* a company looks for industry trends on how much to spend. *Parity* means having equality or similarity. A company studies its competitors' promotions to see if it needs to spend the same amount of money to be competitive. The problem with this method of forming a budget is that each company's objectives may not be same. Copying a competitor's spending pattern may not be realistic if it is based on the other company's promotional budget or objectives.

Objective-and-Task Method

When using the *objective-and-task method,* companies set objectives for their promotion and decide what promotional activities are necessary to reach those objectives. The budget lists all the elements of the company's promotional mix with their corresponding costs. The objective-and-task method actually takes the other methods into consideration. Deciding on the objectives of the promotion takes into account what competitors are doing. It is possible that the total cost for the promotion may be more than the company can afford in relation to its sales. In that case, the objectives would be reviewed to make the plan more realistic and in line with what the company can afford to spend.

Math Check

PROMOTING PROFITS

If Mario's Collector Cards store made $80,000 in sales last year and 5 percent of that will be spent on promotions next year, what will be the promotional budget?

➡For tips on finding the solution, go to marketingseries.glencoe.com.

Quick Check

RESPOND to what you've read by answering these questions.

1. What are the three functions of promotion in sports marketing?_____

_____

_____

_____

2. Explain the promotional mix._____

_____

_____

_____

_____

_____

3. List the three ways to determine a promotional budget._____

_____

_____

_____

Advertising and Sales Promotion

AS YOU READ ...

YOU WILL LEARN

- To identify the roles of advertising and sales promotion in sports marketing.
- To describe the use of technology in promotion.

WHY IT'S IMPORTANT

Advertising and sales promotion provide opportunities for sports events to be communicated to fans and potential customers of sponsored products.

KEY TERMS

- advertising
- promotional advertising
- institutional advertising
- sales promotion

advertising any paid promotion of an idea, good, or service by an identified sponsor

promotional advertising advertising with a goal of selling an item being promoted

institutional advertising advertising with a goal of developing goodwill or a positive image

PREDICT

Name some different kinds of media used by advertisers.

The Role of Advertising

Advertising is one of the four elements of the promotional mix. When companies are deciding on what promotion method will be most effective in reaching a target market, advertising offers many possibilities. Since a company pays for advertising, it has control over the message it wants to deliver. With a variety of media options, there is flexibility in delivering the message.

Advertising Defined

Advertising is any paid promotion of an idea, good, or service by an identified sponsor. Let's look at this definition in more detail. An idea that might be advertised is the concept of getting physically fit. A good is a tangible product, such as a baseball cap. Tickets to sporting events are considered services. Companies must pay for advertising these things. Unpaid promotion is considered free publicity. Advertising rates usually depend on the circulation, or size of the audience, that will be exposed to the ad. The identified sponsor is the advertiser who pays for the ad. There are two types of advertising—promotional and institutional.

Promotional advertising is advertising with a goal of selling the item being promoted. For example, EA Sports advertises its games to make sales. Almost all advertising is promotional advertising because it attempts to make a current sale or set the groundwork for a future sale.

Institutional advertising is advertising with a goal of developing goodwill or a positive image. You may see a newspaper ad by the Yankee franchise at the end of a season that simply thanks fans for their support during the baseball season. This type of advertising is used to generate goodwill. Sports figures are often featured in institutional advertising that advocates certain behavior. For example, Derek Jeter's television commercial advocates not using drugs. The very popular "Got Milk?" ads have used sports celebrities such as Mia Hamm (soccer player) and Kristi Yamaguchi (figure skater). These institutional ads promote milk, but no specific brand or company. Institutional ads are also used to simply remind consumers about a company or industry and to build public confidence.

Types of Media

Advertising media may be grouped according to print, broadcast, direct marketing, and online advertising. Each medium offers specific advantages and disadvantages to advertisers.

GOODWILL HUMOR
Institutional advertising campaigns such as the "Got Milk?" print ads and television commercials keep the consumer aware of the milk industry and generate a positive response through humor. *Do these types of ads include any brand names?*

PRINT Print media consist of many different forms of communication: newspapers, magazines, direct mail, outdoor advertising, station posters, and stadium signage.

- **Newspapers** are generally a local medium, which allows an advertiser to target customers in its home town. Newspapers are geographically selective and inexpensive. Local sports teams and events find newspapers to be very effective in reaching their fans and audiences.

- **Magazines** are more regional as well as national in scope. Therefore, manufacturers advertise in magazines because of the large number of subscribers that they reach who are potential customers. The ability to select a specific audience is a major benefit of magazine advertising. Various Web sites that list magazine subscriptions include the wide variety of sports-related magazines in print. *ESPN The Magazine* and *Sports Illustrated* are two general sports magazines. Other magazines may be specific to a sport. To reach soccer fans, there are several soccer magazines from which to choose. The same is true for bowling, motor sports, fishing, football, golf, hockey, baseball, skateboarding, skiing, and tennis magazines.

- **Direct mail** offers the benefit of a personalized message for the recipient. By using technological tools such as databases, qualified customers can be selected to receive direct-mail pieces. For example,

Sports Via Satellite Radio

Radio is certainly a familiar medium for sports broadcasts. Unlike traditional radio, tuning in to satellite radio requires a paid monthly subscription and special receivers. Two companies that offer satellite-radio service claim that the sound quality is clearer than FM radio signals. Instead of the limited broadcast distance of traditional radio, satellite-radio stations are available nationwide. A satellite-radio receiver is also available for use with a desktop computer.

➡ Describe the typical satellite-radio subscriber after reading information through **marketingseries.glencoe.com**.

CONNECT

Which form of advertising do you think is most effective for sports—print, broadcast, direct marketing, or online advertising? Why?

if you have ever bought season tickets at a particular sports arena or stadium, you may be on a mailing list and receive notices and advertisements from that venue. An up-to-date and categorized mailing list gives advertisers the ability to reach a select group of potential customers who meet their target-market qualifications. The biggest disadvantage of direct mail is that consumers may consider it to be "junk mail." Recipients may not read the direct-mail piece because they throw it away before opening it.

▪ **Outdoor advertising** consists of billboards found on roadways. The major benefit is that it offers the ability to geographically select your audience. For example, in an area where most residents are Hispanic, the billboard can be written in Spanish and designed with Hispanic models wearing athletic shoes for sale. The disadvantage of outdoor advertising is that the message must be short because motorists may be driving past it. Most outdoor advertising acts as a reminder that helps to build brand recognition and may give a specific location (e.g., "Take Exit 32A").

▪ **Station posters** are signs found at public transportation stations, such as airline and railroad terminals. You might see ads for sports drinks targeting thirsty travelers. The benefits of station posters are similar to those of outdoor advertising.

▪ **Stadium signage** includes signs found inside stadiums and sports arenas. With today's technology, these signs can be electronically designed and viewed during television broadcasts. The major benefit of stadium signage is that the sign will be seen frequently by viewers of the sporting event, both in the stadium and on television. The more exposure that the sign gets, the higher the price is for advertising. Some of the stadium signage is granted to corporate sponsors through contracts and licensing agreements.

BROADCAST Radio and television are broadcast media used for advertising. Radio is a medium that allows advertisers to reach a segmented audience based on the radio station or network and the geographic area. Other benefits of radio include its relatively low cost and ability to communicate in many settings, such as in a car or at the beach. The major disadvantage is that radio does not broadcast a visual image. An ad for an exercise bicycle may not be as effective on the radio as it would be on television, where the bike could be demonstrated.

Television advertising is similar to having a salesperson in your home. The major advantage is its sight, sound, and motion, which create dynamic communication. No other medium can do that. Advertisers can also target an audience by selecting a specific TV program. A special form of advertising on television is the *infomercial*. Infomercials are usually 30 minutes in running time and teach viewers how to use a particular product. The educational and entertaining nature of an infomercial helps to sell products.

The major disadvantage of television is the price of advertising. The airtime for most prime-time, 30-second commercials costs about $200,000. However, the cost of running a commercial can be as high as

$600,000 for a 30-second commercial. Other additional costs include the costs of producing the commercial, which increase the total cost of advertising on television.

DIRECT MARKETING Direct marketing uses various media to communicate directly with consumers to make a sale. An advertisement might encourage placing an order or requesting additional information—or it might provide information about where to purchase an advertised item. Various media can be used, such as mail, telephone, or computer. With all these media, a database of people to contact is required. The advertiser can customize a message for the person being contacted. Direct mail may come in the form of letters, flyers, or postcards to potential customers listed in a database. Telemarketing uses telephone solicitation. Federal regulations and a "Do Not Call Registry" program limit this type of marketing. Advertisers also use e-mail to reach online customers who are listed in a computer database.

ONLINE ADVERTISING Online advertising has become another popular medium for advertising. Businesses can purchase banner ads on Web sites, such as espn.com, and may even send special advertising messages directly to consumers through personal e-mail addresses. Many businesses have their own Web sites that they use to promote their products. Some businesses use their Web sites to sell products directly to customers, while others use the Internet to post information, such as where a product can be purchased. Another way businesses get exposure on the Internet is to pay for a listing on portal sites, such as Yahoo!. Special sales promotions function through the Internet as well.

One of the advantages of online advertising is that the number of *hits*, or visits to a Web site, can be counted. The disadvantage of online advertising is that not all members of a target market can be reached through this medium because they may not all use computers.

Case Study — PART 2

CALLING ONLINE ATHLETES
Continued from Part 1 on page 165

With many dot-com businesses failing by the year 2000, Active.com faced new challenges to survive. So, the company refocused its strategies. Active.com CEO Dave Alberga explains that only one-third of the company's business is conducted online. The company was renamed the Active Networks. It now provides software to city recreation and parks departments, helping them to schedule leagues and keep track of participants. Customers include the cities of Austin, Texas, Washington, D.C., and Oakland, California.

Because the Web site is an effective channel for reaching participatory sports athletes, it is also used as a marketing device. Shoe companies, energy bars, and health gurus are only some of the potential customers who pay to take advantage of the site's reach. The site has also started a membership program, in which users can save money on items such as equipment, airfare, and rental cars.

ANALYZE AND WRITE
1. Why would Active.com expand into non-Internet-related business? Explain.
2. Describe the Active.com community of users. What types of businesses would be interested in reaching that market?

Sales Promotion

Sales promotion is a short-term incentive to get consumers interested in buying a product. Sales promotions are usually part of an advertisement or personal sales pitch. There are a variety of different forms of sales promotions. The ones that target consumers include coupons, rebates, samples, premiums, contests, and sweepstakes. The purpose of these sales promotions is to get consumers excited and

sales promotion a short-term incentive to get consumers interested in buying a product

Beyond Bobbleheads

When Dave Coskey, the vice president of the Philadelphia 76ers, first read about Celebriducks, he had a gut feeling they would be huge. Who wouldn't love a rubber duck that looks like a celebrity? For a special promotion, Coskey asked Celebriducks owner Craig Wolfe to manufacture 5,500 rubber ducks in the exact likeness of 76ers star Allen Iverson. Wolfe worked with his daughter Rebecca to recreate Iverson's likeness. The result was a smash hit with fans, and a giveaway craze was born.

HUMBLE BEGINNINGS

Before the ducks caught on with sports fans, Wolfe made a living selling artwork created from animation cels. Then a friend suggested making specialty rubber duckies as a side business. So Wolfe began Celebriducks in 1998 with ducks that looked like cartoon and film icons, such as Betty Boop and Groucho Marx. The success of the Iverson duck then kicked off a new era for the company, marked by increased demand and a focus on sports figures. According to AdAge.com, Celebriducks grew from making 20,000 ducks per year to one million ducks per year after the 76ers promotion in 2002. Wolfe soon signed a deal to make the Celebriduck the official rubber duck of the NBA, and supplied thousands of customized ducks for team giveaways. He then started creating ducks for Major League Baseball, the NHL, and NASCAR.

Despite their recent growth, Celebriducks has an uphill battle to reach the long-term success of other collectible items such as the bobblehead dolls. To achieve this goal, Wolfe has worked to increase demand and product value by limiting production, creating special editions, and distributing selectively. Only time will tell if Celebriducks will last, but for now you can see your favorite sports stars in a bathtub near you.

1. How did Celebriducks grow its business?
2. Do you think the Celebriducks marketing strategy will help the company succeed?

interested enough to become customers and buy a product. Promotional events at sports arenas and ballparks include special events, giveaway items, such as merchandise or food and beverages, contests, reduced ticket prices, and other incentives. **Figure 8.1** lists some successful baseball promotions. Sales promotions that target businesses as customers have the same purpose but may take a different form. Business-to-business promotions often involve sampling products, price incentives, free shipping, and/or free merchandise.

Coupons and Rebates

Coupons and *rebates* offer some type of price reduction or free merchandise. The most significant difference between coupons and rebates is that coupons are usually redeemed at a retail store. Rebates must be sent to the manufacturer for redemption and reimbursement.

One of the benefits of coupons and rebates is the flexibility of use. They can be part of a newspaper or magazine ad, or can be downloaded from a company's Web site. They can be part of or in a product package. Coupons may be distributed in person by store personnel or through direct mail. The advantage of coupons and rebates for a company is that they have an expiration date. The disadvantage is that they are easily copied by competitors. Coupons are

MARKETING SERIES *Online*

Remember to check out this book's Web site for information on sports promotion and more great resources at **marketingseries.glencoe.com**.

Figure 8.1

Major League Baseball Giveaways

Rank	Promotion	Percent Increase in Game Attendance
1	Beanie baby	37.4
2	Beach towel	26.4
3	Umbrella	20.1
4	Coupon	20.0
5	Baseball cap	19.9
6	Fireworks show	19.1
7	Hat (not baseball cap)	17.3
8	Bat	15.0
9	Heritage/Family Days	14.9
10	Beanbag toy	14.4

SOURCE: *Street and Smith's Sports Business Journal 1, no. 25*

EFFECTIVE PROMOTIONS
These popular promotional items have helped to increase attendance at Major League Baseball games. *Do you think these items would be as effective if offered at any sporting event? Why?*

offered for sports products such as equipment and clothing, as well as for sporting events.

Samples and Premiums

A sampling campaign is a fairly common way to promote new products. In a sampling campaign, *samples* of a new product are given away to potential customers. Samples can be distributed with a local newspaper, through the mail, or in person. At sporting events, companies can set up booths for a new product giveaway. In-store demonstrations are also part of the sampling process. Many times, coupons are distributed along with a sample to encourage future purchases.

Premiums are items that are given away free with the purchase of merchandise. For example, Wheaties ran a promotion that included a pack of two 12-ounce Wheaties cereal boxes and a free DVD of the *Greatest NBA Finals Moments* with purchase of the regular cereal. Some other examples might be baseball trading cards included in a box of cereal or gum and free baseball-celebrity bobbleheads given away with the purchase of a McDonald's Happy Meal.

Contests and Sweepstakes

The difference between contests and sweepstakes as sales promotions is that you must perform a task in a contest to win a prize. Sweepstakes participants need only to sign up to be included in the competition.

What is the difference between a contest and a sweepstakes?

Since most contests and sweepstakes are part of an advertising campaign or sponsorship deal, they are presented by a variety of media.

Many contests and sweepstakes take place directly on the Internet through company or sports team Web sites. For example, some notable sweepstakes and contests are associated with the Super Bowl each year. The prize for these winners is free tickets to the Super Bowl. If you go to the Nabisco World Web site and select "sweepstakes" from the menu, you will find several contests and sweepstakes. A recent contest was called "Newton's Ironman Contest," which required a participant to write about someone in his or her life who has "strength, endurance, and passion." The prize was a trip to the 2004 Ironman Triathlon World Championship in Hawaii. The New York Yankees Web site has offered the Continental Airlines' sweepstake, which involved voting for the Yankee ballplayer of the year. Once a vote was cast, the fan was automatically entered to win a trip to a Yankees away-game for two, which included airfare, hotel, and tickets to the game.

Coordination of Sales Promotions

For sales promotions to be effective, they must be coordinated with the other media used in the ad campaign, as well as with the retail businesses involved. For example, an ad campaign might be run on a local radio station advertising a sweepstakes that requires people to visit a certain retail store. The employees of the retail store must be aware of the promotion and have the necessary entry forms for customers who want to enter the sweepstakes. Companies can use other advertising media to support the sweepstakes. For example, the sweepstakes might be advertised in newspapers, magazines, and billboards, or on Internet Web sites. Companies must decide on the amount of media coverage, based on cost and potential return on money invested in the campaign.

Advertising and Promotion Advantage

Companies, teams, and individual athletes have the ability to target their markets and fans with the great variety of media and promotional tools available to sports marketers today.

Quick Check

RESPOND to what you've read by answering these questions.

1. What is the difference between promotional and institutional advertising? _____

_____

2. What are the major types of advertising media? _____

_____

3. List the different forms of sales promotions. _____

_____

Public Relations and Personal Selling

Public Relations

Public relations are activities that promote the image and communications a company has with its employees, customers, investors, and the public at large. **Publicity** is the free mention of a product or company in the media. Publicity differs from advertising because a company does not pay for the exposure it gets in the media. The benefit of free publicity is how the public may view what they see and hear in the media. Since the information is similar to news, it must be objective and believable. The disadvantage of publicity is a company's lack of control over it. Not all news may be positive about a company. Bad publicity gives a company a bad image that must be handled by the company's public relations department. Positive publicity is created by companies and sent to the media in hopes that the media will publish or air it. There are never any guarantees that material sent to the media will be selected or used in its entirety.

The Role of Media in Public Relations

Magazines, newspapers, television, and radio provide outlets for public relations to function. Anything that is newsworthy may be picked up by the media. Sports leagues, franchises, and celebrities, as well as all other businesses and organizations, rely on the media to get the news out. However, it is up to the media to decide on what news will be used on a given day. For example, if something extraordinary occurs, such as an airplane crash, the media will give coverage to that event as top priority over other news originally scheduled for release on that day.

Press Kits and Press Releases

To alert the media in hopes of getting media coverage, companies, teams, and individuals prepare press kits and press releases. A *press kit* consists of promotional materials that can be used by the media, such as fact sheets, background information, press releases, and videotapes. A **press release** is a newsworthy article that provides basic information to answer questions about a subject, such as who, what, where, when, and why. For example, when baseball players are traded, a press release is sent to the media from the baseball franchise. You may see this information in a newspaper article and on the evening news. When companies do something they think should have news coverage, they send out a press release. For example, McDonald's sent a press release describing its plans to put together a team of McDonald's employees to serve the athletes and spectators at the 2004 Olympic

AS YOU READ ...

YOU WILL LEARN

- To identify the roles of public relations and personal selling in sports marketing.
- To explain the types and steps of selling.

WHY IT'S IMPORTANT

Public relations promote and communicate information to the public. Personal selling is an essential part of the promotional mix because it involves two-way communication.

KEY TERMS

- public relations
- publicity
- press release
- personal selling

PREDICT

Does personal selling apply to goods *and* services?

public relations activities that promote the image and communications a company has with its employees, customers, investors, and public

publicity the free mention of a product or company in the media

press release a newsworthy article that provides the basic information to answer questions such as who, what, where, when, and why

Games in Athens, Greece. The press release explained the McDonald's involvement in the Olympic Games and the criteria that it used for choosing the outstanding employees.

Personal Selling

Personal selling is direct communication by a salesperson to potential customers either in person or by telephone. For inexpensive goods, personal selling may not be needed because advertising and other forms of promotion may have already sold customers on the product. For expensive items, face-to-face contact may be needed to educate a consumer about the features and benefits of a product, such as an exercise machine, ski equipment, or event. Personal selling is important as part of the promotional mix because it allows for two-way communication between the buyer and seller.

Types of Selling

There are two types of selling—order taking and order getting. Order taking does not involve much sales ability because consumers generally know what they want and simply ask for it. A salesperson who works in the souvenir shop at a sporting event would be an order taker. An order getter would be a professional salesperson who knows how to follow the steps of a sale, and then follows up after a sale has been completed. A sports agent would be an order getter. Sports agents must have sales and negotiating skills to convince a company to use a sports celebrity for promotion of a product or firm. Think about all the communication that is essential to finalize sponsorship deals and work out the details included in those licensing contracts. Selling advertising space in sports arenas or sports magazines would be order-getting sales also. In both cases, the salesperson must be knowledgeable about the features and benefits of the advertising medium and the audience that he or she would be reaching.

Steps in the Selling Process

Professional selling consists of seven steps: approach, determine needs, present the product, overcome objections, close the sale, perform suggestion selling, and follow up. But before the sale process begins, a salesperson can prepare with prospecting and preapproach strategies.

PROSPECTING Prospecting involves looking for potential customers, or *leads*. Leads can be generated by the salesperson's company or the salesperson. Trade shows generate leads from buyers stopping at the booth and leaving business cards. Advertising can generate leads by asking viewers to write or call for more information.

PREAPPROACH Learning about the products and the potential customers is the basis of the preapproach. For example, sports agents put together sales presentations that highlight the features and benefits of the sports celebrities they represent. Features are attributes of the athlete, such as his or her winning records and winning personality. Benefits are how those attributes will help sell the sponsor's product. For a physical product, such as a pair of Nike athletic shoes, the

personal selling direct communication by a salesperson to potential customers either in person or by telephone

CONNECT

Would you use the same selling skills to sell an athletic shoe as you would use to sell airtime to a television sponsor?

World Market

The High Road to Golf

Some 2,000 years ago, it is possible that an early Roman golfer shouted the Latin word that meant "Fore!" before hitting a leather ball with a bent stick. However, the origins of golf are actually unclear. Many historians believe that the game as we know it began in 15th-century Scotland where the seaside ground provided its own unique *hazards*, which inspired modern-day hazards such as sand traps, earth mounds, and water.

The former Scottish fishing port overlooking the North Sea—St. Andrews—promotes itself as "the home of golf." Each year thousands of golfers from all over the world make the pilgrimage to this 600-year-old historic landmark. The once makeshift course of St. Andrews that grew from heather and grass has evolved into six manicured golf courses. Golfers can still play the Old Course, but today they can make the rounds in trolleys, practice their swings at night on a floodlit driving range, and videotape their entire experience for posterity.

Imagine you live in Scotland during the 15th century. Write a brief press release announcing a "new" golf course of the day.

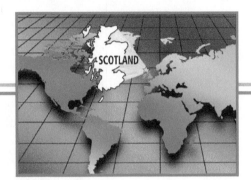

features are the materials that go into making the shoes, the shoes' unique patented design, color, available sizes, and price. The benefits include how those attributes help the customer. For example, the cushioned sole (feature) may make the shoe more comfortable (benefit).

Studying a potential customer requires research and sometimes a telephone call or e-mail. The telephone call may be used to *qualify* the lead, or see if the lead is really a potential customer. If the lead is qualified as a potential customer, then the next step would be to ask for an appointment. **Figure 8.2** on page 180 illustrates the formal steps of personal selling.

STEP 1: APPROACH The approach is the first face-to-face meeting with the potential customer. Its goal is to establish a relationship with the customer. In business-to-business sales situations, a firm handshake and greeting are expected. The initial conversation may be friendly and based on a prior telephone conversation during the preapproach, or it may center directly on the purpose of the visit or the product.

In order-taking situations, such as in a sporting-goods store or concessions stand, the salesperson might ask a question such as "May I help you?" Since customers may already know what they want in this type of situation, this service approach works well. In other sales situations, that approach is not recommended because customers often respond negatively and say they are just looking. In that case, the salesperson does not accomplish the goal of this step in the sales process.

STEP 2: DETERMINE NEEDS Determining needs involves looking, listening, and asking questions. You should attempt to determine needs as early as possible and keep determining needs throughout the

Figure 8.2

Steps of Selling

Using the step-by-step approach to selling is a proven method for making sales that can be applied to selling all sports goods and services. *Is the sale complete when the customer agrees to buy the product? Why?*

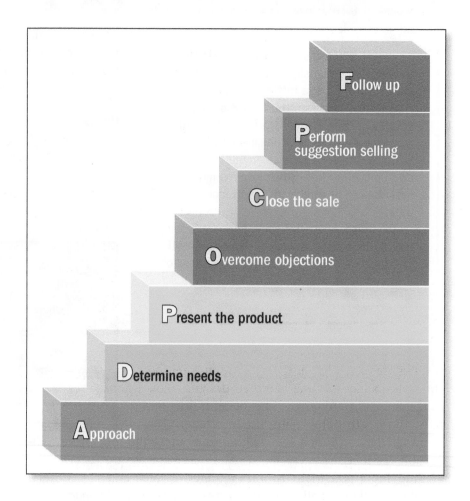

sales process. Look at the customer for nonverbal feedback when presenting the product's features and benefits. Learning to read customers' facial expressions can be helpful in determining what statements made were well received and which ones were not. It is best to do more listening than talking during the sales process. To be a good listener, you need to ask good questions. Some of the basic questions may have been answered during the preapproach. For example, you may know the customer's present need and past experience with the product. More specific questions about the particulars of the product are handled while presenting the product's features and benefits.

STEP 3: PRESENT THE PRODUCT The product presentation should be developed around the customer's needs and wants. The most important feature and benefit of the product should be presented first to create customer interest and desire. Here are a few suggestions to make the product presentation effective: 1) *Involve the customer.* Let the customer handle a physical product if possible. If selling a pair of Nike athletic shoes, let the customer try on the shoes. When selling a sports celebrity to a prospective sponsor, you might want to show a videotape of the athlete in action. 2) *Demonstrate the product.* Sports equipment, like a treadmill, certainly lends itself to demonstration. 3) *Use sales aids.* A videotape or newspaper or magazine article about the product or sports celebrity would be a sales aid. Other sales aids might include swatches of material, a model of the product, such as a shoe or ball cut in half to show the interior materials and construction, or anything else that might be necessary to make a selling point.

STEP 4: OVERCOME OBJECTIONS Overcoming objections involves answering questions or eliminating doubts about a product. Objections provide necessary feedback and help keep communication flowing. In many instances, the objections become selling points

QUESTION

During step three of the selling process, what should be presented first to the customer?

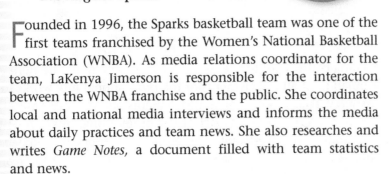

Profiles in Marketing

TAKING IT TO THE BOARDS

LaKenya Jimerson
Media Relations Coordinator
Los Angeles Sparks

Founded in 1996, the Sparks basketball team was one of the first teams franchised by the Women's National Basketball Association (WNBA). As media relations coordinator for the team, LaKenya Jimerson is responsible for the interaction between the WNBA franchise and the public. She coordinates local and national media interviews and informs the media about daily practices and team news. She also researches and writes *Game Notes*, a document filled with team statistics and news.

Experience Counts LaKenya stresses the importance of taking on internships early in your career. Though you may not earn a salary, you will strengthen your networking skills and make important contacts with people who may become your colleagues. "I had at least five internships," she says. "You may not always get what you expect out of an internship. But even if it doesn't fulfill your expectations, there's something to be learned from it—and it looks impressive on a résumé."

Valuable Skills LaKenya recommends strong reading and writing skills, as well as attention to detail. She notes that self-presentation is always noticed. "Conduct yourself with high standards and people will treat you with respect," she adds. "Always have an in-depth understanding of your company's business. Learn your weaknesses and do something to overcome them to be a good, all-around person."

How can internship experience benefit someone interested in public relations?

Career Data:
Promotions Manager

Education and Training Bachelor's or master's degree in communications, public relations, journalism, or sports management

Skills and Abilities Writing skills, networking skills, multitasking skills, and time-management skills

Career Outlook Faster than average growth through 2010

Career Path Internships are especially important in developing contacts that can lead to higher, permanent positions.

because the buyer may have misconceptions or misinformation that need to be corrected or clarified. For example, a customer might be reluctant to buy a treadmill because of lack of storage space. The salesperson could point out that the model folds up easily.

STEP 5: CLOSE THE SALE Closing the sale means getting a commitment from the customer to purchase the product. This step of the sale should occur naturally as the customer's excitement about the product may become obvious.

STEP 6: PERFORM SUGGESTION SELLING Suggestion selling is presenting ideas for additional merchandise sales. The suggested merchandise may be something related to the original purchase, such as batteries for the glow-in-the-dark baseball cap that the customer just purchased at the souvenir stand.

STEP 7: FOLLOW UP In professional selling, especially when a salesperson makes promises during the sales pitch, follow-up is essential. Even if no promises are made, it is good practice to keep in contact with customers by phone, e-mail, mail, or newsletters. A sale is the beginning of a relationship, not the end of one. Developing a relationship with the customer can lead to repeat sales in the future.

Power of the Promotional Mix

Selling contributes to the overall promotional mix. The right combination of all the elements of the promotional mix works to create synergy. That means that all the elements put together can be more powerful than one single aspect of the promotional mix. These marketing strategies—advertising, sales promotion, publicity, and personal selling—can help generate sales, attract more customers and fans, and promote a positive image for everyone involved in the sports business.

Quick Check ✓

RESPOND to what you've read by answering these questions.

1. What are the advantages and disadvantages of publicity? _____

_____

_____

2. Explain the role of media in public relations. _____

_____

_____

3. List and explain the steps in the selling process. _____

_____

_____

Name _____ Date _____

Worksheet 8.1

Promotion, Advertising, and Sales Promotion

Design a bulletin board that illustrates the information in this chapter about the promotional mix. Use a sports-related example for each element of the mix. Make a sketch of your bulletin board below. Share your sketch with your classmates.

Worksheet 8.2

Sports Time Line

1. Choose a sport such as basketball or a team such as the Boston Celtics:

   _____

2. Use the Internet or library for research to learn the history of the sport or team and major media or promotional events that have taken place. Write notes on a separate piece of paper.

3. Create a time line about the sport or team since its beginnings as a franchise.

Portfolio Works

PLANNING A PROMOTIONAL MIX

A minor league baseball team is coming to your community. You are applying for a job as marketing manager of the team. Prepare an outline that describes the promotional mix you plan to use to promote the new team, using the elements discussed in this chapter.

_____

_____

_____

_____

_____

_____

_____

_____

_____

_____

_____

_____

_____

_____

_____

_____

_____

_____

_____

_____

_____

_____

_____

Add this page to your career portfolio.

CHAPTER SUMMARY

Section **8.1** Planning the Promotion

event marketing (p. 166)
promotional mix (p. 167)

- Event marketing includes all activities associated with the sale, distribution, and promotion of a sports event. The activities can be associated with a sports league or be a one-time promotion.

- Promotion for sports products is similar to promotion for other products. Marketers develop an effective promotional mix of advertising, sales promotion, publicity, and personal selling, as well as a corresponding budget. The types of promotions will depend on the organization and particular product.

Section **8.2** Advertising and Sales Promotion

advertising (p. 170)
promotional advertising
   (p. 170)
institutional advertising
   (p. 170)
sales promotion (p. 173)

- Advertising and sales promotion provide opportunities for sports events to be communicated to fans and potential customers of sponsored products.

- Marketers use various technological tools in promotions, including databases for direct mail; electronic signs in stadiums and arenas and on TV; broadcast media; and the Internet for online advertising.

Section **8.3** Public Relations and Personal Selling

public relations (p. 177)
publicity (p. 177)
press release (p. 177)
personal selling (p. 178)

- Public relations techniques are useful for publicizing news about an organization or event. Personal selling is an essential part of the promotional mix because it involves two-way communication, unlike the other aspects of the mix.

- There are seven steps of selling: approach, determine needs, present the product, overcome objections, close the sale, perform suggestion selling, and follow up.

CHECKING CONCEPTS

1. **Define** event marketing.
2. **Identify** the elements in the promotional mix.
3. **Explain** a budget in sports marketing.
4. **Identify** the roles of advertising and sales promotions.
5. **Define** public relations and personal selling.
6. **Differentiate** between contests and sweepstakes.
7. **List** the steps of the selling process.

Critical Thinking

8. **Explain** the role that the various media play in public relations.

CROSS-CURRICULUM SKILLS

Work-Based Learning

Basic Skills—Writing

9. You are the marketing and advertising manager for a company that runs batting cages. A new batting-cage site is opening. Prepare a press kit that announces the opening.

Interpersonal Skills—Negotiating to Arrive at a Decision

10. Work with another student. One of you is a sports agent; the other is a sponsor. "Sell" your client, who is a famous or promising athlete, to the sponsor.

School-Based Learning

Arts

11. Create a colorful graphic organizer or chart of the different types of advertising and sales promotion.

History

12. Use the library or Internet to research the 1919 World Series for baseball. Give a short oral report on the role the media played in portraying one of the players.

Role Play: Promotions Manager

SITUATION You are to assume the role of promotions manager for the Pleasant Stay Seaside Bowl, a new addition to the college, postseason football bowls. Seaside is the name of the resort town hosting the event, and the town is also home to a major university. Pleasant Stay is a national chain of motels. The bowl celebration will include a carnival and the football game. This year neither team playing is from the state.

ACTIVITY Present a promotional plan for the Pleasant Stay Seaside Bowl to the tournament director (judge).

EVALUATION You will be evaluated on how well you meet the following performance indicators:

- Develop a promotional plan for a business.
- Explain the nature of a promotional plan.
- Coordinate activities in the promotional mix.
- Describe the concept of promotion in sports marketing.
- Explain the types of promotion.

INTERNET ACTIVITY

Use the Internet to access an online sports magazine such as *ESPN The Magazine* or *Sports Illustrated*.

- Read two or three articles on sports promotion or sponsorship.
- Choose one, and then write a summary of the article.
- Read the summary to your classmates.

➡️ For a link to *ESPN The Magazine* or *Sports Illustrated* to begin this exercise, go to **marketingseries.glencoe.com**.

Sports Marketing Plans and Careers

Chapter Objectives

- Explain the purpose and function of a marketing plan.
- Identify each element found in a marketing plan.
- Discuss the diversity of career and employment opportunities in sports marketing.
- Identify different career and employment opportunities in sports marketing.

NO SWEAT

Kevin Plank found a product to market to athletes of all types, from skiers to hockey players to football players—and made a career of it.

When University of Maryland special teams captain Plank played football for the Terrapins, he didn't like changing his T-shirt several times during each game. So after graduating in 1996, he designed something better—a skin-tight, high-tech microfiber T-shirt that would stay dry and light. He called the underwear Under Armour. The high-performance gear was picked up by the college football teams of Georgia Tech and Arizona State—and by the NFL's Atlanta Falcons.

By the next year, 12 NCAA Division I-A and ten NFL teams were buying Under Armour, and the gear made its first appearance at the Super Bowl. The year after that, the Baltimore-based business became the official provider to NFL Europe. Variations for hot weather, cold weather, and artificial turf followed. But how could Under Armour maintain an annual growth rate of 300 percent and compete against established brands such as Nike, Reebok, and Adidas?

ANALYZE AND WRITE

1. How did Plank launch his business?
2. How could Under Armour expand its business?

Case Study Part 2 on page 195

POWER READ

Be an active reader and use these reading strategies:

PREDICT what the section will be about.

CONNECT what you read with your life.

QUESTION as you read to make sure you understand the content.

RESPOND to what you've read.

The Marketing Plan

AS YOU READ ...

YOU WILL LEARN

- To explain the purpose and function of a marketing plan.
- To identify each element found in a marketing plan.

WHY IT'S IMPORTANT

A marketing plan provides a road-map for all marketing decisions made by a business and is an important factor in that business's success or failure.

KEY TERMS

- marketing plan
- executive summary
- situation analysis
- SWOT analysis
- marketing strategy
- implementation

marketing plan a written document that provides direction for the marketing activities of a company for a specific period of time

executive summary an overview of the entire marketing plan

Why Write a Marketing Plan?

A **marketing plan** is a written document that provides direction for the marketing activities of a company for a specific period of time. It communicates the goals, objectives, and strategies of a company to its employees. The specifics in the plan inform employees about their responsibilities and timelines for completion, as well as how other resources will be allocated, or given out. In addition, a marketing plan helps a company monitor its performance.

The type of business or organization will determine the complexity of the plan and the period of time covered by the plan. For example, a small sporting-goods retailer may develop a simple marketing plan for a year. However, a large manufacturer of sports equipment with global sales might prepare a marketing plan that covers five years. This longer time period allows for the time it takes to develop new products and the complexities of international marketing.

Some marketing plans are developed for use within a business, while others are prepared to obtain financing from outside investors for a new venture. If outside investors are the focus, the plan serves as a sales tool and must provide more comprehensive financial information.

Elements of a Marketing Plan

Marketing plans may differ from company to company, depending on type of business and products offered. However, there are six basic elements, or sections, found in most marketing plans:

- Executive summary
- Situation analysis
- Marketing goals/objectives
- Marketing strategies
- Implementation
- Evaluation and control

Executive Summary

An **executive summary** is an overview of the entire marketing plan. It briefly addresses each topic in the plan. It also provides an explanation of all the costs involved in implementing the plan.

PREDICT

Why would a sports team need a marketing plan?

The executive summary may also be used to provide information to people outside the organization, especially those who might be investing in the company or organization.

Situation Analysis

A **situation analysis** is a study of the internal and external factors that impact a marketing plan. Internal factors involve the company, its target markets, current performance, and financial resources. External environmental factors that influence the marketing plan include competitive, political, economic, regulatory, legal, technological, cultural, and industry trends. From a study of these factors, an organization will have the information it needs to conduct a SWOT analysis. See **Figure 9.1** for a diagram that organizes SWOT analysis.

A **SWOT analysis** is a study of four factors:

- **S**trengths

- **W**eaknesses

- **O**pportunities

- **T**hreats

Assets that a company possesses, such as talented and well-trained employees, quality workmanship, and an excellent service record, may be part of a company's *strengths*. *Weaknesses* can include anything that creates customer dissatisfaction, such as a poor service record, inexperienced workers, and poor-quality goods. Strengths and weaknesses are internal factors.

situation analysis a study of the internal and external factors that impact a marketing plan

SWOT analysis a study of strengths, weaknesses, opportunities, and threats

Figure 9.1

SWOT Analysis

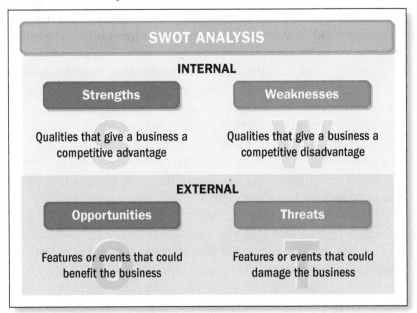

SWOT TEAM **The SWOT analysis helps a business and its employees to organize the factors that influence its success.** *As what factor would you categorize the successful marketing of a competitor's product?*

ETHICAL PRACTICES

Truth or Consequences

Playing by the rules matters in both professional and amateur sports. A young boy from the Dominican Republic came to the United States with a dream of playing baseball. His father presented a false birth certificate stating that his son was 12 years old and, therefore, eligible to play in the Little League. After the boy's team won third place in the 2001 World Series, a reporter discovered the boy's real age. At 14 years old, he was too old to qualify. All of his team's victories were forfeited, and all records they set were erased. As a result of this incident, Little League Baseball came up with new procedures and standards to determine player eligibility.

CONNECT

Does writing down a long-term plan help you accomplish your own goals?

Opportunities and threats are external factors. *Opportunities* are things that occur, which, if handled properly, could be rewarding to a company. For example, a major competitor may receive bad publicity because of defective products that require a recall. As a result, your company may have an opportunity to take sales away from that competitor. Another opportunity may be found in a trend, such as the trend to eat healthy food. Your company may be able to capitalize on, or take advantage of, that trend by developing a new healthy food product for athletes. *Threats* are problems that occur due to any environmental factor that negatively impacts the company. For example, a threat to a company may be the launch of a new product or advertising campaign by a competitor. In that case, a company may have to address that threat with its own new product or ad campaign. Taking this initiative could change that threat to an opportunity.

Objectives

Objectives let everyone know what needs to be accomplished by the marketing plan. These objectives are used to evaluate the marketing plan. To be useful, an objective must:

- Be simple.
- Be single-minded.
- Be specific.
- Be reasonable.
- Be measurable.
- Contain a time frame.

An objective must be *simple,* so that everyone who works on the aspects of the marketing plan finds it easy to understand what is expected.

Single-minded means that only one topic is addressed per objective. For example, you could not include "increasing sales" for regular season tickets and "increasing profits" in the same objective. Each topic would need to be a separate objective.

Specific means that the objective provides enough detail so there can be no misunderstanding. You cannot write that your objective is "to be better than a competitor," because what is "better" to one person may not mean the same thing to another person.

To say an objective is *reasonable* means that the company's objective is realistic and achievable. Setting unreasonable objectives includes setting goals and not including in the marketing plan the means to accomplish these goals.

Measurable means that the objective includes a way to evaluate it. An objective that says that you simply want to "increase sales" is not measurable. In order to make the objective measurable, you would need to identify the specific percent of increase in dollar or unit sales. For example, the objective could be "to increase unit sales of season tickets by 10 percent in six months."

Hot Property

Deportes En Español

Latino Sports Marketing

If you want to advertise to Latino Dodger fans or Spanish-speaking Chargers fans, Latino Sports Marketing LLC (LSM) hopes you'll call them. Founded in 2001 by marketing veteran Anthony Eros, LSM specializes in helping companies such as State Farm, Kraft/Oscar Meyer, and Universal Pictures market to Latino sports audiences.

LSM recognizes that companies of all sizes want to reach the large and diverse Latino market, but are not sure how to do it. LSM helps these firms plan and execute targeted, cost-efficient marketing campaigns designed to speak to Latinos. In addition, they provide training for Latino youths interested in entering the sports marketing field.

LEADERS IN THE MAKING

In partnership with Miller Brewer Company, LSM launched an internship program that gives Latino college students the opportunity to learn about sports marketing from the inside. Students get paid for their work at companies such as Fox Sports World, doing Hispanic outreach, public relations, and many other marketing-related activities. In a press release announcing the program's launch, Eros explained, "This isn't about playing sports or being an avid fan of a sport.... It is about pursuing a career in the sports marketing industry."

The LSM Web site contains a number of facts to explain why students would want to go after this career. For example, a study by Strategy Research Corporation states, "Hispanic males 18–34 [years old] are 59 percent more likely than the general market to frequently attend professional football games." With statistics like these, LSM should have many more companies looking for its help.

1. Why do companies hire Latino Sports Marketing, LLC?
2. How would you create a marketing plan for a specific group of sports fans?

Last, a good objective includes a *time frame*, such as, "We will accomplish our objective in six months" or "as compared to last year's sales at this time." With a time frame, you know when an objective is reached.

Marketing Strategies

A **marketing strategy** is a method that identifies target markets to make marketing-mix decisions that focus on those target markets. The ultimate goal of a marketing strategy is customer satisfaction. Therefore, all strategies need to take the customer's needs and wants into account, as well as the objectives of the marketing plan. As part of the marketing strategy, the marketing plan must possess a *point of difference* in comparison to its competitors. The point of difference could be in the quality of the products, such as golf clubs made of titanium, a superior distribution system, a more creative ad campaign that may have a top athlete endorser, or a more competitive pricing structure. This competitive advantage is what will make the company successful.

marketing strategy a method that identifies target markets to make marketing-mix decisions that focus on those target markets

TARGET MARKETS You know that a target market is a segment of customers or potential customers that share certain characteristics, such as age, income, lifestyle, or interests. Since members of the target market have some common characteristics, marketers assume that they will respond similarly to marketing-mix strategies. A clear picture of the target market for a product will make it easier to make decisions involving the marketing mix to be used for the product.

QUESTION

On what does the marketing mix focus?

THE MARKETING MIX You learned in Chapter 1 that the Four Ps of the marketing mix are product, price, place, and promotion. For a marketing plan to be effective, strategies for each element of the marketing mix must focus on the target market. The needs and wants of that specific segment of the market must be analyzed and used when making these marketing decisions.

Product strategies involve the actual design of the product, as well as its packaging and brand name. They also include a product's warranty, image, and customer benefits.

Price strategies relate to the price the customer will pay for the product. To arrive at an appropriate price, several factors must be taken into consideration, such as cost, competition, economic conditions, and most importantly, what the customer is willing to pay. There are also psychological or emotional factors to consider, such as value, reputation, or prestige. In all marketing-mix decisions, however, it is the customer who plays the key role in deciding the final price of a product. Of the Four Ps, price is the easiest to revise. To be competitive, a company can quickly and easily introduce discount coupons, rebates, and other price promotions. You learned about other considerations and possibilities for making pricing decisions in Chapter 5.

Place Getting the product into the customer's hands involves place or distribution strategies. There are many options available from selling directly to the customer through direct marketing efforts or using intermediaries. Direct channels of distribution may be utilized through a company sales force, company Web site, and/or direct marketing efforts, such as telemarketing or television infomercials. Intermediaries make it easier or more efficient to reach the customer. Agents, wholesalers, and retailers all serve a purpose in a channel of distribution. A company must research how and where members of its target market shop in order to make its decisions regarding place strategies. In some cases, multiple channels of distribution may be appropriate.

Promotion As you learned in Chapter 8, promotion strategies involve communicating with the customer through sales promotional activities, advertising, publicity and public relations, and personal selling. Promotional activities may focus on informing, educating, and/or persuading customers to take some type of positive action.

Implementation

implementation putting the marketing plan into action

Implementation is putting the marketing plan into action. Who will be responsible for each phase of the plan? How much will each activity cost? When will each part of the plan be executed? To execute this element of the marketing plan, marketers develop an organizational outline with a schedule of activities, job assignments, a budget, and details of each activity. This phase of the marketing plan requires a lot of communication between everyone involved.

Evaluation and Control

Evaluation involves answering the question: "Did we accomplish our marketing objectives in the specified time frame?" In the *evaluation* phase, the company reviews sales data, market share, brand-name recall, or any other area from the marketing-plan objectives. Information generated from that review is compared with the objectives to see if the objectives were met. The difference between the planned and achieved performance tells the company which areas need to be revisited. In the *control* phase, the company takes action to reduce the gap between planned and actual performance.

A Sample Marketing Plan

Since marketing plans are usually proprietary, or privately owned information, we will use a hypothetical company as the basis of a sample marketing plan. By reading this sample plan in **Figure 9.2** on pages 196–198, you will see real-world examples and be able to understand how the elements of a marketing plan are applied.

To review, different companies have different marketing plans designed for specific industries and products, as well as target markets. However, most effective marketing plans should include these basic elements:

- Executive summary

- Situation analysis

- Marketing goals/objectives

- Marketing strategies

- Implementation

- Evaluation and control

The hypothetical company is Fairway Fundamentals Corporation, or FFC, a ten-year-old manufacturer of golf equipment. FFC presently makes golf clubs for men and seniors, but none for women or children. Until recently, the company's marketing plan has been limited by budget restrictions. However, a large conglomerate recently took over FFC and wants to make it a "big player" in the golf market.

Case Study · PART 2

NO SWEAT

Continued from Part 1 on page 189

Competing brands such as Nike, Reebok, and Adidas were cutting Under Armour's growth spurt. So in 1999, owner Kevin Plank increased his business's exposure by making a deal with film studio Warner Brothers to supply Under Armour for the football movies *The Replacements* and *Any Given Sunday*. Soon after that the company signed contracts with both Major League Baseball and the National Hockey League. Under Armour began supplying Major League Soccer, the U.S. Ski Team, and USA Baseball. During 2003, television commercials for Under Armour became common. With such an aggressive growth strategy and promotion, as well as prolific research and development, the company has maintained its growth rate and captured a stunning 70 percent of the performance apparel market. As a result, Under Armour enjoyed more than $55 million in sales in 2002, and Plank earned the Ernst & Young "Entrepreneur of the Year" award in 2003.

ANALYZE AND WRITE

1. What marketing strategies did Under Armour use to maintain its growth?
2. How did Under Armour's use by the entertainment industry affect its appeal to its target market?

Figure 9.2

Sample Marketing Plan

MARKETING STRATEGIES A marketing plan outlines specific goals
for a company as well as strategies to achieve those goals. *Read
the sample plan and then list some ways that FFC can evaluate
how well its marketing strategies are succeeding.*

Marketing Plan for Fairway Fundamentals Corporation (FFC)

Executive Summary

Fairway Fundamentals Corporation (FFC) has been acquired by a large conglomerate and now has the financial resources to target women golfers with a new line of golf clubs specially designed for women. The objectives of the marketing plan are to generate sales of $105 million, which will help achieve the second objective of improving its market share from 5 percent to 7 percent within one year. Brand recognition within the first year and being the golf club of choice for women golfers within five years are the other two objectives. These objectives will be evaluated by reviewing sales data and marketing-research focus-group data during the required time periods. To achieve these objectives, a new LPGA (Ladies Professional Golf Association) tour representative will be hired to work closely with the vice president of marketing and the marketing department staff.

Marketing-mix strategies focus exclusively on the new target market and the new line of golf clubs. A set of clubs will be created for beginners, which will be reasonably priced to encourage new golfers to take up the game. More advanced and more expensive golf clubs will be designed for experienced golfers. FFC's current distribution system will be used to launch the advanced line. The beginner's set will be sold in sporting-goods stores, such as Sports Authority. An $18 million promotional budget will permit FFC to sponsor an official LPGA tour, sign a professional LPGA golfer as an endorser of the new line, and create media exposure through advertising, sales promotions, and publicity. Print, online, and broadcast media will be used for the advertising campaign, which will be developed by an ad agency. Retail promotions and special promotional activities, such as demo days, golf-swing analysis, golf clinics, and long-drive contests, will be coordinated with the ad campaign and publicity efforts. FFC's Web site will serve as a communication tool for women golfers and the trade. Exhibiting at the PGA Merchandise Show in Orlando, Florida will help generate excitement and exposure of the new line to the golf pro shop and retailer buyers purchasing the new line.

Situation Analysis

The large conglomerate that acquired Fairway Fundamentals Corporation (FFC) has the financial resources to support an aggressive marketing plan. Presently, FFC enjoys a 5 percent share of the golf-equipment market. Its competitors include Callaway Golf (the market leader), Taylor Made, Nike, Cleveland, Square Two, Titleist, Ping, Mizuno, Tommy Armour, Cobra, MacGregor, and other companies.

Golf is a luxury activity tied to the economy. In 2002, because of the weak economy, the Iraq conflict, and lower consumer confidence, golf-equipment sales either declined or were flatter than in previous years. As the economy improved in 2003, golf-equipment sales improved. Callaway, Nike, and Taylor Made have reported increased unit sales and revenue. With the exception of Callaway, all others—Nike Golf, Taylor Made, and Cobra—are subsidiaries of larger companies, Nike, Adidas-Salomon, and Acushnet Company of Fortune Brands, Inc., respectively. These companies weather economic storms better than small companies. As part of a large conglomerate, FCC is in a position to compete against the market leaders.

One of the major threats experienced by all golf-club manufacturers is counterfeiting. Most knockoffs are made in China, where contract manufacturers make most of the golf clubs for major manufacturers. FFC also has foundries in China where its golf clubs are made. To combat the counterfeiting problem, FFC will engrave serial numbers on the golf clubs and use other technology to identify knockoffs. Another threat is that the number of golfers who take up the sport each year is equal to the number who give it up. Golf is a difficult sport because it takes knowledge and skill to perform well. FFC will attempt to transform this threat into an opportunity through its marketing-mix promotional strategies. Some of the specific promotional strategies will include Demo Days, custom-fitting of golf clubs, long-drive contests, and tips on how to improve your golf game found in promotional literature, as well as on the company's Web site.

There are an estimated 26 million golfers in the United States. The golf-club market is estimated to be around $1.5 billion in wholesale prices. Market-research data indicates growth in the children's and women's golf markets.

Objectives

FFC has four objectives in this marketing plan. They are (1) to generate total sales of $105 million within the first year; (2) to increase FFC's market share from 5 percent to 7 percent by next year; (3) to become a recognizable golf-equipment brand for women golfers within the first year; and (4) to become the golf equipment of choice for women golfers within five years.

Marketing Strategies

To achieve the objectives of this marketing plan, an investment of $18 million will be required.

Target Markets

Men golfers of varying ability levels will continue to be FFC's primary target market. However, this marketing plan will only address the new target market for FFC. The new target market will be women golfers ranging in age from teenagers to older adults. A new line of golf clubs will be designed for and marketed specifically to these women golfers.

Marketing Mix

Product, price, place, and promotion strategies will focus on beginning and advanced women golfers. All golf clubs will come in regular, petite, and long lengths for right-hand and left-hand players.

Beginner golf sets will include clubs such as a sand wedge, pitching wedge, irons, and four woods. The manufacturer's suggested retail price (MSRP) will be $350. The brand name will be the **Lady B** set for beginners. The FFC brand name and model series 150, 250, and 350 will be designed for experienced women golfers. The driver MSRP will be $425, and the fairway woods will be $325 each. The MSRP for the irons will be $100 each. Custom fitting will be offered for these women's golf clubs so that the loft, lie, swing weight, and length are correct for each individual golfer.

With regard to place strategy, FFC will use its current channels of distribution for the experienced golfer. These channels include pro shops and specialty golf retailers. Catalog sales will be introduced in the second year. To preserve the integrity of the channel members, customers will not be able buy directly from FFC. At the FFC Web site, an outlet locator will help customers find a retail store or pro shop close to their homes. The beginner's set will be sold to more general sporting-goods stores, such as Sports Authority.

With an $18 million promotional budget, FFC will launch the new women's golf club line. The FFC series golf clubs will be endorsed by the Ladies' Professional Golf Association and at least one professional golfer, to be announced at a later time.

continued on next page

Figure 9.2

Sample Marketing Plan (continued)

Marketing the new line to consumers will take place on FFC's Web site, as well as through the media with print, cable TV, and broadcast networks included in the mix. *Golf for Women* magazine, cable TV's Golf Channel, and television networks that air professional women's golf tournaments are the media being used. FFC will sponsor one of the LPGA's official tournaments in the next year, which will provide significant exposure. Retail promotions and point-of-purchase displays will complement the national media promotions. Special sales promotions will include more than 2,000 Demo Days and 200 custom-fitting arrangements through golf shops found at private and public golf courses, as well as at large golf driving ranges. At golf courses throughout the United States, 25 long-drive contests will be held for women golfers, as well as swing analysis and clinics on the short game. To help women golfers maintain interest in the game, FFC's Web site and proprietary promotional literature will provide tips on how to play the game. Rules of the game, chipping, pitching, and putting tips, as well as full-swing analysis and instruction will be part of FFC's Web-site design and specially created pamphlets.

For the trade, FFC will be exhibiting the new line at the PGA Merchandise Show in January 2004. At its booth, pro shop, golf retail stores, and other sporting-goods store buyers will have an opportunity to try out the new women's line and speak with the women golf professionals who will be endorsing the new clubs. Swing-analysis equipment will be on display at the booth to draw buyers who want to get an idea of what they do right and what they need to improve in their own golf swings.

Implementation

For the launch of the new women's line of golf clubs, a new LPGA tour representative will be hired who will be responsible for getting professional women golfers to use and endorse the new golf clubs. This person will work closely with the vice president of marketing to secure sponsorship of an official LPGA tournament, as well as sign a tour professional to an endorsement contract with FFC. The LPGA tour professional will be expected to make a certain number of appearances in conjunction with the PGA trade show and some of the special promotions being conducted throughout the United States. An advertising agency will be hired to develop the advertising campaigns and buy the space/time in the media. The marketing department will coordinate the special promotions with a newly hired staff that will be trained for conducting Demo Days, golf clinics, and long-drive contests. The marketing department staff will be responsible for developing relationships with radio and television so the special promotions get publicized. The vice president of marketing and the LPGA tour representative will be in charge of the PGA trade show exhibit.

Evaluation and Control

To assess whether FFC generates total sales of $105 million within one year, sales records will be reviewed at six-month intervals. Shorter-term sales goals will be created each month to keep the sales force motivated. Increasing market share from 5 percent to 7 percent by next year will involve reviewing sales data in comparison to competitors. A market research company will be hired to conduct focus group sessions one year after the launch of the new golf club line with women golfers to see if the FFC brand is recognizable to them. Sales of the new line will be compared to competing women's brands after five years to see if FFC is the number one choice among women golfers. Currently, Callaway Golf holds that position.

BEING FLEXIBLE **A good marketing plan should be flexible enough to accommodate unexpected events.** *What kind of events might be difficult to incorporate in a marketing plan?*

Understanding the Marketing Plan

FFC's marketing plan shown in **Figure 9.2** proposes a strategy for commercial success. It outlines a plan within a set timeline, and it tries to answer all the questions a company might have about existing and new products and services. A good marketing plan should be as detailed as possible about the goals and resources of the company and its employees. Employees who are aware of their specific roles within the marketing plan will know the best way to help their company succeed. There are many different roles and jobs employees can take on to contribute to the success of their company. Section 9.2 will discuss some of the different career opportunities available in sports marketing.

Quick Check

RESPOND to what you've read by answering these questions.

1. Why should a business write a marketing plan? _____
   _____
   _____

2. What is a SWOT analysis? _____
   _____
   _____

3. List the key elements of a marketing plan. _____
   _____
   _____

Sports Marketing Careers

AS YOU READ ...

YOU WILL LEARN

- To discuss the diversity of career and employment opportunities in sports marketing.
- To identify different career and employment opportunities in sports marketing.

WHY IT'S IMPORTANT

By exploring the diversity in the sports marketing industry, you can see how to apply different interests and skills to jobs and careers in this field.

KEY TERMS

- sports venues
- sports agencies

PREDICT

Do you think you need a sports background to work in the sports industry?

Overview of Sports Careers

The sports industry is diverse, encompassing a variety of organizations and types of companies. It includes sporting-goods companies; professional, college, and amateur sports teams and leagues; sports associations and organizations; all media; sports venues; sports agencies; fitness and recreation businesses, as well as special sports events. The kinds of jobs found in these areas are also diverse—and the people who do these jobs come from all walks of life.

You do not have to be an athlete to work in the sports industry, though it is common for athletes to move into other aspects of their industry later in their careers. Like all companies, businesses in the sports industry need marketing personnel to handle advertising, promotions, public relations, and sales. Sports businesses also need managerial staffs to handle finance, operations, and administration. Businesses also need technology specialists, writers, lawyers, and accountants. Regardless of your level of sports expertise, if you have special talent or business experience in any area, you can probably apply it to the sports industry.

Sports Marketing Job Descriptions

Since the sports industry is so broad, there are many job descriptions in the different sports areas. Let's look at a few of the employers and employment opportunities in a variety of sports-related fields.

SPORTING GOODS Sporting goods are sold in both retail outlets and wholesale outlets. Manufacturers, wholesalers, and retailers of sporting goods employ salespeople to get the products out on the market and technical representatives who go to stores to train salespeople. Some familiar sporting-goods manufacturers are Nike, Reebok, Adidas, Wilson, Taylor Made, and Russell Athletic Apparel. Retail salespeople sell to customers. Some familiar sporting-goods retailers are Sports Authority, Champs, and Footlocker.

Large sporting-goods manufacturers and retail chain stores have their own marketing departments staffed with copywriters, artists, media specialists, customer-service representatives, and public relations employees. Advertising campaigns, even if created by an outside advertising agency, need to be approved and coordinated with an in-house marketing department. Outside agencies might come up with special promotions, pursue sponsorship and licensing agreements, and write press releases to create a positive image for the company. Technology associates may also be hired by these firms to create and oversee Web sites and Internet communications.

PROFESSIONAL AND COLLEGIATE SPORTS Professional sports franchises and colleges employ salespeople to solicit corporate, individual, and group ticket sales. Some job titles include:

- Season-ticket sales representatives

- Ticket services manager

- Inside-sales associate

- Corporate/ticket sales personnel

- Account executive

- Group-sales manager

A related job involves seeking out companies to sponsor special promotions and events. This job title might be called "sponsorship sales executive." In all these sales jobs, the goal is to generate revenue for the organization or special event. The marketing department's job is to implement the marketing goals and objectives. Job titles may include:

- Marketing coordinator

- Director of marketing

- Director of communications

- Director of marketing, communications, and promotions

Figure 9.3 on page 205 shows you a sample sports marketing career plan with job descriptions.

SPORTS ASSOCIATIONS AND ORGANIZATIONS The many governing bodies for professional and amateur sports also offer career opportunities. These organizations oversee the leagues, teams, and players with regard to rules, ethics, competition, championships, and playoffs. Most of these organizations have their own Web sites and are involved in licensing agreements for the leagues' teams and players. Some of the major organizations for professional sports include:

- Major League Baseball (MLB)

- National Basketball Association (NBA) and Women's National Basketball Association (WNBA)

- National Football League (NFL)

- National Hockey League (NHL)

- Major League Soccer (MLS)

- National Association for Stock Car Auto Racing (NASCAR)

- Professional Golfers' Association (PGA)

Game Point !

THE BUYING GAME
Companies and organizations spend over $27 billion per year on advertisements at sporting events.

CONNECT
Have you ever noticed any publicity for a school or local sporting event?

THE Electronic CHANNEL

Online Dream Teams
Fantasy sports league participants choose real-life players' names to create their own imaginary teams. The changing real-life statistics of those players determine the rankings of the fantasy teams. With the Internet, statistics are quickly updated, and members can instantly make trades, change salaries, and discuss players and teams online. With over 12 million fantasy participants and the focus on individual players, online fantasy leagues provide new opportunities for sports marketers to explore.

➤Find and describe an online fantasy sports league through **marketingseries.glencoe.com.**

Fast Break to China

Though basketball has been a casual pastime in China for many years, the country has new ambitions for this century-old sport. Preparation starts early. The Chinese Basketball Association (CBA) reports that children who show skills for basketball, as well as for other sports, attend special sport schools in China. They are trained and educated at government expense. The kids work together for years before being introduced to international competition. As the young players develop into first-rate athletes, they are chosen for China's National Team and a shot at the Olympics—specifically, the Summer Olympics 2008 in the capital city of Beijing.

Currently, Chinese television broadcasts basketball games many times a week, and the games are played to packed gymnasiums. In addition, the arrival of star player Yao Ming in the NBA has helped that league market to Asian audiences in China, as well as in the United States. Soon China, the world's most populated country, may boast the largest number of basketball fans—and a profitable new market for sports promoters, sponsors, and the Chinese government.

Do you think that sports in China present opportunities for sports marketers who are just beginning their careers? Why?

Math Check

STATS MATH

Every year MLB awards a silver bat to each player with the highest batting average in his position. If the first baseman from your favorite team won with an average of .323 and had 180 hits, how many times did he go to bat for the season?

➡️ For tips on finding the solution, go to **marketingseries.glencoe.com.**

All college conferences are governed by the National Collegiate Athletic Association (NCAA). Organizations such as the AAU, Little League, or the Special Olympics will have local and national organization branches.

Professional athletes have their own associations, too. Examples include the Major League Baseball Players Associations (MLBPA), National Football League Players Association (NFLPA–NFL Players, Inc.), National Basketball Players Association (NBPA), and National Hockey League Players' Association (NHLPA). All of these organizations provide opportunities for jobs that might include anything from compiling statistics to planning news conferences to providing legal counsel.

BROADCAST, ONLINE, AND PRINT MEDIA Sports are very popular as entertainment. In the United States, media coverage and treatment of sports are extensive and operate through many communication channels. For example, sports-only network ESPN includes a magazine, radio stations, television stations, and a Web site. The Internet has many Web sites devoted to sports and sporting statistics. Many media organizations have marketing writers who provide information about teams, events, players, statistics, and organizations. They also all need sales personnel who are responsible for selling advertising space or time.

Being a sports journalist, announcer, or copywriter requires excellent communication skills. Sports media includes sporting-event news and events, as well as news about individuals or companies involved in the sports industry. Newspapers have separate sports sections; radio and television networks offer sports programming; and sport magazines such as *Sports Illustrated* are plentiful and popular. Sports trade journals such as *Sports Business Daily* provide industry information to sports marketing professionals and others.

SPORTS VENUES Sports venues are facilities or locations, such as stadiums, arenas, parks, or golf courses, where sporting events take place. Venues may be multi-complex facilities. Large venues such as Chicago's Wrigley Field or Manhattan's Madison Square Garden hire people to manage the coordination of events that take place in those facilities. All areas of marketing are used by these facilities, such as selling space in the off-season and coordinating special events, ticket sales, public relations, and sales promotion—as well as safety and security. The logistics for each event must be handled by staff who manage:

- Ticket collection
- Security
- Maintenance
- Parking
- Vendors
- Concessions

SPORTS AGENCIES Sports agencies are organizations that specialize in marketing and managing sports events, sports teams, and professional athletes. Sports agents represent professional athletes in all fields of sports, such as baseball, football, soccer, ice skating, and all of the Olympic sports. They may also handle the promotion and organization of local sporting events such as triathlons and marathons.

TECH
NOTES

Finding Jobs Online
Job seekers interested in a sports marketing career can find many resources online. While some Web sites have job listings for current openings, others offer additional features, such as tips on résumé writing and interviewing.

➡ Search for and list three sports-related jobs and internship opportunities through **marketingseries.glencoe.com**.

sports venues facilities or locations where sporting events take place

sports agencies companies that specialize in marketing and managing sports events, sports teams, and professional athletes

◀ **PLAY-BY-PLAY Sports coverage is often live, and reporters cover all kinds of events.** *Why might a team or athlete's publicist have to do "damage control" with the media after a live event?*

VOLLEYBALL RULES

Stacy Nicks
International Volleyball Player
Position: Middle Blocker

Stacy Nicks has been playing volleyball since she was ten in Spencer, Iowa. Standing 6'3" tall, you might think she would have no trouble being noticed, but she had to learn to market herself to play in college and go on to professional status. With a solid high school program behind her, Stacy applied for a full scholarship offered to female volleyball players at Iowa State University. She put together a package of videotapes, winning stats, and recommendations to earn her place in the Big 12 Conference. While on the college team, she and her teammates were coached on self-presentation in press situations and learned to project a positive team image.

Going Pro After her graduation in 2001, Stacy moved to California where she landed a job coaching teens through a Pepperdine University program. She also got the attention of sports promoter Tim Kelly, founder of Bring It Promotions, a company that organizes tours for international volleyball. In 2002, Stacy turned professional, touring in Europe as she took her own advice: "Be flexible, adaptable, and open to new experiences." After the tour, Stacy again "pitched" herself to Kelly, who drafted her to another team—this time in Basel, Switzerland, where German lessons were part of her 2003 contract.

Stacy realizes that most indoor players retire by age 30. With that foresight, she continues to coach, passing on this wisdom to the next generation: "Believe in yourself." However, she has another dream—to go to grad school and major in sports marketing.

How could Stacy apply her experience as a professional volleyball player to her future career?

Career Data: Sports Marketer

Education and Training Bachelor's or Master's degree in business, marketing, communications, or general education

Skills and Abilities Excellent communication skills, strong organizational skills, and creativity

Career Outlook Faster than average growth through 2010

Career Path Entry-level positions provide experience. Real-world skills are crucial for advancement.

QUESTION

Why is marketing so important to the world of sports?

Sports agents handle contract negotiations with an athlete, a team, and corporate sponsors. Agreements may include endorsements, licensing, promotions, speaking engagements, and personal appearances. Sports agencies can also help companies coordinate sports-related or sponsored events. Some well-known sports marketing and management companies include CMG Worldwide with headquarters in Indianapolis, Indiana, PSP Sports Marketing in New York City, and SFX Sports Group, which has offices in the United States, as well as in Europe and Australia.

Other Careers

Other sports-marketing careers that are growing in popularity are found in health and fitness and recreation industries. Personal-fitness businesses such as Gold's Gym, Bally's Fitness Centers, Family Fitness Centers, and Curves are a few examples of fitness chains that cater to all ages. Jobs in this area include personal trainers and fitness instructors, as well as marketing and sales personnel to generate new customers for these services. These jobs are offered on either a full-time or part-time basis.

Recreation involves all areas of sports for people of every age. Bowling, tennis, yoga, kickboxing, handball, and children's sports programs and camps afford other opportunities in sports-related careers. There are also schools or academies for adults, such as golf and tennis schools. For children, there are camps for all sports, such as soccer, basketball, field hockey, baseball, and swimming. Adult and children's sports camps offer jobs for people who enjoy teaching, as well as marketing and management jobs. Promotional efforts are required to recruit participants for these camps, as well as to manage the camps or schools when they are in full swing.

MARKETING SERIES *Online*

Remember to check out this book's Web site for information on sports marketing careers and other great resources at marketingseries.glencoe.com.

Figure 9.3

A Sports Marketing Career Plan

GO FOR THE GOAL **Jobs related to the sports industry can utilize skills from every profession.** *Why might a sales background be helpful in the world of sports marketing?*

Job Specifications	Team Marketing Assistant	Team Marketing Representative	Team Senior Marketing Representative
Education	High school/GED	Associate degree/ Bachelor's degree	Bachelor's degree or higher
Experience	0–1 years	1–3 years	3–5 years
Duties	• Assist in production of marketing materials. • Provide administrative support. • Provide customer service to vendors and fans.	• Write, develop, and edit marketing materials. • Conduct market research and determine target market. • Create promotional activities in the community.	• Create and evaluate marketing plans. • Represent the team to vendors and media. • Organize staff and resources.

PLANNING AHEAD **Athletes often begin preparing for their careers when they are young, as golfer Michelle Wie has done.** *What is one summer job that might help you to prepare for a sports marketing career?*

Future Careers

Whether you are creating a poster for a local sports team, manufacturing mountain bikes, or promoting a marathon, you are involved in sports marketing. Skills from almost every profession will benefit you if you decide to pursue a career in sports marketing.

Quick Check

RESPOND to what you've read by answering these questions.

1. Is it necessary to be an athlete to work in the sports industry? Why? _____
_____
_____
_____

2. Name different types of businesses or organizations that are part of the sports industry.
_____
_____
_____

3. What are some responsibilities a sports agent might have? _____
_____
_____
_____

Worksheet 9.1

Sample Marketing Plan

Review the sample marketing plan in **Figure 9.2** and answer the following questions.

1. What is FFC's first objective?

_____

_____

_____

2. Describe each element in FFC's marketing mix.

- Product

    _____

    _____

    _____

- Price

    _____

    _____

    _____

- Place

    _____

    _____

    _____

- Promotion

    _____

    _____

3. List three strategies for the implementation of FFC's marketing plan.

_____

_____

_____

_____

_____

_____

_____

Worksheet 9.2

Sports Marketing Jobs

Fill in the chart below with information about sports marketing jobs.

Type of Employer	Types of Jobs
	• • • •
	• • • •
	• • • •
	• • • •
	• • • •
	• • • •
	• • • •

Portfolio Works

WRITE A RÉSUMÉ

You have a special talent or business experience in an area that you think can be applied to the sports marketing industry. Write a one-page résumé to showcase your talent. Then add this page to your career portfolio.

JOB OBJECTIVE

_____

_____

_____

_____

SKILLS

_____

_____

_____

_____

WORK EXPERIENCE

_____

_____

_____

_____

EDUCATION

_____

_____

_____

AWARDS AND ACTIVITIES

_____

_____

_____

CHAPTER SUMMARY

Section 9.1 The Marketing Plan

marketing plan (p. 190)
executive summary
    (p. 190)
situation analysis
    (p. 191)
SWOT analysis (p. 191)
marketing strategy
    (p. 193)
implementation (p. 194)

• A marketing plan provides the basis for all marketing decisions made by a company and is an important factor in a company's success.

• Common elements of a marketing plan are: 1) the executive summary, 2) situation analysis, 3) marketing objectives, 4) marketing strategies, 5) implementation, and 6) evaluation and control.

Section 9.2 Sports Marketing Careers

sports venues (p. 203)
sports agencies (p. 203)

• The sports marketing industry is broad with diverse organizations, companies, and careers. Athletes are not the only people who can work in sports and sports marketing industries. Sports businesses need a variety of personnel with different skills.

• There are a variety of types of jobs and careers in sports marketing. Some sports-related employers include sporting goods, professional and collegiate sports organizations, sports associations and organizations, advertising agencies, broadcast, online, and print media, sports venues, sports agencies, health and fitness, and recreation. There are many jobs including account executive, group-sales manager, sports agent, marketing coordinator, sports writer, advertising writer and artist, venue manager, concessions worker, and numerous others.

CHECKING CONCEPTS

1. **Explain** the purpose and function of a marketing plan.
2. **Identify** the elements of a marketing plan.
3. **Explain** how to conduct a SWOT analysis.
4. **Identify** the guidelines for the elements of a marketing plan.
5. **Name** appropriate marketing strategies for a marketing plan.
6. **Discuss** the diversity of career skills used in the sports marketing industry.
7. **List** five different employment opportunities in the sports marketing industry.

Critical Thinking
8. **Explain** the relationship between threats and opportunities.

CROSS-CURRICULUM SKILLS

Work-Based Learning

Thinking Skills—Knowing How to Learn

9. Make a list of the major headings in this chapter. Beneath each heading, write a short summary of what you read.

Interpersonal Skills—Participating as a Team Member

10. Work with three or four students to create a marketing plan for a new sporting-goods store. Sell the plan to the class using an oral presentation. Include visual aids.

School-Based Learning

Writing

11. Research a sports marketing career that interests you, and then write a brief essay about that career. Include educational requirements and explain why the career interests you.

Language Arts

12. Develop a list of questions you would like to ask someone who has a job that is related to sports marketing.

Role Play: Marketing Professional

SITUATION You are to assume the role of marketing professional in the sports marketing industry. A college student (judge) has scheduled an informational interview to gain more insight into the industry.

ACTIVITY Explain to the student (judge) the best ways to prepare for a career in the sports marketing industry.

EVALUATION You will be evaluated on how well you meet the following performance indicators:

- Describe traits important to the success of employees in the sports industry.
- Explain employment opportunities in sports marketing.
- Describe techniques for obtaining work experience (e.g., volunteer activities, internships).
- Explain possible advancement patterns for jobs.
- Analyze employer expectations in the business environment.

INTERNET ACTIVITY

Use the Internet to access SFX Sports Group.

- Click on one of the areas on the left side of the screen.
- Write a fact sheet from the information about SFX.
- Exchange fact sheets with another student who chose a different area of SFX to research.
- Discuss with each other what you learned about SFX Group.

➡ For a link to SFX Sports Group to begin this exercise, go to **marketingseries.glencoe.com**.

WILL ENDORSEMENT DEALS PAY OFF?

He has been compared to Magic Johnson and put right up there with His Airness, Michael Jordan. Not yet 19, LeBron James is a 6-ft., 8-in. bundle of no-look passes and arching three-pointers who was named by *USA Today* the high-school player of the year for the second time. With James playing guard, his Akron-area high school won three state championships.

The timing couldn't be better. The stars may be in alignment for James to become the Air Apparent. By early May, he is expected to be the first pick in the June 26 [NBA] draft. LeBron James is Big Business in the making. A bidding war has been brewing for months between Adidas and Nike, and eBay is flooded with James-autographed memorabilia.

He's a can't-miss prospect—unless, of course, he misses. That makes James perhaps the biggest crapshoot in sports. The NBA is littered with high-school phenoms whose game never rose to pro levels. Worse yet, there are the superstars who could do it all on the court but couldn't sell tons of sneakers, soft drinks, or burgers. Vince Carter plays in the obscurity of Toronto for a lackluster Raptors squad. Then there's the sad tale of Grant Hill, who has spent most of his career on the disabled list after signing a seven-year, $80 million contract with Fila.

But the future is now for LeBron. "We've had a dozen of them kicking down our door," says James's Cleveland-based attorney, Fred Nance. Nike Chairman Phil Knight flew James's mother, Gloria, up to Beaverton, Oregon, for one meeting, while Adidas star-finder Sonny Vaccaro outfitted James's high-school team with sneakers and other gear.

By all accounts, James should strike it rich. As the first selection, he's guaranteed by NBA rules a three-year, $11 million contract. Whichever shoemaker wins will likely pay him north of $25 million over four years. Nance says soft-drink, fast-food, and packaged-goods companies are also lining up.

But will Nike or Adidas get their money's worth? A lot depends on how they market James. Nike still sells truckloads of Air Jordans—plus shoes endorsed by Gary Payton, Vince Carter, and Yao Ming. Will a kid from Ohio generate buzz among that crowd?

By Ronald Grover with Stanley Holmes

CREATIVE JOURNAL

In your journal, write your responses:

CRITICAL THINKING

1. What are some reasons for Nike's interest in players such as James?

APPLICATION

2. Imagine you are planning endorsements for a young star athlete. Describe the athlete, identifying his or her sport. Then list and describe five products and services for him or her to endorse. Also write one paragraph explaining why this athlete will be worth contracting even though he or she is unproven.

 Go to **businessweek.com** for current *BusinessWeek* Online articles.

UNIT LAB

Dream Machine, Inc.

You've just entered the real world of sports and entertainment marketing. Dream Machine, Inc., is a sports and entertainment marketing company that serves college and professional sports teams, professional athletes, sporting events, sports arenas, and major sports product corporations, as well as performing arts companies, television networks, and movie studios. As an entry-level employee, you will have the opportunity to work on a variety of clients' projects.

Develop a Plan—Write a Marketing Plan for Skates

SITUATION You are employed by Apex, an in-line skating manufacturer. Research indicates that the growth of in-line skating is with recreational and fitness skaters. The owners are looking for innovative products to take advantage of this opportunity. They are counting on you, as director of marketing, to design a new product and to develop a marketing plan for it.

ASSIGNMENT Complete these tasks:
- Research in-line skating manufacturers and their products.
- Research in-line skating competitions and businesses that sell in-line skating products.
- Design a new in-line skate or in-line skating accessory.
- Based on your research, develop a marketing plan for the new product.
- Make a report to the company president.

TOOLS AND RESOURCES To complete the assignment, you will need to:
- Conduct research at the library, on the Internet, and/or by talking to in-line skaters and retailers.
- Have word-processing, spreadsheet, and presentation software.

RESEARCH Do your research:
- Identify target markets for in-line skating.
- Research the in-line skating industry to determine trends and opportunities.
- Research prices for in-line skates and accessories for three major competitors.
- Research new product innovation in in-line skating and related sports.
- Research in-line skating publications, competitions, and televised programs.

REPORT Prepare a written report using the following tools if available:
- *Word-processing program:* Prepare a written marketing plan with a SWOT analysis, target-market analysis, and recommendations for the marketing mix.
- *Spreadsheet program:* Prepare charts of competitors' market share, the annual industry sales for the past five years, and price comparisons.
- *Presentation program:* Prepare a ten-slide visual presentation with key points from your marketing plan, an illustration of your product idea, an advertisement, and price-comparison chart.

PRESENTATION AND EVALUATION You will present your report to the president of the company. You will be evaluated on the basis of:
- Your knowledge of the in-line skating industry and competitors
- Rationale for your product and marketing plan
- Continuity of presentation
- Voice quality
- Eye contact

PORTFOLIO

Add this report to your career portfolio.

UNIT 4

ENTERTAINMENT MARKETING

" Talent hits a target no
one else can hit; genius
hits a target no one else
can see. "

— **Arthur Schopenhauer**
Philosopher

The world of entertainment is diverse, with a variety of types of entertainment and entertainment products, from musical stage shows such as *Cats* on Broadway to the latest electronic game based on a movie. Films, videos, CDs, TV, radio, print publications, live entertainment, museums, and amusement parks—and more—are marketed to target groups of consumers. Chapter 10 focuses on the entertainment marketing for these products as well as the different types of businesses that operate in the entertainment industry. Then Chapter 11 examines entertainment goods and services and how each product is marketed by using media to best reach the audience and consumers of entertainment.

▪ UNIT LAB

Preview

Touring circuses provide family entertainment across the United States. What kind of research do circus companies do when they plan to expand?

Functions of Marketing

Marketing-Information Management · Financing · Selling · Pricing · Distribution · Product/Service Management · Promotion

Foundations

Professional Development · Economics · Business, Management, Entrepreneurship · Communication, Interpersonal Skills

Academic Concepts · Technology

These functions are highlighted in this unit:

- Promotion
- Distribution
- Product/Service Management

The Entertainment Market

Chapter Objectives

- Define entertainment marketing.
- Identify different types of entertainment media.
- Explain the economics of entertainment marketing.
- Discuss the global impact of entertainment marketing.
- Explain types of businesses in the entertainment industry.
- Identify forms of entertainment marketed to consumers.

A LASTING LANDMARK

Landmarks such as the Hollywood Sign are world-famous symbols. Built in the 1920s to advertise Hollywoodland real estate, the sign is often associated with the entertainment industry. In the early 20th century, the industry was expanding, thanks in part to film exhibitors who operated "movie palaces," or theaters, that have also become landmarks. One such theater is Grauman's Chinese Theatre in Hollywood, California.

Created by Sid Grauman, the Chinese Theatre opened in 1927. Resembling a red Chinese pagoda, gold dragons and stone lion-dogs guard the main entrance. The foot- and hand-print tiles that pave the theater's forecourt became a legendary marketing device. This theater has hosted movie premieres that promote films and Hollywood as the entertainment capital of the world.

Over the years movie theaters have changed, due to new technology and multiplex designs. Many movie palaces have closed. How has the Chinese Theatre remained a successful landmark for almost a century?

ANALYZE AND WRITE

1. What business helped the entertainment industry expand in the 20th century?
2. Why have some theaters closed?

Case Study Part 2 on page 231

POWER READ

Be an active reader and use these reading strategies:

PREDICT what the section will be about.

CONNECT what you read with your life.

QUESTION as you read to make sure you understand the content.

RESPOND to what you've read.

Entertainment and Marketing

AS YOU READ ...

YOU WILL LEARN

- To define entertainment marketing.
- To identify different types of entertainment media.
- To explain the economics of entertainment marketing.
- To discuss the global impact of entertainment marketing.

WHY IT'S IMPORTANT

Entertainment marketing is all around us every day. Entertainment is a major part of our lives and our economy.

KEY TERMS

- entertainment marketing
- media
- fad
- cross-selling
- leisure time

entertainment marketing the process of developing, promoting, and distributing products, or goods and services, to satisfy customers' needs and wants through entertainment, or any diversion, amusement, or method of occupying time

PREDICT

What is the meaning of leisure time?

That's Entertainment

Entertainment has existed in many different forms for centuries. Ancient Roman spectators watched gladiators battle at the Coliseum in staged army battles as well as sea adventures enacted in a flooded arena. In ancient Greece 2,500 years ago, the first plays were performed—plays that are still produced and are relevant to audiences today. As early as the 12th century, Chinese operas were performed in public squares. During the late 1500s and early 1600s, royalty and commoners both enjoyed seeing Shakespeare's plays performed at the Globe Theatre in London, England. For centuries, dance in Africa has been a rich tradition. Throughout history and around the world, people have enjoyed music, sport, spectacle, art, and other forms of diversion.

Entertainment Today

Today, on average, people spend almost three hours a day watching television. Ninety-eight percent of all homes have at least one TV set. Thus, with its mass exposure to consumers, television provides many opportunities for marketing. However, television is only one means used for **entertainment marketing**, which is the process of developing, promoting, and distributing products, or goods and services, to satisfy customers' needs and wants through entertainment, or any diversion, amusement, or method of occupying time. The entertainment industry is huge and includes film, television, radio, music and concerts, video games, and theme parks, as ranked below in terms of time spent using the form of entertainment:

1. Television
2. Radio
3. Recorded music
4. Newspapers and magazines
5. Video games (home or arcade)
6. Films (theatrical or home)

Entertainment marketing also includes marketing activities provided by sports and sports marketers, as discussed in Units 2 and 3. The entertainment industry is a $200 billion market of products and services with one goal: to provide diversion, excitement, and amusement. Entertainment today revolves around celebrities, cartoon characters, and concepts such as water parks, video games, concerts, and festivals. For both roller-coaster riders and moviegoers, entertainment provides an enjoyable way to pass the time, and people are willing to pay for it.

Media and Entertainment

Media are the methods used for communicating or transmitting messages, which can be pure entertainment or marketing-related messages. The media is the driving force of entertainment and can dictate product offerings. Media include film, television, radio, publishing media, the Internet, and more. The companies that control the media, such as film and TV studios, publishers, cable companies, or music distributors, influence how the public is entertained.

Entertainment Marketing Jobs

The companies that control the media and media offerings are large businesses, such as Disney, Sony, Universal, and NBC and other television networks, as well as small companies. Hundreds of jobs at these companies and others are associated with entertainment marketing. For example, an agent for a film star, the artist who designs the cover for a CD, the designer who creates the concept of a roller coaster, and the concession-stand worker at the local cinema megaplex all work in areas of entertainment marketing.

The Influence of Entertainment

The clothing we wear, hairstyles, and style in general are influenced by entertainment marketing. Entertainers lend their names and ideas to merchandise lines. Performer Jennifer Lopez started a cosmetics and clothing line, and music producer Sean "P. Diddy" Combs designed a line of clothing. The baggy-pants, hip-hop look was adopted by fashion designers and mass marketed. Cars used in popular movies can lead to increased sales at auto dealerships. For example, sales of the Mini Cooper automobile increased after the car was featured in the film *The Italian Job*.

Everyday expressions are also influenced by entertainment. When Arnold Schwarzenegger spoke the lines "I'll be back!" and "Hasta la vista, baby," in the *Terminator* films, audiences adopted the phrases as popular sayings in everyday life.

Sports also influence nonathletic entertainment. Athletes such as former football star Terry Bradshaw, tennis legend John McEnroe, and others have become successful television announcers. Other athletes such as Michael Jordan (*Space Jam*) and Shaquille O'Neal (*Kazaam*) have acted in films.

Many products or services influenced by entertainment are fads. A **fad** is a short-term popular trend, style, product, or service. For example, the disco music craze of the late 1970s was generated by the 1977 John Travolta film *Saturday Night Fever*. A few years later in the 1980s, the cowboy fashion style became a fad that was initiated by the film *Urban Cowboy*, another Travolta film about a Texas oil-rig worker. Popular styles that you might see in school are influenced by videos, musicians, and current films. These fads are constantly changing, and as soon as the mass culture, or society, adopts them, the trendsetters move on and adopt new fashions.

media the methods used for communicating or transmitting messages

MARKETING SERIES *Online*

Remember to check out this book's Web site for information on entertainment marketing and more great resources at **marketingseries.glencoe.com**.

fad a short-term popular trend, style, product, or service

CONNECT

Describe a recent entertainment-related fad that has already begun to fade in popularity.

Entertainment and the Marketing Concept

Movie and TV studios are constantly striving to anticipate customer wants and needs—which is the function of the marketing concept—and provide what the public wants. Selling entertainment to the public is a challenge. Entertainment usually has a short "shelf life," and it is perishable. For example, when you see a movie at a theater, and the lights go up at the end, your experience is over—you do not take a product home for reuse. Even if you later decide to buy the DVD or video, you will have limited exposure to the product because you probably will not watch the film day after day. The same principle applies to a theme-park or water-park experience. When you leave the park, the experience ends, and the consumer demand drops with it. Therefore, the marketer must cover costs and make a profit immediately.

Profiles in Marketing

ENTERTAINING BUSINESS

Michael Beckett
Theatrical Agent
Andrew Manson Personal
Management, Ltd.

Located in London, England, Andrew Manson Personal Management represents actors and actresses who work in all major media—film, television, theater, and commercials. Michael Beckett works with the firm's stable of clients, which includes internationally known actors.

On a day-to-day basis, Michael makes suggestions for new projects, handles the client's schedule and appointments, and updates "CVs" (a CV is a *curriculum vitae*, a type of résumé that details work done and when).

Michael's work can be hectic, with many tasks needing to be handled at once. "Essential skills are an ability to work methodically under pressure, the ability to communicate on all levels, and having a knowledge of the industry," he says.

The duties of an agent are constantly shifting. Every client is different, and each one needs a different level of attention. No two days are ever the same. "I come from a standard educational background, but to be honest, no amount of qualifications can prepare anyone for the work of an agent," he adds. "I would say that common sense and experience are the most important qualifications."

Why is common sense important in this career?

**Career Data:
Theatrical Agent**

Education and Training
Bachelor's or master's degree in business or communications

Skills and Abilities Writing skills, time-management skills, resourcefulness, and flexibility

Career Outlook Average growth through 2010

Career Path Many agents work for themselves, starting their own agencies after several years of training at an existing firm in an entry-level position.

Selling entertainment is always a gamble because the costs and expenses are paid up front. If the consumer rejects the product (movie, theme park, or video game), the producer has no other source of revenue. The consumer market is fickle, and the public is always looking for the "next big thing." The challenge for studios, theme-park owners, and performers is to keep the customer coming back.

The Economics of Entertainment

Entertainment is in the top ten of the highest-grossing segments of the economy and generates revenue from many sources, goods, and services. It influences and impacts many other areas of the economy. For example, food and beverage makers such as Pepsi rely on popular entertainers such as Britney Spears to sell cola. Apparel retailers such as Gap use entertainers such as Madonna to sell clothing.

Entertainment and Consumer Spending

Entertainment marketing relies on meeting consumer demand for diversion and excitement at a price the customer is willing to pay. Television has been the most popular entertainment diversion for almost half a century. In terms of cost per hour of enjoyment, it is one of the cheapest forms of entertainment. On the other hand, visiting a theme park might be one of the most expensive forms, due to travel, ticket, concessions, and other related costs. To compare, one hour of watching *Entertainment Tonight* might cost 6 cents, whereas one hour of fun at Disney World might cost $35.

Shopping for Entertainment

Shoppers can afford to buy only a limited amount of product before exceeding their budgets. Consumers are constantly faced with trade-offs with so many choices. This is *opportunity cost,* as discussed in Chapter 4: When you make a decision to spend your money in one way, such as going to a concert, you give up the opportunity to spend that money for something else, such as a new band T-shirt. This same situation occurs on many levels—both individual and corporate. For example, Disney Studios can spend millions of dollars to make a big-budget film such as *Pirates of the Caribbean,* or Disney can spend the same money to make two lower-budget films.

The entertainment and sports businesses thrive on getting people to spend their discretionary income. Unlike disposable income, or income that goes to necessities such as food, rent, and medicine, discretionary income is spent as the consumer chooses on a movie ticket, a CD, a DVD rental, or cologne. When people spend their vacation in Orlando, Florida, at Disney World, they use discretionary income to pay for hotels, food, gifts, tickets, and all the other expenses of the trip.

Merchandising and Entertainment

Merchandising is a big part of the entertainment industry. Stars sell products, and products sell stars. Businesses use **cross-selling,** or the method of selling additional related products tied to one name. For example,

cross-selling the method of selling the customer additional related products tied to one name

fast-food restaurants such as McDonald's and Burger King often tie restaurant promotions to current film offerings. Both the restaurant and the film studio benefit from the combined advertising efforts.

Universal Studios uses the popular film character "E.T. the Extraterrestrial" as the theme for a ride as well as souvenirs, apparel, gifts, toys, and food. Entertainment merchandising also relied on cross-selling between Bugs Bunny cartoons sold in the home-video market and the popular *Space Jam* movie, which also included sports superstar Michael Jordan in another tie-in feature. Universal and McDonald's joined forces on a marketing tie-in by selling *Space Jam* toys and meals at the restaurants, while promoting the film. In addition, Universal advertised McDonald's restaurants in its *Space Jam* television promotions.

International Entertainment

Entertainment marketing is international in scope and generates revenue globally as well as nationally. There are thousands of movie theaters, amusement parks, and television sets in other countries. Around the world, people spend money as Americans do when it comes to enjoying **leisure time**, or time free from work or duties.

leisure time time free from work or duties

In fact, the number one American export after agricultural products is entertainment. American films and TV shows are popular in many foreign countries. *The Simpsons* cartoon show is one of the most popular television shows in England. British Prime Minister Tony Blair appeared as an animated character on an episode in 2003. Sometimes foreign entertainment becomes a hit in the American market. For example, *Who Wants to Be a Millionaire* was originally a British television success before it became a top-rated show in the United States.

Global Entertainment Marketing

Entertainment products, including films, television shows, and musical recordings, are one of America's strongest exports. American

CARTOON MANIA
Television shows such as *The Simpsons* have become so popular in America and abroad that they have their own merchandise, including dolls, calendars, clothing, and other promotional items. *Do you think this TV show would have been as popular if it had been a movie? Why?*

Eight-Story Cinema

Sometimes entertainment is larger than life. In 1970, Canadian filmmakers introduced a new and more powerful projection system called IMAX. The result? Mega-sized movies. IMAX theaters draw the audience into the film using vinyl screens up to eight stories high (4,335 times bigger than a TV screen), a wraparound 15,000-watt sound system, and stadium-style seating. "It's almost like being there," viewers explain.

Each year more than 70 million people see IMAX movies, visually traveling to places once only imagined. They rub noses with China's giant pandas, rock with the Rolling Stones, space walk with the NASA astronauts, and enter the world of 3-D animation while wearing special headgear. In the film *Everest,* viewers take a breathtaking mountain hike to the top of the world. This feat was made possible by the IMAX filmmakers—in spite of a camera weighing 42 pounds; jet-stream winds at 70 miles per hour; temperatures of minus 60 degrees—and 11 yaks.

Can you think of any films or film subjects that would not be suitable for IMAX theaters?

companies such as Warner Brothers and The Walt Disney Company are known around the world for their characters, films, books, television, and merchandise. Disney theme parks are successful in Europe and Asia, as well as in the United States. In addition, some American entertainment firms are owned by foreign companies. For example, Universal Studios in the United States is owned by the French company Vivendi, which merged with the U.S. company General Electric. Popular Virgin Records is owned by a British company, Virgin Atlantic.

American film stars such as Sylvester Stallone and Tom Cruise who will not do commercials for television in the United States have appeared in TV commercials on Japanese television.

As developing countries have more income among their citizens, they become attractive markets for American entertainment.

Quick Check

RESPOND to what you've read by answering these questions.

1. What does the term media mean?_____

_____

2. What are fads? _____

_____

3. What product is one of America's strongest exports?_____

_____

Types of Entertainment Businesses

AS YOU READ ...

YOU WILL LEARN

- To explain types of businesses in the entertainment industry.
- To identify forms of entertainment marketed to consumers.

WHY IT'S IMPORTANT

Understanding the scope, structure, and types of entertainment businesses is necessary for marketers to be effective in the many different areas.

KEY TERMS

- break even
- oligopoly
- affiliate
- ratings
- niche marketing
- brick-and-mortar store
- nonprofit organization

PREDICT

Name five entertainment companies that you know.

Business Structures

In the United States, the entertainment industry is concentrated in a number of areas, such as film, TV, radio, music, and theme parks. Most businesses that produce entertainment for consumers are large corporations with many investors and employees. Most of these businesses started out as *single proprietorships* (owned by one person) or *partnerships* (owned by two or more persons) and grew over the years.

In the early 20th century, Walt Disney started as an entrepreneur with artistic talent. The business that he founded is now a giant in the entertainment field, employing hundreds of thousands of people. Entertainment companies are often corporate *conglomerates,* or companies that have merged with or bought other companies and absorbed them into larger, more competitive businesses. Often a company is more competitive because it has bought out competing companies to become the major producer. The company Clear Channel Communications is an example. After years of buying radio stations across the country, this corporation owns over 1,200 stations and controls 60 percent of the rock radio market in the United States.

The Major Companies

There are only a few major companies that produce film, television, radio, music, and print media, as well as Internet-based entertainment and marketing. These companies include The Walt Disney Company, Sony Entertainment, Viacom (Paramount), Time Warner, Vivendi Universal, and The News Corporation (20th Century Fox). These large companies have experienced many mergers and acquisitions to build a wide range of firms to compete in all entertainment areas.

An example is Time Warner. Besides owning the popular Internet server AOL, this company also owns *Time* magazine, Warner Brothers Pictures, the WB Television Network, HBO, *Sports Illustrated* magazine, the Atlanta Braves baseball team, and Rhino Records—and this is only a partial list of associated companies. **Figure 10.1** lists companies owned by The Walt Disney Company, an entertainment-industry conglomerate.

These companies are structured, or organized, with *vertical distribution*. In other words, they create and produce entertainment products and services; they market them; and they distribute them. These companies perform all the functions in the channel of distribution from producer to consumer. A local video-rental shop might be structured differently with *horizontal distribution*. The video-rental shop relies on others for the product and most of the promotion.

Figure 10.1

The Walt Disney Company Ownership

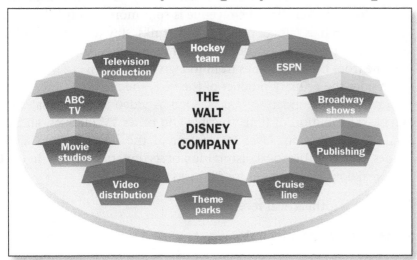

MEGA CONGLOMERATE All of these companies are grouped under The Walt Disney Company umbrella. Each company can influence and support marketing activities for the other companies in the "family." *Which company do you think was most recently acquired by The Walt Disney Company? Why do you think it was bought?*

Movies

Movie production is a multi-billion-dollar operation. Studios create product or release movies for smaller independent producers. The films are released by distributors—usually the studio or a related company—and shown by the theaters, or exhibitors.

The cost of producing films and television programs is so high that most projects are produced by large studios that are corporations with plenty of capital and facilities. Today it costs about $90 million to produce a major studio film and another $40 million to market it. In addition, four out of ten films produced may not **break even,** or have costs and expenses equal the income revenue. Therefore, only large companies can spread out the risk of failure among many offerings. Studios must be assured that a film will appeal to a specific consumer base and will have future ticket sales overseas as well as in the rental market. When a film proposal looks favorable, it is greenlighted, or given approval for production by the studio management.

Major Studios and Indies

Studios including Universal, Disney, Paramount, MGM, and a few others are the core of the film business, which is considered an **oligopoly,** or a business situation in which a few firms affect but do not control an industry. However, independent movie companies, called *indies,* are not affiliated with major studios, but they operate on their own to make films. Lions Gate, Artisan, and New Line Cinema are examples of well-known independent companies. However, many of these companies become subsidiaries of larger studios. For example, Miramax, the company that produced the Best Picture Oscar® winner *Shakespeare in Love,* was acquired by Disney in 1993. Independent films can also be produced by small groups of individuals who form companies. *The Blair Witch Project* is an example of a successful indie film, which was produced for $35,000 but grossed over $141 million.

Game Point !

EVERYONE LOVES THE MOVIES
During the 1990s, revenue from movies nearly doubled—from $12.8 billion to $24.9 billion, with over 500 films released each year.

break even costs and expenses equal to income revenues

oligopoly business situation in which a few firms affect but do not control an industry

Theatrical Distribution

The primary market for film is theatrical distribution. Usually the first week a film is in theaters, all ticket-sale money goes to the distributor, or studio, and after that, the revenue is split more evenly. All concession sales, such as sales of popcorn and drinks, stay with the exhibitor, or theater, and this is a major source of its income. About half of the income from theaters comes from foreign ticket sales.

Besides the primary product of the film, the movie business today also relies on secondary products, such as video and DVD sales and rentals, distribution of films to cable and other TV markets, and foreign TV distribution. Over 50 percent of the revenue from a film comes from nontheatrical distribution of secondary products. In 2000, the breakdown of revenues for film was as follows:

- 26 percent theatrical receipts

- 28 percent television sales

- 46 percent video/DVD sales and rentals

The film business is always a *business,* but one that balances art with the entertainment needs of the audience. Artistic and creative aspects may be sacrificed to make a film that will reach the widest audience or bring in the quickest money. This practice creates an ongoing debate among writers, directors, marketing people, and accountants.

Theme Parks

The first amusement parks, called "pleasure gardens," appeared in Europe around 1550. They were landscaped gardens with games, music, and simple rides. In 1583, the world's oldest amusement park, Bakken, opened near Copenhagen, Denmark. During the 1800s in the United States, parks such as Coney Island with Luna Park in New York were built, as carousels, roller coasters, and Ferris wheels became popular. By 1910, there were over 2,000 amusement parks in the U.S., but within a decade many closed.

It was not until the 1950s and the creation of Disneyland that amusement parks evolved into what they are today. Before that, amusement parks were often unclean and unsafe, and employees were known to be rude and poorly trained. Walt Disney noticed this while taking his own young daughters to amusement parks. So, he developed the idea of a grand park with a variety of areas, each with a theme—fantasy, the Wild West, the future, and cartoons. Disney planned Disneyland to have exhibits and attractions for all ages—rides, different types of foods, many shops, bands, and other entertainers. Other services included a kennel to house visitors' pets while they were in the park as well as a post office. Cleanliness, organization, and friendly employees were a major part of the whole experience for customers, called "guests."

Disney went even further. To help pay for building Disneyland, he signed sponsors to contribute funds for different rides and exhibits. Companies such as Pepsi, Goodyear, and Kodak signed on to sponsor attractions at Disneyland. The sponsors benefited by being associated

CONNECT

Do you watch more movies on TV, in theaters, or on video/DVD?

Math Check

RECEIPTS FOR FUN
Theme parks collect $5.5 billion per year in receipts, and the average ticket costs about $25. Estimate how many people buy tickets per year on average.

➡️ For tips on finding the solution, go to marketingseries.glencoe.com.

Hot Property

Bigger Isn't Always Better

How do you build a better entertainment studio? For Steven Spielberg, Jeffrey Katzenberg, and David Geffen, you focus on quality and creativity, instead of speed and extravagance. When the trio announced their new venture in 1994, each was at the top of his game. Spielberg had established a worldwide reputation as the director of films such as *Jaws, Jurassic Park,* and *Schindler's List.* Katzenberg earned his reputation as chairman of Walt Disney Studios, guiding hits such as *The Little Mermaid* and *The Lion King.* Geffen was legendary for rising through the ranks of Hollywood to build his own record label, Geffen Records.

Despite success in their respective fields, each was dissatisfied with his role in Hollywood. Spielberg craved more creative freedom. Katzenberg wanted a greater leadership role. Geffen wanted to focus on making deals behind the scenes. Together, they tailored DreamWorks SKG into the entertainment business of their dreams.

BOUTIQUE WITH BUCKS

Since its inception, DreamWorks has consistently chosen to develop projects carefully, rather than churn out products at the pace of major studios. While some major studios produce 25 to 30 films per year, DreamWorks usually makes 10 or less. Though they have not avoided failures, they have enjoyed more than their share of critical successes with films such as *Saving Private Ryan* and *American Beauty.* In addition, they have strategically partnered with other studios on hits such as *Gladiator* and *Meet the Parents* to lessen their investment risk. Looking to the future, they hope to find more big-cash generators such as *Shrek,* which took extra care to develop but became a franchise-starting blockbuster.

1. What strategy does DreamWorks use to reduce economic risk?
2. What is DreamWorks' approach to producing successful films?

---

with a popular theme park and having exposure to millions of people each year who visited the park.

Since the 1950s, theme parks have grown around the world. Universal Studios, Knott's Berry Farm, Six Flags, Dollywood, and others are national and international tourist destinations.

The Price of Rides

The cost of creating new rides in theme parks is very high. A new roller coaster can cost $50 million. Rides must be carefully designed and have themes, such as *Batman* or *Jurassic Park,* to draw the customers. Each new ride must be bigger and better to succeed. Today there are over 600 amusement parks of various sizes in the United States. Some focus more on thrill rides, such as those at Six Flags. Others offer a wide variety of activities: Sea Life Park in Orlando, Florida, started out with whale and animal shows and expanded to include rides and water sports.

Water Parks

In the late 1980s, the water park idea developed, with flumes, pools, wave-making machines, and waterfalls as prime attractions. These parks continue to grow in popularity. However, the average yearly gross of about $450 million for water parks is small in comparison to the gross receipts of theme parks, which total over $5.5 billion each year.

Television

Television is the number one entertainment medium for many Americans. Adults spend on average three hours a day watching television, teenagers spend four to six hours, and children spend almost 25 hours a week watching TV. This does not go unnoticed by marketers and advertisers who realize that television is an important medium to reach the consumer. Television offers diversion and information to many people, but it is also a link to the world and can influence consumer behavior. Viewers who admire certain television personalities buy products that they use and wear styles they wear. MTV knows this and spends millions of dollars to plan programming and shows, such as *The Real World*, that will appeal to teens and young adults, which attracts advertisers who buy airtime on the network for promotional spots.

Because advertising sponsors support television networks, television shows either survive or get cancelled according to the size of their audiences. The shows with large viewerships continue, and shows with few viewers do not. Shows such as *Friends, Will and Grace,* and *Survivor* have had consistently high ratings, and thus, the networks that air those shows are able to charge high rates, with *Friends* at $473,500 for a 30-second commercial spot.

TV Production

Television programs originate from a variety of sources. Networks or services such as NBC, CBS, HBO, or Discovery Channel may produce their own products or shows. Studios such as Paramount or Disney may produce products as well. A television program can be a major feature film bought from a studio after it has been in theaters. Television stations can be independently owned or owned by a major network (e.g., ABC TV). As you have learned, many networks are owned by bigger entertainment conglomerates. For example, ESPN is owned by Disney.

The producers of shows are not necessarily the distributors. Just as movie studios do not usually own the theaters where their films are shown, TV stations may have no connection to a producer of a program. An independent station may decide to become an **affiliate**, which is an independent broadcaster that contracts with larger national networks for programming. The larger networks pick up the programming, while still acquiring independently produced programming. For example, at one time, NBC dropped the popular lifeguard program *Baywatch* due to poor **ratings**, which are the rankings of TV show or radio show popularity in a certain time period. The show was then produced independently and sold to independent stations around the country and the world. This strategy proved very successful, and *Baywatch* was produced for many years after being officially cancelled by its original network, NBC.

Zoo Cams

A number of zoos around the nation broadcast streaming video footage of their animals. While allowing researchers to monitor the animals' behavior, the live Web cams also offer potential visitors a peek at what each zoo has to offer through the zoo's Web site. For example, Cheyenne Mountain Zoo in Colorado Springs, Colorado, established the first Internet zoo camera, which keeps watch over the giraffe compound.

➡️View a zoo cam through **marketingseries.glencoe.com.** Name other entertainment venues that might benefit from using Web cams.

affiliate an independent broadcaster that contracts with larger national networks for programming

ratings the rankings of TV-show or radio-show popularity in a certain time period

TV Ratings

Ratings are a type of market research that determines if a program stays on the television schedule or is dropped. The most famous rating company is Nielsen Media Research. Through surveys of viewers, electronic data collection, and other methods, Nielsen ranks the popularity of a TV program within its time slot and geographic area. A show with a low rating means that it does not have enough viewers, and thus, advertising is not reaching an audience. A low rating usually means that advertisers will not buy time during the show, and the station or network will not make money. A show with a low rating will most likely be dropped, or cancelled.

TV Commercials

A typical television show runs for 30 minutes. Out of that, 22 minutes includes the content (program), and eight minutes are devoted to commercials. This advertising time can be split between national ads and local ads, depending on arrangements between the local station and the network. *Prime time* is the most expensive advertising time charged for the programming in the evening from 8 P.M. to 11 P.M. This is the time when the majority of people watch television. Advertisers are willing to pay more to place their ads on popular shows during this timeframe because they feel it will pay off.

Selling Airtime

The size of the market also influences the price of advertising, as well as the rating of the show. Advertising on *Friends* in the New York metropolitan area would cost far more than would advertising during a low-rated show in a small-town market. The most expensive TV ad time is for the Super Bowl. For example, a 30-second spot during the 2004 Super Bowl program sold for $2.25 million. Compare this to a 30-second local spot at 2 A.M., which might cost as little as $50 in a small-town market. TV networks use major events such as the Super Bowl as primary vehicles to advertise their prime-time line-ups of shows.

Marketing is involved in all aspects of television programming: planning, production, selling ad time, promoting the show, promoting products related to the show, planning residuals, reruns, and overseas distribution. **Niche marketing** is a type of marketing that focuses on a small target market of consumers who have very similar interests. This type of marketing has expanded in television marketing with many cable channels and specialized TV networks aimed at specific target markets. For example, the WB Channel focuses on teens and young adults. The WE Channel (Women's Entertainment Channel) provides programming aimed at women. ESPN focuses on sports enthusiasts who are primarily men. MTV aims at the teenage market. The target market is narrowed down further by the type of show offered on each network and its time slot.

Radio

Radio stations function as television stations do—as either independent stations or part of national networks. Both radio and television stations book local advertising, national ads, or both, depending

ETHICAL PRACTICES

A Different Kind of Rating

In the mid-1960s, America was in the midst of social change that would affect not only the nation but the movies as well.

In a decade marked by political and civil unrest, filmmakers began loosening their restraints. Hollywood's censorship board, the Production Code Administration, was dissolved after having authority for over 30 years. Street language and sexuality began to filter into films. Responding to public outcry in 1968, the Motion Picture Association of America set up what is known as the Voluntary Movie Rating System. It was created so that adults and children could identify the type of content that might be included in a film by letters such as G, PG, and R.

niche marketing a type of marketing that focuses on a small target market of consumers who have very similar interests

QUESTION

Why is prime time important to marketers?

on affiliation with national networks. Independents can obtain programming from national networks or develop their own programming. Radio stations rely on market research to determine popularity of radio programming. The Arbitron Rating Service and Nielsen are two businesses that evaluate the popularity of radio stations and their programs.

Radio programming categories include rock, hip-hop, call-in talk shows, classical, country, oldies, easy listening, and many others. Each category, or format, has a specific target market. For example, the people who listen to classical music are usually not the same people who listen to hip-hop music—and advertisers know this. Advertisers place commercials on stations that reach their audience, or target market.

Prime-Time Radio

Prime time for radio is different from prime time for TV. For radio, it is the morning-drive-to-work period of time with the captive commuter audience hungry for entertainment. Radio stations charge the most for ad spots during this time, which is usually between 6 A.M. and 9 A.M. Again, low ratings lead to show cancellation or format changes. For example, a country-music station could become an easy-listening rock station if a market shifts or if the ratings do not support country music—or vice versa.

Music Industry

The music industry is dependent on record companies to sign artists and produce and release albums. A record company is also called a *label.* The music business is risky because many albums and songs that are released do not make a profit. In addition, the musicians who are financially successful absorb the costs of those who are not.

The industry is always looking for new talent while trying to release new music from the established names. Labels such as Sony, Asylum, and others continually bring acts such as Coldplay, the Dixie Chicks, and many others to music stores or to online stores such as the e-tail store at Amazon.com.

Music and TV

In the early 1980s, MTV (Music Television channel) appeared and revolutionized the music business with music videos. Before videos, labels relied on airplay on the radio to promote sales of records and tapes. After videos became popular, artists had to promote their music by getting airplay on both radio and television. Record companies make large profits from successful artists who rely on up-front payments and royalties, or money paid to the owner, or author, label, or performer for material that has been copyrighted—in this case, music. In addition, if another artist *covers,* or records the same song, the company must pay the author for the use of that song. Whenever an artist's music is played on the radio or television by other bands or orchestras, or even as elevator music, the author receives royalties. This use of the music is tracked and documented by ASCAP (American Society of Composers, Authors, and Publishers) and BMI (Broadcast

Music, Inc.), two major organizations that collect royalties and distribute them to the artists.

Music and the Internet

The music industry has lost money as a result of illegal file sharing and downloading of music for free off the Internet, which was once done through Web sites such as the former Napster site. This practice bypasses the royalties and copyrights of musicians and record labels. The record labels, songwriters, and performers enforce copyrights to make sure payment is made for the use of their music. Some legal download services, such as iTunes, are operating with a positive response from the public.

Live Performance

In addition to radio and CD sales, musicians and performers often perform live and go on tour. This activity generates revenue from ticket sales, supports album sales, and provides public exposure with publicity in local communities. Touring provides an opportunity to make personal appearances and connect with fans. Performers will often visit local radio stations and talk with DJs to stimulate fan interest. Labels often provide free tickets as prizes to be given away on air, which also creates demand for concerts.

Performing Arts

From major productions on Broadway—the theater district in New York City—to plays in local venues, theater is a popular entertainment provider. Performance art is a very centralized business today, because a producer selects the play to be performed as well as the director, cast, and musicians. Producers work with theater owners to arrange the promotion, stage crew, box office, ticket sales, and other functions for a production.

Shows such as *Cats* and *Phantom of the Opera* earn millions of dollars each year. With the high cost of production today, many plays or productions are financed and produced by the same large entertainment companies that produce films or television. For example, Disney has financed the musical productions *Aida* and *The Lion King* on Broadway.

The Shows Go On

Many shows that prove successful on Broadway later tour around the country. These engagements can earn about 80 percent of the revenues for a successful play. Of course, many Broadway hits began as

Case Study — PART 2

A LASTING LANDMARK

Continued from Part 1 on page 217

During the 1980s and 1990s, the number of new theaters increased by 111 percent. With the development of multiple-screen theaters located in shopping malls and other nontraditional sites, many older single-screen movie theaters went out of business. Just before this expansion, the Chinese Theatre was bought by Ted Mann of Mann's Theatres chain, who began restoration of the theater and renamed it Mann's Chinese Theatre. However, by 2000–2001, Mann's Theatres chain went bankrupt, as did other chains such as Carmike Cinemas, Loews Cineplex Entertainment, and United Artists. The problem was too many theaters with too few customers.

However, the Chinese Theatre had its special appeal as a tourist destination and continued to sell tickets and promote special events. So it was bought by a subsidiary of Time Warner Entertainment Company for $91 million in 2001. As of November 2001, the original and legendary name, Grauman's Chinese Theatre, appeared once again above the world-renowned marquee.

ANALYZE AND WRITE

1. What significant event occurred in the film exhibition business during 2000–2001?

2. What has allowed the Chinese Theatre to stay in business with competition from new theaters?

Figure 10.2

Major Entertainment Awards

AWARDING ENTERTAINMENT
The Academy Awards are just one type of recognition given by the entertainment industry. *How might an entertainment marketer use an award to sell or promote an entertainment product?*

Award	Category
Academy Award (Oscar)	Excellence in all aspects of film, presented by the Academy of Motion Picture Arts and Sciences (AMPAS)
Golden Globe	Excellence in all aspects of film and television presented by the Hollywood Foreign Press
Emmy	Excellence in television programming, presented by the Academy of Television Arts and Sciences (ATAS)
Grammy	Excellence in musical performance, song-writing and composing, and producing, presented by the National Academy of Recording Arts and Sciences (NARAS)
Tony	Excellence in all aspects of theater production, presented by the American Theatre Wing

plays that toured the country or one or two cities before finding success on Broadway.

Popular theater productions may be adapted for film. For example, *Romeo and Juliet, Chicago,* and *Les Misérables* were all popular Broadway shows that became films. In addition, sometimes movies become successful plays. For example, the film *The Producers* was made into a blockbuster musical comedy that won many Tony Awards for its creator, Mel Brooks. (See **Figure 10.2** for examples of major awards given for different types of entertainment.)

The Internet and Computers

Research shows that teens spend more time on the Internet than watching television. Internet users can watch movies, listen to music, communicate with friends through instant messaging, access newspapers from around the world, and track information instantly.

Advertisers are constantly looking for ways to reach Web users through ads, banners, pop-ups, and spam (e-mail ads sent to Internet subscribers). Shopping on the Internet has increased since the early 1990s, yet it has not replaced brick-and-mortar retailing, as was often predicted. A **brick-and-mortar store** is a retail business with a physical location or store site.

brick-and-mortar store a retail business with a physical location or store site

Computer Games

The growth of the video and computer game industry has been steady and expansive. The first games were inspired by pinball machines and shooting gallery games, as a young TV engineer Ralph Baer began inventing game models in 1951. At the time, only researchers, scientists, and military personnel had access to computers and video technology, which were experimental and expensive.

By 1958, nuclear researcher William Higinbotham came up with the first video game *Tennis for Two*. Such games consisted mainly of blips and dots on a screen. Then in 1962, the world was introduced to the first interactive video game *Spacewar*. A Harvard University employee, Stephen Russel, is credited with creating that game. Later games such as *Space Invaders* were designed mainly for arcade machines during the 1970s. Baer's early experience was applied to the first home video-game system *Odyssey*, made by Magnavox in 1972. That opened the door to other developers such as Coleco and Atari, which experienced success with *Pong* in the 1970s. Sales of interactive computer games exploded in the 1980s due to game consoles such as Nintendo.

Moving into the 21st century, inspiration for new games comes from fiction adventure as well as movie tie-ins. The computer game industry continues to expand with online gaming earning at least one-third of the total revenue for the whole industry. With Nintendo's Game Boy, Microsoft's Xbox, and Sony's PlayStation game systems growing in popularity every year, the electronic entertainment industry is earning over $7 billion annually.

Other Entertainment Businesses

The circus has been another popular form of entertainment for decades, but it has competed, first, with movies, then with TV— and now with the Internet. However, innovative circuses, such as

◄ NEW CIRCUS In the tradition of diverse street performers, the Cirque du Soleil revived and reinvented the traditional circus with its goal "to entertain, uplift, and enlighten audiences the world over." *Who do you think is the target market for Cirque du Soleil?*

Cirque du Soleil have attracted a new audience through the use of magical and fantasy-themed shows. The circus business faces high costs of moving people, equipment, and supplies from city to city, and doing advance promotional work to draw the audience.

Marketing plays a major role in promoting theme restaurants. When you dine at Hard Rock Café or Planet Hollywood, you have stepped into the world of "eatertainment," where the food is often secondary to the environment of rock music, memorabilia, and souvenir merchandising.

Opera and ballet are also long-standing forms of entertainment with more limited markets. These productions are usually staged in larger metropolitan areas and attended by an educated audience with higher incomes. Many of the companies that produce these performances are publicly funded, nonprofit organizations. A **nonprofit organization** is a non-governmental organization that focuses on providing a service rather than a profit. Unfortunately, costs for the elaborate production of operas and ballets can be so high that the limited audience does not provide enough ticket revenue to make the production successful. Nevertheless, opera, ballet, and dance companies continue to provide live entertainment to many people, who are also targeted by entertainment marketing.

nonprofit organization a non-governmental organization that focuses on providing a service rather than a profit

Variety of Markets

With so many forms of entertainment—film, TV, computer games, print media, music, theme parks, and performing arts—marketing professionals have unlimited products to offer to almost any target market. Understanding the characteristics and economic aspects of the types of media and forms of entertainment will help to ensure successful marketing plans.

Quick Check

RESPOND to what you've read by answering these questions.

1. What is an indie movie company? _____
_____
_____

2. What is prime time for television? _____
_____
_____

3. What are royalties? _____
_____
_____
_____

Name _____ Date _____

Worksheet 10.1

Entertainment Businesses

Choose a major entertainment company such as The Walt Disney Company or Vivendi
Universal. Research on the Internet or at the library to learn about the other companies it
owns. Then make a graphic organizer or chart that illustrates the different media companies
owned by the one large corporation. For example, include these categories in your chart:

- Theme parks
- Television
- Computer games

- Internet
- Music
- Radio

- Film
- Performing arts
- Print

Name of company: _____

Worksheet 10.2

Entertainment Spending

For two weeks, use the chart below to keep track of your entertainment spending.

Entertainment	Amount Spent
Theme parks	_____
	_____
	_____
	_____
Performing arts	_____
	_____
	_____
	_____
Internet and computer games	_____
	_____
	_____
	_____
Movies	_____
	_____
	_____
	_____
Entertainment magazines	_____
	_____
	_____
	_____
Recorded music	_____
	_____
	_____
	_____
Total money spent:	_____

Portfolio Works

TV LOG

For one week, keep a log of times that you watch television and what you watch. For at least one day, write down all of the commercials that are on before, during, and after the program(s) you watch. Then answer the following questions.

1. How much time did you watch TV in one week?

_____

2. On average, how much time did you watch TV in a day?_____

3. What is your favorite TV program and why?

_____

_____

_____

_____

4. Name three of the products advertised and describe the advertisements used to sell those products.

_____

_____

_____

_____

5. Do you think these ads are effective? Why?

_____

_____

_____

_____

6. Do you or does anyone in your family buy any of the products you see advertised on TV? If so, which ones?

_____

_____

_____

_____

Add this page to your career portfolio.

CHAPTER SUMMARY

Section 10.1 Entertainment and Marketing

entertainment marketing
(p. 218)
media (p. 219)
fad (p. 219)
cross-selling (p. 221)
leisure time (p. 222)

- Entertainment marketing is the process of developing, promoting, and distributing products, or goods and services, to satisfy customers' needs and wants through entertainment, or any diversion, amusement, or method of occupying time.

- Entertainment media, or the methods used for communicating or transmitting messages, can include film, television, radio, publishing media, the Internet, and more.

- Entertainment impacts many areas of the economy. A significant source of revenue is merchandising entertainment products. Businesses cross-sell and market products tied to one name.

- Entertainment marketing impacts the global economy and generates revenue in the United States and abroad. The number one American export after agricultural products is entertainment.

Section 10.2 Types of Entertainment Businesses

break even (p. 225)
oligopoly (p. 225)
affiliate (p. 228)
ratings (p. 228)
niche marketing (p. 229)
brick-and-mortar store
(p. 232)
nonprofit organization
(p. 234)

- Entertainment businesses include companies that create and market film, TV, radio, music, theme parks, and the performing arts. The film industry is considered an oligopoly because it is strongly influenced but not controlled by a few major studios. Independent companies, or indies, also produce and market films. The music industry is dependent on major record companies.

- A variety of forms of entertainment are marketed to consumers, including movies, TV shows, music, radio programs, theme parks, ballet, opera, theater, computer games, museums, circuses, and theme restaurants.

CHECKING CONCEPTS

1. **Define** entertainment marketing.
2. **Identify** types of media.
3. **Name** two consumer products that are influenced by entertainment.
4. **Describe** an oligopoly.
5. **Identify** types of entertainment businesses.
6. **Explain** why many films produced do not break even.
7. **Define** ratings.

Critical Thinking
8. **Describe** how cable TV uses niche marketing.

CROSS-CURRICULUM SKILLS

Work-Based Learning

Resources—Allocating Money

9. If Environco has an annual television advertising budget of $8,000,000 and revenue of $138,000,000, what percentage of revenue is spent on advertising?

Thinking Skills—Reasoning

10. Your company makes home-improvement products, such as carpet and wallpaper. Someone suggested advertising on MTV because it has a large audience. Do you think this would be an effective advertising strategy? Why?

School-Based Learning

History

11. Using the Internet or an encyclopedia, find out when the first radio and television programs were broadcast.

Language Arts

12. Use a dictionary to find out how the meaning of the word *broadcast* has changed over time.

Role Play: Marketing Manager

SITUATION You are to assume the role of marketing manager for an independent music production company. Your company records music and distributes it through music stores, festivals and concerts, and the Internet. Your boss (judge) has noticed an increase in downloading of songs by your artists on the Internet and is concerned about pirating.

ACTIVITY Present to your boss (judge) a plan for the release of an artist's album that will protect the product from illegal distribution.

EVALUATION You will be evaluated on how well you meet the following performance indicators:

- Identify factors affecting a business's profit.
- Determine factors affecting business risk.
- Explain the concept of competition.
- Describe the impact of pirating.
- Explain legal considerations in distribution.

Use the Internet to access the Sony Web site and answer the following questions:

- What were annual sales for the last fiscal year?
- Name three of Sony's U.S. businesses.
- How many people does Sony employ worldwide?

➡ For a link to the Sony Web site to help you answer these questions, go to **marketingseries.glencoe.com.**

Chapter 11

Entertainment Products and Marketing

N

Chapter Objectives

- Identify types of entertainment products.
- Define evergreen products.
- Describe location-based entertainment (LBE).
- Explain the significance of impulse spending.
- Explain why marketing is involved in entertainment product development.
- Discuss the difference between primary and secondary markets.
- Explain the importance of programming.

MASTER OF TICKETS

When people consider products, they often think of tangible goods such as toys or clothing. Services are also products. The entertainment industry offers a great variety of services, including live and filmed entertainment on TV and in theaters. Ticketmaster sells tickets for events as an entertainment service.

When Ticketmaster formed in 1981, the company was a "group of college students with bright ideas." Under the guidance of entrepreneur Robert Leonard, its goal was to upgrade phone systems in each of its clients' box offices. It would create a network of ticket offices where, for a fee, customers could buy tickets for just about any event. The business took off. It became the exclusive supplier of tickets for the majority of professional sports events, dance performances, concerts, shows, and plays. In 1990, Ticketmaster bought out Ticketron and dominated the industry. Then the popular rock band Pearl Jam filed a lawsuit that questioned Ticketmaster's prices, but the proceeding was discontinued in 1995. However, Ticketmaster was about to face its next challenge—the growing popularity of ticket sales through the Internet.

ANALYZE AND WRITE

1. Are tickets entertainment products? Why?
2. What was a challenge to Ticketmaster?

Case Study Part 2 on page 255

POWER READ

Be an active reader and use these reading strategies:

PREDICT what the section will be about.

CONNECT what you read with your life.

QUESTION as you read to make sure you understand the content.

RESPOND to what you've read.

Types of Entertainment Products

AS YOU READ ...

YOU WILL LEARN

- To identify types of entertainment products.
- To define evergreen products.
- To describe location-based entertainment (LBE).
- To explain the significance of impulse spending.

WHY IT'S IMPORTANT

There are many entertainment products, including goods and services, available to consumers. Understanding the variety helps in creating effective marketing strategies to merchandise these products.

KEY TERMS

- concessions
- evergreens
- record clubs
- rack jobbers
- location-based entertainment (LBE)
- impulse spending

concessions snack-bars that sell refreshments such as popcorn, soda, and candy

PREDICT

Give an example of impulse spending.

Entertaining Products

You learned in Chapter 1 that products can include both tangible goods and intangible services. The entertainment industry produces both very successfully, in part due to the efforts of entertainment marketers. This chapter discusses many of the products available and how they are marketed. Media-based entertainment goods include films on DVDs and videos, music on DVDs and CDs, video and electronic games, and books and magazines, as well as toys, T-shirts, concessions, and other goods related to entertainment products. Media-based entertainment services include television shows, movies in theaters, and concert and theater performances. Recreation-based entertainment services are offered at amusement parks, zoos, museums, and even snack bars. All of these things are entertainment products that are often marketed more extensively than products such as cars, cereal, or shoes.

Film and Music Merchandising

Theaters provide their media-based services—motion pictures, plays, and musical productions—for which customers pay and receive tickets. Theaters also provide services at **concessions**, or snack-bars that sell refreshments such as popcorn, soda, and candy. Studios also issue related or extended products of films, such as character toys, games, and clothing goods.

The home-entertainment industry sells media-based goods such as films in DVD and video formats. In addition, there is a vast segment of retailers that buys prerecorded entertainment software to sell to the public. Retailers of entertainment goods range from Wal-Mart, the largest retailer in the world, Best Buy, and Sam Goody to many small, local shops. These companies buy billions of dollars of inventory, or entertainment product, every year from producers. Because of volume buying, the larger stores buy DVDs and CDs for a lower price than the smaller stores pay. The large stores pass the lower prices on to the customer. In addition to these brick-and-mortar stores, Internet versions of the same stores and e-tail stores, such as Amazon.com, sell these entertainment goods.

DVD/Video Rentals and Sales

Film producers have two choices for DVD and video distribution—to rent or to *sell through,* which is selling to the customer. Currently about 40 percent of revenue for DVDs and videos comes from sell through. Thus, many customers buy films in DVD and video formats as entertainment goods for home use. Studios promote first-run films more than they promote DVD and video sales at stores such as Blockbuster. In-store sales promotion and television advertising are key methods of marketing rentals and creating sales.

Evergreens, or films or products that are popular year after year, are important primarily because new generations of viewers who may be unfamiliar with the films buy them. For example, the Disney films *Aladdin, The Little Mermaid,* and *The Lion King* fall in the evergreen category. For the baby-boom generation, MGM's *The Wizard of Oz* and Warner Brothers' *Casablanca* are also evergreens. These products will continue to generate steady revenue.

Have you ever gone to rent a video and noticed many titles that you have never seen before? Those may be movies that did not succeed at the box office after release and were pulled from theaters. Some films are made for release straight to video rental or to the overseas film and television markets. These products will generate revenue if they are marketed very carefully.

Marketing media is challenging because technology changes so quickly. For example, in the 1950s, television put some theater owners out of business. Currently, pay-per-view and on-demand film rentals from cable-TV providers are threatening rental-store business. People stay home and rent recently released films through their cable-TV providers or through online providers such as Netflix.com, and they avoid the trip to the video rental store. Many people prefer to relax at home instead of going out. Convenience is a major selling point for this entertainment service.

Music CDs and Distribution

Worldwide sales of recorded music total about $40 billion a year. Both music specialty stores and large retailers such as Tower Records and Wal-Mart sell music CDs, which are media-based entertainment goods. In addition to in-store sales, the marketing efforts of record clubs and rack jobbers also contribute to sales of CDs. **Record clubs** are organizations in which members receive free records if they agree to purchase additional records within a certain time period. These clubs focus on direct-mail and print-media campaigns to sell their products and have expanded to the Internet with companies such as BMG.com and Columbia House.

Rack jobbers are independent vendors who distribute, price, and control their own inventory within a store. For example, they come into retail stores and set up displays and a limited assortment of CDs and tapes. Rack jobbers work in convenience stores, small discount stores, and variety stores.

With the many online companies marketing music alongside retail stores and clubs, it is easy to see why so much money is being made selling these entertainment goods.

TECH
NOTES

High-Tech Tickets
Touchscreen technology may eliminate long lines at cinema box offices. Patrons can speed up the process of purchasing movie tickets and snack items by using interactive kiosks. For those who haven't decided which movie to see, kiosks also feature preview videos at the touch of an onscreen button. Besides providing faster service, kiosks may also increase sales. Studies have shown that moviegoers often spend more money when paying with credit cards.

➡️Name some benefits of installing kiosks at movie theaters after reading information through **marketingseries.glencoe.com.**

evergreens films or products that are popular year after year

record clubs organizations in which members receive free records if they agree to purchase additional records within a time period

rack jobbers independent vendors who distribute, price, and control their own inventory within a store

Hot Property

Quirky Entertainment Products

 How do you go from selling records out of your car to being part of a multinational corporation? Like Richard Foos, you find a loyal audience and create products they desire. Foos opened the Rhino Records store in 1973 to sell old records and cult classics that he had collected at sales and swap meets. The store found an enthusiastic market of music fans hungry for Foos's finds. Then in 1978, he teamed up with his star salesman Harold Bronson to produce the first record on the Rhino label. The novelty single *Go to Rhino Records* caught on with listeners and put the new record company on the map.

BRANCHING OUT

Of course, one funny song does not make a record label. Foos and Bronson expanded their catalog to include reissues, anthologies, and a various artists series. If you wanted a pristine copy of a Monkees record, Rhino had it on its roster. If you were looking for a rare jazz album or a comedy recording, you could find it as a Rhino release.

By 1985, Rhino expanded to include a video division, which packaged and sold cult movies such as *Attack of the Killer Tomatoes* and television shows such as *The Brady Bunch*.

The corporate world took notice of Rhino's success, and in 1998, Rhino Entertainment became part of the Warner Music Group, a division of Time-Warner. Though part of a large conglomerate, Rhino Entertainment has retained its quirky personality and dedication to social causes. For example, employees receive days off to perform community service. It is a unique approach from a company that thrives on selling unique products.

1. Name the Rhino Entertainment products that contributed to the company's growth.
2. Do you think marketing to a small but loyal audience can succeed as well as marketing to a mass audience? Why?

Electronic and Video Games

Video and electronic games as media-based entertainment products have been growing in popularity since they were first introduced. At about $10 billion a year, the gross sales of video games for game consoles, such as PlayStation® and Xbox™, rival the sales of music CDs. In most DVD and video rental shops, such as Blockbuster, 40 percent or more of the space is devoted to video-game rentals.

Many major producers of games are large conglomerates. Examples are Sony and Vivendi Universal, who have sophisticated marketing and distribution operations. Microsoft is also aggressively pursuing the game market because it realizes the potential for profits.

Electronic Arts, the largest independent developer of electronic games, competes with major movie studios in terms of creative output. The company has flexibility because it produces games that can be played on game systems such as Xbox, PlayStation, and Game Boy®. This flexibility broadens the buyer market and increases sales.

Marketing Games With Music

Cross-marketing in video-game distribution is common. Gamemakers work with films, television shows, sports teams, and cartoon characters. Popular music has a big role in video games. For exam-

CONNECT

Have you played an electronic game related to a film?

ple, Trent Reznor of the band Nine Inch Nails began making music for games in 1996 with the video game *Quake*. He has also composed music for the game *Doom III*. Music provides a background for the video games and is in high demand by the game players. Sony, the maker of the top-selling PlayStation2, released separate CDs of music from the game *Grand Theft Auto: Vice City* with music tracks by Ozzy Osbourne and Iron Maiden.

At rock festivals such as Lollapalooza and the Nintendo Fusion Tour, video games are part of the appeal. At Lollapalooza, a huge inflatable dome was created for fans who played games at over 100 Xbox video-game terminals while the bands played outside on stage. Xbox and the software creators have their markets clearly targeted. The game target market is young: Four out of ten players are under 18, and 40 percent of them are 18–35 years old.

Electronic Game Tie-Ins

The potential is huge for tie-ins with films, music, and sports as well as related merchandise such as apparel and accessories, because the game buyers are also the primary market for all of these forms of entertainment. "Advergaming" is the marketing concept that drives video-game marketing. Advertisers see the games as a good way to reach target markets, and they create games that are really ads but look and play like games. For example, Daimler-Chrysler knows that over 60 percent of PlayStation2 players are over 24 years of age. This is Chrysler's key market. The Jeep, Dodge, and Chrysler automobile brands have been placed in online games created by Chrysler to entertain—and sell products.

Print Books and Magazines

Second to theater, the print media—books, magazines, comics, newspapers—is one of the oldest sources of entertainment. In fact, despite the computer age, customers are now buying more books and magazines (media-based entertainment goods) than ever before. In 2003, the record for first-day sales of fiction books was broken when *Harry Potter and the Order of the Phoenix* went on sale. Crossing media lines, singer-performer Madonna also entered the print media world by selling millions of copies of her children's books, such as *The English Roses*.

Book Categories

Trade books are published for general bookstore sales and public library circulation. This group of books includes fiction, humor, poetry, arts, music, how-to, self-help, and many other types. The fiction category of books is best known for its escape-from-reality entertainment value— and fiction accounts for most books sold. Genres, or types, of fiction books include romance, science fiction, mystery, fantasy, horror, and western.

Romance publishers such as Harlequin Enterprises sell over 700 titles a year in supermarkets, drugstores, and book retail chains. These entertainment products are written with a story formula that success-

Game Point

ISN'T IT ROMANTIC? According to the Romance Writers of America, fans of romantic novels may read three to six books per week.

QUESTION

What type of entertainment is a theme park?

location-based entertainment (LBE) entertainment that includes amusement, theme, animal, and water parks

fully reaches its target market of women over 50 in suburban and mid-western communities.

Many fiction titles are adapted and tied in to films and vice versa. For example, the novel *The Firm* was printed with Tom Cruise's face on the cover after the film that starred Cruise was a success. Other novels and book series, such as *The Shawshank Redemption* by Stephen King, *The Lord of the Rings* trilogy by J.R.R. Tolkien, and the *Harry Potter* series by J.K. Rowling, have also been successfully translated into box-office hits.

Magazines

As entertainment products, magazines offer a good opportunity to marketers who are looking for ready-made target markets. There are many specific groups of customers who buy certain magazine titles. In fact, there are over 20,000 magazine titles on the market appealing to different groups. However, only 160 of those titles earn 85 percent of the total magazine revenue.

Some magazines are considered evergreens. Examples include *The New Yorker, Time, National Geographic, Good Housekeeping, Newsweek, Life,* and *BusinessWeek* magazines, though they are also subject to the ups and downs of consumer spending. Many entertainment-industry magazines and trade publications are well-established, such as *Rolling Stone, Billboard, Variety,* and *The Hollywood Reporter.*

Major media corporations that own film and television studios also own magazines and other print media. Time Warner, Hearst Corporation, General Electric, and Viacom, to name a few, include newspapers, magazines and book publishing companies on their corporate rosters. With the development of Internet publishing and e-zines, many printed publications also have electronic versions of the magazines on Web sites. The potential for reaching a greater global market is huge for print media.

Theme Parks and Water Parks

Theme parks and water parks not only provide recreation-based entertainment services, but they also sell tangible goods. Disney owns or controls five major theme-park operations as well as many smaller parks around the world. Other companies are also involved in the amusement-park industry. Paramount Studios owns five amusement/theme parks, and Six Flags, Inc., owns 39 regional theme parks in the United States and Europe.

Location-based entertainment (LBE) is the industry term for entertainment that includes amusement, theme, animal, and water parks. LBEs have evolved into major entertainment forms, and they are local, regional, or national attractions. For example, people may travel from North Dakota to Walt Disney World in Florida, which is a national attraction, but they might not travel to New Hampshire to visit Canobie Lake Park, a local attraction. Six Flags promotes the fact that it has a park within eight hours from the homes of 98 percent of the American population.

World Market

Danish Amusements

In 2003, one of the world's most beautiful amusement parks, Tivoli Gardens, celebrated a landmark anniversary—its 160th. Concerts, performances by the New York City Ballet, and a year-round discount offer commemorated the event.

In 1843, Tivoli Gardens opened outside the city of Copenhagen, Denmark. The king had granted permission for its construction, believing that a ride on a merry-go-round might distract the people from plotting *regicide*—or "murder of a king." The park was designed so that the buildings could be torn down easily in the event of war. As Copenhagen grew in size, the city soon included the 21-acre park, which became an urban oasis.

The old structures still stand today. Each year, five million visitors enjoy a variety of amusements, including theater and concerts performed among flowers, lakes, 115,000 lights, and Saturday-evening fireworks. For children of all ages, there are 25 rides that will turn you upside-down, throw you around, or drop you from on high. In addition, Denmark's highest and fastest roller coaster was built in 2004 to thrill and entertain visitors.

Can you name any U.S. amusement parks that are similar to the historic Tivoli Gardens?

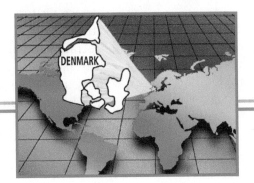

In the 1990s, the major park operators began promoting theme parks as destinations and resorts, trying to get tourists to stay for more than one day at the parks and thus spend more money. Once in the park, visitors are basically a "captive audience" of spenders. In addition to admissions fees, which can be over $50 for adults, visitors buy food, gifts, souvenirs, and apparel. Customers' **impulse spending**, or buying without prior planning, is common since the park environment is set up to urge patrons to spend money at every opportunity.

impulse spending buying without prior planning

Theme-Park Tie-Ins

LBE venues are usually owned by major entertainment conglomerates, and they use themes, characters, stories, and other intellectual property of their owners. Intellectual property is an idea, concept, or written or created work that is unique and is protected by copyright laws. It also has value in the marketplace. For example, nonowners can license the use of characters or popular films or stories in exchange for fees. The ability of LBE owners to cross-sell products in their parks has made them very popular with marketing managers. For example, at Disneyland in Anaheim, California, shops sell souvenirs based on current and past Disney movies. Thus, the movies are promoted throughout the park as well. As another example, one of Disneyland's oldest and most popular attractions, *Pirates of the Caribbean*, was adapted as a blockbuster movie.

Theme-park owners have also found that for the price of one new roller coaster, they can build a whole water park in or next to their property. Water parks are low-cost fun centers that the whole family can enjoy—and once again visitors are a captive buying audience and will purchase other products while at the park. Water parks are one of the fastest-growing entertainment services in the LBE area.

Edutainment

Other related destinations that provide recreation-based entertainment services are linked to education, called "edutainment." Art museums, natural history museums, zoos, and historic sites not only provide entertainment, but these recreational facilities also focus on learning as part of the experience.

MUSEUMS During the 1990s, museums experienced worldwide expansion with greater public interest in cultural and educational activities as forms of entertainment. Thus, museum marketers and administrators became more aware of their markets and strategies to attract visitors. In fact, most museums have two main goals—to attract more visitors and to generate more income to support their operations, which include acquiring collections, maintaining physical facilities, supporting staff, and marketing activities. Many museums have developed extensive Web sites to provide services and information.

ZOOS As another form of edutainment, zoos and animal parks have also enjoyed increased popularity along with increased awareness of marketing strategies. Around the world, millions of people visit zoos every day. The American Zoo and Aquarium Association reports that over 134 million people visit zoos and aquariums each year, which is a greater attendance than that of NFL, NBA, and Major League Baseball events combined. Moreover, students make up a large part of that total. More than nine million students attend onsite education programs at zoos and aquariums every year. Many of these programs are free of charge, supported by donors and some government funds. About 800,000 animals are cared for in zoos, which maintain strong conservation programs. Besides the social, cultural, and educational value of this form of entertainment, zoos also provide jobs and generate income for local communities through tourism.

THEATERS Film theaters have stepped into the world of "edutainment" by offering special events in connection with popular commercial films shown in theaters. For example, the Regal Entertainment Group owns the largest theater chain with 562 locations in the United States. It has developed the first digital theater network that can link up via satellite. This capability has enabled Regal to create CineEducation, which combines education with entertainment. In 2003, students across the country participated in a live interactive video classroom designed around the film *Ghosts of the Abyss*. Through events such as this, education becomes very entertaining and learning increases.

CHAMPIONSHIP ENTERTAINMENT Ice shows have been a source of entertainment for many years. The best and the brightest champions headline these shows. *Why do you think a show of this type is an entertainment service?*

Special Entertainment Events

Special entertainment events such as circuses, state fairs, pageants, and ice shows all provide entertainment services. Each event also supplies a venue for selling related entertainment products, such as concessions and souvenirs. Ice shows such as *Disney on Ice, Stars on Ice,* the *Sesame Street Show,* and *Champions on Ice* are a blend of sports and performance entertainment. Costumes, sets, music, story, and skating skills are combined to provide family-style shows for all ages. These shows are often headlined by former Olympic skating champions such as Tara Lipinski and Michelle Kwan. Similar to the circus, or bands on tour, the ice shows are constantly moving to different arenas across the country, providing its entertainment service to eager audiences.

Quick Check ✓

RESPOND to what you've read by answering these questions.

1. Why are evergreens important to the film industry? _____

   _____

   _____

2. What are three forms of location-based entertainment (LBE)? _____

   _____

   _____

3. What is a rack jobber? _____

   _____

   _____

Media Product Marketing

YOU WILL LEARN

- To explain why marketing is involved in entertainment product development.
- To discuss the difference between primary and secondary markets.
- To explain the importance of programming.

WHY IT'S IMPORTANT

Being aware of entertainment product marketing methods is important for success in a marketing career.

KEY TERMS

- primary market
- secondary market
- exhibitors
- gross revenue
- trailers
- syndication
- programming
- payola
- jingle
- ad campaign

PREDICT

Look at the main headings in this section and describe the topics of this section.

Media Marketing Channels

The major media include film, TV, radio, print publishing, and the Internet. These different media are the channels for marketing entertainment products. These media are also forms of entertainment in themselves and serve as sources of entertainment as well as channels for marketing messages. As you learned in Units 2 and 3, the sports entertainment industry is dependent on all media, though sporting events are often live with spectators at venues. The media control what gets through to the viewer or listener, and the media also shape opinions and consumer wants and needs. Marketers know this. In fact, marketing teams are usually involved in the development of most entertainment products, or goods and services.

Marketing Film and Distribution

When a studio or indie develops and produces a film, it usually focuses on the goal of getting the film seen by as many paying customers as possible. Therefore, a large part of planning a film involves marketing and merchandising. The movie is a product that has many accessory products, or product extensions, associated with it. For example, the *Star Wars* films were planned with many products that tie in with the films and that greatly increase the profit potential. Planning takes place to design and market toys, games, books, comics, posters, clothing, and many other items related to a movie.

Selling the music from a soundtrack is also a major moneymaker for film studios. The cross-marketing between film and music is important to the success of both products. The film producers also plan the DVD and video marketing as well as the strategies for cable TV and international distribution. This planning usually starts well before filming begins.

Primary and Secondary Markets

The film market is divided into primary markets and secondary markets. The **primary market** in film distribution is the target audience which is the theaters that show films in first release. The **secondary market** is the target audience after a film has been in first run at theaters, and it includes foreign theatres, television, discount theaters, home rental and sales, cable TV, and airlines. There is a basic film distribution system with many steps. A studio or independent production company creates the product, or film. It is then shopped to the **exhibitors,** or theaters that sell tickets and show films to an audience—or the primary market.

Every year at the ShoWest Convention, all major studios and hundreds of exhibitors from over 50 countries meet and look at the new studio offerings. It is here that many of the films you see in your local theaters are booked and scheduled. Movies go into *limited release* or *wide release* when they come out. Limited release, or platforming, places the films in only a few theaters in the whole country to showcase them and create "buzz," or public interest. Later they go into wide release and are booked in thousands of theaters nationwide. Some films come out and go directly into wide release. Films such as *Finding Nemo, Armageddon,* and the *Rush Hour* series are examples of wide-release films.

Film Exhibitors

The field of exhibitors is primarily made up of large theater chains. Eight major chains control about 20,000 theaters and 65 percent of the screens in the United States. They bring in eight out of every ten dollars earned at movie theaters. One company is Regal Entertainment, which owns Regal Cinemas, United Artists Cinemas, and Edwards Theatres; other companies are Loews Cineplex and AMC.

The exhibitor's **gross revenue** is total income from sales before costs, expenses, and taxes are deducted. The exhibitor breaks down gross revenue sources in two areas:

- 70 percent from ticket sales

- 30 percent from concessions sales

The price for the tickets and concessions are decided by the exhibitor. Theaters have found that home entertainment, such as videos, DVDs, and video games, have not reduced ticket sales. The experience of going to a theater to see a film is part of the film-going experience and is not the same experience as watching at home; film-going involves social interaction. The exhibitors also know that 60 percent of the theater audience is within the 14- to 29-year-old age group.

Studios and independents begin promoting their upcoming film ideas to exhibitors before filming has begun. This generates interest and advance bookings. Both ends of the distribution channel need each other. The studio needs outlets for the films, and the exhibitors need popular films to sell tickets and put people in the seats. The film studio and the exhibitor also use **trailers,** or previews of coming movies shown before the main feature, to create interest in new releases.

Marketing Television

As you learned in Chapter 10, television is the number-one entertainment medium used by Americans. Entertainment producers are constantly trying to develop programming that will result in high ratings and attract advertisers. Most television shows that run in prime time (8 P.M. to 11 P.M.) are created by major studios. These shows bring in the greatest advertising revenue with the most people watching at this time. (See **Figure 11.1** on page 252.)

ETHICAL PRACTICES

A Classic Film Monopoly

Long before independent filmmakers, there was the Big Five—a group that monopolized the movie industry. Warner Brothers, Paramount, RKO, MGM, and Fox were the Hollywood studios that controlled all areas of film development and distribution. They not only owned theaters, they also required other theater owners to rent packages of their B movies, or less popular films, in exchange for showing the blockbuster movies. This monopoly in the motion picture industry ruled until the late 1940s, when the U.S. government broke it up.

primary market in film distribution, the target audience, which is the theaters that show films in first release

secondary market in film distribution, target audience after a film has been in first run at theaters

exhibitors theaters that sell tickets and show films to an audience

gross revenue total income from sales before costs, expenses, and taxes are deducted

trailers previews of upcoming movies shown before the main feature

CONNECT

On average, how many trailers do you see before the main feature?

Reruns, or previously aired shows, are a great source of revenue for studios and networks because the basic costs of production are already paid, and the show can be televised in different markets over and over, continually generating profits. A TV series or sitcom (situation comedy), such as *Everybody Loves Raymond*, makes money in reruns and syndication after its original network run.

Syndication is selling television programs to individual stations, not networks. Many actors make more money on reruns than on the original shows. Some programs, such as *All in the Family* and *Seinfeld*, replay for years in the United States and abroad. Actors collect payments called residuals every time shows are aired up to a certain number of times.

Marketing television differs for "reality shows" such as *Survivor* and *The Bachelor*. While they cost little to produce and have earned strong advertising revenue for the networks up front, they have limited rerun value. This means that earning potential will diminish when these shows are no longer popular.

Television target audiences are specialized by **programming**, which is the schedule, or times, for broadcasting shows on television. Companies with products to sell to kids target Saturday morning shows. Shaving cream marketers might target sports programming or prime-time sitcoms. Programming is determined by the top network executives.

Marketing Radio

R adio is one of the best ways to target your advertising message to an audience. Before TV, there was radio. By the 1920s most people had a radio in their homes. Advertisers bought time and paid for radio programming by sponsoring shows. This practice set the trend for TV in the 1950s.

Today there are over 11,000 commercial radio stations in the United States with over 2 million listeners and many more around

syndication selling television programs to individual stations, not networks

programming the schedule, or times, for broadcasting shows on television; or on radio, also the music style and playlist

---

Figure 11.1

TV Time Slots

THE BEST TIME OF DAY
Besides determining advertising costs, time slots also tell marketers how many people are watching. *If you wanted to advertise your product to many people, but you had a limited budget, what daypart slot might you choose?*

Dayparts	Time
Early morning	5 A.M. – 9 A.M.
Daytime	9 A.M. – 3 P.M.
Early fringe	3 P.M. – 5 P.M.
Early news	5 P.M. – 7 P.M.
Access	7 P.M. – 8 P.M.
Prime time	8 P.M. – 11 P.M.
Prime time on Sundays	7 P.M. – 11 P.M.
Late news	11 P.M. – 11:30 P.M.
Late fringe	11:30 P.M. – 1:00 A.M.

Profiles in Marketing

KEEPING IT COOL

Mike Kappus
Founder and President
The Rosebud Agency

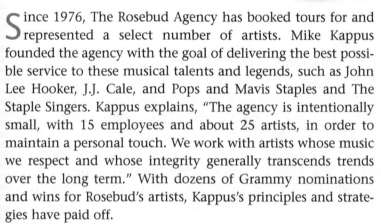

Since 1976, The Rosebud Agency has booked tours for and represented a select number of artists. Mike Kappus founded the agency with the goal of delivering the best possible service to these musical talents and legends, such as John Lee Hooker, J.J. Cale, and Pops and Mavis Staples and The Staple Singers. Kappus explains, "The agency is intentionally small, with 15 employees and about 25 artists, in order to maintain a personal touch. We work with artists whose music we respect and whose integrity generally transcends trends over the long term." With dozens of Grammy nominations and wins for Rosebud's artists, Kappus's principles and strategies have paid off.

Indeed, principles guide Kappus's professional practices in the music business—a business in which many people do not always follow through. "Just by doing what you say you will do, and advising quickly if you cannot, sets you apart from others in this business and builds respect." He believes that hard work and doing his best to live up to commitments have benefited Rosebud and its clients. Community awareness and service are another guiding principle. Rosebud was the first facility in the music industry to become fully solar-powered. Kappus helped produce benefit CDs for the environmental organization Earthjustice. Also, Rosebud is active with MuST (Music in Schools Today).

Kappus advises students, "If you are interested in a specific career area, such as the music business, then absorb everything you can about it." Kappus started promoting concerts at the age of 19 and gained on-the-job experience in booking, management, and record production. He explains, "I wasn't always the best student, but I now realize that subjects that did not seem practical have actually been helpful and important." While also realizing the appeal of the music industry, Mike Kappus admits, "We all need adventure in our lives, but we should take advantage of the great opportunities we have to learn."

How has Kappus blended personal values and community service to market Rosebud's products?

Career Data: Musical Artist Agent or Tour Promoter

Education and Training
Associate's, bachelor's, or master's degree in business or music, or many other majors; on-the-job training; legal knowledge

Skills and Abilities
Communication skills, writing skills, people skills, math skills, foreign language skills, attention to detail, and book-keeping or accounting skills

Career Outlook As fast as average growth through 2010

Career Path Entry-level positions at record companies, agencies, and concert venues can lead to more advanced positions in the industry.

the world. Each station has a primary style of music or entertainment it provides, and each style usually appeals to a specific market segment. Fans of country music will listen to country stations, whereas rock and classical listeners will listen to stations providing their favorite music. Programming for radio is determined by the style of music and playlist or type of program on the radio station. Programming is the key to successful radio marketing. Competition for airplay is intense as most radio stations add only three or four new songs to their playlists every week.

Marketing the Music

The music industry earns $40 billion a year worldwide. Of all the entertainment businesses, the music business affects the most nationalities, cultures, and income levels. It includes recorded and live music heard on CDs and soundtracks, in large concert halls and small nightclubs, and at free concerts in the park. Music is marketed by many labels, such as Columbia, MCA, Def Jam, and Elektra. Labels distribute their music to retail stores or Internet retailers.

Producing a commercial album can cost $125,000 to $225,000 and more. Production costs may include studio time and professional musicians' fees but do not include marketing and promotion costs, which may be five times the production costs. Each year an average of 8,000 albums are released, but 90 percent of them do not make a profit. The element of risk, or the potential to lose money, is high in the industry. For a label to stay in business, a few successful albums need to make enough money to cover losses from unsuccessful releases and still make a profit. The performers, or talent, may receive up to the top royalty rate of 15 percent of the retail price of each album sold. The percentage amount can be reduced for new or less popular acts.

Getting on the Air

Airplay, or time on the radio, is very important to record companies because if a performer's music does not get airtime, the music does not sell. Radio is still the primary means of introducing new artists as well as new music by established acts. It is also a major tool to promote upcoming concerts and acts in the local area.

To create a successful music act, performers need radio exposure. In prior years, payola was the key to having DJs play a record. **Payola** is an illegal payment by record companies, or labels, to radio stations to persuade them to play the label's records. Studios and agents would go to stations and pay the DJ or station manager to play an artist. The federal government declared payola to be commercial bribery, and it was deemed illegal in 1960. Today record labels might hire independent agents to promote records to stations and provide gifts to station personnel to encourage them to play the music on the radio.

Music Promotion Strategies

To create hits, record labels develop focused marketing strategies. Promotion is concentrated on radio play in major markets, which are areas with the largest listening audience for a specific target market.

Math Check

ROYALTY RATES

If the band OutKast sold 378,000 units, or CD albums, at the top royalty rate, and each CD sold for $12.95, how much would the band earn?

➡ For tips in finding the solution, go to **marketingseries.glencoe.com**.

---

payola an illegal payment by record labels to radio stations to persuade them to play the label's records

---

marketingseries.glencoe.com

There are only about 300 stations that fit this important category. Other marketers will focus on specific stations with specific *formats,* or certain styles of music, because they want to reach a particular target market. **Figure 11.2** on page 256 lists the variety of radio stations in the United States. Record labels also rely on Internet advertising, MTV, VH1, and magazines such as *Spin* and *Rolling Stone* for promotion.

PERFORMERS AS MARKETERS Today popular music is integrated with other media. For example, popular bands or performers sing product jingles. A **jingle,** or a catchy tune or song that promotes a product, accompanies television, radio, or Internet advertisements. Cross-marketing of music and merchandise helps sales of both. For example, when Sting used a Jaguar automobile in a video for his song "Desert Rose," it impressed Jaguar's ad agency, and the agency created an ad campaign around the song/car connection. An **ad campaign** is a promotional plan that combines selling, advertising, public relations, and the use of different media to reach the target market. The result was higher CD sales for Sting and greater interest and sales for Jaguar cars.

Many performers are aware of the need to use all possible media to market their art. For example, the band Aerosmith has a flashy Web page that includes information about the band, concert footage, a shop to buy Aerosmith merchandise, and other band publicity. In 2003, Aerosmith teamed up with the band KISS to do a national tour. KISS also has a similar, very professional Web site. The two bands realize that they need to reach fans and potential fans by using all media.

Other media exposure is important. TV appearances on talk shows such as *Late Night With Conan O'Brien, The Tonight Show With Jay Leno, Late Show With David Letterman,* and MTV's *TRL,* in addition to radio interviews with local DJs, are key activities for getting publicity. Other good marketing tools include interviews with reporters for local newspapers, record signings at music stores, and Internet chat-room discussions. Aerosmith also donated time and money to charitable activities such as Save the Music. Performers and artists realize that they are also businesspeople and marketers. They have to sell by using various media.

Internet Marketing

The Internet is popular as a source of music. As a result of free illegal music downloads and file sharing, record labels and broadcasters revised their practices. Some Web sites, such as Apple's iTunes Music Store and MusicMatch, are offering downloading services for reasonable prices per song.

Case Study | PART 2

MASTER OF TICKETS
Continued from Part 1 on page 241

With the medium of the Internet allowing ticket-selling businesses to operate, the old Ticketmaster needed to adapt to cyberspace. So it created a network capable of handling hundreds of thousands of hits, or customer orders, at the moment tickets go on sale for an event. Customers can see and choose seat locations by viewing online layouts of arenas and concert halls. It also allows users to create profiles so they will be warned before their favorite tickets go on sale. The system gives an option of printing tickets at home to save the customers time and the cost of mailing. Ticketmaster has also begun an online auction service in an effort to regain profits lost to scalped, or resold, tickets. In 2003, customers were able to bid on the best seats at sporting events, concerts, and other functions.

ANALYZE AND WRITE
> **1.** Do online ticket sales benefit the entertainment events? Why?
> **2.** How do you think Ticketmaster's online auctions will affect ticket prices?

jingle a catchy tune or song that promotes a product and accompanies television, radio, or Internet advertisements

ad campaign a promotional plan that combines selling, advertising, public relations, and the use of different media to reach the target market

QUESTION
Give an example of cross-marketing music with another product.

Figure 11.2

Radio Diversity

SOMETHING FOR EVERYONE
Radio stations have become increasingly specialized for certain groups of listeners. Advertisers and marketers take advantage of these ready-made target markets that are categorized by type of music. *Do you think musical tastes are related to buying habits? Why?*

Rank	Format	Number of Stations
1	Country	2088
2	News/Talk/Business	1224
3	Oldies	807
4	Adult Contemporary	692
5	Hispanic	628
6	Adult Standards	497
7	Contemporary Hit Radio (CHR)	491
8	Sports	429
9	Classic Rock	425
10	Hot AC	399
11	Religion	347
12	Soft Adult Contemporary	336
13	Rock	273
14	Black Gospel	253
15T	Classic Hits	237
15T	Southern Gospel	237
17	R&B	207
18	Modern Rock	189
19	Contemporary Christian	167
20	Urban AC	128
21	Ethnic	102
22	Alternative Rock	99
23	Jazz	90
24	R&B Adult/Oldies	66
25	Gospel	64
26	Pre-Teen	60
27	Modern AC	51
28	Variety	36
29	Classical	32
30	Easy Listening	18
31	Other/Format not available	1

SOURCE: M Street Corp., © 2003

Marketing Print Media

The print media, which include books, magazines, and newspapers, also use all types of media for marketing. Global trade shows and book fairs have been very successful venues for showcasing new books in the past, though fewer retailers attend these events today. National book fairs such as Book Expo and the New York City Book Fair are still effective. Book-signing events and book tours by authors generate publicity and interest. Book reviews also serve as marketing tools. TV talk shows and radio interviews with a book's author are another marketing strategy for books. For example, in the 1990s, Oprah Winfrey's book choices for her book club on her television show increased book sales. In addition, if a book is sold for adaptation to film, its sales increase due to increased media exposure.

Direct marketing of magazines through direct mail is also used if a target market is very specific. Magazine subscription lists are very effective for gathering information to create a target customer profile.

The Internet and Print Media

E-publishing once seemed futuristic, but by the end of the 20th century, most print media became available to consumers on the Internet.

Though book publishing still remains a primarily paper-and-ink print medium, some Web publishers such as mightywords.com have been able to earn revenue through secure Web sites with unprintable Web pages. For example, in 2000, this publisher sold over 400,000 copies of a Stephen King short story, "Riding the Bullet."

E-zines, or magazines on the Internet, also have a presence in cyberspace. Examples are numerous, including *PC Magazine* and *BusinessWeek*. Revenue is earned from advertisers more than from subscribers. However, many e-zines are free to users, and the publishers make money as a result of number of hits on the Web site, or number

TALKING PR Labels make sure their artists are heard on the radio through airplay and talk radio. *What other media besides radio do artists use to be seen and heard?*

of visitors to the site. With more users, the publisher can charge higher advertising fees.

Today, almost all major newspapers, from the *New York Times* to the *Los Angeles Times*, also have corresponding Web sites. Many newspapers have found that the Web sites can serve as marketing tools to gain subscribers to their print publications. Moreover, the costs of operating a cyber publication are far less than the expense of putting out daily print newspapers. In addition, there are e-newspapers exclusive to the Internet.

Media and Marketing

For all types of entertainment, the media are not only sources of pure entertainment products, they are also effective entertainment marketing tools. With the great variety of media and entertainment product available, good marketing requires planning and being aware of different marketing strategies and those best suited to these media and products.

Quick Check

RESPOND to what you've read by answering these questions.

1. What is the difference between the primary market and the secondary market in film distribution?

_____

_____

_____

_____

_____

2. What is gross revenue?_____

_____

_____

_____

_____

3. Define programming. _____

_____

_____

_____

_____

_____

Name _____ Date _____

Worksheet 11.1

Marketing the Music Industry

Visit your favorite music store and see how many different labels are on the market. Choose 12 of your favorite artists and write their names, the names of their CDs, and their labels. Note whether any artists recorded under more than one label with different CDs.

Artist	CD Name	Label
1. _____ _____	_____ _____	_____ _____
2. _____ _____	_____ _____	_____ _____
3. _____ _____	_____ _____	_____ _____
4. _____ _____	_____ _____	_____ _____
5. _____ _____	_____ _____	_____ _____
6. _____ _____	_____ _____	_____ _____
7. _____ _____	_____ _____	_____ _____
8. _____ _____	_____ _____	_____ _____
9. _____ _____	_____ _____	_____ _____
10. _____ _____	_____ _____	_____ _____
11. _____ _____	_____ _____	_____ _____
12. _____ _____	_____ _____	_____ _____

Worksheet 11.2

Marketing the Evergreens

Visit your favorite video store to learn about evergreens, or classic films. Write a list including what you think are at least six movie titles and the film studios that produced them.

1.   **Movie Title**   **Film Studio**

_____   _____

_____   _____

_____   _____

_____   _____

_____   _____

_____   _____

_____   _____

_____   _____

2. What do these movies have in common?

_____

_____

_____

_____

_____

_____

_____

_____

3. Why do you think these movies are still popular after so many years?

_____

_____

_____

_____

_____

_____

_____

Portfolio Works

FILM PRODUCT MARKETING

You are the marketing manager of a major film studio that is about to release a film for a high school audience. In a meeting with your marketing department, you want to present secondary products—goods or services. Think of a real or imagined film title and use the concept map below—or create one of your own—to show the movie's secondary products. Then add this page to your career portfolio.

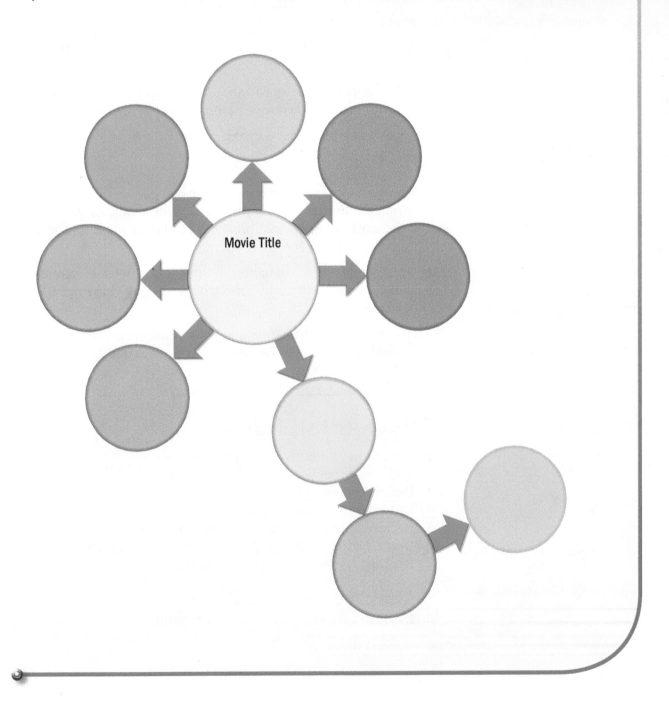

CHAPTER SUMMARY

Section 11.1 **Types of Entertainment Products**

concessions (p. 242)

evergreens (p. 243)

record clubs (p. 243)

rack jobbers (p. 243)

location-based entertain-
    ment (LBE) (p. 246)

impulse spending (p. 247)

- Retailers are part of the vast market for marketing entertainment products, or goods and services, that include live shows, movies, TV shows, radio programs, recorded music, toys, clothing, DVDs and videos, and electronic games.

- Evergreen products, such as classic films and television shows, are popular year after year, and they continue to generate revenue.

- Theme parks with location-based entertainment (LBE) have evolved into major entertainment forms.

- Theme parks and other LBE sites depend on impulse spending by customers to generate substantial revenue.

Section 11.2 **Media Product Marketing**

primary market (p. 251)

secondary market
    (p. 251)

exhibitors (p. 251)

gross revenue (p. 251)

trailers (p. 251)

syndication (p. 252)

programming (p. 252)

payola (p. 254)

jingle (p. 255)

ad campaign (p. 255)

- Media marketers are the dominant media players in the entertainment business and use the resources of media. As part of developing entertainment products, marketing plans for those products help to generate maximum revenue.

- Primary markets are audiences of films in first release; secondary markets include the customers who rent or buy video and DVDs or watch TV.

- Programming for television and radio is important because it determines how many viewers or listeners are tuning in and are being exposed to paid advertising.

CHECKING CONCEPTS

1. **Name** three entertainment products.
2. **Explain** primary and secondary markets.
3. **Define** evergreen products.
4. **Describe** impulse spending.
5. **Differentiate** between theme parks and water parks.
6. **Describe** the customers of electronic and video games.
7. **Explain** the importance of programming.

Critical Thinking

8. **Explain** why you think large media companies have so much control over entertainment.

CROSS-CURRICULUM SKILLS

Work-Based Learning

Basic Skills—Writing

9. You are a freelance writer who has a film script to sell to a major studio. Write a one-page summary of your script.

Interpersonal Skills—Teaching Others

10. Work in pairs of students. Each of you takes one section of the chapter and teaches that section to the other. Include a short quiz. Know the correct answers to the quiz.

School-Based Learning

Language Arts

11. If your life were going to be made into a form of entertainment, what would it be? Write a short essay about it.

Arts

12. Use copies, clippings, sketches, and so on to create a collage of entertainment forms. Discuss it in class.

Role Play: Product Manager

SITUATION You are to assume the role of product manager for *Lady,* a new animated family movie about a ladybug. The test marketing predicts great success if this movie is released during the summer. Your boss (judge) asked you to brainstorm ideas for generating income from the movie.

ACTIVITY Plan the product extensions of the movie *Lady* and present them to your boss (judge).

EVALUATION You will be evaluated on how well you meet the following performance indicators:

- Explain the nature and scope of the product/service management function.
- Explain the concept of product in entertainment marketing.
- Explain the nature of product extensions in services marketing.
- Determine merchandising opportunities for an entertainment event.
- Explain the concept of product mix.

INTERNET ACTIVITY

Use the Internet to access one of the major megaplex theaters in your region.

- Create an illustrated pamphlet that lists and describes the movies playing.
- Also include other services offered, such as teleconferencing and space rental.
- Display your pamphlet in the classroom.

➡For a link to begin this exercise, go to **marketingseries.glencoe.com.**

LIGHTS, CAMERA, WEB SITE

Mutants are everywhere in *X-Men: The Movie.* But even more lurk in the computers of 20th Century Fox, the studio that released the flick. Months before, Fox wrote articles for a faux news Web site, mutantwatch.com, featuring a campaign by one of the movie's villains, Senator Kelly, to stamp out mutants. Visitors were asked to find mutants and get them to register on the site. More than 65,000 folks "reported" friends who exhibited mutant behavior, such as "an affinity for Spandex." Silly? Sure, but it provided Fox with a gold mine of data, from e-mail addresses to demographics, that the studio can use to hawk videos or create buzz for a new film.

One-Two Punch

It's all part of the most elaborate Internet marketing blitz ever to hit Hollywood. In post-Blair Witch Internet marketing, Fox has few peers in mastering the interactive power of the Web to boost interest in its films. Fox used online games, chat-room talks with the stars, and even a series of fake news articles of mysterious events to whip up online chatter.

The Web campaign capped a $50 million marketing program that helped *X-Men* gross more than $150 million. Fox exit polls showed that 28 percent of those who saw the film had visited the *X-Men* Web site—nearly five times the number of moviegoers who usually surf movie sites, say Hollywood marketing experts. "This was a movie that was just meant for the Internet," with its young, male-oriented audience, says Jeffrey Gozsick, Fox's executive vice-president for publicity and promotion. "And we tried to exploit it early and often."

What makes Fox marketers far more crafty than their studio brethren is simple: They understand the emotional one-two punch of the Internet's instant, two-way communication combined with the old-fashioned lure of a good story. "Most studios simply put up promotional sites for their movies and figure fans will go there and want to see the movie," says Phillip Nakov, co-founder of Countingdown.com, a movie fan site. "Fox gets it. They involve people emotionally. They make their promotional sites as much about entertainment as the movie itself."

By Ronald Grover

CREATIVE JOURNAL

In your journal, write your responses:

CRITICAL THINKING

1. What unique method of marketing did Fox use to promote *X-Men*?

APPLICATION

2. Choose one of your favorite films. Write down and describe three different elements you would include on a Web site to promote your favorite film.

 Go to **businessweek.com** for current *BusinessWeek* Online articles.

UNIT 5

ENTERTAINMENT MARKETING MIX

> **❝** The person who makes a success of living is the one who sees his goal steadily and aims for it unswervingly. That is dedication. **❞**
> — Cecil B. DeMille

UNIT OVERVIEW

The entertainment industry is made up of a diverse mix of businesses, goods, and services enjoyed by the public. Strategies for developing marketing plans for entertainment products include creating a marketing mix. This unit focuses on the Four Ps of the marketing mix—product, price, place, and promotion. Chapter 12 examines product and pricing in entertainment marketing. Research and identifying target markets are reviewed in Chapter 13, along with the factors for choosing venues and outlets. Chapter 14 focuses on images and licensing. Chapter 15 discusses promoting and advertising entertainment. Chapter 16 examines marketing plans and business plans. The text concludes with a discussion about marketing-related careers.

■ UNIT LAB

Preview

The children's market for DVDs and videos is expanding. Understanding this target market can contribute to a successful product design.

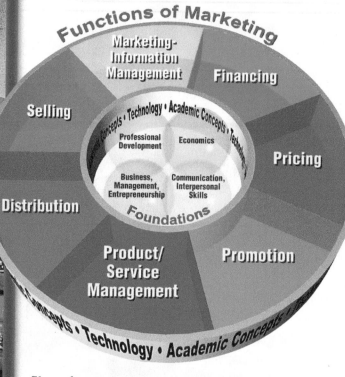

These functions are highlighted in this unit:
- Promotion
- Selling
- Marketing-Information Management
- Products/Service Management
- Pricing

UNIT OVERVIEW

The entertainment industry is made up of a diverse mix of businesses, goods, and services enjoyed by the public. Strategies for developing marketing plans for entertainment products include creating a marketing mix. This unit focuses on the Four Ps of the marketing mix—product, price, place, and promotion. Chapter 12 examines product and pricing in entertainment marketing. Research and identifying target markets are reviewed in Chapter 13, along with the factors for choosing venues and outlets. Chapter 14 focuses on images and licensing. Chapter 15 discusses promoting and advertising entertainment. Chapter 16 examines marketing plans and business plans. The text concludes with a discussion about marketing-related careers.

■ UNIT LAB

Preview

The children's market for DVDs and videos is expanding. Understanding this target market can contribute to a successful product design.

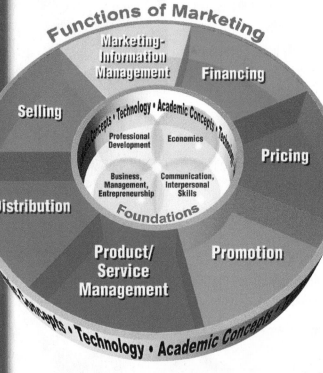

These functions are highlighted in this unit:

- Promotion
- Selling
- Marketing-Information Management
- Products/Service Management
- Pricing

Product and Price Decisions: Entertainment

Chapter Objectives

- Explain entertainment brand identity, brand marks, and trademarks.
- Identify brand strategies used by entertainment companies.
- Explain how celebrities are brands.
- Define gross profit and net profit.
- Identify different pricing goals.
- Identify factors that determine CD and concert ticket prices.

Case Study — PART 1

MUSIC MATTERS

The *Star Wars* films and related products have distinct brand indentities that consumers and moviegoers recognize. Creating a brand identity for entertainment products and companies such as record labels is an important factor for successful marketing.

Realizing that getting a record deal was a long shot for their band, Ian MacKaye and Jeff Nelson formed Dischord Records in 1979. They planned to create a record label that would record the local music scene, treat musicians fairly, and sell records at a fair price.

Since then the independent Washington, D.C., label has released 7-inch singles, records, CDs, and videos by unknown bands, splitting profits 50/50 and charging only $5 to $12 for a mail-order CD. In fact, Dischord has released albums from some of the most popular bands in their category. Dischord promotes its bands through independent magazines and sidesteps radio conglomerates and MTV. The bands play in smaller, all-ages clubs. They have also influenced mainstream music. As a result, major labels began competing by marketing similar bands.

ANALYZE AND WRITE

1. How might Dischord's brand identity differ from a major label's identity?
2. What pricing decisions did Dischord make?

Case Study Part 2 on page 275

POWER READ

Be an active reader and use these reading strategies:

PREDICT what the section will be about.

CONNECT what you read with your life.

QUESTION as you read to make sure you understand the content.

RESPOND to what you've read.

Branding and Entertainment

AS YOU READ ...

YOU WILL LEARN

- To explain entertainment brand identity, brand marks, and trademarks.
- To identify brand strategies used by entertainment companies.
- To explain how celebrities are brands.

WHY IT'S IMPORTANT

Brands and brand identification are a major part of entertainment marketing and help the consumer to identify products, which increases sales.

KEY TERMS

- brand identity
- brand mark
- soundmark
- motionmark
- brand extension
- entertainment franchise
- crossover

PREDICT

What types of things can be trademarked?

brand identity a consistent image or feeling that consumers recognize when encountering the brand

The Role of Branding

Branding and packaging are among the most important product elements of the marketing mix in today's business world. Whether it is labeling cars, an airline, soup, or movies, the brand name speaks volumes. For example, the name *Campbell's* means soup, and the name *Disney* suggests wholesome family entertainment. Popular brand names are vital to the success of companies and products. They represent trust, reliability, style, and prices that are familiar to the customer.

Origins of Branding

The use of brands has been around for thousands of years. The earliest known brands were seen on paintings of cattle in cave murals in southern France. They date back to the Stone Age. Five-thousand-year-old pottery is marked with signs that identify its maker. In 1266, England passed a law that required bakers to mark their breads for identification. During the Industrial Revolution in the 1700s and 1800s, the growth of consumer products led to increased need for manufacturers to distinguish their products from their competitors' products. Brand identity as we know it today was in the infant stages.

Brand Identity Today

Today choosing a brand identity is an important product decision. You learned in Chapter 7 that a brand may include all the feelings and experiences you have regarding a particular company, product, or service. **Brand identity** is a consistent feeling or image that consumers recognize when encountering the brand. As a consumer, you may accept the product and possibly buy it with no product knowledge beyond brand-name recognition. The name may be familiar and have reassuring connections to previous purchases associated with the name.

For example, many fans of the *Star Wars* film series will see the latest installment no matter what the critics say about it. They already accept the characters and story. Moreover, true fans feel a sense of community and association with other *Star Wars* fans. *Star Wars* is a motion picture that revolutionized the movie industry because it emphasized the marketing benefit of tie-ins and related merchandising. In addition to seeing the movies many times, fans will buy associated *Star Wars* merchandise, such as toys, books, memorabilia, and many other products.

Entertainment companies that are developing brands work on many levels. They must develop an identifiable **brand mark**, or a brand name and symbol. Sometimes a slogan, or catchy phrase, is developed with the brand name.

DIFFERENT IDENTITIES It can be difficult for some companies to develop a consistent brand identity. For example, Universal Studios has an eclectic, or varied and widespread, mix of entertainment products. The studio has made films in all genres for all ages. It also has a theme park associated with the films. Because of these different identities, Universal does not have a clear-cut identity. Entertainment consumers may not refer to a movie and say, "Oh, that's a Universal film," with the same certainty they might say, "It's a Disney film."

Over the years The Walt Disney Company has developed a reputation for G-rated, family-style entertainment. Disney's identity as a family-friendly company has been carefully developed and marketed. This identity is worth millions of dollars to Disney. The company could lose money if this identity were compromised and lost. Because some companies such as Universal do not have a similar consistent image, they must work to establish individual identities for every film they produce, so that each movie can establish its target market.

FIXED BRAND IDENTITY Having a consistent brand identity can lead to more focused marketing, but it can sometimes be a drawback. For example, in the 1980s, Disney realized that making only family films limited its market. There were millions of consumers who wanted more than the G-rated family films and entertainment Disney offered. There were also consumers who wanted to see popular entertainers not normally featured in family films. However, if Disney started making films that were for more mature audiences or using controversial actors in its films, the company would risk alienating their carefully built market of family audiences. To get around this, Disney decided to create other companies owned by the Disney Corporation—but not identified with the Disney name. In the 1980s, Disney set up other production companies, such as Hollywood Pictures and Touchstone Pictures, to produce films for more mature audiences. Touchstone's first film was *Splash*, starring Darryl Hannah and Tom Hanks. Another film from a Disney subsidiary was *Dick Tracy* starring Warren Beatty, Al Pacino, Madonna, and other actors not normally seen in Disney films. Touchstone also produced the western film *Open Range* with Kevin Costner in 2003.

The Value of Trademarks

Symbols that you see every day help identify companies and goods and services you buy. For example, in most parts of the world, you can find the "golden arches" that represent McDonald's restaurants. You might turn on the TV and see a peacock logo and know that you are watching NBC. At the beginning of a movie, you might see a mountain and recognize the Paramount Studios trademark. These *trademarks* are extremely important and signify ownership.

THE Electronic CHANNEL

Sneak Preview

You know that the Internet distributes information through multiple methods: text, audio, and visual. The Web's multimedia capability makes it the ideal place to market a movie. Both major and independent films have created Web sites that often offer Internet-only features, such as downloadable clips, Internet-only trailers, and extended cast and crew profiles—all in one place. People come to the Web for the promise of exclusive content—and word-of-mouth travels far and fast.

➥ Discover some Internet-only features offered by a current or previously released-movie site through *marketingseries.glencoe.com*.

brand mark a brand name and symbol

MARKETING SERIES *Online*

Remember to check out this book's Web site for product and pricing information and more great resources at *marketingseries.glencoe.com*.

Hot Property

Toys Worth Keeping

Equity Marketing

Have you ever bought a kid's meal at a fast-food restaurant just to get the toy? If so, you've probably seen Equity Marketing's work. This company helps clients develop promotional items that grab consumers' attention and encourage them to buy. For example, Burger King sold about three times more kid's meals by including a toy (created by Equity Marketing) from *The Lion King*.

Many promotions tie in with entertainment properties such as *The Lion King* or *The Simpsons*. In these cases, Equity Marketing works with the entertainment studio to get licensing rights, design a product, and then coordinate its manufacture and distribution for the client.

EXPANDING TO SUCCEED

Equity Marketing started small in the promotion business in 1983, but it began to expand as high-level clients such as Arby's and Coca-Cola signed on. After working at Equity for several years, Stephen Robeck and Don Kurz bought out Equity Marketing's founder in 1991. They set their sights on growth, moving the company to Los Angeles to be close to the entertainment industry and the manufacturers in Hong Kong. They sold company shares to the public and started their own line of consumer products based on popular licensed characters. In addition, they acquired companies that would improve their marketing capabilities and increase their roster of clients.

To cement their prospects, they also signed long-term deals with companies such as Burger King. These strategies have built Equity Marketing into a company that has earned over $200 million in revenue over the last few years.

1. Name three clients that have benefited from Equity Marketing's services.
2. How has Equity Marketing taken advantage of branding to succeed?

---

soundmark a trademark identified by a sound associated with a brand or company

motionmark a trademark identified by specific movement associated with a brand or company

CONNECT

Can you think of another example of a soundmark?

Other Marks

Trademarks are not just logos or pictures. There are other legal "marks" that identify brands or companies besides designed logos and pictures. For example, the roaring lion that you hear at the beginning of an MGM film is a **soundmark**, or a trademark identified by a sound associated with a brand or company. What about the winged horse that almost leaps off the movie screen at the beginning of a Tri-Star film? The moving horse is a **motionmark**, or a trademark identified by specific movement associated with a brand or company. The Mickey Mouse-ears hat sold at Disney theme parks and stores is also trademarked. Shapes such as the chocolate Hershey's kiss and the Coke bottle design are trademarked.

You learned in Chapter 7 that trademarks provide legal protection for a company's brand as well as any products or creations such as movies or TV shows. Since trademarks ensure that the company holds the sole and exclusive right to the brand, other companies or individuals must get permission to use the brand or symbol. In exchange, they usually pay a royalty or license fee for its use. If a retailer ties its everyday product, such as a cheeseburger, toy, or video game, to a major motion picture, that product receives great exposure due to the film brand. These licensing arrangements can be very profitable, or generate a lot of money, for the licensor, which is the film company. For example, licensing revenue from Universal Studios' film *Jurassic Park* merchandise amounted to over $50 million. Disney had similar success with licensing merchandise rights for the film *The Lion King*.

Entertainment Brands on the Internet

Branding on the Internet and in e-commerce is just as important as in conventional marketing. The Internet's multimedia capabilities make it an ideal channel for marketing entertainment. Having a domain name is necessary for a company's Web site.

Music and the Internet

In 2003, the Recording Industry Association of America (RIAA) began to bring lawsuits against people who engaged in distribution and file sharing, or downloading, music from the Internet without paying for the music. The industry believed that this exchange of files was violating the copyrights of artists and record companies. Some artists, such as the heavy-metal band Metallica, agreed with the crackdown. Other musicians, such as Moby and Roger McGwinn of the Byrds, felt that people would always find a way to get free music. Therefore, any exposure that was generated was good publicity. Then in 2003, Apple Computer, Inc., with its iPod system began to sell single songs for 99 cents each and found it was an effective way to distribute digital music to Internet users. The record companies know that technology is always changing. Thus, maintaining control of music distribution and gathering royalties are a constant challenge.

 SOUNDMARKS **Many movie-goers take the lion for granted, but if asked, they will usually recognize MGM as the owner of the "roar."** *What do you remember best—sound, symbols, or moving pictures? What is the most effective brand mark?*

Celebrities as Brands

brand extension the development and introduction of new products that expand the brand and take advantage of the recognition and image of an established brand name

Celebrities recognize that they are not just performers, but they are also "brands" who have monetary value, just as the brands Nike, Pepsi, or Warner Brothers do. Clothing lines by celebrities are examples of the brand strategy called brand extension. **Brand extension** is the development and introduction of new products that expand the brand and take advantage of the recognition and image of an established brand name.

Performer Madonna was hired by the clothing company Gap, Inc., to do a series of commercials for its chain of stores. Gap believed that Madonna, who appeals to many age groups, would project the idea that Gap sells products for all generations. Actress and singer Jennifer Lopez developed her J. Lo clothing line, as did music producer and performer Sean "P. Diddy" Combs (Sean John clothing), performers Jay-Z (Rocawear clothing), and Eminem (Shady clothing). They are all selling clothing and accessories they designed or helped design. This capitalizes on their popularity as celebrities and their public personas.

Actors are also seen as being "brands." They have identities in the eyes of the public. In fact, stars can carry films because of their identity profiles. For example, Julia Roberts is sometimes identified as "the girl next door" and may play various roles that capitalize on that image. Harrison Ford, who has played characters in *Star Wars* and the *Indiana Jones* film series, is identified with wholesome action adventure. Such actors are cast in certain films that will appeal to specific audiences, because producers and film studios depend on the stars' appeal as brands to generate profits.

Franchises

entertainment franchise a series of films, programs, or character portrayals planned to expand the character's activities in a series

The concept of *franchise* is different in Hollywood than it is in the retail world. While it is another brand strategy, an **entertainment franchise** is a series of films, programs, or character portrayals planned to expand the character's activities in a series. For example, the film *Scream* was the beginning of a franchise that would continue to reach the same fan base over and over. Planning a franchise is an important part of making entertainment product decisions.

Film Franchises

Franchising is similar to making sequels, but it is planned from the beginning of the series. A *sequel* is a film made to take advantage of the popularity of the first film and might not be planned from the beginning. *The Mummy 2* was made to appeal to the audience of the first *The Mummy*. The marketers found a profitable target market with the unexpected success of the first film. They knew they would have a ready-made audience for the second film. This worked for *Jurassic Park* and its sequels in the 1990s. The most famous and successful of all sequels that developed into a franchise is the James Bond film series, which has earned billions of dollars since the first film, *Dr. No*, in the early 1960s. For over 40 years, the character of James Bond has

QUESTION

Why might sequels be easier to market than first-run films?

transcended the many different actors who have played the part and has retained audiences while attracting new fans.

The films *Triple X* with Vin Diesel and the *Lara Croft: Tomb Raider* series with Angelina Jolie are examples of franchise films. Unfortunately, the success of the first film does not guarantee success of the second film in a franchise. For example, the second installment of the *Lara Croft: Tomb Raider* series was not as successful as the first one. As in all areas of business, there are no guarantees in the entertainment industry. However, Hollywood has discovered that creating sequels and franchises does provide more financial security than producing single films.

Television Franchises

Television uses the same marketing strategy. The original *Star Trek* series paved the way for *Star Trek: The Next Generation,* which in turn generated *Star Trek: Voyager* and other popular spin-offs. Again, there is no guarantee of success. For example, the popular *Seinfeld* TV sitcom series in the 1990s led to shows for its characters after the original show stopped production. The producers hoped there would be an audience based on the original *Seinfeld* success. However, the spin-offs, starring supporting cast members, did not draw the same number of viewers and were cancelled, and those actors experienced success in other televised presentations.

Trends and styles associated with entertainers can be short-lived. This year's favorite star may be forgotten six months from now. Such celebrities may be the focus on shows such as VH1's *Where Are They Now?* when their marketability as performers has passed.

Case Study — PART 2

MUSIC MATTERS
Continued from Part 1 on page 269

With major labels marketing once avant-garde music as mainstream, Dischord's position was challenged. Dischord reacted to the commercialization of its style of music by continuing business as usual—and the label remained steady. Why? Both faithful and new customers are loyal to Dischord's attitude: "It's not about the money; it's about the music." In 2002, the label released a belated 20th anniversary box set of CDs that features songs from every record it has released. Dischord succeeded by continuing to document Washington, D.C.'s music scene. It also set an example for other independent record labels around the world. MacKaye notes, "People often measure the value of music and art in terms of sales." However, Dischord's success can also be measured by its loyal following.

ANALYZE AND WRITE
1. What is Dischord's brand identity?
2. How has this small entertainment company remained in business?

Crossover Artists

Another aspect of entertainment marketing that is related to a performer's image or brand is crossover, which is used as a brand strategy. **Crossover** is an expansion of the popular appeal of an artist or work by achieving success in another market or style. Performers who already have a specific audience sometimes use their talents to appeal to other market segments. For example, Shania Twain began her career as a country singer, but she was able to appeal to the pop market and many non-country music fans. No Doubt singer Gwen Stefani transitioned into film acting, drawing her music fans into the movie theaters. Basketball player Shaquille O'Neal has performed rap music and has acted in film. Celebrities continue to expand their markets as much as possible to increase mainstream exposure and stay in the public eye.

crossover an expansion of the popular appeal of an artist or work by achieving success in another market or style

Archived Brands

The use of archived brands is another brand strategy. Some performers such as Marilyn Monroe and Elvis Presley have become classic brands. Their legendary status has grown over the years since their deaths, and they have become marketing icons. In fact, their estates are worth millions of dollars more today than when the stars were alive. Elvis Presley's recordings and movies continue to sell, along with memorabilia and merchandise. Marilyn Monroe's image is sold on items such as posters, mugs, key chains, and DVDs. Recent pop stars such as Madonna and others have mimicked Monroe's style. If you look around, you can see other examples of golden oldies that have continuous marketability. Another example is the English rock band Pink Floyd. Their *Dark Side of the Moon* album has never left the *Billboard* Top 100 chart since its release over 30 years ago.

Film Vaults

The vaults, or archives, of a studio contain entertainment properties that are part of its brand and product line. The accumulation of

Figure 12.1

Classic Brands in the Film Vaults

VINTAGE GOLD **This chart lists only a few movies owned by three top movie studios. These film libraries still generate revenue and recognizable brands.** *Can you think of any brand extensions created from these films? Give some examples.*

Decade	MGM	Universal	Warner Brothers
1920s	Bulldog Drummond	Phantom of the Opera	The Jazz Singer
1930s	Gone With the Wind	Frankenstein	Scarface
	The Wizard of Oz	All Quiet on the Western Front	42nd Street
1940s	The Best Years of Our Lives	Sherlock Holmes	Casablanca
	The Secret Life of Walter Mitty	Hamlet	The Maltese Falcon
1950s	Some Like It Hot	Pillow Talk	Damn Yankees
	Guys and Dolls	The Incredible Shrinking Man	Rebel Without a Cause
1960s	The Apartment	Psycho	Bonnie and Clyde
	The Graduate	To Kill a Mockingbird	My Fair Lady
	James Bond films	Spartacus	The Music Man
1970s	The Goodbye Girl	Jaws	Superman
	Logan's Run	The Sting	Dirty Harry
1980s	Bill and Ted's Excellent Adventure	E.T.: The Extra-Terrestrial	Batman
	The Terminator	Back to the Future	National Lampoon's Vacation

movies and television shows is worth billions of dollars. Universal Studios has over 4,000 titles, ranging from *Frankenstein* to *Jaws* to *E.T.*. (See **Figure 12.1**.) The studio's properties include cartoons such as Woody Woodpecker and television shows such as *Leave It to Beaver*, *Magnum P.I.*, and *The Munsters*. The total value of Universal's library of titles is estimated at $14 billion. Any title can be re-released. Since most of the production costs were paid years ago, the only real expenses to re-release are for new film negatives and marketing and distribution costs. Similar to Universal Studios archives are the Disney, Paramount, and MGM film vaults, filled with valuable and recognized brands worth billions of dollars that continue to be marketed.

Quick Check ✓

RESPOND to what you've read by answering these questions.

1. Why can a performer be considered a brand? _____

_____

_____

_____

_____

_____

_____

_____

2. What is brand extension? _____

_____

_____

_____

_____

_____

_____

_____

3. What is meant by a crossover artist? _____

_____

_____

_____

_____

_____

_____

Price Decisions

AS YOU READ ...

YOU WILL LEARN

- To define gross profit and net profit.
- To identify different pricing goals.
- To identify factors that determine CD and concert ticket prices.

WHY IT'S IMPORTANT

Pricing is critical to the success of any business, and it is important as a marketer to be aware of different factors affecting prices.

KEY TERMS

- product placement
- gross profit
- net profit
- profit margin
- reach and frequency

product placement the appearance of a product as a prop in a film or TV show, in exchange for a fee paid by the product's advertiser

gross profit revenue minus the cost of the goods sold

net profit gross profit minus expenses

PREDICT

Is entertainment a business of high risk and high return?

Revenue, Profit, and Loss

Revenue is the total income brought in through the sales of goods and services. It can include ticket sales, merchandise sales, or concessions sales. It can be advertising income from selling radio or television spots. It might include money for **product placement**, which is the appearance of a product as a prop in a film or TV show, in exchange for a fee paid by the product's advertiser. For example, the German auto maker BMW paid $15 million to MGM to have its automobiles placed in James Bond movies. MGM includes this money as part of its revenue for the film. A film such as *Cat in the Hat* can earn large revenue from product placements with more than 40 products appearing in the movie.

Profit is viewed in two ways—gross profit and net profit. **Gross profit** is revenue minus the cost of the goods sold. Examples of costs for the film industry are film production and film negatives; and for theater, examples are producing a play, actors' salaries, and stage production. **Net profit** is gross profit minus expenses, or those costs beyond the costs of production. These include taxes, advertising, public relations, and selling costs. Net profit is kept by the entertainment company, much as your take-home pay from your paycheck is the money you keep. Prices for entertainment products are calculated to make profits.

Pricing Strategies and Goals

Pricing in the entertainment field is similar to retail pricing for goods. Entertainment pricing is also similar to sports pricing for intangible services. As with all price planning, marketers must determine the goals of their pricing strategies. Setting prices can be based on recovering costs, getting a specific return on investment, hitting profit goals, or meeting or beating the competition. Once the goal is decided, the planning process focuses on reaching the objectives.

Recovering Costs

As you learned earlier, it is not easy to make a profit in the entertainment industry. For example, most CDs released by record companies do not recover the cost of production and distribution. Therefore, prices of CDs must be set high enough to recover costs. In addition, the profits from the successful CDs help to pay for the losses incurred by the unsuccessful CDs. One successful album may have to pay for 20 unsuccessful albums—and make a profit.

Return on Investment

Another goal is return on investment. This simply means that for every dollar the company puts into a project, the goal is to get the maximum return. For example, an entertainment company could look at these options:

- One dollar put in a bank might bring a return of two to four cents on the dollar, before taxes, with very little risk.

- One dollar could be invested in producing a CD by a new band and earn five to ten cents per dollar, with a very high risk of total loss of investment—or the slim chance it could earn millions of dollars.

Movie production pricing is similar to music production pricing. The failure rate is high for such entertainment products. Film marketers must look at a variety of pricing goals.

Competition Pricing

Another pricing goal might be to meet or beat the competitor's price. In 2003, Universal Music, one of the largest recording companies in the industry, changed its business practices when it lowered the cost of top-line CDs by about 30 percent to $12.99 per CD. The company believed that by doing so, sales would increase, and loss of revenue due to the lower retail price would be recovered. Also, lower prices might discourage illegal downloads off the Internet.

Other music labels were then forced to decide whether to lower their prices to catch up with Universal. The danger in price slashing is that if it does not work and sales are still flat, there are few other options. It is especially difficult to raise prices 30 percent if the product is not even moving at the reduced price.

Net Profit Pricing

Some entertainment companies set net profit pricing goals so that their prices will bring the desired net profit, providing they sell enough units. Movie exhibitors (theaters) do this when they plan to take 70 percent of the ticket revenue after the movie has been at the theater for two weeks. By knowing the estimated costs and expenses of running the theater, they can estimate their **profit margin**, which is the difference between the expenses and the retail price, expressed as a percentage or a dollar amount. For each ticket sold, the profit margin might be from one to three dollars.

Pricing in Television and Radio Advertising

One of most famous prices in television is the cost of Super Bowl advertising. Every year the prices go up, and the ad buyers and the public wonder if it is worth it. As discussed in Chapter 10, the cost of a 30-second national spot was $2.25 million in 2004. Companies

TECH NOTES

Broadband Bundling

Faced with increasing competition from satellite providers and phone companies, cable companies have caught on to *price bundling*. Besides cable television, customers can also purchase phone service and high-speed Internet access from the same company. Some subscribers feel they are getting more for their money and may receive only one bill for all services.

➡ Describe a bundled-service package after reading information through **marketingseries.glencoe.com**.

profit margin the difference between the expenses and the retail price, expressed as a percentage or a dollar amount

Game Point

NEW WAVES
The Federal Communications Commission reports there are over 12,500 U.S. radio stations filling the airwaves. In only ten years, the Internet is now transmitting over 1,500 stations such as Kerbango.com in cyberspace.

Figure 12.2

Price and Payoff

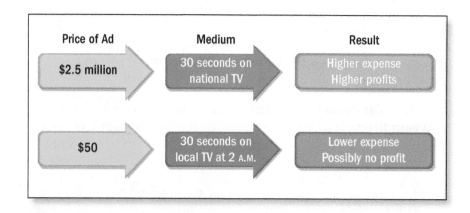

Price of Ad	Medium	Result
$2.5 million	30 seconds on national TV	Higher expense Higher profits
$50	30 seconds on local TV at 2 A.M.	Lower expense Possibly no profit

pay the price because the Super Bowl is the number one rated television show every year, and it is seen by billions of people around the world. In fact, marketing surveys find that 8 percent of the viewers are not interested in the game but tune in to watch the commercials. On the other end of the television advertising price scale, a local ad broadcasted on a small-town television station at 2 A.M. could cost as little as $50 for 30 seconds. (See **Figure 12.2**.)

For media-ad purchases, reach and frequency are the key elements to consider in planning. **Reach and frequency** is an advertising term meaning the number of people exposed to an advertisement and the number of times they are exposed to it. On average, it takes three exposures to have a successful ad.

reach and frequency the number of people exposed to an advertisement and the number of times they are exposed to it

Radio and Promotions

Record labels take a different approach. They may pay radio stations up to $1 million in promotional airplay costs before a record is a hit. This covers a lot of radio stations in major metropolitan areas throughout the United States. The radio stations can make more money from payoffs by record-company representatives to play their artists than they can from ad revenues.

Pricing in the Television Industry

For producing television shows, the general rule is that if a series can stay on the air for three years and/or complete production on 60 episodes, it is a financial success. This puts the series in line to go into profitable reruns and syndication on local television stations and cable systems. The real profits are generated in reruns because most production costs have already been paid, and the product is known to the public and has a ready audience. Unfortunately, only about one in five shows last long enough to produce 60 shows before being cancelled due to low ratings.

Some of the longest-running television shows are not neccessarily aired as reruns. Some examples are:

Profiles in Marketing

OLD-TIME MOVIE MAGIC

Mark Mazrimas
Director of Marketing
Classic Cinemas

ocated in Downers Grove, Illinois, the Classic Cinemas theater chain operates 12 theaters. While many large chains build new state-of-the-art facilities from the ground up, Classic Cinemas restores historic theaters, giving patrons the feel of a bygone era.

Mark Mazrimas, who spent years working in large theater chains, now handles marketing for the company. "I supervise all marketing, which includes our newspaper ads, film promotions, theater expansion programs—whether we're opening a new theater or expanding screens," he says. His job also includes making sure marketing materials such as posters and displays are properly installed at each theater location.

Mark has been working in the film industry for 30 years and supervises a small staff, including an in-house graphic artist and a community marketing manager, who handles press releases and the company Web site.

Love What You Do Mark has a bachelor's degree in radio, television, and film from the University of Indiana, but he credits real-world experience and a personal love of the movies as his most important qualifications.

Like most marketing professionals, Mark considers communication skills to be very important. "Deliver—with a lot of schmoozing," he says. "Make your customer feel special."

Mark also stresses an upbeat and fun attitude in keeping with the nature of the product he is offering. "The business that I'm in is *entertainment*," he says. "You've got to have a sense of humor. It's the movies, it's fun—and it's people."

How can having a sense of humor be helpful in an entertainment marketing career? Why?

Career Data: Director of Marketing

Education and Training Bachelor's degree in marketing, communication, or the arts

Skills and Abilities Writing and communication skills and creativity

Career Outlook Faster than average growth through 2010

Career Path Entry-level positions at large chains or at smaller companies, where diverse skills can meet more than one need, are typical career paths.

- *The Tonight Show*—50 seasons

- *60 Minutes*—36 seasons

- *Monday Night Football*—34 seasons

- *20/20*—27 seasons

Math Check

MUSIC MARKUP

If a distributor sells CDs with a basic cost of $11.90 per CD and a markup of 26 percent, what is the retail price of a CD?

➡ For tips on finding the solution, go to **marketingseries.glencoe.com**.

➡ For tips on finding the solution, go to **marketingseries.glencoe.com**.

QUESTION

What profit margin do concert merchandise items usually have?

➤ **ENTERTAINMENT EXPENSES Most movie-goers will pay for tickets to get in the theater. Once inside, they spend more money on food, drink, and souvenirs.** *Would you go to see movies more often if theaters offered special sale prices on tickets, as clothing stores offer special sale prices?*

Pricing in the Film Industry

Sources of revenue in the film industry include profits from tickets, rentals, video and DVD sales, foreign distribution, toys, CD sound-tracks, books, video games, merchandise, tie-ins, and many other spin-offs. The profit margin for spin-offs varies. Profits at the box office may be very slim, while home DVD sales can provide high margins.

Breaking down the cost and profit potential for each dollar of movie-ticket sales reveals that after paying the distribution fees, ads and publicity, and theater costs, an average of 31 cents remains to cover production and film negative costs—and for the studio to still make a profit. This does not allow much room to squeeze in the cost of film production. Seven out of ten films made do not make a profit at the box office.

On the exhibitor's side, 10 to 20 percent of that ticket dollar goes to the *house,* or to support the theater itself. Other profits are generated from popcorn and other concession sales. These items can generate high gross-profit margins. That $6 box of popcorn might cost the theater only 30 cents, not including labor and other expenses, which may only add another 12 to 18 cents to the cost. Thus, concession sales can be very profitable.

Pricing in the Music and Recording Industries

Selling music in CD form through retail stores and e-commerce is a risky business. As you learned, most new albums and singles do not make profits, and record companies must make a lot of money on a few CDs to cover losses from the majority of releases. Like movie and television studios, record companies try to control the costs of production to increase the potential profit.

 marketingseries.glencoe.com

World Market

Entertaining Ecology

If you're looking for a unique entertainment adventure, then you'd probably enjoy Brazil's Amazon region. Each year ecotourism, an industry promoting travel that helps preserve the natural world and its inhabitants, invites travelers to explore the world's mightiest river, the Amazon, and its rainforest. Occupying two million square miles of the Earth's land mass and about two-thirds of Brazil, the Amazon offers something for everyone. For as little as $1,000, you can hunt alligators with a spotlight, fish for the toothy piranha, hike jungle trails, drift lazily downriver in a houseboat or canoe, or visit the Isana Indians and experience their culture first-hand. You might even snap the picture of a life-time, if you're lucky enough to spot the rainbow plumage of the hook-billed macaw or colorful butterfly swarms gathering—sometimes by the thousands—on the damp sands of the riverbank.

List some of the expenses that might be included in the pricing of an ecotour.

On average, the cost of production for a popular album (including studio time, equipment, and staff) is a minimum of $125,000. Other costs include marketing and promotion, album-cover design and graphics, the pressing of CDs, and shipping costs. The marketing costs can include free CDs, T-shirts, posters, billboards, in-store displays, and promotional kits with free giveaways.

Additional costs include *junkets,* one or more publicity trips that band members take to major market centers, or cities. They make public appearances at radio stations, at record stores, and on television talk shows. These costs can range from $100,000 to $500,000 and more. Some stores require 5+1 or 6+1 deals, which mean that for every five or six items they buy, they get one free. In addition, there are the promotion payments that record companies pay to the radio stations to get critical airplay. This can amount to many thousands of dollars. Every year over 7,000 albums are released. The competition is fierce for exposure, especially when radio stations normally play only a few new songs per week.

Enough for Profits

The bottom line is that the large production and marketing costs must be covered, and there must be enough money left from the gross revenue for the artist's royalty payments per album as well as profit for the record company. The artist's royalty is about 15 percent of the retail price of the album for each album sold.

On the wholesale level, retailers might pay $11 to $12 for a CD that they will mark up to a retail price of $15 to $19. This provides a profit margin of 27 to 37 percent for a retailer.

Concert Pricing

Pricing concert and other public performances relies on estimating public demand and trying to match what others are charging for the same basic entertainment product. Some bands, such as the Rolling Stones, can charge more because they are in high demand by the public and can get away with charging higher ticket prices. Also, the size of the venue and the cost of production, staging, transportation, and employees are included in ticket prices. Contract arrangements with arenas or theaters can include a guaranteed performance fee plus a percentage of the ticket sales and sometimes a percentage of concessions to be paid to the artist and possibly the record company representing the artist. The performers may also have total control of the merchandising sales. These include T-shirts, posters, and other memorabilia, which may have a 60-percent profit margin or even higher.

The risk for some acts is booking a location, or venue, that has too many seats for the act's expected *draw*, or audience. Then costs will far exceed the *gate*, or ticket sales. It is hoped that an act on tour will have enough profitable stops to make up for any concert stops that lose money.

Brands and Pricing

Customers' perceptions of an entertainment brand identity can affect purchasing decisions and the price of an entertainment product. There are many factors that affect entertainment product pricing for film, television, radio, music, and other products; but most often, costs will be determined by what the customer is willing to pay.

Quick Check

RESPOND to what you've read by answering these questions.

1. What are some of the strategies entertainment companies use when planning prices?

_____

_____

_____

2. How does gross profit differ from net profit? _____

_____

_____

_____

3. What factors influence the prices of concert tickets? _____

_____

_____

_____

Worksheet 12.1

Tracking Brand Names

For one week, look for trademarks, soundmarks, and motionmarks for entertainment products. Find at least ten. When you notice one, record it below. Identify the item marked by a trademark, soundmark, or motionmark, and then write in the symbol used.

Item	Trademark	Soundmark	Motionmark
1. _____	_____	_____	_____
2. _____	_____	_____	_____
3. _____	_____	_____	_____
4. _____	_____	_____	_____
5. _____	_____	_____	_____
6. _____	_____	_____	_____
7. _____	_____	_____	_____
8. _____	_____	_____	_____
9. _____	_____	_____	_____
10. _____	_____	_____	_____
11. _____	_____	_____	_____
12. _____	_____	_____	_____
13. _____	_____	_____	_____
14. _____	_____	_____	_____
15. _____	_____	_____	_____

Worksheet 12.2

Using Surveys

Create a survey with questions to ask people what they think about celebrities and brand extension. Include the celebrity's name and product(s) in your survey. Administer the survey to students your age and to older members of your community.

Review your results and create a chart on a separate sheet of paper that shows the beliefs about celebrities and brand extension in your community.

Survey Questions   **Answers**

1. _____   _____
   _____   _____
   _____   _____

2. _____   _____
   _____   _____
   _____   _____

3. _____   _____
   _____   _____
   _____   _____

4. _____   _____
   _____   _____
   _____   _____

5. _____   _____
   _____   _____
   _____   _____

6. _____   _____
   _____   _____
   _____   _____

7. _____   _____
   _____   _____
   _____   _____

8. _____   _____
   _____   _____
   _____   _____

Portfolio Works

COMPARING PRICES

You are the owner of a music store. You have decided to advertise on local radio and television. Your budget is limited, but you want favorable *reach and frequency*.

Contact local radio and television stations to learn about their prices for ads. Choose the medium for your ads—television, radio, or both. Decide on the number of ads you will run and when they will run. Explain your choices.

1. Describe your ad campaign.

_____

_____

_____

_____

_____

_____

_____

_____

_____

_____

_____

_____

_____

2. Explain your choices.

_____

_____

_____

_____

_____

_____

_____

_____

_____

Add this page to your career portfolio.

CHAPTER SUMMARY

Section 12.1 Branding and Entertainment

brand identity (p. 270)
brand mark (p. 271)
soundmark (p. 272)
motionmark (p. 272)
brand extension (p. 274)
entertainment franchise
  (p. 274)
crossover (p. 275)

- Brand identity is a consistent feeling or image that consumers recognize when encountering the brand. A brand mark is the brand name and symbol of the brand. They have trademarks that signify a company's ownership. Other types of trademarks are soundmarks and motionmarks.

- Some brand strategies include the use of brand extension. Entertainment franchises are another brand strategy. Crossover and archived properties can also be brands that can help market other products.

- Celebrities can be considered brands with brand identities. Some may capitalize on their images to sell clothing or other merchandise.

Section 12.2 Pricing Decisions

product placement
  (p. 278)
gross profit (p. 278)
net profit (p. 278)
profit margin (p. 279)
reach and frequency
  (p. 280)

- Gross profit is revenue minus the cost of goods sold; net profit is gross profit minus expenses such as taxes, advertising, public relations, and selling costs.

- Different pricing goals can include recovering costs, return on investment, competition pricing, and net profit pricing.

- Many new record albums are unsuccessful. There are many expenses to produce a CD, and recording companies must have a few releases that are big hits to be able to cover losses from the majority of releases. Concert ticket sales depend on estimating demand and matching what others are charging.

CHECKING CONCEPTS

1. **Define** brand identity.
2. **Name** two branding strategies.
3. **Explain** why celebrities can be considered brands.
4. **Differentiate** between gross profit and net profit.
5. **Discuss** the different pricing goals used by entertainment companies.
6. **Explain** how retail CD prices are set.
7. **Explain** the factors that determine concert ticket prices.

Critical Thinking

8. **Explain** why you think the courts have judged that downloading certain music from the Internet without paying is illegal.

CROSS-CURRICULUM SKILLS

Work-Based Learning

Thinking Skills—Decision Making

9. Create a chart to organize the information on pricing methods used in the entertainment industry.

Interpersonal Skills—Teaching Others

10. Form a group of three students. Each student will write down two headings and keypoints from Section 12.2. Discuss the material with your group.

School-Based Learning

History

11. Use the Internet or library to research any discrimination in the music industry. Write a one-page essay.

Arts

12. Using computer graphics or art supplies, create a new trademark, soundmark, or motionmark for your favorite entertainment product. Display your design in class.

 **CONNECTION**

Role Play: Account Executive

SITUATION You are to assume the role of account executive at the Maintown Arena, an indoor facility that seats 10,000 people and hosts 150 events each year. The Star Circus will be booked for one week, with evening shows during the week and a matinée and evening show on the weekend. Five dollars of each ticket will cover the arena's expenses. The Star Circus will keep 60 percent of each ticket. There are three tiers, or levels, inside the arena: low, medium, and high seats.

ACTIVITY Present to your boss (judge) a pricing schedule for tickets to the Star Circus at the Maintown Arena.

EVALUATION You will be evaluated on how well you meet the following performance indicators:

- Explain the concept of price in entertainment marketing.
- Set event prices.
- Adjust prices to maximize profitability.
- Explain factors affecting pricing decisions.
- Select promotional pricing strategies to adjust base prices.

 **INTERNET ACTIVITY**

Use the Internet to access the *Billboard* Top 100 charts.

- Click on one of the charts on the left side.
- Write a fact sheet about the information on the chart.
- Wait one week and repeat the exercise using the same chart.
- Wait one more week and repeat the exercise using the same chart.

How did the information change? What can you conclude about recording artists staying at the top of the charts?

➡️ For a link to *Billboard*'s Web site to begin this exercise, go to **marketingseries.glencoe.com**.

Entertainment Market Research and Outlets

Chapter Objectives

- Explain how market research is used to identify target markets.
- Discuss how demographics are used in entertainment marketing.
- Explain the use of primary and secondary data.
- Explain the difference between qualitative and quantitative research.
- Identify methods of conducting entertainment market research.
- Identify criteria for selecting outlets and venues.

BANDS ONLINE

Finding an audience and venue for a band is the marketer's job. Market research is one way to target consumers for entertainment products, including music, film, or video games. Then marketers must match the product with the right outlet, whether it's an outdoor concert in Dallas, Texas, or a well-designed Web site, so that consumers will have access to the entertainment they want.

In 1994, ARTISTdirect.com was launched to help musicians reach their fans. Bands such as *NSYNC, the Backstreet Boys, and Korn have used the site to sell collectibles, limited-edition CDs, advance tickets to concerts, and other merchandise. ARTISTdirect.com also maintains the Ultimate Band List reference database and a comprehensive search engine allowing users to access information about artists, genres, and time periods.

However, as the Internet industry has grown, bands have started to form their own Web sites for their specific target audiences. Has ARTISTdirect.com succeeded in the face of such competition?

ANALYZE AND WRITE

1. What services does ARTISTdirect.com offer musical artists and fans?
2. What development might threaten the Web site's success?

Case Study Part 2 on page 295

POWER READ

Be an active reader and use these reading strategies:

PREDICT what the section will be about.

CONNECT what you read with your life.

QUESTION as you read to make sure you understand the content.

RESPOND to what you've read.

Targeting Entertainment Markets

PREDICT

What are some ways that entertainment marketing research might be similar to sports marketing research?

The Importance of Market Research

There is no foolproof formula for marketing a product successfully. A product can work well and be priced competitively, but if the consumer does not like it, the marketing effort will fail. Before investing money in developing and marketing a product, marketers want to know what kind of consumer is likely to buy the product and why. Market research can help determine how to best approach the consumer. Market researchers gather, record, and analyze data about an industry, a product, or market in which specific businesses sell products. This information allows marketers to target products to the consumers who will buy them.

Marketers want to know who is in the market for their product, what these consumers want, and how best to give it to them. These potential consumers comprise the *target market*. A customer's decision to buy or not to buy a product is based on many factors. The product may or may not be attractive or interesting; it may or may not meet a need or desire; or the customer may or may not be aware of the product. The entertainment marketer's goal is to understand the target market's needs and tailor the product and the message to that market. Market research can help the marketer achieve this goal.

Entertainment Products and Market Research

Unlike typical consumer products, entertainment products are based on creative ideas, such as a melody, an image, a story, or a character. Products based on creative ideas are more difficult to target to a single group of consumers. Because each song, book, movie, amusement ride, video game, play, or toy is unique, each product will appeal to a unique group of consumers. For example, consumers who listen to music by Mozart may attend an opera instead of a Rolling Stones concert.

Discovering what works for a particular entertainment market is a complicated job. The goal of an entertainment product is to entertain. The product works if consumers are entertained by it. However, different things are entertaining to different people. Therefore, it is essential to know your product, know to whom it appeals, and understand what that market wants and needs.

The Market Research Process

Market research helps business leaders understand their markets. When planning for market research, marketers think about their products. They decide what information they want to gather and create specific questions to answer. Then they conduct the research using in-house staff, or they hire a market research company to compile and interpret the answers to the questions. Conducting market research can involve five steps:

1. **Identify information needs:** Decide what you want to know.

2. **Create research objectives:** Create questions you want answered.

3. **Create a plan to meet your objectives:** Outline research methods.

4. **Design a method for collecting and interpreting data:** Compile results.

5. **Summarize and apply findings:** Adjust marketing strategy based on data.

Consumer Demographics

Knowing consumers requires market research to understand who they are and how they think. Consumer groups can be divided into market segments that are categorized by demographic characteristics such as age, income, occupation, gender, ethnicity, education, marital status, geographic location, and lifestyle choices.

How consumers think involves psychographics. **Psychographics** are studies of consumers based on their attitudes, interests, and opinions. For example, the term *family values* may refer to a particular psychographic group that consists of suburban families who are active in religious, school, and community activities. They consider themselves family-oriented and their opinions may reflect their political and moral values. This psychographic group may respond well to products perceived as promoting a family value that fits in with their lifestyle and beliefs such as G-rated films.

Demographics in the Entertainment Market

In the entertainment industry, researching demographic information is important when marketers want to know who is watching, attending, listening to, reading, or buying their merchandise. With this knowledge, marketing professionals can more effectively develop, package, and promote their products to their target markets. They can also sell advertising to clients who market to the same demographic group. Furthermore, demographic research alerts marketers to new or expanding markets to include in their marketing strategies.

Selling to a Target Demographic

As mentioned in previous chapters, television networks rely on a rating system known as the Nielsen ratings. The Nielsen ratings determine which demographic groups are watching particular shows. Nielsen researchers take segments of the U.S. population and monitor their viewing habits. Households are randomly selected to participate in Nielsen surveys. These data are classified by the demographic characteristics of the households surveyed. The survey notes what television shows are playing, where they are playing, and when they are playing. Marketers get a complete picture of what shows viewers choose to watch out of the other choices airing at the same time.

psychographics studies of consumers based on their attitudes, interests, and opinions

Math Check

TV MARKET SHARE

There are 105 million TV households in the U.S. One Nielsen ratings point represents 1 percent of those households. If a new show has a 10.0 rating, how many households are tuned in?

➡ For tips on finding the solution, go to **marketingseries.glencoe.com**.

Nielsen survey information can help businesses direct their advertising to a specific target demographic group. For example, a movie studio that is promoting an action film aimed at 18- to 49-year-old males will not run ads for the film during daytime television. The studio knows that this time slot traditionally attracts viewers in the 25- to 54-year-old female demographic group. Similarly, advertisements for a children's electronic game would not run during *Monday Night Football* when most young children are on their way to bed.

Creating Product for Target Markets

If a prime-time network show earns high Nielsen ratings, it means more viewers are watching that show. For this reason, companies with a product that interests that target market will buy advertising space during this time. Most people from the demographic group of adult men and women, aged 25 to 49, are viewing during prime time (8:00 P.M. to 11:00 P.M.). Marketers create product for this demographic group because these adults have a greater earning and spending ability than other groups. The networks benefit by charging more for advertising space during their prime-time shows.

Special-Interest Cable Channels

Teens and young adults with part-time jobs make up a demographic and psychographic group with discretionary income. This group has large spending potential as well as after-school leisure time, social life, and a culture that values a variety of entertainment and leisure products. Popular programs result in more advertising dollars for networks, so creating programming that appeals directly to this emerging demographic group is important. Channels such as MTV, Comedy Central, Nickelodeon, and the Cartoon Network have opened up advertising possibilities to advertisers who market to this group.

Special-interest cable channels carry this idea further. For example, channels such as BET (Black Entertainment Television) appeal directly to the African-American demographic. Lifestyle and do-it-yourself

➤ **KNOWING YOUR MARKET**
Some children's entertainment is made for one demographic group but marketed to another—the parents.
What factors might a children's entertainment company consider when marketing products in a multi-ethnic population?

channels appeal to adult homeowners. Channels such as Lifetime and Oxygen appeal to female demographic groups. Other special-interest cable channels include sports, animals, science, health, and travel. Each one reaches and targets a specific demographic group.

Psychographics

Psychographics refers to a certain demographic group's attitudes, interests, and opinions. These are important elements for knowing who makes up the demographic. Different demographic groups respond to products in different ways, based on their attitudes and behavior. These differences are important to think about when developing a brand, slogan, logo, or the packaging for a product. For example, an electronic game may have the same appeal to everyone in the 18- to 25-year-old male demographic group, but gamers in urban areas may have different expectations about how a game should be packaged and designed. This difference can be as simple as a difference in taste or exposure to more diverse design and advertising ideas in the city versus the suburbs. If the wrong package keeps a game on the shelf in New York City but the product sells well in Shaker Heights, Ohio, it is important to find out why. This is where primary research is valuable.

Primary Research

You learned in Chapter 6 that primary research is original research done to answer a specific question or solve a problem. Usually marketers do primary research on a single product, and the research is ordered by the particular company making the product. By using primary research, marketers can solve problems or answer questions about the product before it is released to consumers.

Product testing is an example of primary research used by marketers. **Product testing** is assessment of a product to see if it works, meets industry standards for safety, and is user-friendly. In market research, however, researchers are more interested in finding out how customers will react to the product—and if it will sell. Instead of designers and engineers testing a product to see if it works, potential consumers test a product to see if they like it and would buy it. The information collected from primary research is called **primary data**, or information collected from primary or original research used specifically for an issue under study.

Case Study PART 2

BANDS ONLINE
Continued from Part 1 on page 291

ARTISTdirect.com was offering the same information provided by band Web sites. So, it expanded and established two labels, or record companies. ARTISTdirect Records, which develops new artists and distributes their releases, is headed by CEO Ted Field, who was instrumental in launching the careers of Eminem and Dr. Dre. This label distributes music online as well as in traditional CD format.

The second label, Imusic, signs established artists on a per-album basis, eliminating costly multi-album deals, trimming research and expensive marketing costs, emphasizing artists' ownership of songs, and ensuring fair profit-sharing. In addition to the two music labels, ARTISTdirect.com offers musical downloads, features music news, sells marketing opportunities, and organizes tour packages for its artists.

ANALYZE AND WRITE
1. Do record labels consider market research as an expense?
2. Describe the demographic group who might buy ARTISTdirect CDs.

CONNECT
What are some demographic groups to which you belong?

product testing assessment of a product to see if it works, meets industry standards for safety, and is user-friendly

primary data information collected from primary or original research used specifically for an issue under study

trend a pattern, habit, or tendency following a general course

secondary data information collected from secondary or preexisting research for a purpose other than the current study

QUESTION

What do researchers want to find out through product testing?

Secondary Research

Secondary research is research that already exists on a product or a market and has been gathered by a research group. Secondary research is used to understand trends in a market. A **trend** is a pattern, habit, or tendency following a general course. **Secondary data** are information collected from secondary or preexisting research for a purpose other than the current study. These data can provide information on a number of trends in a market, including consumer buying trends, such as seasonal or economic buying trends; information on sales and products of other businesses in an industry; and general demographic information about consumers.

The Nielsen group also collects secondary data. Television companies use these data to answer questions about their products, markets, and competition. The U.S. Census Bureau is also a good source of secondary data. Entertainment marketers use these data to target consumer groups. Trade magazines, such as *Variety* and *The Hollywood Reporter,* or consumer reports published by industry organizations are also excellent sources of secondary data.

Gathering information through different methods is part of the entire market-research process. It utilizes demographics and psychographics to identify and target consumers for entertainment products.

Quick Check ✓

RESPOND to what you've read by answering these questions.

1. How do entertainment products differ from other consumer products? _____

_____

_____

_____

_____

_____

2. List the steps that marketers outline before conducting research. _____

_____

_____

_____

_____

_____

_____

_____

3. Product testing is an example of what type of research? _____

_____

Research Methods

Information Advantage

Have you ever been in a shopping mall when someone with a clipboard stopped you to ask you questions about a product or store? Maybe you have visited a Web site and a pop-up survey appeared and asked you to rate the content or design of the site. These are just two examples of the many methods that market researchers use to obtain primary and secondary data. In the entertainment industry, finding out how an audience member, game player, music fan, or reader will react to a product before its release is vital to entertainment companies and marketing professionals.

Market Testing

Through market testing, marketers can find out if their products will get a favorable response. The question on every marketer's mind when he or she conducts market research is: Will this product sell? Testing consumer reaction to a product gives marketers a chance to make adjustments to their marketing plans. This is how they help their products sell.

Qualitative and Quantitative Research

Most entertainment marketing professionals are interested in finding out both qualitative and quantitative data about their product and industry. This information gives marketers a complete picture of how consumers respond to the product, both before and after it is released.

Qualitative research is data that measure qualities, such as people's reactions or perceptions. These data are not based on numerical information. It is important to note that qualitative data can be expressed using numbers: "Three out of four people on the ride thought it was exciting" is an example of a qualitative statement expressed by using numbers. However, the information itself is based on *qualities*, such as excitement, rather than numbers. **Quantitative research** is data expressed as amount in numbers, such as the number of people visiting a stadium.

Information about how many people chose a particular ride at an amusement park is quantitative; information about whether they thought the ride was exciting is qualitative. The marketer's choice of research method will depend on whether the information he or she needs is qualitative or quantitative. For example, does the marketer want to know *why* the demographic will visit the amusement park or *how many* will visit?

AS YOU READ ...

YOU WILL LEARN

- To explain the difference between qualitative and quantitative research.
- To identify methods of conducting entertainment market research.

WHY IT'S IMPORTANT

Market research is vital to the entertainment business, which relies on consumer trends. Matching a research method with a product ensures successful marketing.

KEY TERMS

- qualitative research
- quantitative research
- respondent
- mall intercept
- survey
- statistics
- observational research
- traffic count
- mystery shopper
- ethnography

qualitative research data that measure qualities, such as people's reactions or perceptions

quantitative research data expressed as amount in numbers

PREDICT

Why do you think Internet surveys are useful to marketers?

Filmmakers and marketers know that teens and young adults make up the biggest movie-going audience. This group of 12- to 18-year-olds and 20- to 25-year-olds will increase twice as fast as the total population.

respondent a consumer who participates in personal interactive interviews or other research methods

Research Methods in Entertainment Marketing

Marketers use several research methods to collect both qualitative and quantitative data. These research methods include interviews, focus groups, mall intercepts, surveys, and observational research. However, certain methods are better suited to collecting certain types of data.

Methods of Qualitative Research

In entertainment marketing, qualitative research provides information about consumer perceptions, opinions, or feelings about a product or service. The best way to find out how people think and feel about a product or service is to ask them. In qualitative research, interviews and surveys are two methods of obtaining this feedback.

PERSONAL AND INTERACTIVE INTERVIEWS Personal and interactive interviews are done in a number of ways with different levels of consumer participation. Researchers can use personal or online interview methods to obtain information from consumers about products and services by using personal and online focus groups, as well as mall intercepts. A **respondent** is the consumer who participates in personal interactive interviews or other research methods.

At the beginning of the interview, the questions are usually general. The questions become more specific as the interview progresses, depending on what the marketers want to find out. The purpose of screening questions at the beginning of the interview is to find out more about the respondent. Many interviews start with questions such as:

- How old are you?

- What do you do for a living?

- How much do you earn a year?

- Are you single, married, or married with children?

- Do you consider yourself a liberal or a conservative person?

The respondent's answers to the screening questions help researchers determine to which demographic and psychographic groups the respondent belongs.

Once that information is established, interviewers begin to ask more specific questions designed to collect research information. For example, movie marketers would ask questions such as:

- Do you go to theaters to see movies, or do you rent or buy films?

- How much do you spend each month on movie tickets and/or movie rentals and purchases?

- Do you prefer going to the movies or watching films on video or DVD at home?

- Do you prefer comedies, action films, or dramas?

Hooray for Bollywood

Bollywood—Hollywood's Indian counterpart—is finding a profitable new outlet for its films. More than a century ago, India released its first movie, a six-scene, ten-minute silent film. Today the Bombay-based, Hindi-language film industry, known as Bollywood, is the world's largest. The Bollywood audience isn't just at home in India. Foreign money and interest are already helping India's pop culture to reach larger audiences.

The typical Bollywood film is a musical melodrama and can include fight scenes, song-and-dance routines, and simple romance, comedy or adventure stories. Though Bollywood films are popular in many parts of the world, to expand its global reach to Western audiences, Bollywood has begun to produce more sophisticated plots and cross over to the English language.

The change has "wowed" the American film industry. In 2002, the Indian film *Lagaan: Once Upon a Time in India* was nominated for an Academy Award for Best Foreign Language Film. The sleeper hit *Monsoon Wedding* earned millions of dollars and was turned into a Broadway show. Andrew Lloyd Webber's musical *Bombay Dreams* is another Broadway show influenced by Bollywood. In its first joint venture, Hollywood and India's film industry are coproducing this musical comedy. A happy ending is one tradition Indian movies haven't left behind.

Why might Bollywood films appeal to so many different cultures?

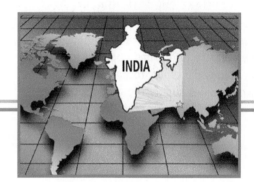

By analyzing the results of these questions, researchers develop a profile of preferences and buying habits of different demographic groups.

FOCUS GROUPS The most in-depth form of interview is known as a focus group. A *focus group* is made up of consumers brought together in a controlled environment to discuss or try products or services. A focus group is made up of between six to ten participants. First, researchers screen participants to find out what they know about the product and to identify their demographic characteristics. A moderator, or person leading the group, questions the participants in detail. The moderator will ask for a group member's opinion about the product or service being tested. The marketer wants to know if each consumer likes the product and in what way it needs improvement. Researchers want to find out if participants would buy the product after trying it.

ONLINE FOCUS GROUPS Online focus groups are also used to measure consumer opinions. An online focus group functions in the same way a face-to-face focus group functions, except that the participants exchange their views and opinions in an online *chat room*, an online site where users can converse in real time. Researchers stream video, graphics, or music to the chat room. Then, respondents send back their reactions to the material they see.

CONNECT

Have you or anyone you know ever participated in a focus group? What product was discussed?

Hot Property

Placement Is Everything

NMA

In *GoldenEye*, James Bond zoomed across the screen in a flashy BMW, instead of his usual Aston Martin. Viewers took notice. Norm Marshall & Associates (NMA) made sure of it. Founded in 1979 by Norm Marshall, NMA is an entertainment marketing agency that focuses on getting its clients' products placed in movies and television shows. It also helps create off-screen promotional tie-ins. The car placement in *GoldenEye* and the accompanying commercial campaign marked an award-winning success for NMA and its client BMW.

CONNECTIONS MAKE THE DIFFERENCE

How does NMA get those key placements? NMA executives explain that they review about 650 scripts per year to find prime opportunities. Often they encourage clients not to pay for placements. Instead, companies supply the product for free and pay only NMA's retainer fee. In return, they get a widely distributed ad that doesn't seem like advertising to viewers.

To drive the message home further, companies can agree to sponsor off-screen promotions that feature entertainment properties. Sometimes this works better, especially in cases of period and fantasy films. For example, NMA worked with Baskin-Robbins and DreamWorks SKG to create an integrated campaign of in-store *Shrek* decorations and ice cream flavors. Together they created nationwide commercial coverage to spread the word. It didn't matter whether Shrek ate ice cream in the film, as long as he did in the promotion. As a result, Baskin-Robbins got the opportunity to increase sales, and DreamWorks the opportunity to reach more family viewers. What a sweet deal!

1. What other product placements or promotions would work for a James Bond film?
2. How might market research help determine the best products to place in particular films?

---

mall intercept a market research interview conducted in a public place, such as a mall

MALL INTERCEPTS A **mall intercept** is a market research interview conducted in a public place, such as a mall. Researchers stop people and ask shoppers questions about the product they are researching. This method is called mall intercept because the practice was introduced in shopping malls. Asking questions in person gives researchers a chance to interact with consumers and gather information that is more difficult to get through noninteractive methods. Researchers can ask standard questions and follow up with in-depth questions, based on the consumer's responses.

With mall intercepts, the participant groups are not screened beforehand. They are chosen at random. This can be both an advantage and a disadvantage. On one hand, the participants are a truer representation of the customers who are buying products in malls. On the other hand, researchers know less about a participant's *bias*, which is a personal and sometimes unreasoned judgment about something. Bias can surface in many ways. For example, if you do not like jazz music, you will not provide very specific information when you are asked to review a jazz artist's new album, based on her previous collection of work. Without screening beforehand, researchers find it difficult to identify respondents' psychographic information. These biases can skew, or distort, the results of the survey, especially if the survey is looking for very specific information.

SURVEYS Surveys are a good way to collect qualitative data on consumer preferences or opinions. A **survey** is a questionnaire or series of questions designed to collect specific information. Questionnaires are completed by the participant or by a researcher asking the participant questions and filling in his or her responses. A survey is only as effective as the questions it asks.

The questions are designed to collect specific information set within specific parameters, or guidelines. The parameters determine how many people will be surveyed; types of questions to be asked, such as open-ended, multiple-choice, true-or-false, or yes-or-no questions; and the demographics to be included or excluded.

Marketers can deliver surveys by mail, conduct interviews over the phone, or post them online. These methods have the advantage of being less expensive than in-person interviews. However, recruiting survey participants can be very difficult. Only a small percentage of mail and Internet surveys are completed and returned by participants. It is difficult to get participants to complete and return mail and Internet surveys because they require interest and effort on the part of the participants. To make it easier for participants to complete and return surveys, marketers design questionnaires that are attractive, interesting, and easy to understand—and have prepaid postage. In addition, many marketing firms and businesses offer incentives for participating in surveys, such as gift certificates or free prizes.

Methods of Quantitative Research

As mentioned earlier, quantitative research data are usually expressed in numbers. There are two effective methods used in quantitative research to find the numbers marketers need: surveys and observational research. Though both methods provide the marketer with information that can be tallied, the manner in which the data are collected differs.

SURVEYS Surveys are very effective at collecting quantitative data that relates to consumer behavior. When survey results are tallied, or added up, they are converted into statistical information. **Statistics** are a collection of numerical data that can be compared, analyzed, and interpreted. Again, the quality of the information gathered depends on the kinds of questions that are asked. For example, a simple yes-or-no question can show that 85 people out of 100 surveyed answered *yes* when asked if they buy CDs online.

OBSERVATIONAL RESEARCH **Observational research** is a method of collecting data by observing respondents in contrived or natural settings. Cameras or spotters are placed in the research environment to gather this type of information. They observe consumer behavior in different situations, or in relation to a product. The data collected are used to evaluate the effectiveness of promotions, design, or products. For example, a **traffic count** is a measure of how many people stop or do not stop to look at an ad or store display.

CONTRIVED AND NATURAL SETTINGS *Contrived settings,* or settings that are set up and prearranged, are created in a research facility where client products are tested along with a sample of other

survey a questionnaire or series of questions designed to collect specific information

QUESTION

What is the difference between statistical and observational research?

statistics a collection of numerical data that can be compared, analyzed, and interpreted

observational research a method of collecting data by observing respondents in contrived or natural settings

traffic count a measure of how many people stop or do not stop to look at an ad or store display

products chosen by the researchers. Researchers observe the respondents through a one-way mirror or on camera. Their choices and reactions to the products are noted. In the contrived-setting method, researchers might display five or six competing products for their respondents to try and then choose the product they prefer. However, in a real store, these respondents would have access to many more products. The contrived situation is artificial because the choices of products and location do not reflect the choices and factors involved in a real shopping situation.

In a *natural setting*, researchers can watch how consumers behave and shop without affecting their choices. Two methods used to observe consumers in a natural setting are mystery shoppers and ethnography. Each method involves researchers immersing themselves in the shopping situation to observe how consumers react to certain products.

mystery shopper a market researcher who poses as a shopper to observe how consumers and retailers behave in a shopping situation

MYSTERY SHOPPERS AND ETHNOGRAPHY A **mystery shopper** is a market researcher who poses as a shopper to observe how consumers and retailers behave in a shopping situation. For example, researchers use mystery shoppers to see how many customers in a music store stop to look at a new-release display, how many buy that new release, and how the salespeople promote the item during the shopper's time in the store.

ethnography the study of social and cultural behavior and habits

Ethnography is the study of social and cultural behavior and habits. Researchers immerse themselves in the culture or society of a particular group to better understand their habits and behavior. For example, if researchers were interested in the music and beverage choices of urban 21- to 30-year-old men and women, they might visit a nightclub or venue frequented by this demographic group and observe their behavior and buying habits.

Media Entertainment Research

Media entertainment products include movies, music videos and DVDs, commercials, and electronic games. Media entertainment marketing firms use a variety of qualitative and quantitative methods to test their products on consumers and observe their reactions. One method used to collect this research data is the screening room. **Figure 13.1** on page 304 lists several entertainment products, research firms, and their various methods for collecting data.

SCREENING ROOMS Media entertainment marketers use screening rooms to show consumers previews, TV shows, movies, commercials, and movie trailers. Some screening rooms look like mini-movie theaters. These screening rooms are designed to simulate the experience of seeing a film on a big screen with theater-quality sound. Some screening facilities provide real-time behavior-response panels, which are small remote-control devices that respondents hold as they watch a screening. The panels have buttons that can indicate whether the respondent likes or dislikes the product. As a respondent presses a button on the remote device during the screening, the marketing team can instantly analyze the data the respondent enters.

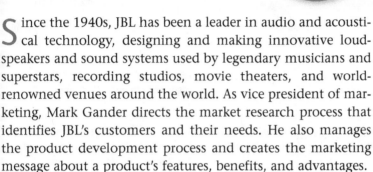

Profiles in Marketing

MARKETING SOUND QUALITY

Mark Gander
Vice President of Marketing
Harman JBL

Since the 1940s, JBL has been a leader in audio and acoustical technology, designing and making innovative loudspeakers and sound systems used by legendary musicians and superstars, recording studios, movie theaters, and world-renowned venues around the world. As vice president of marketing, Mark Gander directs the market research process that identifies JBL's customers and their needs. He also manages the product development process and creates the marketing message about a product's features, benefits, and advantages.

The key to Mark's success has been an intimate understanding of the products and how customers use them. Knowing his different customers' individual personalities and professional needs is crucial. "The things I like most about my job are the variety of product applications and management challenges and creating solutions for them—and the involvement with music and creative people."

ECLECTIC TRAINING While studying sciences and electrical engineering coupled with marketing, music, and broadcasting at Syracuse University, Mark also gained real-world experience at the college radio station. After graduating he worked in concert promotions and live sound production. He then went on to further studies at Georgia Institute of Technology where he earned a master's degree and began his marketing career.

Mark's advice applies to students interested in any career: "Choose something that you are passionate about. Find ways to study all aspects of it in formal classes, through reading, seminars, and other activities. Observe professionals performing the job that interests you. Find ways to volunteer and help those working in your career area so you can get experience. Find something you love and immerse yourself in all aspects of it."

List some of the ways a marketer might do market research for professional sound equipment.

Career Data: Vice President of Marketing

Education and Training
Bachelor's or master's degrees in business, marketing, or general education

Skills and Abilities Excellent communication skills, strong organizational skills, multi-tasking skills, and creativity

Career Outlook Faster than average growth through 2010

Career Path Entry-level positions provide experience. Real-world skills are crucial for advancement.

Figure 13.1

Entertainment Research Methods

COLLECTING DATA Think about the media entertainment products you own or enjoy viewing. *Which research methods would you use to discover how others view these products?*

Products	Firm	Methods	Facilities
Movies and trailers Music videos TV commercials	MCR Group Las Vegas, NV	Focus groups, Internet, telephone, and on-site surveys	In-house theater and screening facilities are equipped with real-time behavior response panels. Participants use these panels to electronically record their responses to what they view.
Publishing Television Broadcast media	RIVA: Research in Values and Attitudes Bethesda, MD	Focus groups and in-depth interviews	Moderated focus groups result in lively respondent participation and feedback in conference rooms.
Electronic games	Hugh Bowen and Associates Interactive Research	Focus groups, chat groups, Web surveys, and online panels	Respondents are from a six-city national network online.
Travel, tourism Recreational theme parks	SIS International Research Sarasota, FL	Focus groups, Internet and telephone surveys, in-depth interviews, specialty panels surveys, Mystery Shopping	Computer-assisted telephone surveys, real-time online interviewing, international respondents, bilingual moderators, and on-site Mystery Shoppers conduct research. Conference rooms and test rooms with one-way mirrors facilitate feedback.
Theater Performing arts Nightlife venues Travel and tourism Museums Parks	Audience Research and Analysis New York, NY	Focus groups; in-depth interviews; pre-testing; online surveys; mail, telephone, and Internet surveys	Multi-lingual questionnaires, concept-designed pre-paid mail surveys, and video-conferencing interviews allow research to be gathered.

These data are then combined with other respondents' data. The data then form a graph that shows the larger audience's response to the product, such as a film or commercial. Media entertainment marketers use the graphed data to promote their products to specific target markets.

Live-Action and Recreational Entertainment Research

Live-action and recreational entertainment products include concerts, theme parks, and casinos. Because many of these sources of

TEST SCREENING Film studios do test screenings in different cities months before a movie's release date. During these screenings, researchers test the audience's reaction. Sometimes after a test screening, parts of films are changed or re-shot. *Why might the results of a test screening cause the release date of a film to be changed or cancelled?*

entertainment are travel and tourist destinations, marketers learn about tourists' behavior while visiting these attractions. This information helps marketers effectively promote their products. For example, Disney marketers may want to know how people in Europe perceive the American Disney World versus EuroDisney. Are both theme parks equally exciting destinations? What attracts visitors to each venue? The answers to these questions and other market research help marketers evaluate and create successful marketing strategies.

Quick Check

RESPOND to what you've read by answering these questions.

1. Name two research methods that might be used to find quantitative data in the entertainment market._____

_____

_____

2. Explain the difference between contrived settings and natural settings. _____

_____

_____

_____

3. What methods do media entertainment marketers use to test their products?_____

_____

_____

_____

Entertainment Outlets and Venues

AS YOU READ ...

YOU WILL LEARN

- To identify criteria for selecting outlets and venues.

WHY IT'S IMPORTANT

Awareness of the important aspects of outlets or venues and their risks helps to ensure successful events.

KEY TERMS

- outlet
- venue
- capacity

outlet a place where a marketed product is released and made available

venue a place where live events are presented

PREDICT

How might understanding demographics relate to choosing a concert venue?

Other Entertainment Marketing Businesses

Entertainment marketing research firms make up a large portion of the marketing industry. They are a segment of the marketing industry focusing on entertainment product. Market research also affects decisions regarding entertainment outlets and venues, which are other large segments of the entertainment marketing industry.

Outlets and Venues

An **outlet** is a place where a marketed product is released and made available, or where it is placed—another one of the "Ps" in the marketing mix. In the case of movies and video games, the outlets would be a theater and arcade.

A **venue** is also an outlet, but it is a place where live events are presented. In the music industry, a venue for a concert might be a stadium, an amphitheater, or a club. The outlet and venue managers are in charge of marketing their locations to the entertainment companies that produce concerts, movies, live events, and shows. Their first function is to win a contract to host that company's event. Once outlet and venue managers secure those deals, they are also involved in ticket sales, promoting, and event management for shows held at their locations. Types of entertainment outlets and venues include:

- Movie theaters
- Live performance theaters
- Concert halls, amphitheaters, and stadiums
- Nightclubs, restaurants, and dancehalls
- Video-game arcades
- Arenas and stadiums for sports and nonsports events
- Galleries and museums
- Amusement parks

Size, Location, and Population

Outlet and venue marketers try to match the entertainment event with the appropriate venue. They consider factors such as the venue size, location, and population. Booking the Rolling Stones to play a

400-seat high school auditorium in a small midwestern town might be exciting, but it would create problems. There is no doubt the Stones would draw a crowd, but the size of the crowd would be more than the capacity of the venue and the location. **Capacity** is the maximum number of people that a venue or outlet can accommodate. For example, Madison Square Garden in New York City is better equipped to put on a show of that size and move the crowd in and out safely. When venue marketers consider booking an act, they consider the limitations and the advantages of their venues.

Entertainment marketers also want to find the correct outlet for the correct event. The type of event and the target demographic group it will attract dictate where an event can take place. Entertainment marketers and venue promoters consider several factors when matching an event to an outlet. **Figure 13.2** lists some of these factors. For example, a music label may want a new, lesser-known band to play an intimate concert in a nightclub whereas a popular, well-established band might be better suited to play in a large stadium.

CONNECT

Name two venues in your town or state.

capacity the maximum number of people that a venue or outlet can accommodate

Figure 13.2

Choosing the Right Venue

LOCATION, LOCATION, LOCATION **Many factors go into deciding on the right venue for an entertainment event.** *Think of one venue in your town or neighborhood. What types of events could you market to the population residing in your neighborhood?*

Size	Location	Population
• Seating capacity	• Geographic location: Is the venue located near a large metropolitan area such as New York City or Boston, or is it in a more isolated metropolitan area?	• Population interests: What kinds of events do they want to see: sports, theater, or movies?
• Standing-room capacity	• Size of the surrounding town or city: Is it in a rural, suburban, or urban area?	• Population support for the venue: Will people attend events, support the construction of venues in their neighborhood, and welcome out-of-towners attending events?
• Ticketing and merchandising outlets capacity	• Available amenities: Are there hotels, shopping, and restaurants needed to accommodate eventgoers?	
• Parking capacity	• Accessibility of location: Are highways, public transportation, trains, and airports accessible?	• Population size and income level: Can the target audience afford tickets, taxes for maintenance, and cleanup costs?
• Restroom and food facilities	• Safety of the location: Is the area well-lit and built-up, or economically depressed?	• Population size: Can the surrounding community provide venue employees?
• Number of emergency exits and safety precautions for house capacity		• Local businesses and merchants: Will venue contribute to or compete with local employers and retailers?

The Future of DVD Technology

Your home is a kind of entertainment venue where products are placed. As an entertainment product for the home, DVDs offer viewers more choices and additional content. Most DVDs contain bonus features such as deleted scenes, unaired episodes, commentaries, subtitles, language options, trivia games, and quizzes. The DVD market is still dominated by feature films, but some believe that the interactive format will lead to more "made-for-DVD" titles for niche markets.

➡ Discuss the future of DVD technology with your classmates after reading the article through marketingseries.glencoe.com.

QUESTION

What is the biggest challenge to keeping a venue profitable?

Income From Venues

Venues can create hundreds of jobs through their construction and their operation. Venue construction can be essential to urban revitalization programs. However, venue construction and management can be risky.

VENUE RISKS AND CONSIDERATIONS Key factors must be in place before construction is planned:

- The local population must be willing and able to support a venue.

- The venue must be safe and functional.

- The venue promoters must be able to book shows and fill seats.

Many stadiums are funded through a combination of private investment and taxpayer money. The benefits of an income-generating venue make projects worthwhile to taxpayers. However, if private investors withdraw, a town can go into debt. A sound business plan and binding contracts need to be in place before work can start.

Construction of a venue requires a great deal of planning and execution. Facilities must be safe, functional, and able to handle the number of people using them. Construction must be insured against accident, fire, and malfunctioning equipment to protect the venue promoters and managers in the event of an accident.

The most difficult part of making a venue profitable is keeping events booked and selling the venue to capacity. This means full houses for shows, games, films, or concerts.

Successful Marketing Strategies

Understanding your product, your customer, and your product outlets is essential to creating a successful marketing strategy. Marketing professionals gain this understanding by conducting market research. By using market research firms or conducting primary and secondary research, marketers can be fully informed about their products, customers, and outlets before making marketing decisions that will affect the success of a product or service they sell.

Quick Check ✓

RESPOND to what you've read by answering these questions.

1. List three examples of entertainment venues. _____

_____

2. Name the main three factors used to classify outlets and venues. _____

_____

3. What key factors must be in place prior to new venue construction? _____

_____

Worksheet 13.1

Choosing a Target Market

For one week, chart products and their target markets. Watch television commercials, listen to radio ads, and look at newspapers and magazines. Use the chart below or design your own. Chart at least ten products and their target markets. Pay attention to the clues that show what market is being targeted. Think about demographic characteristics such as gender, age, and ethnicity.

Product	Media	Target Market	Clues
1. _____	_____	_____	_____
2. _____	_____	_____	_____
3. _____	_____	_____	_____
4. _____	_____	_____	_____
5. _____	_____	_____	_____
6. _____	_____	_____	_____
7. _____	_____	_____	_____
8. _____	_____	_____	_____
9. _____	_____	_____	_____
10. _____	_____	_____	_____

Drawing Conclusions

11. To what category do most products belong (e.g., sportswear, personal-care products, food and beverages, etc.)?

_____

12. To what age group are the majority of products targeted?

_____

Name _____ Date _____

Worksheet 13.2

Taking a Survey

For one week, track the television viewing habits of your family and friends. Ask at least six people what programs they watch from 8:00 A.M. to 10:00 P.M. Use the chart below or design your own to write down your findings. Review your results and then rank each show, with number one being the most-watched show.

Rank	Program Name	Network	Day	Time
_____	_____	_____	_____	_____
_____	_____	_____	_____	_____
_____	_____	_____	_____	_____
_____	_____	_____	_____	_____
_____	_____	_____	_____	_____
_____	_____	_____	_____	_____
_____	_____	_____	_____	_____
_____	_____	_____	_____	_____
_____	_____	_____	_____	_____
_____	_____	_____	_____	_____
_____	_____	_____	_____	_____
_____	_____	_____	_____	_____
_____	_____	_____	_____	_____
_____	_____	_____	_____	_____
_____	_____	_____	_____	_____
_____	_____	_____	_____	_____
_____	_____	_____	_____	_____
_____	_____	_____	_____	_____
_____	_____	_____	_____	_____
_____	_____	_____	_____	_____
_____	_____	_____	_____	_____
_____	_____	_____	_____	_____
_____	_____	_____	_____	_____
_____	_____	_____	_____	_____

Portfolio Works

ASSESSING YOUR LISTENING SKILLS

Effective market researchers need good listening skills. This means being an active listener and giving the person you are interviewing complete attention when he or she is speaking.

The simple assessment below will help you assess your active listening skills. Read each statement. Then check **Yes** or **No** based on whether these statements relate to you.

		Yes	No
1.	My intention is to be an active and effective listener.	_____	_____
2.	I concentrate on the meaning and not on every word.	_____	_____
3.	I focus on the speaker and use eye contact.	_____	_____
4.	I am aware of emotions and nonverbal behavior.	_____	_____
5.	I withhold judgment until I hear the entire message.	_____	_____
6.	I am open to new information and ideas.	_____	_____
7.	I seek to understand the speaker's point of view.	_____	_____
8.	I do not interrupt, argue, or plan my response. I listen.	_____	_____
9.	I am mentally and physically alert and attentive.	_____	_____
10.	I paraphrase to clarify my understanding.	_____	_____
	Total Yes responses:	_____	

Count your Yes responses. If you marked Yes to seven or more questions, you are well on your way to becoming an active and effective listener. If you did not, you have some work to do to improve those skills. Learn more about active listening. Then add this page to your career portfolio.

CHAPTER SUMMARY

Section 13.1 Targeting Entertainment Markets

psychographics (p. 293)
product testing (p. 295)
primary data (p. 295)
trend (p. 296)
secondary data (p. 296)

- Market researchers seek to identify their target markets by using demographic information and psychographic information.

- Demographic characteristics such as age, income, gender, and ethnicity are used to categorize consumers into market segments.

- Primary data is information collected from original research to apply to an issue being studied. Secondary data is collected from preexisting research to provide information about trends.

Section 13.2 Research Methods

qualitative research
   (p. 297)
quantitative research
   (p. 297)
respondent (p. 298)
mall intercept (p. 300)
survey (p. 301)
statistics (p. 301)
observational research
   (p. 301)
traffic count (p. 301)
mystery shopper (p. 302)
ethnography (p. 302)

- Quantitative research refers to data expressed as numbers; qualitative research refers to data that measure qualities based on reactions or perceptions.

- Methods of research include personal interactive interviews, such as focus groups. Other methods include surveys, observational research, screening rooms, mystery shoppers, and ethnography.

Section 13.3 Entertainment Outlets and Venues

outlet (p. 306)
venue (p. 306)
capacity (p. 307)

- Marketers and promoters consider various criteria when deciding on a venue for an entertainment event, including the size and location of the venue, and the population of the community.

CHECKING CONCEPTS

1. **Explain** the importance of market research.
2. **Describe** the market research process.
3. **Define** demographics and psychographics.
4. **Explain** primary research and secondary research.
5. **Compare** qualitative and quantitative research.
6. **Describe** methods of qualitative research.
7. **Name** two types of observational research.

Critical Thinking

8. **Explain** how demographics can be used to market a CD.

CROSS-CURRICULUM SKILLS

Work-Based Learning

Information—Acquiring and Evaluating Information

9. A computer game company wants to expand its selection. What form of research should the company use to find out which new games to add, and why?

Interpersonal Skills—Working With Diversity

10. How might ethnography help your local newspaper sell more subscriptions to non-English-speaking customers?

School-Based Learning

Math

11. If 852 of 1,600 men surveyed prefer actor Viggo Mortensen over Bruce Willis in films, what percentage prefer Mr. Mortensen?

Language Arts

12. Create an event poster for a concert by your favorite music group and use a language other than your native language.

Role Play: Marketing Researcher

SITUATION You are to assume the role of marketing researcher for a theme park. The food service manager (judge) wants feedback on the current food service, including customer service, food quality, and food selections, in an effort to improve.

ACTIVITY Develop a plan of market research to evaluate the current food service and present it to the manager (judge).

EVALUATION You will be evaluated on how well you meet the following performance indicators:

- Describe the nature of target marketing in entertainment marketing.
- Identify information used for marketing decision making.
- Collect marketing information from others (e.g., customers, staff, and vendors).
- Describe techniques for processing marketing information.
- Describe the use of technology in the marketing-information management function.

INTERNET ACTIVITY

Use the Internet to access Hollywood.com and click on About Us.

- List two movies being advertised at this Web site.
- Name the corporate owner of Hollywood.com and identify one other business belonging to this owner that conducts market research for the entertainment industry.

➡️For a link to Hollywood.com to do this exercise, go to **marketingseries.glencoe.com.**

Chapter 14

Images and Licensing

Section 14.1

Images and Merchandising

Section 14.2

Licensing and Royalties

Chapter Objectives

- Define the term image.
- Describe the role of merchandising in entertainment marketing.
- Discuss how the United States government controls endorsements.
- Describe the role of sponsorship in entertainment marketing.
- Explain the importance of entertainment product licensing.
- Explain aspects of royalties.

THE CIRCUS REINVENTED

When Cirque du Soleil was started by French-Canadian street performers in 1984, the circus business was stagnant. Discarding animal tricks and other acts, the troupe concentrated on human feats of acrobatics and dance. The group did away with unnecessary speech, choosing to communicate through tonal songs instead. The Cirque du Soleil became a hit at home and on the road, playing to about 270,000 people a year from 1984 to 1989.

The award-winning show has grown to include members from 34 countries who speak more than 40 languages. Many of the founding members have stayed with the group: The founding president is a fire-breather, and the director of creation is a stilt-walker. As the show has evolved, so has the demand. The circus now has nine shows, including three North American tours, a Japanese tour, a European tour, three permanent shows in Las Vegas, and a permanent show in Orlando, Florida. How has the Cirque du Soleil supported such growth?

ANALYZE AND WRITE

1. Why might the Cirque du Soleil have an international cast?
2. What kind of sponsorship might Cirque du Soleil attract?

Case Study Part 2 on page 321

POWER READ

Be an active reader and use these reading strategies:

PREDICT what the section will be about.

CONNECT what you read with your life.

QUESTION as you read to make sure you understand the content.

RESPOND to what you've read.

Images and Merchandising

AS YOU READ ...

YOU WILL LEARN

- To define the term image.
- To describe the role of merchandising in entertainment marketing.
- To discuss how the United States government controls endorsements.
- To describe the role of sponsorship in entertainment marketing.

WHY IT'S IMPORTANT

Images and public perception of celebrities and companies affect the success of merchandising, which is a major source of revenue for entertainment companies.

KEY TERMS

- image
- merchandising
- return

image a mental picture or concept of something or someone

merchandising the variety of promotional activities and materials that complement and support the advertising effort

PREDICT

Describe the meaning of *image* in your own words.

The Impact of Image

Imagine waking up and going through your day with people watching you every moment. Then imagine having them comment publicly on what you wear, what you say, and what you eat. Famous personalities often endure this routine 365 days a year. As long as they are the source of people's curiosity, celebrities are subject to public scrutiny. The public's fascination with the everyday lives of favorite musicians, movie stars, and athletes exists because of curiosity. The media feeds the public's fascination with images of these famous people through television, radio, magazines, and newspapers. However, the images portrayed by the media are often false. Articles and reports may contain *slander,* or false and damaging statements that can affect a person's public image.

An **image** is a mental picture or concept of something or someone. Celebrities in the public eye constantly consider how they look, what they say, and what they wear in order to portray a positive public image. The public images of celebrities can make the difference between success and failure. To capture or recapture public recognition, many celebrities change or enhance their images to appeal to different markets.

Selling the Image

When a celebrity or a company is in the public eye, there is an increase in the opportunity to make a profit from merchandising. **Merchandising** is the variety of promotional activities and materials that complement and support the advertising effort. Marketers develop merchandising strategies that involve packaging, displaying, and publicity of a product, theme, or personality.

Merchandising can be direct and indirect. For example, marketers for the 2003 motion picture *Finding Nemo* used direct merchandising involving toys and plastic figures, such as the Nemo and Bitin' Bruce figurines. Examples of indirect merchandising strategies are placing logos on bedding, such as a Nemo comforter, drinking glasses, and clothing.

Merchandising is a multibillion-dollar industry that has made huge profits for motion pictures. In fact, successful merchandising can earn as much money as box-office revenue. Motion picture industry research shows that there is a five-year period to make money through merchandising. For example, the 1995 release of *Toy Story* had a four-year run of selling merchandise before the 1999 release of *Toy Story 2.* Merchandising added multimillion-dollar profits to both Disney film projects.

In addition to direct and indirect merchandise, marketers develop merchandise tie-in promotions between two or more parties. This popular marketing strategy is practiced by the fast-food chain McDonald's, which frequently gets involved in merchandise tie-ins with major motion picture studios such as Disney. For example, McDonald's offered figurines from the Disney film *Finding Nemo* with Happy Meals to appeal to children. This type of merchandising tie-in is mutually beneficial to McDonald's and the studio, because food and merchandise sales as well as product recognition increase. Other motion pictures with merchandise tie-ins have included *Star Wars*, *Batman*, *Dick Tracy*, *101 Dalmatians*, *The Lion King*, *The Lord of the Rings*, *Harry Potter*, *Peter Pan*, and numerous other films. Consequently, some parents report their children experience *toy fatigue,* or loss of interest in the toys, from all of the merchandise that is being offered with products such as Happy Meals.

Endorsements

In addition to merchandising, celebrities can also improve their images by involving themselves in other forms of promotion. For example, it is common to see television commercials with celebrities supporting and giving their approval for certain products. This type of support is considered an *endorsement* if the person in the commercial is acting as himself or herself and not as a character.

The Federal Trade Commission (FTC), a U.S. government organization whose purpose is to ensure that the American free-trade market system follows legal and fair exchanges, defines an endorsement as any type of advertising done by a person who reflects his or her own opinions, beliefs, findings, and experiences that are separate from those associated with the product's company. In fact, the FTC has set guidelines by which to identify endorsements (see **Figure 14.1** on page 318). For example, if actor Ben Affleck decides to endorse the American Automobile Association (AAA), he would have to be a legitimate user of its services; and he would have to be allowed to provide his opinion about its services without being told what to say by the organization. It is important that the endorsement be from the actual person, otherwise the authenticity of the endorsement is jeopardized.

Controversy of Endorsements

Consider how difficult it can be for celebrities and companies to make sure that problems from endorsements do not occur. Golfing celebrity Tiger Woods' endorsement of Nike's golf club was jeopardized when the professional golfer decided to go against his five-year, $100 million contract with Nike by switching back to his older Titleist golf club. Music celebrity Madonna agreed to endorse Pepsi by doing three commercials. But when she was asked to drink Pepsi in public, she refused to be seen drinking the beverage.

Endorsements can get more complex and risky when entertainers become involved and endorse political issues and groups. Although there is no rule against celebrities involving themselves in political issues, a statement or endorsement of a political nature can have

ETHICAL PRACTICES

The True Target
Advertisements on television often target children. Advertising companies may use the help of child psychologists to come up with images that will capture the attention of America's youth. Advertisers know that children can influence how the family will spend money. However, crispy marshmallow cereals are not the only kid-targeted products. Car commercials have also been geared toward children with expectations that they will influence their parents. The advertising industry is divided over this issue. Some experts believe this form of advertising goes overboard, while others believe that different standards should be set for children and for adults.

CONNECT
Do you think celebrities' images are negatively affected by doing TV commercials?

Figure 14.1

Endorsement Guidelines

TO ENDORSE OR NOT? **The FTC has set guidelines that must be followed for a promotion to be considered an endorsement.** *Why do you think the government is so concerned with regulating endorsement?*

1. Endorsements must always reflect the honest opinions, findings, beliefs, or experience of the endorser. Furthermore, they may not contain any representations which would be deceptive or could not be substantiated if made directly by the advertiser.

2. The endorsement may neither be presented out of context nor reworded so as to distort in any way the endorser's opinion or experience with the product. An advertiser may use an endorsement of an expert or celebrity only as long as it has good reason to believe that the endorser continues to subscribe to the views presented.

3. The endorser must have been a legitimate user of (the product) at the time the endorsement was given.

4. The advertisement should clearly and conspicuously disclose what the expected performance (or limitations) would be in the depicted circumstances.

5. Advertisements presenting endorsements by what are represented to be "actual consumers" should utilize actual consumers.

6. The endorser's qualifications must (show) the expertise that is represented in the endorsement.

7. The endorsement must be supported by an actual exercise of expertise in evaluating product features or characteristics with respect to which they are an expert and which are both relevant to an ordinary consumer's use of or experience with the product and also are available to the ordinary consumer.

8. An organization's endorsement must be reached by a process sufficient to ensure that the endorsement fairly reflects the collective judgment of the organization.

9. If a connection between the endorser and the seller of the advertised product exists that might materially affect the weight or credibility of the endorsement, then full disclosure of the connection must be revealed.

10. If the product changes, the company must notify the endorser, who must continue to use and believe in the revised product.

SOURCE: Federal Trade Commission

MARKETING SERIES Online

Remember to check out this book's Web site for images and licensing information and more great resources through marketingseries.glencoe.com.

damaging effects on a celebrity's career. For example, fans may boycott a star or band if they do not agree with public political statements. Also, a celebrity's image does not seem to match his or her public opinions, then fans may react with disapproval.

When a company seeks endorsement of its product, chances are very good that it wants a well-known person who represents its product to have a favorable image. Aside from product usage, personal characteristics need to be considered to appeal to a market. Using the earlier example of Ben Affleck to endorse AAA (American Automobile Association), the target market for that type of audience would most likely be people born between the 1970s and 1980s. Because of Affleck's age and the culture he represents in his image, AAA's target market would be a driver between the ages of 16 to 30 years. This

Advertising on the Side?

A *Japander* (Japan + pander) is defined as a Western celebrity who uses his or her image and fame to make large sums of money in a short time by advertising products in Japan. In other words, it is a quick way for stars to make millions of dollars without "losing face" in the United States. Many top celebrities often refuse to do commercials in the United States. However, it's a hard offer to refuse in Japan, especially since the commercials cannot be shown in the United States—that is, until recently.

Now, thanks to several Web sites, curious fans can log on to their computers and see actors and musicians hawking everything from jewelry to airlines. For example, Pierce Brosnan pitches lipstick; Mariah Carey sells coffee;

George Clooney peddles cars; Brad Pitt offers blue jeans; and Penélope Cruz markets hair-care products. One Web site features more than 100 celebrity ads. The developer says that his motivation for posting the ads online was to show the "stark contrast" of the usual onscreen images with "people doing strange and potentially embarrassing things for money."

Do you think the stars should be able to shut down these Web sites? Why or why not?

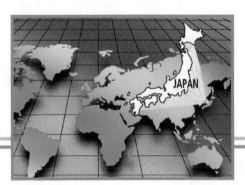

group will be more influenced by Affleck's views than, say, celebrity Paul Newman, who is considerably older and has little in common with people in this age group. As long as the FTC rules are followed and Affleck has a favorable image, then there is no reason he would not be able to endorse the AAA.

Sponsorship

Celebrities are also known to involve themselves in sponsorship. As discussed in Chapter 7, *sponsorship* occurs when a company supports an event, activity, or organization by providing money or other resources that are of value to the event. In return for money or other resources, the sponsor is typically provided with some type of advertising at the event.

Sponsorship is perhaps one of the most crucial aspects in sports and entertainment marketing because it is one of the most popular methods that companies use in promotion. When considering how many 30-second commercial spots there are for all of the major events that occur each year on television plus all of the other major television shows that draw high numbers of viewers, a large amount of money is seen exchanging hands though sponsorship. Consider all of the other events and broadcasts that occur and use sponsorship, such as award shows including the Academy Awards, TV programs that get high ratings, especially with season-finale episodes, and popular interview shows.

TECH NOTES

Web Site Works Magic

Released in 1999, *The Blair Witch Project* became a cult-classic film almost immediately. The film's instant success is often attributed to its official Web site, which featured original content not included in the film itself. The official Web site created an air of mystery about the film by promoting the movie as a documentary, rather than as a work of fiction.

➡ Do you think *The Blair Witch Project* would have been popular without its official Web site? Why? Answer this question after reading information through **marketingseries.glencoe.com.**

The Need for Sponsorship

Sponsors can also be seen in a variety of entertainment events such as music concerts. When musicians go on tour, they are essentially promoting their image in order to increase their record sales. Although ticket sales may be considered high to the consumer, the money from ticket sales does not cover the complete cost of the tour for the musician. Musicians have several costs and fees that they incur from various sources when they are on tour:

- Sets
- Transportation
- Arena
- Rentals
- Lights
- Concessions
- Programs

- Shirts
- Security
- Food
- Hotel
- Support staff
- Taxes

A musician has to find a way to pay these expenses not covered by ticket sales. Fortunately there are companies willing to help the musician by providing them with sponsorship money.

In exchange for their money, companies may ask for advertising space on the stage, concessions, T-shirts, and event programs. To ensure that the money used to sponsor the musician is well spent, marketing personnel for the sponsoring company spend time analyzing the feedback from the concert. In other words, marketing personnel might keep track of how many times fans would see the sponsor's name at the event, or they might track how much sales increase for their product after the concert. For example, an electronic games company may advertise at a concert that draws electronic-music fans. Marketers would then monitor sales of their products. If the company feels that it has been well represented, given the amount of money spent on sponsorship, then there is a good return on its money.

Why Sponsor?

Return is the amount of profit that is given back to the sponsor for the sponsor's initial investment or sponsorship. For example, imagine putting $100 in your savings account. You might deposit money into your savings account to save for future use. While your money is in your savings account, the bank uses it to make other investments (e.g., loaning money to other people). In exchange for allowing the bank to use your money, the bank provides you with a return on your investment known as *interest*. Interest rates are usually expressed in percentages and refer to the proportion of money you can earn on your investment. After letting your $100 sit in your savings account for one year, you decide to withdraw all of your money to make a purchase. When you

QUESTION

What is the difference between sponsorship and endorsement?

return the amount of profit that is given back to the sponsor for the sponsor's initial investment or sponsorship

withdraw your money that has earned 2 percent interest, or $2, your return will be about $102.

This amount of interest return is determined by using loan calculators that can be found at your local bank or on the Internet. For the company sponsoring a music concert, the return may not be as easy to calculate as investing money in the bank. However, if sales increase for the company, then this can be just as good as, if not better than, investing in a savings account.

The Right Representative

A sponsoring company wants to make an investment in a person or group that is best suited to represent the company. This person or group does not have to use the product. However, they are representing the product by allowing the company to sponsor them. For example, McDonald's is a major sponsor for the Olympic Games. Although the athletes may not eat at McDonald's, they are still best suited to represent the products because the athletes project images of champions and winners. In return for their sponsorship, which pays for uniforms, hotel space, and various fees, McDonald's receives several commercial spots on television and radio. In addition, McDonald's will have several billboards in various arena locations giving McDonald's increased name recognition and increased sales.

Case Study | PART 2

THE CIRCUS REINVENTED
Continued from Part 1 on page 315

In 2003, the nine Cirque du Soleil productions were to play for audiences numbering more than 7,000,000 on three continents. To support growth, the troupe erected an international headquarters with training rooms, dance studios, exhibition areas, office space, and retail stores. The Montreal facility was awarded the city's Orange Prize for its urban renewal. It is also home of the Place du Chapiteau, where a big top is raised for local performances. The Cirque du Soleil is also diversifying its business, starting projects in film, publishing, and merchandising markets as well as contracting special performances for private events.

ANALYZE AND WRITE

1. Why would the Cirque du Soleil require a large headquarters facility?
2. What are some possible merchandising and sponsorship possibilities for the Montreal troupe?

LENDING AN IMAGE **Many celebrities refuse to do commercials if they think doing so might affect their public image.** *Do you think a celebrity such as Sandra Bullock would represent any product? Why?*

Sponsorship Risks

Sponsorship does have risk and can have damaging outcomes. Consider what would happen if a musician who has numerous sponsors suddenly finds himself or herself in legal trouble, or gives poor-quality performances. Sponsorship will most likely decrease, as companies do not want to be associated with a person who has a poor public image or whose popularity is decreasing.

Government Restrictions

In addition to the risks associated with the person or group, consider the risks of the industry. For example, when the federal government passed various laws forbidding wealthy tobacco and alcohol companies from advertising at events appealing to children and teens, sponsorship was reduced and various venues were in jeopardy. As federal laws dealing with tobacco and alcohol become stricter, the opportunities for funding various events decreases, and seeking sponsors becomes more challenging.

On the other hand, these types of laws passed by our government are intended to protect citizens from negative influences that are brought on by tobacco and alcohol consumption. In addition, the federal government is able to regulate the practices of wealthy companies that may sponsor events that could be inappropriate for children and teens.

Quick Check

RESPOND to what you've read by answering these questions.

1. What is merchandising? _____

_____

_____

_____

_____

2. What is the purpose of the FTC? _____

_____

_____

_____

_____

3. Give an example of what a company might gain in return for sponsoring a musician. _____

_____

_____

_____

Licensing and Royalties

Overview

Licensing and royalties are major aspects of both the sports and entertainment marketing industry, involving large amounts of money. Consider how many fans wear clothing or own merchandise that are imprinted with images of their favorite teams, athletes, or celebrities. As you learned in Chapters 7 and 8, sports marketers may place a team name or image on a product to increase the value of the product. An average T-shirt might appeal to some people, but add a picture of basketball player LeBron James, and the appeal and value of the T-shirt may increase.

Merchandising

Entertainment-related companies also utilize merchandising. For example, an image of a popular band, such as the Dave Matthews Band or Coldplay, might be placed on T-shirts to sell at concerts. The Grateful Dead band has profited tremendously over the years from the band's image on products and concession items.

Amusement parks offer new rides with adjacent retail areas to encourage people to buy merchandise when they disembark from the rides. For example, Paramount Studios' theme park, Kings Island in Ohio, boasts that The Beast is the world's longest wooden roller coaster on 7,400 feet of track, reaching speeds of over 60 mph through dark tunnels—and it's a twin helix. After being on this whirlwind ride, people are excited. Paramount's marketers have found that at the moment people get off the ride, they want to remember it in a way that could not be captured in a T-shirt. As a result, Paramount has set up an area where you can buy a Kodak photograph of your expression as you race 135 feet down the first hill at a 45-degree angle. If you purchase the picture, you also get a frame imprinted with The Beast logo. If you still have an urge to purchase The Beast T-shirts and other merchandise, you have the opportunity to do this throughout the park. All of these items are **licensed products**, or goods or services that legally use logos or images owned by other companies or people.

Licensing

Licensing is required when the owner of an original image (such as a logo) or a product (good or service), including creative works, gives legal permission for a fee to another company or person to copy, manufacture, market, and sell reproductions of the original item. The most recognizable example of licensing can be seen in your

licensed products goods or services that legally use logos or images owned by other companies or people

PREDICT

Do you think products with popular movie images are sometimes more profitable than the movies themselves?

> **EXTENDING THE PRODUCT**
A theme park may promote its popular rides through advertising and merchandise such as T-shirts and photographs. *Can you think of some other well-known theme-park rides that could benefit from merchandising? What kinds of products could be developed?*

CONNECT

Name a song that has been recorded by more than one artist.

Math Check

SOURCES OF INCOME
BMI collects for and pays music writers' royalties. Alicia wrote a two-minute song that was used on a prime-time TV show on a major network. What is her royalty payment if she is paid $11.50 per station for 45 seconds or more of airplay—and the network has 532 stations?

➥For tips on finding the solution, go to **marketingseries.glencoe.com.**

classmates' clothing. Do you ever see your classmates wearing clothes with images such as a picture of Mickey Mouse, The Simpsons, a favorite band, a film logo, a famous actor or actress, or a theme-park logo? Each of these images represents an opportunity for licensing. When The Beast logo is printed on various pieces of merchandise, Paramount Studios, the owner of The Beast, grants permission to manufacturers and vendors to sell products with The Beast name on the products. As a result of this agreement, Paramount makes money from its logo by means of a licensing fee, and the manufacturers and vendors also make money by means of their merchandise production and sales of products.

Licensing Music and Royalties

Licensing can also apply to music, software, motion pictures, and video. A songwriter and publisher of a song may charge a licensing fee when an artist and label want to record that song. For example, as a result of her work on the soundtrack for the 1992 motion picture *The Bodyguard*, singer and actress Whitney Houston received Grammys for Single of the Year, Best Female Pop Vocal, and Album of the Year. The song that earned Houston the Single of the Year award is called *I Will Always Love You.* Country star Dolly Parton wrote and sang the original version in the early 1970s. She and her publishing company received a licensing fee. The version that Houston sang 22 years later sold 16 million copies and held the top spot in the pop charts for 14 weeks. Although Houston benefits from the 1992 version of the song when her record sells, Parton owns the rights to the song. When Houston's version is sold or broadcast, Parton benefits and receives royalties. When Parton was asked if she

Hot Property

The Magic Words

Harry Potter The image of the little boy who discovered he was a wizard first appeared to J.K. Rowling in scribbles. She was teaching English to children in Portugal where she spent afternoons writing about her favorite character Harry Potter and creating the world of Hogwarts wizardry school, Quidditch, muggles, and the wicked Lord Voldemort.

Upon returning to England, Rowling finished her first book that would make publishing history—*Harry Potter and the Philosopher's Stone* (*Sorcerer's Stone* in the U.S.). Published in 1997, it won awards and enchanted readers who found it on *The New York Times* Best-Seller List. With three more books, Harry went on to charm the world and capture the children's book market for publisher Scholastic. However, when Rowling's fifth book *Harry Potter and the Order of the Phoenix* was released in 2003, it made all other records vanish by selling five million copies the first day in bookstores and online.

MARKETING MAGIC

What is the secret to Harry's success? Children and adults alike respond to the child who discovers the power to fight evil, but critics also praise Rowling's "wonderful, textured writing" and "tirelessly inventive imagination." However, good marketing has worked its magic as well. The publisher creates a cloak of secrecy around plots before book releases, creating anticipation. Scholastic also offers a variety of products, such as DVDs, CD-ROMs, and even a Harry Potter plush doll. In addition, Warner Brothers has produced top-grossing films of the books.

It's easy to recognize Harry's image with this marketing mix for children—but surprisingly, 43 percent of purchases have been made by adults. Thus, the children's book publisher has found a new target market, aged 18 to 35, and designed savvy ads featuring bikers, skateboarders, and "couch potatoes" for magazines such as *Rolling Stone*. Whatever the reason for his popularity, Harry Potter has ignited a fire for reading—with people of all ages standing in line to buy 800 pages at a time.

1. Name three Harry Potter products that require licensing.
2. Would you classify the character Harry Potter as an image? Why?

---

was upset that Houston won a Grammy for a song that she wrote, Parton responded by laughing and exclaiming, "Are you kidding?" In this case, the song *I Will Always Love You* benefits the writer (Parton) and her publishing company, the singer (Houston), and the record company (BMG/Arista Records).

Labels have rights through contracts that are signed between the original artist and the record company. In return for use of the music, the artist may receive royalties, or a percentage of the record sales. In addition, the artist may receive an up-front sum of money based on his or her popularity and public image. The label also provides the artist with funding for the production and promotion of the music. However, there can be several agents between the artist and the record company, offering a variety of legitimate services that deduct more money from the profits.

Game Point

FUNNY IS MONEY
The New Yorker online Cartoon Bank offers its famous cartoons and artist services for a fee—a licensing fee. Businesses and individuals can find hundreds of cartoons to use for books, cups, or T-shirts.

Figure 14.2

Band Expenses and Profits

A SMALL PIECE OF THE PIE This chart lists some real-world figures for an imaginary band with a Gold® record. After expenses are paid, a band member may earn as much as an average worker earns. If illegal copies of the CD are distributed, the band earns no money from those CDs. *What might be some strategies to increase revenue for this band?*

Band	STONE MUFFINS
Number of members	4
Royalty rate to band	15%
Number of CDs sold	500,000
Price per CD	$16.98
Gross	**$8,490,000**
Deductions:	
Packaging costs @ 25%	$2,122,500
Giveaways @ 15%	$1,273,500
Actual Gross	$5,094,000
Royalty to band	*$764,100*
Expenses:	
Advance to band	$100,000
Production costs	$150,000
Advance to producer	$ 50,000
Video production	$100,000
Payment to producer	$153,760
Royalty subtotal	*$210,340*
Manager fee	$ 46,551
Attorney @ 2% of gross	$101,880
Royalty Balance	*$161,909*
Royalty per band member	**$ 40,477.25**

THE Electronic CHANNEL

Music to Your Fingertips

Internet service providers such as AOL often have content agreements with major music labels—in AOL's case, Warner Music Group. The sharing of content works both ways: The music draws people to the Web site, and subscribers are exposed to the music. Music marketing is integrated into the regular user interface, or the program that lets users navigate the Web. Users can do more than just listen to a new album: They can download exclusive tracks, artist information, and interviews.

➡️Visit a site to see an example of integrated music marketing through marketingseries.glencoe.com.

Paying for Entertainment

When people think of the entertainment industry, they often think of celebrities. However, celebrities make up a small portion of the entire industry. The entertainment industry employs over one million people who depend on income that may come from purchases of music and software, tickets for movies, or video rentals from authorized retailers. Some people do not want to pay for these products, if they can be obtained free. Why should users pay for them? The reality is that profits from these entertainment products pay for the expenses of producing the products, with only a portion going to the artists themselves (see **Figure 14.2**).

Consequences

When music, movies, and software are illegally downloaded and distributed from the Internet or products are pirated and copyrights are

Profiles in Marketing

BIG NAME BRANDING

Seth M. Siegel
Chairman, Licensing
The Beanstalk Group

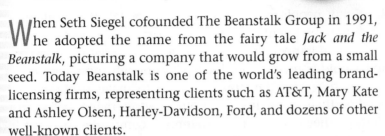

When Seth Siegel cofounded The Beanstalk Group in 1991, he adopted the name from the fairy tale *Jack and the Beanstalk*, picturing a company that would grow from a small seed. Today Beanstalk is one of the world's leading brand-licensing firms, representing clients such as AT&T, Mary Kate and Ashley Olsen, Harley-Davidson, Ford, and dozens of other well-known clients.

"When the company was beginning, I spent more time as a licensing agent," Siegel recalls. "Because the company has grown, I now spend more of my time managing other people who work as agents, and I develop new ideas for the company. I focus on the company's vision, what tomorrow's ideas are going to be, and on making sure that every employee is working toward a similar goal."

Seth points out that a licensing agent needs to be a strategic thinker and needs to do research. Handling the sales side of the business is also important—approaching new prospects, making presentations, and handling ongoing relationships. "An agent must make sure the products are in coordination with the brand message and that the products are of good quality."

Siegel also oversees hiring: "There are four traits that I look for when hiring employees," he offers. "They must be smart, hardworking, ethical, and honest, and be able to solve problems creatively."

Nonprofit Profits In addition to his duties running Beanstalk, Seth Siegel makes it a point to spend one hour a day working on not-for-profit activities. "It's technically not part of my job, but I've made it part of my job—it's important to be a player in our community."

Of the four traits Siegel looks for in a new employee, which one is your strongest trait? Which one is your weakest?

Career Data: Licensing Agent

Education and Training
Bachelor's or master's degrees in advertising, marketing, public relations, or sales

Skills and Abilities
Interpersonal skills, time- and project-management skills, resourcefulness, and problem-solving skills

Career Outlook Faster than average growth through 2010

Career Path Entry-level positions can lead to advanced positions.

violated, many people are affected, including the musicians, the makeup artist, the lighting technician, the sound technician, the costume designer, the set decorator, the caterer and others.

The user of the product is also affected. If prosecution occurs, consequences might include job termination, incarceration, and fines up to $250,000. Such consequences can become part of a permanent record that can affect future prospects. You may wonder why prices for movie tickets, textbooks, software, and video games increase. There are many factors that determine pricing, but these entertainment businesses also pass on the cost of illegal actions to the public in order to pay expenses and stay in business.

Making It "Big"?

Many people have talents. Some are talented athletes; others may be talented singers or actors. Have you ever considered what would happen if you became a professional musician or actor? How would you earn your income? Although some performers earn salaries, they also have opportunities to make additional income, based on their public image, through endorsements and sponsors. In addition, they and other entertainment companies can earn income through merchandising, licensing, and royalties.

Quick Check

RESPOND to what you've read by answering these questions.

1. What are three types of entertainment companies that use merchandising?_____

_____

_____

_____

_____

_____

2. Explain the meaning of licensing. _____

_____

_____

_____

_____

_____

3. Who are at least three participants in a record who may share royalties?_____

_____

_____

_____

_____

_____

Worksheet 14.1

Images and Licensing

Match the key terms to the correct description. Write the correct letter on the line beside the description.

_____ 1. licensing

A. fee paid to copy and sell original

_____ 2. merchandising

B. mental picture or concept of something or someone

_____ 3. return

C. sponsor's profit

_____ 4. royalties

D. celebrity approval of product

_____ 5. image

E. artists' pay

_____ 6. sponsorship

F. promotion strategy involving packaging, displaying, and publicity of a product, theme, or personality

_____ 7. endorsement

G. company supports an event

Name _____ Date _____

Worksheet 14.2

Licensed Products

For one week pay attention to licensed products that your friends wear. Use the chart below or design one of your own to chart the licensed products and licensor. Find as many as you can.

Type of Product	Name of Movie, Band, or Licensor
_____	_____
_____	_____
_____	_____
_____	_____
_____	_____
_____	_____
_____	_____
_____	_____
_____	_____
_____	_____
_____	_____
_____	_____
_____	_____
_____	_____

Observations and Conclusions

1. What types of movies or music produced the most licensed products? Why do you think this is so?

   _____

   _____

2. What type of product did you notice the most? Why do you think this is so?

   _____

   _____

Portfolio Works

CREATING AN IMAGE

Celebrities who are in the public eye have to consider how they look, what they say, what they wear, and how they act in order to portray a positive public image. In your world, you have also created an image by how you look, what you say, what you wear, and how you act. Complete the following exercises. Add this page to your career portfolio.

1. Write about the image you now portray to the rest of the world.

_____

_____

_____

_____

_____

_____

_____

2. Write about the image you would like to portray.

_____

_____

_____

_____

_____

_____

_____

3. List some steps you need to take to portray your ideal image.

_____

_____

_____

_____

_____

_____

_____

CHAPTER SUMMARY

image (p. 316)
merchandising (p. 316)
return (p. 320)

- An image is a mental picture or concept of something or someone. The public image of celebrities can make the difference between their success and failure.

- Merchandising is a type of promotion and can be direct or indirect. Merchandising increases profits as marketers develop merchandising strategies involving packaging, displaying, and publicity of an entertainment product.

- The Federal Trade Commission has set guidelines for endorsements, which are any type of advertising done by a person who reflects his or her own opinions, beliefs, findings, and experiences.

- Sponsorship occurs when a company or celebrity supports an event, activity, or organization by providing money or other resources. It is one of the most popular promotion methods.

licensed products
   (p. 323)

- Licensing is an important aspect of the entertainment industry. Licensing is required when the owner of an original image or product gives legal permission to copy, manufacture, market, and sell reproductions of the original item for a fee.

- Royalties are paid to authors, writers, songwriters, composers, and others who create or own products. For example, recording artists may receive royalties from record companies. However, there are many expenses involved in producing entertainment products, which are paid out of profits.

CHECKING CONCEPTS

1. **Explain** how image affects the entertainment business.
2. **Describe** how merchandising develops from a successful image.
3. **Define** sponsorship in entertainment marketing.
4. **Differentiate** between sponsorships and endorsements.
5. **Describe** the returns associated with sponsorship.
6. **Define** licensing.
7. **Explain** why illegal downloading may have harmed the music industry.

Critical Thinking
8. **Discuss** the importance of licensing in the entertainment business.

CROSS-CURRICULUM SKILLS

Work-Based Learning

Basic Skills—Writing

9. Cutbacks have forced your school to drop some programs. You must find sponsors for one of these programs—athletics, drama, or music. Write a letter asking for sponsorship.

Interpersonal Skills—Negotiating to Arrive at a Decision

10. Work with another student. One of you will defend free downloading of music from the Internet; the other will oppose it. Negotiate a possible solution and present it to the class.

School-Based Learning

History

11. Use the Internet or phone to research an entertainment company such as Pixar. Create a timeline with at least seven events to illustrate the history of the company.

Math

12. Your album has sold 5,000 copies at $15.95 per CD. What are your royalties if they are 15 percent of the gross?

Role Play: Agent

SITUATION You are to assume the role of agent for a child television star in a family sitcom. This actor (judge) is popular with kids ages 8–12. The character's image endorses toys, food, and clothing. The actor just turned 18. At the end of this season when the contract expires, the actor would like to leave the television show, go to college, and do more grown-up, dramatic roles. However, the show is a hit, and endorsement companies wish to continue the relationship.

ACTIVITY Present a marketing plan for approval to the actor (judge).

EVALUATION You will be evaluated on how well you meet the following performance indicators:

- Explain the nature of endorsements.
- Select strategies for maintaining fan support.
- Develop a public relations plan.
- Explain the nature of a promotional plan.
- Explain the nature of risk management.

Use the Internet to access information about one of your favorite entertainers, and then answer the following questions:

- What is the URL of the Web site you found?
- What image does this entertainer project?
- What does the entertainer do to project this image?
- Do you think this is a good image for the entertainer? Why?

➡For more resources, go to **marketingseries.glencoe.com**.

Chapter 15

Entertainment Promotion

Chapter Objectives

- Explain the promotional mix in entertainment marketing.
- Identify the role of advertising in entertainment promotion.
- Discuss the importance of public relations in entertainment marketing.
- Explain personal selling and promotions in entertainment marketing.
- Compare media and non-media advertisements.
- Describe how other promotional methods are used in entertainment marketing.
- Explain the importance of reaching diverse markets.

MUSICAL PROMOTIONS

Advertising and public relations are two elements of the promotional mix that were used by the film marketers of the hit movie *Toy Story 2*. There are a variety of ways to promote any entertainment product such as a film, TV show, or musical group.

Jessica Hopper learned about the music industry by working in an independent record label's mailroom in Minneapolis, Minnesota. Upon graduating high school, she moved to Los Angeles but found that she did not like working for the major labels. So she returned east to Chicago and started her own independent public relations (PR) company, Hopper PR, because, as she says, "Talking on the phone about music was one of my marketable skills." She notes that many bands who record for small labels and tour in vans do not have budgets for big-time agencies. She works with bands to make sure they get exposed to small music publications and college radio stations. While working under the radar of larger companies without playing politics and lacking famous clients, how has Hopper PR survived?

ANALYZE AND WRITE

1. What are some promotional methods used by Hopper PR?
2. Why would a band prefer to be marketed to small magazines and radio stations?

Case Study Part 2 on page 345

POWER READ

Be an active reader and use these reading strategies:

PREDICT what the section will be about.

CONNECT what you read with your life.

QUESTION as you read to make sure you understand the content.

RESPOND to what you've read.

Promotional Mix

AS YOU READ...

YOU WILL LEARN

- To explain the promotional mix in entertainment marketing.
- To identify the role of advertising in entertainment promotion.
- To discuss the importance of public relations in entertainment marketing.
- To explain personal selling and promotions in entertainment marketing.

WHY IT'S IMPORTANT

Applying the promotional mix in entertainment marketing, using advertising, public relations, as well as personal selling, is key to successful promotion.

KEY TERM

- release date

PREDICT

Recall the four components in the promotional mix.

Entertainment and the Promotional Mix

Promotion is any form of communication that a business or organization uses to inform or persuade people to buy its products. One of the most recognized aspects of marketing involves promotion. When asked to describe promotion, many people mention advertising. However, promotion involves four components in the promotional mix—advertising, publicity, personal selling, and sales promotion. As discussed in Chapter 1, the four components of promotion work together to provide a marketing professional with a promotional plan. A promotional plan exists when two or more of the components from the promotional mix are used together. As an example, Tower Records promotes its stores and merchandise through paid advertisements on television, in newspapers, and on Internet Web sites. In addition to advertising, Tower also uses personal selling when sales personnel assist customers in its stores and also recommend products and services. Because two components, advertising and personal selling, work together, a promotional mix exists.

To better understand each of the four parts of promotion—advertising, publicity, personal selling, and sales promotion—we will examine each component of the promotional mix as used in entertainment marketing.

Advertising

Advertising is any paid form of non-personal presentation and promotion of ideas, goods, or services by an identified sponsor. Advertising can occur almost anywhere. Different categories of advertising outlets include:

- Print
  - Newspaper
  - Magazine
  - Direct mail
  - Directory
  - Outdoor
  - Transit

- Broadcast
  - Television
  - Radio

- Online and specialty

Market research shows that the average person is exposed to more than 2,000 advertisements in a week. If you find this hard to believe, consider the many types of advertisements. Even some of your clothing functions to advertise. Companies such as Nike, Adidas and Quiksilver sell clothing with their imprinted names. Each article of clothing is considered an advertisement because it displays the company's name.

Advertising is the most expensive form of promotion. Recall that a 30-second television advertisement for Super Bowl 2004 cost $2.25 million, and that a one-page print advertisement can cost as much as $80,000.

Disney Ads Everywhere

Perhaps one of the most-advertised amusement parks is Walt Disney World in Orlando, Florida. By using a variety of television, radio, magazine, newspaper, and billboard mediums, Disney is able to reach a variety of target markets, including adults, children, and newlyweds. Once a person arrives at the amusement park, the advertisements continue with commercials in hotel rooms that promote the variety of rides, shows, and restaurants available in the park. Disney's advertisement has become so successful that many organizations, including athletic teams and other amusement parks, have imitated Disney promotions.

Advertising Jingles

Advertising campaigns can be heard on the radio or on television. These advertisements often use a jingle, which is a short tune or song with catchy repetition. Whether it is for a fast-food restaurant, a local car dealer, or a furniture store, these kinds of advertisements are easy to remember. Although we may not be interested in buying the products at that moment, the advertisement is placed in our memories. Marketing personnel who can successfully combine a particular radio or television station's target market with the appropriate ads can develop a loyal following for a product.

Public Relations and Publicity

Public relations include any activity designed to create a favorable image toward a business, its products, or its policies. It involves promotion of a product through a marketing group that involves the public and answers questions and concerns. Public relations are an essential type of promotion that helps sell products. When publicity is negative, the organization that provides the product needs to change the negative to a positive as quickly as possible. For example, when a product is considered dangerous for use, such as a toy, the problem must be solved, or the product must be recalled and fixed. Amusement parks provide other examples. If a ride malfunctions or a controversial group holds a convention in a park, the park management is quick to respond by using its public relations department to address any negative situations.

TECH NOTES

Harry Potter and the Web
On June 26, 2003, author J.K. Rowling appeared at Royal Albert Hall in London, England, to promote her latest book *Harry Potter and the Order of the Phoenix*. The event was broadcast live over the Internet and watched by an estimated 1.6 million people. In addition to reading an excerpt from the new book, Rowling answered questions that had been submitted by e-mail from fans around the world.

➥View an article and write a short paragraph about Rowling's historic reading through marketingseries.glencoe.com.

CONNECT

Can you think of a news report that gave negative or positive publicity to an entertainment company, event, or personality?

Hot Property

The Personal Touch

MUCH and HOUSE Public Relations

"It's important to have a passion for what you're doing," says Elizabeth Much, partner with Sharon House at Much and House Public Relations. A small full-service agency, Much and House is the inspired creation of both women. They used their PR expertise as vice presidents of entertainment and corporate at Wilkinson/Lipman PR to buy that firm and transform it into Much and House.

As a small agency, Much and House is able to provide personalized attention to its accounts, which include high-end celebrities in the mainstream and on the cutting edge. A roster of corporate clients, such as clothing companies and health-and-fitness businesses in their Lifestyle division, also call on the agency's creative services.

MEDIA BLITZ

The field of public relations is very competitive, and honesty and hard work are keys to staying in business. But creating innovative publicity campaigns has also kept Much and House in demand by high-profile professionals. For example, the agency designed a campaign for actress Alicia Silverstone and the film *Clueless*. Much and House's promotion plan was built around cover photos on magazines, articles in *Rolling Stone* and other magazines, appearances on popular talk shows, and extensive televised promotions on MTV. Much notes that planning, development, and execution for such feature-film promotion can take about six months. The agency has also co-ordinated entertainment promotions for television shows, films such as *City Slickers,* and many other movies.

Since 1996, this small, media-savvy publicity firm has created innovative publicity campaigns and has kept its clients large in the public eye.

1. What types of media do Much and House utilize to create publicity campaigns?
2. What other media might the agency use to promote its clients and clients' products?

Publicity is a specific type of public relations that involves placing positive and newsworthy information about a business, its products, or its policies in the media. Perhaps the most common type of publicity can be seen in the news when information is reported to the public. In entertainment marketing, when a motion picture is reviewed by industry critics on television, the review is considered publicity because the name and the content of the motion picture are being presented in a promotional format to inform the public. Since this type of promotion occurs at little or no financial cost to the motion picture business, it becomes a rewarding way to promote a movie. However, the review of the movie can be either positive or negative. When publicity is used in this manner, people find it believable because it is unbiased information.

Perhaps the most successful publicity comes from receiving recognition on various awards shows. When music albums, motion pictures, television shows, and plays win awards, there is often an increase in sales from positive publicity. Promoters use these awards to promote their products to the public. Various print, radio, or TV advertisements will mention a film has won five Golden Globe Awards or an Oscar for Best Motion Picture. These types of awards are very influential in convincing the public to spend money and to go see movies.

MARKETING SERIES *Online*

Remember to check out this book's Web site for promotions information and more great resources at **marketingseries.glencoe.com**.

marketingseries.glencoe.com

Figure 15.1

Entertainment Ad Agencies

Entertainment Company	Advertising Agency
Disney Studios	Western Media, Division of Interpublic
Columbia Pictures	McCann Erickson
Universal Studios and Theme Parks	DDB Worldwide
Warner Brothers Studios WB Network *Entertainment Weekly* and *People* magazines	Grey Advertising
ABC TV Network	TWBA, Division of Omnicom
Showtime Viacom Blockbuster Video Sony Electronics	Young & Rubicam

HIRING OUT Major entertainment companies rely on professional marketers for advice and strategies. These companies are represented by top ad agencies. *Why might a film studio hire an agency outside of its own company?*

Many entertainment companies use advertising agencies, research firms, direct-marketing companies, public relations firms, and Internet agencies outside of their companies to assist in their promotions and advertising efforts. **Figure 15.1** lists some of the major entertainment companies and their out-of-house agencies.

Personal Selling

Personal selling is any form of direct contact between a salesperson and a customer. It involves salespeople making individual contact when they promote a product. Once a person is attracted to a product, personal selling finalizes the sales process. As discussed in Chapter 8, the most important part of personal selling, and the reason that it is the most common form of promotion, involves two-way, personalized communication.

In entertainment marketing, for example, when a person calls Ticketmaster to order concert tickets, the salesperson may try to increase the quality of tickets as well as the cost of the tickets so that the company makes more money and the customer has a more enjoyable experience. You can find other examples of personal selling at special events, such as the Barnum & Bailey Circus, where merchandise vendors encourage customers to buy souvenirs and products beyond what they may intend to purchase. Customers are often anxious to buy products and souvenirs, such as concert T-shirts, CDs, or dolls, because they want to remember an event. Book-signing events held at bookstores are also presented as promotions to sell books at the events.

ETHICAL PRACTICES

False Paper Trail

Some people in the media will go to great lengths to promote a celebrity, film, or themselves—often stretching the truth. Even respected news sources are vulnerable to this trend. In 2003, a *New York Times* reporter allegedly stole material from other news sources to write articles and create phony interviews with people he had never met. Though he resigned, the scandal caused the executive and managing editors to resign after long careers.

ENTERTAINMENT HANDLER

Leslie Stewart
Publicist
Leslie Stewart Media Relations

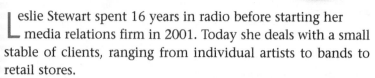

Leslie Stewart spent 16 years in radio before starting her media relations firm in 2001. Today she deals with a small stable of clients, ranging from individual artists to bands to retail stores.

"I work primarily in the area of publicity, so I basically coordinate artists with the media as a way of promoting their upcoming concerts, albums, or events," she says. "My job involves a wide range of duties: writing artist biographies, arranging photo shoots and interviews, sending out press releases about upcoming appearances, transporting the artists themselves to the various media interviews, and serving as the spokesperson for the artist or organization."

Stewart majored in music with an English minor at Eastern Kentucky University. She says communication skills are crucial in her line of work. "That includes good writing skills, good personal communication skills, and diplomacy—or being able to smooth over difficult situations and make everyone feel comfortable when a crisis arises," she adds.

"Mental and emotional flexibility are necessary. Sometimes flight schedules delay an artist's interview availability, or a performer gets sick, or there may be a last-minute conflict with contract negotiations. You have to be able to deal with those situations in a professional manner that presents a positive outcome to all parties involved."

According to Stewart, the most rewarding aspect of her job is getting to know and work with artists, those who are well known as well as the "up-and-comers."

Why is flexibility important for a publicist?

Career Data: Entertainment Publicist

Education and Training Associate's or bachelor's degree in communications, general business, marketing, or subject related to field

Skills and Abilities Excellent communication skills, writing skills, and strong organizational skills

Career Outlook Faster than average growth through 2010

Career Path The field is open to freelancers. Many entertainment publicists work for themselves, but most begin their careers with an established company.

QUESTION

What is sales promotion?

Personal selling takes place all around Disney theme parks. While walking up Main Street in the park where scents of popcorn and cotton candy fill the air and cheerful music is amplified in the street, it is very easy for customers to respond to Disney's salespeople and products. When you feel an urge for food or candy, is it difficult to resist a person selling these products? When you pass by a toy store with appealing and colorful products, is it difficult to resist a salesperson offering a Mickey Mouse hat for a souvenir? With these advantages at a theme park, the job of personal selling is easy for salespeople who provide personal attention to the customers.

Sales Promotion

As in all marketing situations, sales promotion in entertainment marketing represents the promotional marketing activities other than personal selling, advertising, and public relations. Sales promotions typically involve short-term incentives that encourage a customer to buy a product. One of the most common sales promotions is a premium known as the coupon. Students are entitled to various discounts and privileges that adults do not get. For example, a student discount at a museum or a special event is common because the management of these places is encouraging frequent visits by this target market to increases sales and recognition. The discount you receive is considered a sales promotion. Another type of sales promotion can be seen when you purchase the extra-large popcorn or soft drink at a movie theater in order to get a sweepstakes game piece or promotional CD that might be offered.

Sales promotion for Disney is evident through the coupons found in travel guides, airlines, car rental agencies, and hotels. Disney's theory is quite simple: Attract the customer to the park with discounted hotel, car rental, or park-admission fees, and the customer will make up the difference by purchasing merchandise and food. Besides coupons and adult discounts, Disney theme parks also use discounts as sales promotion tools for children's admission to the parks (see **Figure 15.2**).

Cross Promotion

Disney also works with other companies to promote their products. For example, Disney and Delta Airlines, which is the official airline of Walt Disney World, work together to promote both of their products in one package known as the Delta Vacations, Disney's Winter Dream Maker™. These types of sales promotions draw customers with reduced prices.

Math Check

FUN ON A BUDGET

Your parents are taking you and your cousins, who are eight and nine years old, to Summerland Water Park Resort. The promotion to stay for three days is $195 per child (to age nine), a savings of $60 each—and $495 per adult, a savings of $250 each. How much money would all five tickets cost if not discounted?

➡For tips on finding the solution, go to marketingseries.glencoe.com.

Figure 15.2

Promotional Discounts

DISCOUNTED PACKAGES
Many theme-park resorts offer special promotional discounts to adults and children to encourage business, especially if park attendance is down. *Do you think promotional discounts help increase profits? Why?*

Television shows will often have online forums, or places on the show's official Web site where fans can interact with one another—and sometimes with writers and creators. Fans enjoy this because they can discuss anything from plot points to that week's wardrobe selection. Thus, fans feel as if they influence the show. Media companies like online forums because they can measure interest in their shows and use that information to come up with marketing strategies.

➥Visit a major TV show's Web site and learn how to participate in an online fan message board through **marketingseries.glencoe.com**.

release date the day a film is first shown in theaters

Promotional Case Study

Each of the four parts of the promotional mix—advertising, publicity, personal selling, and sales promotion—creates a promotional plan, which is the combination of two or more of the promotional mix elements. In entertainment marketing, before a new motion picture is released, marketers go to work creating a promotional plan.

Film Promotions

Before the film *S.W.A.T.* was released in theaters in 2003, several forms of promotion took place. Advertisements began months before the August 2003 release date, or the day a film is first shown in theaters, with short previews in theaters and on television. Print advertisements were posted in magazines and on billboards.

A week before the release date, publicity began on major television talk shows, such as CBS's *Late Night with David Letterman,* NBC's *The Tonight Show with Jay Leno,* and NBC's *The Today Show.* On each talk show, Sony Pictures arranged to have *S.W.A.T.* celebrities Samuel L. Jackson, Colin Farrell, and James Todd Smith (aka LL Cool J) make personal appearances and preview film clips from the movie. These interviews were publicity because the celebrities were invited to appear on these talk shows specifically to promote the new movie. Additional publicity for *S.W.A.T.* included positive reviews by television film critics on shows such as *Ebert and Roeper,* with ratings of two "thumbs up," as well as reviews in magazines such as *Entertainment Weekly.*

A third type of promotion was sales promotion. Sony Pictures authorized various companies to use merchandise to promote *S.W.A.T.* For example, cellular-phone service provider Nextel offered a *S.W.A.T.* performance pack to customers—a *S.W.A.T.* Nextel cell phone and an opportunity to win merchandise signed by the actors.

These types of promotional mixes have also been used for other major motion pictures such as *Star Wars* (1977 and 1997), *Titanic* (1997), and *The Matrix* (1999). Successful mixes have also promoted television shows such as *M*A*S*H, Seinfeld, Friends,* and *Survivor,* as well as other forms of entertainment.

Quick Check ✓

RESPOND to what you've read by answering these questions.

1. Define promotion. _____

_____

2. Give an example of publicity in entertainment marketing. _____

_____

_____

3. What kinds of sales promotion are offered by Disney parks? _____

_____

_____

Variety of Promotional Methods

Media Advertising

Considered the most expensive promotional method, **media advertisement** is any form of advertising that uses media such as television, radio, the Internet, newspapers, or magazines to promote ideas, goods, or services. Many media advertising campaigns have produced some popular and memorable ads and commercials. Some of the most famous phrases used in everyday communication originated in such advertisements.

For example, "Where's the Beef?" was a phrase that was popular during the 1980s. Actress Clara Peller originally spoke the phrase in a television commercial for the Wendy's chain of hamburger restaurants. After being given a small burger from a competitor, Peller angrily exclaimed, "Where's the beef?!" The humorous advertisement and Peller's memorable character gave the slogan a life of its own, and it was repeated in countless TV shows, films, magazines, and other media outlets. In the 1984 U.S. Democratic Party primary, former Vice President Walter Mondale even used the phrase when he stated that his opponent's policies made him wonder, "Where's the beef?"

Media and the Promotional Mix

Media has also helped to enhance promotional plans. When Apple released iTunes in the spring of 2003, it became the first protected music-download Web site that required subscribers to pay for each song. Apple promoted its software and service by signing popular recording artists who agreed to make only certain songs available through the Apple Web site. In addition, the songs were encoded in a way so that they would be protected from illegal distribution. These expensive promotional tactics were effective as Apple reported over one million downloads during its first day.

Targeting the Audience

Aside from iTunes, the Internet itself has become one of the most effective advertising tools for marketers since the mid-1990s. With the help of Web sites such as Yahoo!, advertisers are able to target specific groups of people. For example, when using Yahoo!, a person might click "Entertainment" on the home page. At the top of the Web page, there might be an advertisement called a banner ad, as well as additional advertisements on the sides of the Web page. These advertisements are targeted at the person clicking on these links. This means that the user of these entertainment links may be sent advertisements from *Entertainment Weekly, ET Online,* or any other company that marketers feel is appropriate.

non-media advertisement
any form of advertising that uses methods other than the media to promote ideas, goods, or services

Non-Media Advertising

If you have been to an outdoor concert, event, or the beach, you have probably seen airplanes and blimps flying overhead with banners attached to them. A **non-media advertisement** is any form of advertising that uses methods other than the media to promote ideas, goods, or services. These advertisements, such as airplane banners, are good promotional tools because they are unique in comparison to media-style promotions. Other non-media promotions include direct-mail promotions in your mailbox as well as flyers handed out at various events or near popular attractions.

Disney has used both media and non-media promotional strategies successfully. Through several media sources, Disney promotes its products to its target markets. You can see examples in its television, radio, newspaper, and magazine advertisements. Internet advertisements run on Disney's partner companies' Web sites for Delta Airlines, Hilton Hotels, and National Car Rentals. Disney also participates in non-media promotions such as direct mailings that distribute promotional videos and DVDs that explain how to plan a trip to Walt Disney World.

Other Promotional Methods

There are several other methods of promotion used by companies trying to get in touch with consumers. A company uses these methods when there are special circumstances that allow for extra benefits in the promotion. Customers are rarely aware of these promotional methods until they are pointed out in a marketing or business context. As mentioned in Chapters 2 and 10, three methods are among the most popular: tie-ins, cross-selling, and product placement.

Tie-Ins

It is quite common to see promotions from two or more companies that combine as a tie-in. For example, many tie-in promotions for everyday purchases are found at places such as McDonald's. McDonald's is able to use tie-in promotions with various companies to appeal to their customers. With the help of a sweepstakes campaign, McDonald's is able to sell food products with an added tie-in that allows lucky customers to win a car, a TV, or an electronic game. These promotional tie-ins allow for many companies to benefit while serving a main purpose, such as to sell a large-sized drink. Marketers often use ties-ins for motion picture promotions. For example, the film *Finding Nemo* (2003) was promoted using a tie-in with McDonald's Happy Meal©, which helped to increase awareness and sales of both the products.

Cross-Selling

As a form of promotion, cross-selling allows a company to promote or link products within its own product assortment. In entertainment marketing, cross-selling occurs when you buy tickets for a concert or a movie. The backside of the ticket may offer discounts at the concession stand where food and drinks are sold. Thus, customers buy more than one product—tickets, food, and drinks.

Placing Products

You are probably most familiar with product placement as a promotional method. As discussed in Chapter 12, *product placement* is the locating and negotiating of prominent placements for a company's product or name as a prop in media, such as film, television, or radio.

The 1982 motion picture *E.T., The Extra-Terrestrial* is famous for being one of the first films to use product placement when the two main characters, Elliott and E.T., ate Hershey's Reese's Pieces. Of course, the brand name of the candy was visible onscreen. As this promotional strategy caught on and was proven successful, the 1993 motion picture *Wayne's World 2* satirized the practice of product placement when the two main characters vowed not to "sell out" to various companies, such as Pizza Hut and Pepsi, while they were actually showing and using the products onscreen. As a result, Pizza Hut and Pepsi successfully contacted their target market of teens who were watching the film.

Critics of product placement may say that the practice contributes to over-commercialization and detracts from the entertainment. Others might argue that good product placement lends realism to films and TV shows.

Case Study — PART 2

MUSICAL PROMOTIONS
Continued from Part 1 on page 335

To serve her expanding roster of clients who were looking for an alternative to big PR firms, which charge $1,500 or more per month, Jessica Hopper moved her business out of her living room. She set up a loft space with computers and enlisted the help of interns who were interested in the business of independent music.

To stay in touch with the current scene, Hopper often goes to shows, writes for independent music publications, and publishes her own music publication, *Hit It or Quit It*. She has also expanded her services to promote reissued music, organizing interviews with members of musical groups that had disbanded.

ANALYZE AND WRITE

1. What other promotional methods does Hopper PR use?
2. Who are some non-musical clients that a company such as Hopper PR might represent?

INDIRECT SALES The promotional practice of product placement is very popular in films. James Bond films also take advantage of the promotional method. *Do you think product placement in an entertainment presentation prevents people from enjoying the show?*

It's a Beautiful Way

It's not all about rock and roll for Ireland's Bono. Born Paul Hewson in Dublin, Ireland, Bono, the lead singer of the award-winning band U2, has a mission to help ease the suffering of the world's people. Bono reasons that celebrity is a powerful key to open doors: "Use this spotlight to shine on bigger problems"—such as disease, famine, and poverty.

The 40-something rock musician promotes his message on the road from pulpits, at truck stops, and on talk shows such as *Oprah*. Millions of people worldwide get the message, as do heads of state—including the U.S. presidents, South African President Tuabo Mbeki, Pope John Paul II, and British Prime Minister Tony Blair. Fans have come to expect inspirational performances and compassionate lyrics from this artist. Bono sings in his song *American Prayer:* "Give me your tired, your poor, and huddled masses / All are yearning to be free." In 2003, the GRAMMYs took a backseat when Bono was unexpectedly nominated for the Nobel Peace Prize for the second year in a row.

Do you think it is appropriate for entertainers to promote a cause while promoting their art? Explain.

IRELAND

Reaching Diverse Markets

Another aspect of marketing involves reaching specialized markets or diverse target markets to promote a product. Diverse markets include groups that vary in their ethnic, national, cultural, and geographic characteristics. For example, when promoting a product to a Hispanic group, marketers must learn the traits and habits about this target market. As the largest minority group in the United States, the Hispanic population has made a substantial impact in entertainment marketing. Several Hispanic television stations, such as Telemundo and Univision, were created for the Spanish-speaking U.S. market who watches Spanish-speaking broadcasts such as newscasts, game shows, talk shows, and soap operas. Not only have these stations been successful at attracting a diverse market, but they have also become very appealing to companies who want to promote and sell products to this market.

Products and Diversity

Since promotion is one of the most expensive aspects of marketing, it is important to consider the variety of diverse markets that might be interested in a product. For example, Tommy Hilfiger discovered that while marketing efforts to appeal to upper-income Caucasian men were unsuccessful, African Americans were becoming the largest buyers of his product line.

Similar situations have occurred regarding entertainment marketing for motion pictures, musical bands, and television shows. Marketers for the television show *The Simpsons* originally thought that its target market was adults. However, market research in the beginning seasons reported that the show also appealed to teenagers. This unexpected market became a huge target for merchandise and advertisements that increased revenue for the Fox network. Therefore, it is crucial for marketers to learn as much as possible about a target market and to be aware of the wide and diverse world of marketing.

Global Appeal and Markets

International entertainment products, such as music, books, TV, and films, may require specialized promotion and marketing, but the possibility for generating revenue and worldwide recognition is great. For example, the release of the 2003 motion picture *Bend It Like Beckham* was extremely appealing to many geographic markets outside the United States. With global appeal and a diverse cast, the film was made in England and starred two teenaged British actresses—one with British heritage and the other with Indian heritage.

Several effective marketing strategies were used to take advantage of the global potential of this film. Because of the appeal of this motion picture to soccer fans, the movie was released in the U.S. market over a year after it was first released in primary markets in Europe, Asia, and South America. Though soccer is a popular sport in the United States, its appeal is broad outside the country. The promoters of *Bend It Like Beckham* considered the U.S. market a secondary market in this case.

Promoters also determined that this audience would be teenaged female athletes. To appeal to this target market in the U.S., promoters believed that overseas success would serve as effective publicity for influencing American teens. In addition, the number of theaters that

QUESTION

What is the largest minority group in the United States?

ROCK AROUND THE WORLD **Musical artists such as Bruce Springsteen have audiences all over the world. Press conferences and advertisements are a few methods of promoting a new CD or tour.** *Name some other promotional strategies.*

showed *Bend It Like Beckham* was small in comparison to the number of theaters that would show a major studio's film in the United States.

As a result of these strategies, *Bend It Like Beckham* was one of the more successful motion pictures during the blockbuster months of 2003.

Promoting Entertainment

By using the four components of the promotional mix— advertising, publicity, personal selling, and sales promotion— entertainment companies can promote their products using a variety of strategies targeted to their markets. Products that might otherwise go unnoticed can generate huge profits, experience box-office success, and reach the widest audience possible in the United States and abroad.

Quick Check ✓

RESPOND to what you've read by answering these questions.

1. Give three examples of non-media advertisements. _____

_____

_____

_____

_____

_____

_____

2. What is a banner ad? _____

_____

_____

_____

_____

_____

_____

3. What are three promotional methods? _____

_____

_____

_____

_____

_____

_____

Name _____ Date _____

Worksheet 15.1

Mixing the Promotional Mix

The four components that make up the promotional mix—advertising, publicity, personal selling, and sales promotion—work together to provide entertainment marketing personnel with a marketing plan. Use the chart below or create one of your own to add facts about each component.

Advertising	Publicity	Personal Selling	Sales Promotion

Name _____ Date _____

Worksheet 15.2

Media and Non-Media Promotion

I. Choose from the list of terms below and match each term to its description. Write the correct answer in the space provided. Some terms are used more than once.

  a. media advertisement
  b. tie-in
  c. product placement
  d. non-media advertisement
  e. cross-selling

1. _____ Shown in movies

2. _____ Seen on television

3. _____ Links another product with product line

4. _____ Internet advertising

5. _____ Toys from a movie given to kids at McDonald's

6. _____ Blimps and airplanes with flying banners

7. _____ Seen in newspapers and magazines

II. Write a paragraph using the five terms in this exercise to describe a promotional plan for a new zoo in town.

_____

_____

_____

_____

_____

_____

_____

_____

_____

_____

_____

_____

_____

Portfolio Works

EXPLORING VERBAL SKILLS

Working in the entertainment promotion industry requires good speaking and writing skills. Answer the following questions. Then add this page to your career portfolio.

Taking Stock

1. What are your strengths in writing and speaking?

_____

_____

_____

2. What would you like to improve?

_____

_____

_____

3. What are your feelings about writing and speaking?

_____

_____

_____

Application

4. How can you demonstrate to employers that you have effective writing and speaking skills?

_____

_____

_____

Documentation

5. In your portfolio, keep examples of letters, essays, speeches, and other samples of your writing skills. Have someone you know, such as a teacher or employer, write a letter of recommendation for you that recognizes that you have learned good verbal communication skills.

CHAPTER SUMMARY

Promotional Mix

release date (p. 342)

- Promotion is any form of communication that a business or organization uses to inform, persuade, or remind people about its product. The promotional mix includes four components: advertising, publicity, personal selling, and sales promotion.

- Advertising is one of the four components of the promotional mix. Advertising uses all media, including print, broadcast, and online.

- Public relations and publicity are main components of the promotional mix, and are used to promote films, TV, theme parks, and personalities.

- Personal selling and sales promotion are crucial for an effective promotional mix to sell and promote entertainment products.

Variety of Promotional Methods

media advertisement (p. 343)
non-media advertisement (p. 344)

- Media advertisements are the most expensive promotional method, but they can also be the most effective. Non-media advertisements, including banners and direct-mail promotions, are useful because they are unique and distinctive.

- Other promotional methods, such as tie-ins, cross-selling, and product placement, are used by companies to reach their target markets.

- A challenging part of marketing involves reaching specialized or diverse target markets. Since promotion is one of the most expensive aspects of marketing, it is important to consider how a product might appeal to a variety of diverse markets.

CHECKING CONCEPTS

1. **Define** promotion.
2. **Name** the four components of the promotional mix.
3. **Describe** advertising.
4. **Identify** different types of media advertisements.
5. **Explain** the difference between publicity and public relations.
6. **Identify** a promotional method that uses more than one product or company.
7. **Define** diverse markets.

Critical Thinking

8. **Explain** how personal selling is different from other types of promotion.

CROSS-CURRICULUM SKILLS

Work-Based Learning

Interpersonal Skills—Participating as a Team Member

9. In groups of three or four students, develop a promotional mix for a school play or concert. Present it to the class.

Thinking Skills—Decision Making

10. Choose a target market in your community. Decide how to promote a school art exhibit to your target market and develop and write a promotional campaign.

School-Based Learning

Arts

11. Using markers, crayons, computer graphics, paper, or other materials, create a brochure to promote your favorite theme or amusement park. Include a discount coupon or other sales promotion strategy.

Computer Technology

12. Plan a Web page for an imaginary record company. Explain how your Web page could help promote its recording artists.

 CONNECTION

Role Play: Promotion Manager

SITUATION You are to assume the role of promotion manager for a television production company. Your company is releasing a new half-hour sitcom next fall targeted to families. The show centers around two grandparents raising two grandchildren in a resort town near a beach. The cast includes two major television stars as the grandparents.

ACTIVITY Develop a plan to promote the show to viewers and advertisers and present it to your boss (judge).

EVALUATION You will be evaluated on how well you meet the following performance indicators:

- Describe the concept of promotion in sports and entertainment marketing.
- Explain the types of promotion.
- Coordinate activities in the promotional mix.
- Explain the nature of a promotional plan.
- Develop a promotional plan for a business.

 **INTERNET ACTIVITY**

Use the Internet to access the Web site for the publication *Advertising Age* and click on Special Reports.

- Choose one Special Report related to the entertainment industry.
- Write a brief summary of the article.

➡For a link to the *Advertising Age* Web site to do this exercise, go to marketingseries.glencoe.com.

Chapter 16

Entertainment Marketing Plans and Careers

Chapter Objectives

- Explain an entertainment marketing plan.
- Describe a business plan.
- Explain a promotional plan.
- Describe educational preparation for a career in marketing.
- Identify career areas in entertainment marketing.

NEW ADVENTURE

Entertainment is one of America's top exported products to the world. The industry provides jobs and includes many forms of entertainment, from movies and video games to theme parks. Each of these forms of entertainment can inspire related products. Disney cartoons and films were the foundation for the original Disneyland, the first modern theme park.

In the 1990s, The Walt Disney Company developed plans to create a theme park next to Disneyland in Anaheim, California. Called California Adventure, it would have a "Golden State" theme with attractions blending familiar amusement park rides with state-of-the-art technology. When it opened in 2001, it received mixed reviews. Some people said the tickets were too expensive with half of the attractions. Other critics called it "Disney lite" and thought the new park was created to make more money from Disneyland tourists. In addition, the southern California economy was slowing down, and tourism was decreasing due to fewer visitors from Asia and other areas. Thus, park attendance was less than expected.

ANALYZE AND WRITE

1. If you were designing a marketing campaign for California Adventure, list the criticisms you would address.
2. Write two possible promotions for California Adventure.

Case Study Part 2 on page 361

Be an active reader and use these reading strategies:

PREDICT what the section will be about.

CONNECT what you read with your life.

QUESTION as you read to make sure you understand the content.

RESPOND to what you've read.

Section 16.1

Entertainment Marketing Plan

AS YOU READ ...

YOU WILL LEARN

- To explain an entertainment marketing plan.
- To describe a business plan.
- To explain a promotional plan.

WHY IT'S IMPORTANT

Understanding the elements of a marketing plan can help an entertainment company realize a business plan.

KEY TERMS

- fiscal year
- business plan
- viability
- promotional plan
- slogan
- media mix

The Importance of a Marketing Plan

To be successful in entertainment marketing, you must develop and present a well-thought-out, sensible marketing plan. As discussed in Chapter 9, a marketing plan outlines the marketing objectives for a business. It also outlines the strategies that marketers will use to meet those objectives and communicates strategies to company decision makers, investors, and clients. A good marketing plan is essential for winning budget approval, an investment opportunity, or a new contract. While there is no absolute format, a marketing plan should be tailored to identify the products it is selling and how to sell them to the target market.

Developing a Marketing Plan

Marketing plans are created for many reasons. Primarily, marketing plans present an organized and informed approach to marketing all products—including entertainment products. A marketing plan consists of two main parts—a market overview and a marketing strategy.

Market Overview

A market overview is a research report that details:

- The economic climate in which the business is operating.
- Market trends for the industry and the company's market share.
- Current goods or services and performance.
- Current target customers and their buying habits.
- Current distribution channels and their reach.
- Competition and competing companies' performance.
- New opportunities and ways to improve performance.

The market overview is essential to a marketing plan. The market overview informs the marketing team about economic and market trends. It clearly defines the goods and/or services being sold and the business's customers or audience. The market overview also helps determine whether marketing efforts will reach the target market. Finally, it outlines the competition and the company's competitive position.

Marketers gather overview data by conducting primary and secondary research. For example, a studio may use focus groups to discover audience reaction to a film or particular scenes in a film. These data help marketers analyze a product's past or future performance.

PREDICT

What do you think is meant by a marketing mix?

Marketing Strategy

In Chapter 13, you learned that a marketing strategy is the action plan that outlines the tactics marketers use to meet their marketing objectives. These objectives are based on the conclusions made from the market overview. Each objective should be a goal that can be measured and proven. For example, a conclusion may be that your company is not targeting a potential demographic group and is losing market share to the competition. An objective would be to increase market share by 2 percent over the next year by targeting a new demographic group. Your marketing strategy would outline how to achieve this objective. Marketers use the four components of the marketing mix to meet their marketing objectives:

- **Product** Positioning a product to make it stand out from the competition

- **Price** Pricing a product competitively and highlighting value

- **Place or distribution** Making a product easily accessible to target consumers

- **Promotion** Advertising a product's qualities and brand to a target group

Figure 16.1 on page 358 illustrates how marketers meet their marketing objectives by making adjustments in product, price, place, and promotion. A promotional plan would also be included within the promotion component. For example, a plan for a new film would include advertising and release strategies.

Putting It Together

A marketing plan is a combination of the market overview and the marketing strategy. Marketers usually include a time frame for executing the marketing plan, along with an outline of the budget and the resources needed to make the plan work. Marketing plans are usually developed before the launch of a new project, or at the beginning of a **fiscal year**, which is a 12-month accounting period.

Developing a Business Plan

Marketing plans are just one element of an overall business plan; a business plan is a broader map of a business as a whole. A **business plan** is a proposal that describes a new business to potential investors and lenders. It is used to describe the purpose of a business, its products, how the business is structured, and how it will compete with others in the same market.

A business plan is an important part of a proposal to secure funding from investors. Before decision makers invest their money, they want to see that marketers have fully developed their ideas. Business plans are a way of presenting **viability**, or the possibility of successful operation and profitability of a business. **Figure 16.2** on page 359 illustrates the structure and the elements of a business plan.

TECH NOTES

TV by E-Mail

Cable channels are using e-mail newsletters to keep viewers informed and to promote their services. In addition to providing program schedules, the newsletters often contain links to quizzes, contests, and products for sale, and other content from the channel's Web site. Avid viewers can also use sites such as Yahoo! TV to create personalized listings and set up e-mail reminders for their favorite shows.

➡ Subscribe to an e-mail newsletter and describe its layout through marketingseries.glencoe.com.

fiscal year a 12-month accounting period

business plan a proposal that describes a new business to potential investors and lenders

viability the possibility of successful operation and profitability of a business

MARKETING SERIES Online

Remember to check out this book's Web site for marketing plan information and more great resources at marketingseries.glencoe.com.

Figure 16.1

Marketing Strategies

SELLING ENTERTAINMENT There are many different ways to adjust entertainment marketing strategies to meet goals. *How does outlining objectives help the marketing team focus and plan tactics for improving sales?*

Product	Conclusion	Objective	Tactic
Classic movie formatted for home viewing	Sales have dropped for home-viewing versions of the classic movie.	To achieve 25 percent increase in sales of video and DVD version of the classic movie.	• Adjust product to increase sales by digitally remastering VHS version. • Re-release on DVD with added scenes and director comments to increase sales.
Recording artist	Early albums are not selling competitively.	To increase sales of early albums to compete with new album sales.	• Adjust pricing to increase sales. • Create greatest hits box set with more tracks for a fixed price.
Theater tickets	Box-office sales show that mainly local audiences buy tickets.	To increase ticket sales to out-of-town audiences by 10 percent.	• Adjust distribution to increase sales. • Hire group booking service or develop Web site to increase distribution to out-of-town consumers.

Developing a Promotional Plan

promotional plan a detailed strategy of how to focus advertising and marketing communication efforts

A **promotional plan** is a detailed strategy of how to focus advertising and marketing communication efforts. This plan can be part of the marketing plan. It is not enough to get the word out about a product. You want consumers to remember your brand name, logo, and goods or services when they choose between the many products available. A single print ad or television commercial may not accomplish this objective. To run an effective promotional campaign, you need to have a promotional plan. The major goals of a promotional plan are to create or identify a brand and communicate the brand to consumers.

CONNECT

How would you promote an event taking place at school?

Brand

Identify the message you want to send to target customers. What do you want customers to think or feel when they see your business name and logo? Branding creates identification with a business name or image in a potential customer's mind. You also want your products to have positive brand identification. This means you want customers to think of something good when they consider buying your product. To do this, you can use a positive sales pitch or slogan. A **slogan** is a catch phrase or small group of words that are combined in a special

slogan a catch phrase or small group of words that are combined in a special way to identify a product or company

Figure 16.2

Elements of a Business Plan

PLAN FOR SUCCESS A good business plan will help ensure the success of any business, including a movie production company or a theme park. *Which element would you develop first in a business plan?*

I. Executive Summary
A brief introductory outline that highlights the key ideas of the business plan
(Investors can quickly read this "attention grabber" to understand the plan before getting into the specifics.)

II. Mission Statement
An outline of the business's purpose and the products and services it will offer
(The marketing team explains its business idea to the investor.)

III. Industry Overview
An analysis of the industry and markets in which a business will compete, and the factors affecting the business
(The marketing team demonstrates its knowledge of the industry. It is similar to a market overview, but it gives a macro view, or the big picture or overview.)

IV. Competitive Analysis
An analysis of the direct competitor's market position and its strengths and weaknesses
(The marketing team plans how it will carve out a place for the business in a competitive market.)

V. Marketing Plan
A detailed outline including a market overview and an outline of the business's market strategy
(The marketing team maps out its marketing objectives and explains how it will position, price, distribute, and promote its product or service.)

VI. Organization Plan
An organizational plan that details the business's key managerial roles and legal structure
(The marketing team explains the business structure.)

VII. Operating Plan
An operational plan that details a business's location, facilities, equipment, supplies and suppliers, and staffing requirements
(The marketing team outlines what it will need for the business to operate.)

VIII. Financial Plan
An outline of the business's profit and loss projections, cash flow, operating costs, funding needs, and how funds will be used to run the business
(The marketing team estimates the amount of money it needs to run the business, and how it will be spent.)

IX. Appendices and Exhibits
Any additional information that will help to prove the feasibility of the business plan, such as market studies, key players' résumés, credit reports, and tax statements
(The marketing team provides information that demonstrates it is qualified to create a business plan and that the business plan is feasible.)

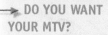
DO YOU WANT YOUR MTV?

MTV went on the air in August 1981 with a promotional ad campaign instructing young people to call and give this message to their local cable TV operators: "I want my MTV."

way to identify a product or company. A memorable slogan makes consumers interested in a product. Attached to a brand, the slogan creates a memorable brand.

- "Just Do It."

- "Where's the Beef?"

- "The happiest place on Earth"

These are all effective slogans that Nike, Wendy's, and Disney have developed. When creating your promotional plan, develop a slogan that will get people's attention so that your product is remembered.

Communicating Brand

The next step in creating a promotional plan is outlining how to communicate a brand and its message to the target market. Marketing a product is more than just advertising. As discussed in Chapter 15,

Hot Property

M-I-C-K-E-Y M-O-U-S-E

Has there ever been a mouse more famous than Mickey? More than just a cartoon character, Mickey Mouse introduced the world to the Disney brand. Walt Disney created the squeaky-voiced character in 1928, a few years after he began making short comedies with his brother Roy. Soon after that, Disney expanded his stable of long-running characters to include Donald Duck, Goofy, and Pluto.

Walt Disney then moved beyond this beloved bunch to create full-length animated features, state-of-the art production facilities, and Disney-brand theme parks. He also created live-action films and television programs that embodied his family-friendly ideals. These ideals, along with a flair for cross-promotion, formed the foundation of The Walt Disney Company.

MICKEY MADE OVER

Years after Walt Disney's death in 1966, the company began to struggle. Michael Eisner, who had guided Paramount Pictures to the top of the box office, signed on as chairman and CEO of Disney in

1984. The Walt Disney Company launched many plans to boost revenue and extend its international reach. Successful strategies included re-releasing old favorites (evergreens) for home audiences, aggressively merchandising entertainment properties, and buying live-action film production companies like Miramax. Disney also focused on animation efforts. The company was rewarded with international hits including *Beauty and the Beast* and *The Lion King*. The Walt Disney Company bought the ABC television network, and acquired ESPN as part of the deal. By 2002, the company employed over 100,000 people in its numerous worldwide divisions.

As an indication of its value, by 2004, Disney was offered $54 billion to sell the company. Through it all, the Disney brand identity has remained strong.

1. How did The Walt Disney Company grow?
2. How do you think a long-lasting brand such as Disney maintains its appeal to young audiences?

some promotional methods to communicate a brand to consumers include:

- Marketing materials

- Advertising

- Sales and promotions

- Publicity

- Tradeshows and industry events

The **media mix** is a combination of two or more promotional methods. Marketers often use more than one promotional option to communicate their marketing messages and promote their products to target markets.

MARKETING MATERIALS Businesses can use various marketing materials for promoting products. These materials display a company's logo and slogan and are distributed every time business is transacted. Marketing materials are a great way to communicate a brand and any information about a company to vendors, suppliers, and new and existing clients and should be part of a marketing plan. Some marketing materials include:

- Company-letterhead stationery

- Business cards

- Brochures

- Company Web sites

ADVERTISING Different media can advertise, or communicate, a brand to a large number of consumers. Various advertising media that can be incorporated into market plans include:

- TV

- Newspapers and magazines

- Radio

- The Internet

- Movie previews

- Product placement

- Billboards

Case Study   PART 2

NEW ADVENTURE
Continued from Part 1 on page 355

By 2001, the California Adventure theme park, as part of Disneyland in southern California, was experiencing a reduction in park attendance. By 2003, this trend continued for most theme parks. However, Disneyland began to show an increase in attendance of 7 percent from local residents, who spend less on hotel accommodations and food than do tourists visiting California. Though Disney's earnings were healthy in its movie and other divisions (up 9.9 percent), its theme parks were suffering from a depressed global travel industry. To encourage more business, Disney offered special promotions with discounted travel packages and ticket prices. A four-day pass into Disneyland and California Adventure was priced at half off the regular admission price. Though these promotions may reduce profits, the hope is that the good deals will open the gates to a steady stream of guests at the Magic Kingdom.

ANALYZE AND WRITE

1. What trend outside of the theme-park industry has affected Disney's park attendance?

2. What marketing strategies has the company used to encourage more business?

media mix a combination of two or more promotional methods

QUESTION

Do marketing materials communicate a brand only to customers?

- Location ads on buses, subways, and benches

- Direct mail

- Telephone books

- Window and in-store displays

- Live-event advertising

However, advertising is only effective if it reaches the target market. Marketers should identify the best way to reach their target markets when they choose advertising methods.

SALES AND PROMOTIONS When Disney World offers discounted tickets and a theater offers free passes to a film, they are conducting sales and promotions. Buy-one-get-one-free promotions and coupons encourage potential customers to use a product and recognize a brand. These types of promotions would also be included in marketing plans.

PUBLICITY Publicity can take many forms, such as press releases, news stories, and articles about a product that communicate the brand to a wider audience. Sponsoring events, such as CD-release parties, community or charitable events, book signings, movie premieres, and product-launch parties, are effective ways to gain positive publicity for a company or event. In addition to inviting the press to these events, companies can promote their products by handing out product samples, promotional items, or free merchandise that feature the company logo and slogan.

 **MARKETING FAME People who create entertainment products are often on display. J.K. Rowling, author of the Harry Potter series of books, makes public appearances at book signings.** *How can a celebrity take advantage of being in the public eye?*

TRADESHOWS AND EVENTS Marketers promote their products and services to vendors and distributors at these conferences and venues. This type of presentation provides exposure for a brand. There are film expositions in which new filmmakers and companies can market their movies to a vast number of producers and studios. A good marketing plan for a film might incorporate this type of promotion.

The Whole Package

A good business plan will include a well-researched and outlined marketing plan. Entertainment marketing plans consist of a marketing overview and a marketing strategy. Within this marketing plan there will be a focused and clear promotional plan. The business plan outlines the business; the marketing plan outlines the product and how to sell it; and the promotional plan describes exactly which channels will be used to communicate a marketing message to target consumers. All three plans work together to develop a profitable business.

Quick Check ✓

RESPOND to what you've read by answering these questions.

1. Describe a marketing plan. _____
_____
_____
_____
_____
_____

2. Name two events that could generate publicity for an entertainment person, company, or product.
_____
_____
_____
_____
_____

3. What are some promotional methods used to communicate a brand? _____
_____
_____
_____
_____
_____

Entertainment Marketing: Education and Careers

AS YOU READ...

YOU WILL LEARN

- To describe educational preparation for a career in marketing.
- To identify career areas in entertainment marketing.

WHY IT'S IMPORTANT

Knowing the educational resources for an entertainment marketing career will help you develop a career path. Knowing the variety of career opportunities will help you make informed choices.

KEY TERMS

- internship
- networking

PREDICT

Do you have to be in the workplace to network?

The Value of Education

Education is important for anyone to be successful in any field. Learning is an ongoing process valuable to any career. Through education, you can accumulate the knowledge, information, and skills necessary to succeed in your chosen field. To be an entertainment marketing professional, you need to know about marketing and marketing plans, as well as the entertainment industry. However, education does not always mean years and years of expensive schooling and degrees. Some level of formal education is necessary, but much of what you need to know about the industry can be learned through work experience. This section will examine some of the ways you can educate yourself about the entertainment marketing industry.

Educational Resources

There are several ways to acquire an education about marketing, in general, as well as about entertainment marketing, in particular:

- High school courses
- Undergraduate and graduate programs
- Internships and work experience
- Industry training programs, workshops, and seminars
- Industry publications and journals

High School Courses

Courses on entertainment marketing are taught in many high schools. High school marketing students cover some or all of the following functions of marketing: marketing-information management, market analysis, financing, pricing, promotion, product/service management, distribution, and selling. A course in entertainment marketing will also help you plan the steps to take to pursue a career in this field. High school courses provide a range of information. Taking a course is a good way to find out if you are truly interested in a career in entertainment marketing.

Undergraduate and Graduate Programs

Many universities offer undergraduate and graduate degrees in marketing and marketing communications. There are even entire schools within universities that are dedicated to marketing and business disciplines. Degrees can be earned online or by attending classes, conducting research, and writing theses, or graduate papers.

At the graduate level, marketing courses are offered within the context of a master's degree in business administration or a master's degree in marketing. Students can also go on to earn doctorates in business and marketing. There are several Web sites that list marketing degrees and graduate programs offered at schools around the United States. Be sure to research a marketing program's curriculum to see if entertainment marketing is covered, because some university marketing programs do not offer entertainment marketing courses.

CONNECT

What kind of person might take on an internship?

Internships and Work Experience

The best way to educate yourself about entertainment marketing is to work in the field. An internship is a great way to find out how things really work, what job opportunities exist, and what skills are required to work in entertainment marketing. An **internship** is a temporary paid or unpaid position giving students direct work experience and exposure to various aspects of a career. An intern often does basic tasks, such as filing, while learning how things work

internship temporary paid or unpaid position giving students direct work experience and exposure to various aspects of a career

World Market

All the World's Their Stage

With a name like the Royal Shakespeare Company (RSC), it's not hard to guess what is on the theatrical program. The RSC is one of the most prestigious theater groups in the world. Dedicated to presenting Shakespeare's plays, the company's roots go back more than 125 years— to the dreams of one man. In 1875, Charles Flower, a Stratford beer maker, donated a two-acre site to construct a theater in the town where Shakespeare was born and died (1564–1616).

Over the years the theater company grew, attracting critical acclaim as it nurtured artistic talent such as the late great actors Sir Laurence Olivier, Vivien Leigh, and Richard Burton. In the last decade, the RSC has given over 19,000

performances, sold 11 million tickets, and played in 150 towns around the world. As a result, new fans of Shakespeare are born. About one-quarter of the RSC's current audience includes fans under the age of 25.

The RSC is an ensemble company, and so everyone from the director to go-fers works as a team. How might this approach be helpful to someone just starting out?

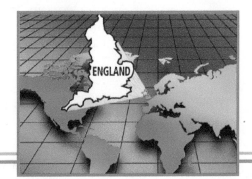

Virtual Actors

Actors' unions require benefits and minimum pay according to their contract terms with major studios. At times, contract disputes have delayed or cancelled production of films and television shows. However, the 21st century may see more virtual actors on the set. Unlike live actors, computer-generated casts do not legally require salaries or medical insurance. Since 1996, when the director of *The Frighteners* hired programmer Stephen Regelous to develop software to create virtual crowd scenes, Hollywood has been moving toward cyber actors. In fact, to bring J.R.R. Tolkien's *The Lord of the Rings* trilogy to the screen, Regelous gathered computer-designed characters called "agents" to fight the great battles—and they did their own stunts.

QUESTION

Do you have any aptitudes that could be applied to an entertainment career? Name them.

within the company. Many marketing firms, such as The Leverage Group, offer entertainment marketing internships.

Sometimes companies offer paid internships, but you should be prepared to work without a paycheck. However, your unpaid labor might be rewarded. Some companies will offset your costs by offering a stipend for travel and food expenses. Most universities and colleges will grant college credit for the work you do as an intern.

There are also non-student interns. Non-student interns are people who want to work in the industry and are interning in hopes of making contacts at an entertainment firm to be eventually hired. However, because of the low-paying or unpaid nature of internships, it is best to intern when you are a student or have a part-time job. The contacts you make and the skills you learn as a student intern will help you when you enter the work force.

Industry Training Programs, Workshops, and Seminars

Many large companies as well as marketing and public relations associations offer training programs for executives and marketing professionals. These programs can include:

- **Training** in marketing and management skills

- **Workshops** with peers and instructors on marketing concepts and practices

- **Seminars** with academic and professional speakers on new developments in the industry

- **Conferences** and networking events where marketing professionals can meet, pitch ideas, and share news and information on entertainment marketing

Many associations, such as the American Marketing Association (AMA), offer information, courses, and resources to both professionals working in the industry as well as marketing students.

Industry Publications and Journals

Marketers stay informed about developments in entertainment marketing by reading trade and marketing magazines and journals. This is an easy way to educate yourself about the aspects of, and the people who work in, the entertainment field. Many trade marketing magazines and journals exist both in print and online:

- *Variety* is a trade magazine about the entertainment industry.

- *TMS News* is a newsletter from MOBE (Marketing Opportunities in Business and Entertainment).

- *Internetnews* is a Web site for Internet advertising news.

- *Newsreel* is a Web site you can search for headlines on entertainment and marketing.

Industry journals and books are available in the business and careers section of your local library. Film and television sections in bookstores and libraries are also good resources for related information. No matter how successful or knowledgeable you are in an industry, you can always learn more.

Entertainment Marketing Careers

Entertainment marketing is a large and diverse field. In an industry where there are so many different kinds of products, media, outlets, and venues, many different opportunities exist for skilled marketers. Working in marketing is not limited to sitting in a room with a product and writing slogans all day long. There are several areas of entertainment marketing in which to specialize.

Marketing is important on every level of the entertainment industry. For example, a box-office manager at a local theater engages in marketing by advertising a half-price ticket promotion or a new play opening next week. In the entertainment industry, marketing affects goods and services from development to distribution. This means there are many paths to explore to find a career in entertainment marketing and many types of careers available.

Careers in Entertainment Marketing

There are several career areas of entertainment marketing on which you can focus. Some areas include:

- Public relations
- Advertising
- Merchandising
- Brand development
- Facility design
- Sponsorship and endorsement contract negotiation
- Event planning and marketing
- Ticket group sales and distribution
- Publicity and promotions
- Product and market research
- Licensing and copyright
- Talent management

These areas of marketing exist in every company that produces entertainment products. This means you can be an entertainment marketer for sports teams, television production companies, theatrical touring companies, amusement parks, electronic-game manufacturers, concert promoters, record labels, and artist and athlete management firms.

The list can also include areas of entertainment law and accounting. These particular fields focus on the legal and tax issues involved in entertainment marketing. Some strategies for building a successful career in entertainment marketing include:

1. Identify your areas of interest: film, sports, amusement parks, theater, music, or other areas.

2. Identify your skills: advertising copy writing, contract negotiation, ticket sales, event planning, or other skills.

3. Map out your education. Ask yourself if there are specific areas of knowledge or skills that you need to learn to build a career in marketing. Find out if certain degrees or training will help you get the job you desire. Apply for courses or night school, attend seminars, and work as an intern to help build your marketability as a potential employee.

4. Research the companies you would like to work for and investigate the types of products and services they provide. Research job positions, salaries, and career paths available.

5. Make contacts and network with people in the entertainment industry. Arrange informational and job interviews.

What Are Your Resources?

How do you find a job? How do you research job titles, salary ranges, career paths, and companies? The following resources will help you focus on specific areas within entertainment marketing.

IDENTIFY YOUR INTERESTS Choose an area of the entertainment industry that interests you. Identify your areas of interest by watching TV, reading books and magazines, listening to music, playing sports, going to games, and watching movies and plays. You may not be very good at marketing opera season tickets if you do not know anything about opera. Be sure to choose a career that involves promoting products that you enjoy.

GET EXPERIENCE Take a variety of marketing courses in school, or take internships that cover several fields of marketing. This is a no-risk way to discover your strengths and what you like. The earlier you identify your strongest skills, the sooner you can polish those skills to help your career. Take writing courses, volunteer at promotional events, and read about legal entertainment issues such as copyright law. These activities can help you improve your knowledge of the entertainment industry. Ask for feedback from your teachers, coworkers, employers, and friends about what you do well.

RESEARCH Visit public, business, and industry libraries to find listings of marketing firms that specialize in entertainment. Research the companies' histories, areas of specialty, and client lists via their Web sites. Identify specific careers in entertainment marketing and read job descriptions to find out the skills needed for those careers. Marketing association listings, such as those on the AMA Web site, are great resources for job seekers and marketing students, providing information on salaries and job titles.

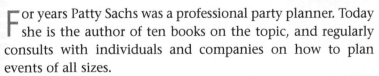

Profiles in Marketing

ENTERTAINING CELEBRATIONS

Patty Sachs
Party Planner
Author of *Don't Wait ... Celebrate!*

For years Patty Sachs was a professional party planner. Today she is the author of ten books on the topic, and regularly consults with individuals and companies on how to plan events of all sizes.

"It's a wonderful career," she says. "There's plenty of room for planners—the busier people get, the more they rely on someone to help them. And people are celebrating more. It has occurred to people that it's very good for them to celebrate. The value of a planner is becoming more evident."

According to Patty, attention to detail is one of the most important traits a party planner can possess. "Making lists and being organized, that's key," she says. "Creativity is helpful, and a lot of creative people think they might like to get into event planning, but then they get into it and realize how much detail there is."

She also recommends that aspiring party planners take as many courses as they can on sales and marketing. "Most planners, before they get a chance to plan, have to sell someone on the ideas. If you're in marketing or PR, you get such an insight into the whole business side of it."

The Human Touch Patty also says that knowledge of psychology and human relations is very helpful. "When you're dealing with personal parties, weddings, and christenings, people are emotional.

"When it comes to weddings, it's good if you can be an arbitrator. A wedding is usually at least 12 people's dreams come true—the bride being one of the people, but not the only one. You're dealing with parents and grandparents. It's emotional, and they often hire a planner to plan the event, and then end up using the wedding planner as an arbitrator."

Why would negotiation and diplomacy skills be useful to an event planner?

Career Data: Event Planner

Education and Training
Associate's or bachelor's degree in communications, public relations, or marketing

Skills and Abilities
Organizational skills, people skills, time-management skills, and multitasking skills

Career Outlook Faster than average growth through 2010

Career Path Many planners are self-taught, but degrees in sales and marketing are helpful in running a business and advancing in a career.

MAKE CONTACT When you know what you want to do and with whom you want to work, you can begin networking. **Networking** is the practice of finding contacts among people you know, including family and friends, employers, and professional people you know personally. Meet and talk with other professionals in your field to develop relationships and share ideas. Talk to your teachers and industry

networking the practice of finding contacts among people you know, including family and friends, employers, and professional people you know personally

professionals. Ask your friends, family, and coworkers about contacts in the marketing and entertainment marketing field. If they do not have contacts at the companies in which you are interested, see if their contacts do. Then set up an informational interview for the purpose of asking questions about what a company does. Along with networking, use the Internet to look for opportunities posted on company Web sites, marketing and PR association Web sites, and job sites. You can also check with your school guidance counselor or local employment office.

LIKE WHAT YOU DO Many interests and hobbies can lead to exciting marketing careers. *To what careers might an interest in music lead?*

Getting the Job

Once you are working in the entertainment marketing field, you will be exposed to the specific jobs and skills required to market entertainment products. From within the industry, it is possible to move into other positions. You might find that you are better suited for research than for sales. However, all marketing knowledge and skills are valuable, regardless of the industry. Knowing how to sell a product effectively is a skill in any industry. However, knowing how to sell the dynamic, exciting products of sports and entertainment is not only a great skill, it's a great career.

Quick Check ✓

RESPOND to what you've read by answering these questions.

1. Name four areas of entertainment marketing careers. _____

_____

_____

_____

2. What are some ways to find out about personalities and companies in the entertainment world?

_____

_____

_____

3. What is an informational interview?_____

_____

_____

_____

_____

Name _____ Date _____

Worksheet 16.1

Elements of a Business Plan

Use the graphic organizer below, or create one of your own, to illustrate the connection among the business plan, the marketing plan, and the promotional plan. Write the function of each in the space provided.

Business Plan _____

_____

_____

_____

_____

_____

_____

Marketing Plan _____

_____

_____

_____

_____

_____

_____

Promotional Plan _____

_____

_____

_____

_____

_____

Worksheet 16.2

Personal Interests, Aptitudes, and Skills

1. Make a list of your personal interests, aptitudes, and skills. Personal interests are the activities and pursuits that you enjoy most. An aptitude is your natural capability to do certain things. A skill is your capability to do certain things—things that you can learn to do and improve. For example, you may have an aptitude for math. That is a natural ability for you. You also may possess musical skills. Musical skills can be enhanced and improved through practice.

Personal interests:

_____

_____

_____

_____

_____

Aptitudes:

_____

_____

_____

_____

_____

Skills:

_____

_____

_____

_____

_____

2. Look at your personal interests, aptitudes, and skills. Then list five areas of entertainment marketing that might be best for you.

_____

_____

_____

_____

_____

_____

Portfolio Works

BUILDING A SUCCESSFUL CAREER

To build a successful career in entertainment marketing, you need a plan of action. Follow the steps and answer the questions below to create your own plan. Then add this page to your career portfolio.

1. Identify your areas of interest, such as films, music, theater, and other areas.

_____

_____

_____

2. Identify your skills. For example, are you skilled in writing, personal selling, or event planning?

_____

_____

_____

3. Map out your education. Go online to find out what degrees or training you need.

_____

_____

_____

4. Research the companies you would like to work for and investigate the type of products they sell.

_____

_____

_____

_____

5. Make a list of potential contacts and networking opportunities.

_____

_____

_____

_____

CHAPTER SUMMARY

Section 16.1 Entertainment Marketing Plan

fiscal year (p. 357)
business plan (p. 357)
viability (p. 357)
promotional plan
    (p. 358)
slogan (p. 358)
media mix (p. 361)

- An entertainment marketing plan outlines the marketing objectives for a business and the strategies for meeting those objectives. It consists of two main parts: a market overview and a marketing strategy.

- Marketing plans are one element of a business plan, which is a much broader map of a business as a whole. Business plans are used to help secure funding from investors.

- A promotional plan is a detailed strategy of how you intend to focus your advertising and marketing communication efforts.

Section 16.2 Entertainment Marketing: Education and Careers

internship (p. 365)
networking (p. 369)

- To be an entertainment marketing professional, you should be educated about the entertainment industry. You can obtain this education in high school, in college, through internships, and on the job. You can also read industry publications and access entertainment-related Web sites.

- Marketing is important at every level of the entertainment industry. Areas you can specialize in include public relations, advertising, brand development, and talent management.

CHECKING CONCEPTS

1. **Explain** the importance of a marketing plan.
2. **Describe** the components of a marketing plan.
3. **Name** the elements of a business plan.
4. **Define** branding.
5. **Explain** the value of education.
6. **Identify** the resources that can provide an entertainment marketing education.
7. **List** three people in your network.

Critical Thinking

8. **Identify** two careers in entertainment marketing that interest you and explain why you think they sound interesting.

CROSS-CURRICULUM SKILLS

Work-Based Learning

Thinking Skills—Reasoning

9. Describe a tactic for a strategic adjustment to the product, price, place, or promotion of a hip-hop artist whose albums have had slow sales.

Basic Skills—Math

10. Last year tickets for concerts at the Razzmatazz cost $35, $55, and $75. If ticket prices increase by 10 percent and are rounded to the nearest dollar, how much will tickets cost this year?

School-Based Learning

Language Arts

11. Write a mission statement for an entertainment venue (theater, concert hall, amusement park) in your community. It should be brief—two to three sentences.

History

12. Use the Internet or an encyclopedia to find out the names of some of the first films and dates they were shown.

 **Role Play: Agent**

SITUATION You are to assume the role of agent for a high school-age band. This band is well-known and well-liked throughout its school, and its members would like to pursue music as a part-time career. The leader of the band (judge) is looking for a plan to make money for the next year.

ACTIVITY Present a year-long marketing plan for the band (or company) to its leader (judge).

EVALUATION You will be evaluated on how well you meet the following performance indicators:

- Develop company objectives (for a strategic business unit).
- Develop strategies to achieve company goals/objectives.
- Explain external planning considerations.
- Develop a business plan.
- Explain the nature of risk management.

 **INTERNET ACTIVITY**

Use the Internet to access the American Marketing Association's Web site and research the information, courses, and resources available for students.

- Describe the information available for job seekers at the Career Center.
- Explain where to begin your search for seminars, conferences, or workshops.

➡For a link to the American Marketing Association's Web site to do this exercise, go to **marketingseries.glencoe.com.**

BusinessWeek News

HOLLYWOOD HEIST

Premiere day was fast approaching for *The Hulk*. The film's budget had already climbed to more than $150 million, including an extra $20 million for George Lucas' special effects company to give the giant green hero an extra dose of ferocity. The 11th-hour nitpicking was nothing compared with an earlier uproar at Universal Pictures: Two weeks before *Hulk*'s June 20 release, pirated versions of the blockbuster hopeful were circulating on the Internet. Worse yet, the film was getting nasty reviews.

For Hollywood moguls, that script is more terrifying than anything they could ever put on the big screen. More and more, the first showings of the latest Julia or Mel flicks aren't in just the local cineplex. They're on KaZaA, Morpheus, or iMesh—Internet sites known for music file-sharing but now for snapping up pirated movies. Within a few days of Keanu Reeves battling his first black-suited bad guy in theaters in *The Matrix Reloaded,* an estimated 200,000 folks had already taken in the action, downloading the long-awaited sequel in their dens and dorms.

It's all too reminiscent of the monster that ate the music business. For a town that loves a good sequel, that's one repeat performance Hollywood isn't keen to produce. Only five years ago, music sales were booming. Today the industry is nearly paralyzed by piracy. The speed at which music was brought to its knees makes Hollywood execs tremble.

Can Hollywood avoid getting Napsterized? Execs are energized by the success of Apple's iTunes Music Store. At 99 cents apiece, more than five million songs have been sold in two months. The moguls see iTunes as proof positive that consumers are willing to accept limits on copying if the price is right.

Many studios are already laying the foundation for digital delivery. Five Hollywood studios began offering movies through Movielink last November. And CinemaNow began selling films on the Web in early 2001. Come this October, Walt Disney Co. launches tests of its MovieBeam service.

Media moguls are realizing that what they really need to do is turn pirates into paying customers. That's why, for so many in the industry, Apple's iTunes has become a demarcation between eras. When it comes to entertainment, you have to give the people what they want.

By Ronald Grover and Heather Green with Tom Lowry, Catherine Yang, and Cliff Edwards

CREATIVE JOURNAL

In your journal, write your responses:

CRITICAL THINKING

1. Name some advances in technology that are affecting the entertainment industry. Do you think these advances are beneficial? Why?

APPLICATION

2. Imagine and describe in one paragraph a new film or music CD project. In developing a plan, what considerations would you make for Internet downloading? Why?

 Go to businessweek.com for current *BusinessWeek* Online articles.

UNIT LAB

Dream Machine, Inc.

You've just entered the real world of sports and entertainment marketing. Dream Machine, Inc., is a sports and entertainment marketing company that serves college and professional sports teams, professional athletes, sporting events, sports arenas, and major sports product corporations, as well as performing arts companies, television networks, and movie studios. As an entry-level employee, you will have the opportunity to work on a variety of clients' projects.

Develop a Plan—Write a Marketing Plan for a Young Child's DVD

SITUATION You are employed by Cinema Stage, an independent production company. Due to the popularity of *Baby Einstein* DVDs and videos, your company has decided to venture into that type of entertainment. As the director of marketing, you will develop a marketing plan for the introduction of a new DVD that targets parents of infants and young children. The vice president believes the company can compete with the *Baby Einstein* series of DVDs. She expects you to design a competing DVD as well as a creative marketing plan for it.

ASSIGNMENT Complete these tasks:
- Research producers and retailers of baby toys and entertainment.
- Talk to parents to learn what products entertain their children.
- Design a DVD that will entertain infants or young children.
- Develop a marketing plan for the product.
- Make a report to the vice president.

TOOLS AND RESOURCES To complete the assignment, you will need to:
- Conduct research at the library, on the Internet, and by talking to parents of infants and young children.
- Have word-processing, spreadsheet, and presentation software.

RESEARCH Do your research:
- Identify target markets for infant and young children DVDs.
- Research the baby products industry to determine trends and opportunities.
- Research competitors' prices for DVDs.

REPORT Prepare a written report using the following tools, if available:
- *Word-processing program:* Prepare a written marketing plan that includes a SWOT analysis, target-market analysis, and recommendations for the marketing mix.
- *Spreadsheet program:* Prepare a chart of the market share of competing companies and a chart of price comparisons.
- *Presentation program:* Prepare a ten-slide visual presentation with key points from your marketing plan, an illustration of your product idea, a sample advertisement, and chart of competitors' prices.

PRESENTATION AND EVALUATION You will present your report to the vice president. You will be evaluated on the basis of:
- Your knowledge of the baby entertainment industry and competitors
- Rationale for your new product idea and marketing plan
- Continuity of presentation
- Voice quality
- Eye contact

PORTFOLIO
Add this report to your career portfolio.

Glossary

A

ad campaign a promotional plan that combines selling, advertising, public relations, and the use of different media to reach the target market

advertising any paid promotion of an idea, good, or service by an identified sponsor

affiliate an independent broadcaster that contracts with larger national networks for programming

amateur athlete a person who does not get paid to play a sport

ancillary product a product related to or created from the core product

B

brand a name, word or words, symbol, or design that identifies an organization and its products

brand equity the value a brand has beyond its actual functional benefits

brand extension the development and introduction of new products that expand the brand and take advantage of the recognition and image of an established brand name

brand identity a consistent image or feeling that consumers recognize when encountering the brand

brand mark a brand name and symbol

brand name a word or words, letters, or numbers representing a brand that can be spoken

break even costs and expenses equal to income revenues

brick-and-mortar store a retail business with a physical location or store site

bundle pricing selling several items as a package for a set price

business goods goods purchased by organizations for use in their operations

business plan a proposal that describes a new business to potential investors and lenders

C

census a study that counts everyone in the research population

channel of distribution the path a product takes from the producer to the consumer

co-branding a branding strategy that combines one or more brands to increase customer loyalty and sales for each product

commercialization process that involves producing and marketing a new product

competition as a characteristic of free enterprise, the struggle among companies for customers

concessions snack-bars that sell refreshments such as popcorn, soda, and candy

consumer goods goods purchased and used by the ultimate consumer for personal use

consumer loyalty consumers' attitude that occurs when they are happy with a company and become repeat customers

consumers people who use products

convergence the overlapping of product promotion

copyright the legal protection of a creator's intellectual property or products

core product the main product, such as sports event, movie, stage show, or book

cost-plus pricing pricing products by calculating all costs and expenses and adding desired profit

crossover an expansion of the popular appeal of an artist or work by achieving success in another market or style

cross-promotion any form of communication through which one industry relies on another industry to promote its product

cross-selling the method of selling the customer additional related products tied to one name

D

demographics statistics that describe a population in terms of personal characteristics

direct channel the path a product takes without the help of any intermediaries between the producer and consumer

direct marketing marketing activities to sell products directly to customers through the use of a customer database

discretionary income money left to spend after necessary expenses are paid

E

economics the study of the choices and decisions that affect making, distributing, and using goods and services

endorsement approval or support of a product or idea, usually by a celebrity

entertainment franchise a series of films, programs, or character portrayals planned to expand the character's activities in a series

entertainment marketing the process of developing, promoting, and distributing products, or goods and services, to satisfy customers' needs and wants through entertainment, or any diversion, amusement, or method of occupying time

ethnography the study of social and cultural behavior and habits

event marketing all activities associated with the sale, distribution, and promotion of a sports event

evergreens films or products that are popular year after year

executive summary an overview of the entire marketing plan

exhibitors theaters that sell tickets and show films to an audience

extreme sports sports that involve nontraditional, daring methods of athletic competition

fad a short-term popular trend, style, product, or service

fiscal year a 12-month accounting period

focus group a panel of six to ten consumers who discuss opinions about a topic under the guidance of a moderator

GDP (gross domestic product) the value of all goods and services produced within a country

generic brand a brand that represents a general product category and does not carry a company or brand name

grassroots marketing marketing activity on a local community level

gross profit revenue minus the cost of goods sold

gross revenue income from sales before costs, expenses, and taxes are deducted

image a mental picture or concept of something or someone

implementation putting the marketing plan into action

impulse spending buying without prior planning

indirect channel the path a product takes using intermediaries between the producer and consumer

infrastructure the physical development of an area, including the major public systems, services, and facilities of a country or region needed to make a location function

institutional advertising advertising with a goal of developing goodwill or a positive image

intangible product a nonphysical service such as tennis lessons, personal training, or sports camps

intermediary brand a brand that carries a name developed by the wholesaler, retailer, or catalog house

internship temporary paid or unpaid position giving students direct work experience and exposure to various aspects of a career

jingle a catchy tune or song that promotes a product and accompanies television, radio, or Internet advertisements

kinetoscope a device used to view a sequence of moving pictures

leisure time time free from work or duties

licensed products goods or services that legally use logos or images owned by other companies or people

licensing an agreement that gives a company the right to use another's brand name, patent, or other intellectual property for a royalty or fee

location-based entertainment (LBE) entertainment that includes amusement, theme, animal, and water parks

loss-leader pricing pricing an item at cost or below cost to draw customers into the store

mall intercept a market-research interview conducted in a public place, such as a mall

manufacturer brand a brand owned by the producer of the product

market potential customers with shared needs who have the desire and ability to buy a product

market research the process of systematically collecting, recording, analyzing, and presenting data related to marketing goods and services

market segmentation a way of analyzing a market by specific characteristics to create a target market

market share the percentage of the total sales of all companies that sell the same type of product

marketing the process of developing, promoting, and distributing products, or goods and services, to satisfy customers' needs and wants

marketing concept idea that organizations need to satisfy their customers while also trying to reach their organizations' goals

marketing mix a combination of four basic marketing strategies, known as the 4 Ps—product, price, place, and promotion

marketing plan a written document that provides direction for the marketing activities of a company for a specific period of time

marketing strategy a method that identifies target markets to make marketing-mix decisions that focus on those target markets

markup difference between the retail or wholesale price and the cost of an item

media the methods used for communicating or transmitting messages

media advertisement any form of advertising that uses media such as television, radio, the Internet, newspapers, or magazines to promote ideas, goods, or services

media mix a combination of two or more promotional methods

merchandising the variety of promotional activities and materials that complement and support the advertising effort

motionmark a trademark identified by specific movement associated with a brand or company

mystery shopper a market researcher who poses as a shopper to observe how consumers and retailers behave in a shopping situation

NCAA (National Collegiate Athletic Association) a national organization that governs college athletics and oversees important decisions pertaining to athletics

needs a lack of basic necessities such as food, clothing, or shelter

net profit gross profit minus expenses

networking the practice of finding contacts among people you know, including family and friends, employers, and professional people you know personally

niche marketing a type of marketing that focuses on a small target market of consumers who have very similar interests

non-media advertisement any form of advertising that uses methods other than the media to promote ideas, goods, or services

non-price competition competition between businesses based on quality, service, and relationships

nonprofit organization non-governmental organization that focuses on providing a service rather than a profit

observation method research technique that involves watching actual behavior and recording it

observational research a method of collecting data by observing respondents in contrived or natural settings

odd-even pricing pricing goods with either an odd number or even number to match a product's image

oligopoly business situation in which a few firms affect but do not control an industry

opportunity cost the loss of the opportunity that is passed up in order to receive something in exchange

payola an illegal payment by record labels to radio stations to persuade them to play the label's records

personal selling direct communication by a salesperson to potential customers either in person or by telephone

piracy the unauthorized use of an owner's or creator's music, movies, or other copyrighted material

point of difference a unique product characteristic or benefit that sets it apart from a competitor

press release a newsworthy article that provides the basic information to answer questions such as who, what, where, when, and why

prestige pricing pricing based on consumer perception

price the value placed on goods or services being exchanged

price fixing an illegal practice whereby competitors conspire to set the same prices

price lining selling all goods in a product line at specific price points

primary data information collected from primary or original research used specifically for an issue under study

primary market in film distribution, the target audience which is the theaters that show films in first release

primary research original research conducted for a specific marketing situation

product a good or service that any for-profit industry sells to its customers

product item specific model or size of a product

product line a group of closely related products manufactured and/or sold by a company

product mix the total assortment of products that a company makes and/or sells

product placement the appearance of a product as a prop in a film or TV show, in exchange for a fee paid by the product's advertiser

product testing assessment of a product to see if it works, meets industry standards for safety, and is user-friendly

product tie-in use of ancillary products such as merchandise as promotional tools

professional athlete an athlete who has the will and ability to earn an income from a particular sport

profit the money left after all costs and expenses of a business are paid

profit margin the difference between the expenses and the retail price, expressed as a percentage or a dollar amount

programming the schedule, or times, for broadcasting shows on television; or on radio, also the music style and playlist

promotion any form of communication used to persuade people to buy products

promotional advertising advertising with a goal of selling an item being promoted

promotional mix any combination of advertising, sales promotion, publicity, direct marketing, and personal selling

promotional plan a detailed strategy of how to focus advertising and marketing communication efforts

psychographics studies of consumers based on their attitudes, interests, and opinions

public relations activities that promote the image and communications a company has with its employees, customers, investors, and public

publicity the free mention of a product or company in the media

qualitative research data that measure qualities, such as people's reactions or perceptions

quantitative research data expressed as amount in numbers

rack jobbers independent vendors who distribute, price, and control their own inventory within a store

ratings the rankings of TV-show or radio-show popularity in a certain time period

reach and frequency the number of people exposed to an advertisement and the number of times they are exposed to it

record clubs organizations in which members receive free records if they agree to purchase additional records within a time period

release date the day a film is first shown in theaters

repositioning changing a product's image in relation to a competitor's image

respondent a consumer who participates in personal interactive interviews or other research methods

return the amount of profit that is given back to the sponsor for the sponsor's initial investment or sponsorship

revenue gross income

risk management a strategy to offset business risks

risks unforeseen events and obstacles that can negatively affect business

royalty a payment for material that has been copyrighted, or legally declared as belonging to the creator

sales promotion a short-term incentive to get consumers interested in buying a product

sample a number of people who are representative of a study's population

secondary data information collected from secondary or preexisting research for a purpose other than the current study

secondary market in film distribution, target audience after a film has been in first run at theaters

secondary research published data that have been collected for some other purpose

situation analysis a study of the internal and external factors that impact a marketing plan

slogan a catch phrase or small group of words that are combined in a special way to identify a product or company

soundmark a trademark identified by a sound associated with a brand or company

sponsorship the promotion of a company in association with a property

sports agencies companies that specialize in marketing and managing sports events, sports teams, and professional athletes

sports consumer a person who may play, officiate, watch, or listen to sports, or read, use, purchase, and/or collect items related to sports

sports franchise an agreement or contract for a sports organization to sell a parent company's (i.e., a national sports league) good or service within a given area

sports marketing all the marketing activities designed to satisfy the needs and wants of sports consumers

sports products the goods, services, ideas, or combination of those things related to sports that provide satisfaction to a consumer

sports venues facilities or locations where sporting events take place

statistics a collection of numerical data that can be compared, analyzed, and interpreted

survey a questionnaire or series of questions designed to collect specific information

SWOT analysis a study of strengths, weaknesses, opportunities, and threats

syndication selling television programs to individual stations, not networks

synergy a combined action that occurs when products owned by one source promote the growth of related products

tangible products physical goods that offer benefits to the consumer

target market a specific group of consumers that an organization selects as the focus of its marketing plan

target pricing pricing goods according to what the customer is willing to pay

Title IX a law that bans gender discrimination in schools that receive federal funds

trademark a device that legally identifies ownership of a registered brand or trade name.

traffic count a measure of how many people stop or do not stop to look at an ad or store display

trailers previews of upcoming movies shown before the main feature

trend a pattern, habit, or tendency following a general course

vendors sellers of products

viability the possibility of successful operation and profitability of a business

wants things that people desire based on personality, experiences, or information about a product

yield-management pricing pricing items at different prices to maximize revenue when limited capacity is involved

Index

Index

Index

Index

Index

Index

Credits